UNITED STATES

EXPLORING

EXPEDITIONS.

E PLURIBUS UNUM.

ChapinDel

Richardson Sc. N.Y.

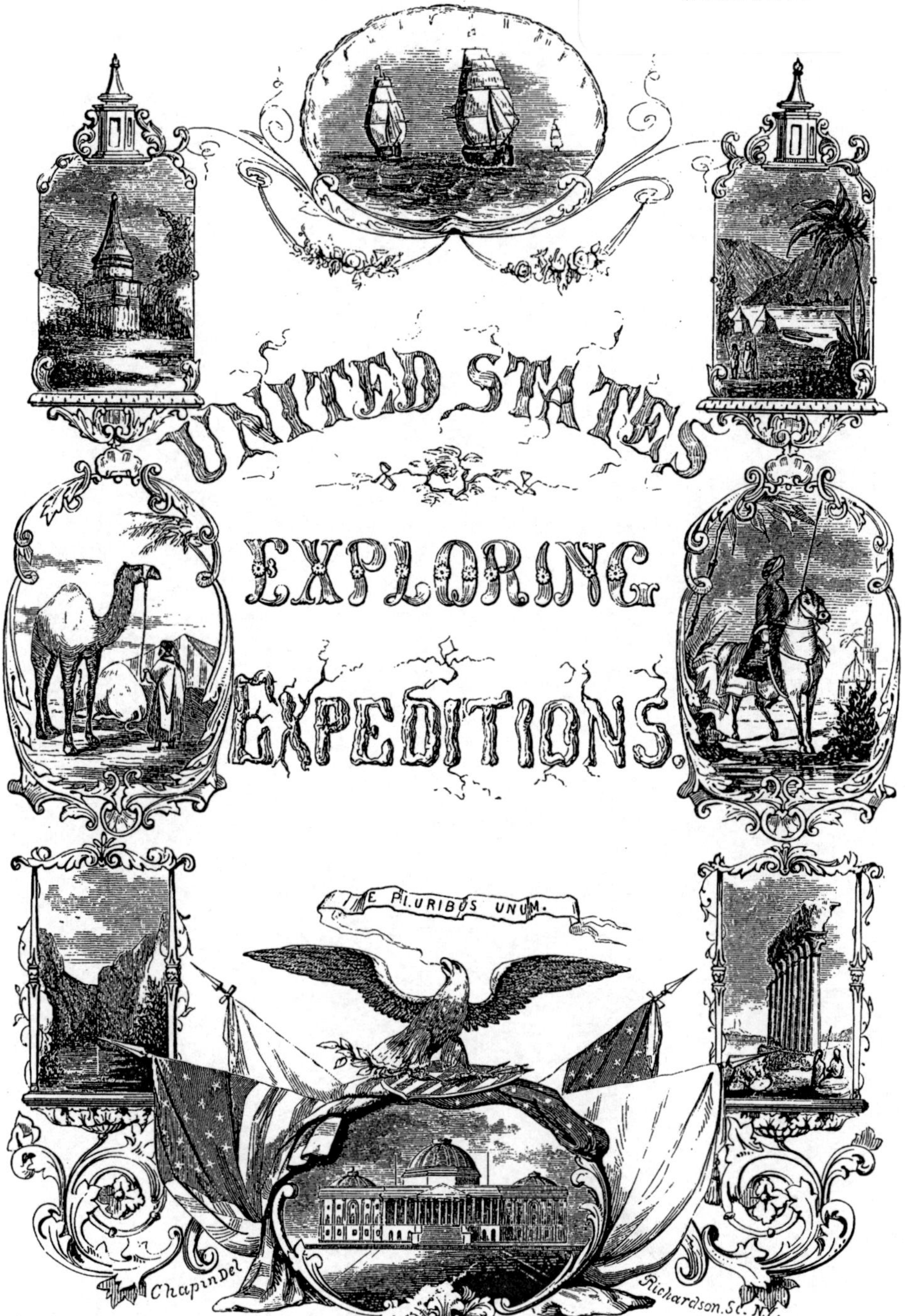

F. C. GUTIERREZ, PRINT. 51 JOHN ST. N.Y.

UNITED STATES EXPLORING EXPEDITIONS.

VOYAGE

OF THE

U. S. EXPLORING SQUADRON,

COMMANDED BY

CAPTAIN CHARLES WILKES,

OF THE UNITED STATES NAVY,

IN 1838, 1839, 1840, 1841, AND 1842:

TOGETHER WITH

EXPLORATIONS AND DISCOVERIES MADE BY

ADMIRAL D'URVILLE, CAPTAIN ROSS,

AND OTHER NAVIGATORS AND TRAVELLERS;

AND AN

ACCOUNT OF THE EXPEDITION TO THE DEAD SEA,

UNDER LIEUTENANT LYNCH.

BY JOHN S. JENKINS,

AUTHOR OF "THE LIFE OF SILAS WRIGHT," "POLITICAL HISTORY OF NEW YORK,"
"HISTORY OF THE WAR WITH MEXICO," ETC., ETC.

WITH NUMEROUS ILLUSTRATIONS.

AUBURN:

JAMES M. ALDEN.

1850

STEREOTYPED BY T. B. SMITH
216 WILLIAM STREET.

PREFACE.

~~~~~~~~

I⊤ has been my main object, in the preparation of this work, to present, in an attractive and condensed form, an account of the various Expeditions mentioned in its pages, with such other information touching the places and localities described, as might be of interest to the general reader; and if the public approve of the design, additions will hereafter be made to it, treating of similar enterprises undertaken by the American government.

So far, however, from being an abridgment of the published narratives of Messrs. Wilkes and Lynch, this volume will be found to contain a very large proportion of facts not embraced in either of them. These have been obtained from divers sources. While engaged in preparing the work, I have consulted the Voyages of D'Urville, Ross, Beechey, King and Fitzroy; Ellis' Polynesian Researches; Crawfurd's Indian Archipelago; Darwin's Journal of Researches; Williams' Missionary Enterprises; Kidder's Sketches of Residence and Travels in Brazil; Bingham's Sandwich Islands; Mrs. Meredith's Sketches of New South Wales; Earl's Enterprise in Tropical Australia; Greenhow's History of Oregon and California; the travels of Hall, Mier, Moerenhout, Clarke, Elliott, Stephens, Robinson, and Fisk; and a

number of other books of voyages and travels, some or all
of which are referred to in the notes. It would be unjust,
too, not to acknowledge, in this connection, my indebtedness
to the official narratives of Commanders Wilkes and Lynch.
I have, as a matter of course, been essentially benefited by
them, though I have found that of the former encumbered
with frequent errors. Something may, indeed, be conceded
to haste in preparing a work for the press; but it is hardly
excusable that any writer should be so far wrong in his
geography as to confound San Salvador with Rio Janeiro, or
so much at fault as to mistake a Peruvian *montaña* for a
forest.

It would have been easy for me to have swelled the size
of the Second Part of the book, by inserting the stereotyped
gleanings of almost every modern traveller who has visited
the Holy Land, which have, from continued repetition,
become familiar to every reader; but I could not find any
justification for taking that course. The important results,
and the actual information, obtained by the Dead Sea
Expedition, may be reduced within a very narrow compass;
and the account of it seemed to me appropriately to terminate
with the breaking up of the Encampment on the shores of
the lake.

Anachronisms of frequent occurrence may be found in
these pages; but as my desire has been to impart information, they have appeared to me to be justifiable. The Expeditions of Wilkes and Lynch have been, as it were, the
threads upon which I have strung the facts procured from
different sources, many of which are not accessible to the
majority of readers, or, if accessible, few have the leisure to
examine them. Many of these facts relate to periods long
subsequent to the date of the Expeditions with which they

are connected, but no one can be misled by this arrangement; and if the reader is as much profited by the perusal of this work, as I have been by the examinations necessary to its preparation, he will not, I am confident, be inclined to doubt that I have rendered him an acceptable service.

CONTENTS.

PART I.

CHAPTER I.

CHAPTER II.

1*

CHAPTER III.

CHAPTER IV.

CHAPTER V.

CHAPTER VI.

CHAPTER VII.

CHAPTER VIII.

CHAPTER IX.

CHAPTER X.

CHAPTER XI.

CHAPTER XII.

CHAPTER XIII.

CHAPTER XIV.

CHAPTER XV.

CHAPTER XVI.

CHAPTER XVII.

CHAPTER XVIII.

PART II.

CHAPTER I.

CHAPTER II.

CHAPTER III.

PART I.

EXPEDITIONS IN THE PACIFIC

AND THE SOUTH SEAS.

EXPLORING EXPEDITIONS

IN THE SOUTH SEAS.

CHAPTER I.

(1.) WHEN the Genoese navigator and philosopher sailed with his little fleet, from the harbor of Palos,—on the 3d of August, 1492,—and directed his course over the fathomless waste of waters outside the pillars of Hercules, in search of the bright realms of Zipango and Cathay, he marked a new era in maritime discovery and adventure. The voyages of the Phœnicians, like those of the Scandinavian navigators at a later day, do not seem to have been productive of much benefit to the world at large ; or to have stimulated any extraordinary spirit of enterprise, unless among those immediately interested in their results,—but the discoveries of Christopher Columbus aroused the whole Continent of Europe, and adventurers pushed out from every port and haven, in quest of the fair land of promise beyond the dark bosom of the Atlantic.

Expeditions were fitted out in England, France, Spain, and Portugal,—all having the same object, and prompted by the same motives. A new world was found in the far-off West, presenting a

"Sweet interchange
Of hill and valley, rivers, woods, and plains;"

and rich in mineral wealth, in majestic forests, and a virgin soil. It was a happy thought, that, when this country—thus, as it were, called into existence—had become peopled, and advanced to greatness and distinction, she should repay the debt of gratitude which she owed, by her discoveries in the same field in which the enlightened nations of the old world have been constantly employed for more than three hundred years. The Coast Survey of the United States—first proposed in 1806, by the late Professor Patterson, and warmly favored, at that time, by Albert Gallatin, and other scientific and learned men, but not commenced until the year 1832—is a great work, and one from which other countries, as well as our own, will unquestionably derive the most important benefits. The comparatively limited information possessed in regard to the great Southern Ocean, in which such a vast amount of the capital of our countrymen was employed, in whaling and other commercial enterprises, next attracted the attention of the American Congress.

(2.) On the 18th of May, 1836, an act was passed authorizing an Expedition to be fitted out—the first, of a similar character, undertaken by the national government—for the purpose of exploring and surveying the Southern Ocean, " as well to determine the existence of all doubtful islands and shoals, as to discover, and accurately fix, the position of those which [lay] in or near the track of our vessels in that quarter, and [might] have escaped the observation of scientific navigators."* Liberal appropriations were made for accomplishing the objects of the Expedition, and it was at first organized under Commodore Thomas Ap Catesby Jones, of the United States Navy: he subsequently resigned the station, and was succeeded, in turn, by several different officers, until, finally, on the 20th of March, 1838, Lieutenant Charles Wilkes assumed the command.

The novelty of the undertaking occasioned numerous delays and hindrances; but, early in the month of August, 1838,

* Three other Exploring Expeditions were undertaken in the South Seas, at the same time; two English, and one French.

the expedition was ready to sail,—though, as it afterwards appeared, some of the vessels were not in as good condition as they should have been. The squadron consisted of the sloop of war Vincennes, the flag-ship of the commander of the expedition ; the sloop of war Peacock, Lieutenant William L. Hudson ; the brig Porpoise, Lieutenant Cadwalader Ringgold; the store-ship Relief, Lieutenant A. K. Long ; and the tenders Sea-Gull and Flying-Fish. As it was deemed important to divest the expedition of all military character, the armament provided for it was adapted merely for defence against the savage and warlike inhabitants of the South Sea islands. The boats of the vessels were all clinker-built, with the exception of the launches, like those used by whalers and sealers.

A full corps of scientific gentlemen, consisting of philologists, naturalists, conchologists, mineralogists, botanists, horticulturists, taxidermists, and draughtsmen—all employed by the government—accompanied the Expedition. An ample supply of books, and a complete set of charts and instruments, of the most approved character and workmanship, were also furnished ; and several able reports of philosophical and other societies, together with a memorandum transmitted to the Navy Department by Vice-Admiral Krusenstern, of the Russian Navy, were placed in the hands of Lieutenant Wilkes.

All things being in readiness, on the 9th of August, the squadron, which had been fitted out at Norfolk, dropped down to Hampton Roads and anchored. On the 12th instant, they were joined by the tenders, and on the 17th Lieutenant Wilkes received his final instructions from the Navy Department. Signal was at once made that the squadron was under sailing orders. At three o'clock in the afternoon of the following day, the vessels weighed anchor ; but as the breeze soon fell away, they anchored again at the Horse-shoe. In a couple of hours the wind freshened, and the whole squadron stood down the bay in company. During the night the breeze slackened once more, and they made very little progress. Early in the morning of the 19th, how-

ever, they passed Cape Henry Light, and at nine o'clock hove
to, and discharged their pilots. The ships then stood out to
sea together. This being Sunday, all hands were called to
muster at eleven o'clock, and an impressive sermon was delivered on board the Vincennes, by the Chaplain, Mr. Elliot.
He alluded, in eloquent terms, to the arduous nature of the
enterprise in which they had embarked, and the probably distant period when they would be permitted to return to the
bright shores then rapidly sinking below the western horizon ;
and appropriately cautioned his hearers, through weal and
woe, to put their trust in Him who holds the tempest in the
hollow of his hand.

(3.) The instructions issued to Lieutenant Wilkes, required him, in the first place, to shape his course to Rio
Janeiro, crossing the line between longitude 18° and 22°
West, and keeping within those meridians to about latitude
10° South, in order to determine the existence of certain
vigias, or shoals, laid down in the charts as doubtful. Having replenished his supplies at Rio,—the longitude of which,
as well as of Cape Frio, was to be determined,—he was directed to make a particular examination of the Rio Negro,
which falls into the South Atlantic ; and then to proceed to
a safe port, or ports, in Tierra del Fuego, where the larger
vessels were to be securely moored, while he explored the
South Antartic, to the southward of Powell's Group, and between it and Sandwich Land, with the brig Porpoise and the
tenders. In the meantime, the officers left at Tierra del Fuego
were to make accurate examinations and surveys of the bays,
ports, inlets, and sounds, in that region.

On rejoining the vessels at Tierra del Fuego, Lieutenant
Wilkes was ordered to stretch towards the southward and
westward, with the whole squadron, as far as the Ne Plus
Ultra of Cook, or longitude 105° West, and to return north-
ward to Valparaiso, where a store-ship would join them, in
March, 1839. From that port, he was to direct his course
to the Navigator's Group,—so disposing his vessels, in the
latitudes where discoveries might be reasonably anticipated,

as that they should sweep the broadest expanse of ocean practicable,—and thence to the Feejee Islands, where he was to select a safe harbor for whalers and public vessels of the United States, and make such arrangements as would insure their being furnished with supplies.

From the Feejee Islands, he was to proceed to the port of Sydney, and then make a second attempt to penetrate within the Antartic region, south of Van Diemen's Land, and as far west as longitude 45° East, or to Enderby's Land. The squadron was then to rendezvous at Kerguelen's Land, usually called the Isle of Desolation, and proceed to the Sandwich Islands, where a store-ship from the United States would meet them, in April, 1840. Thence they were to sail to the Northwest Coast of America, and make surveys and examinations of the coast of Oregon and California. From this coast, they were to repair to that of Japan,—taking as many doubtful islands as possible on their route,—and make a particular examination of the Sea of Japan, and the Sea of Sooloo, or Mindoro. Having completed this examination, Lieutenant Wilkes was instructed to ascertain the disposition of the inhabitants of the islands of that archipelago for commerce, their productions and resources; after which he was to proceed to the Straits of Sunda,—pass through the Straits of Billiton,—touch at Singapore, where he would meet a store-ship,—and then return home by the way of the Cape of Good Hope.

In addition to the orders necessarily suggested by the foregoing instructions, Lieutenant Wilkes directed every officer of the Expedition to keep a journal, in which everything that occurred during the voyage was to be carefully noted. These journals were to be weekly submitted to him for inspection, and, on the return of the Expedition, to be disposed of according to the directions of the Secretary of the Navy. The scientific gentlemen were admonished to lose no opportunity to procure information in their several departments. Meteorological observations were required to be taken four times daily; and particular instructions were given to measure and observe, all astronomical and atmospherical phenomena, and every unusual appearance connected with the weather, such as shooting stars, zodiacal lights, aurora borealis, rainbows, halos, water-spouts, the Magellanic clouds,* lightning, and rain.

After several days' trial, the store-ship Relief was found to be so dull a sailer—the other vessels being frequently required to lie to for her—that Lieutenant Wilkes determined to part company. Lieutenant Long was therefore ordered to proceed, with all practicable dispatch, to Porto Praya, in the island of St. Jago, and thence to Rio Janeiro. In case of separation, the remaining vessels of the squadron were directed to rendezvous at Madeira.

(4.) Immediately after leaving the Capes of Virginia, the influence of the cold polar, or counter-current, flowing parallel to the coast, close to the inner edge of the Gulf Stream, from Davis' Straits as far south as Cape Hatteras, was sensibly felt.† In crossing the Gulf Stream, the squadron were highly favored. They had light winds, and their progress was so slow, that they were forty-eight hours in passing it, although they were most of the time sailing at right angles to its direction. When they entered the stream, a sudden rise of the temperature of the water was indicated by the thermometer, which went up from 77° to 83° in a few hours, but soon fell again to a mean temperature of about 80°,—thus showing that the stream is considerably warmer towards the inner edge than on the outer. Its breadth, where the squadron crossed it, on the parallel of 34° 30′, was ascertained to be fifty-three miles, and its velocity two miles per hour. These data are not very reliable, however, as it is now well settled, that both the breadth and velocity fluctuate very materially.‡

* The *Magellanic clouds* are three conspicuous nebulæ, bearing the appearance of thin white clouds, situated near the south pole. They derive their name from Magellan, the distinguished Portuguese navigator.

† This current is sometimes called the eddy of the Gulf Stream; but the great difference in the temperature shows conclusively that the idea is erroneous.

‡ The observations of the officers of the Exploring Expedition, while in the Gulf Stream, were, necessarily, very limited; consequently, they do not appear

(5.) On the 25th of August, the squadron laid its course towards the island of Madeira. The winds had been light and the sea smooth, but on the night of the 26th there came up a squall, during which the Peacock and the Flying-Fish parted company with the other vessels.

The first days in September were clear, bright, and beautiful; immense shoals of flying fish disported about the prows of the ships, or darted through the air to escape from their voracious pursuers; and beautiful dolphins, and " deep-sea" sharks, were seen in every direction. In the morning of the 6th, they encountered a huge cotton-wood tree, one hundred and twenty feet in length, and fourteen feet in circumference; all covered over with barnacles, and much eaten by the teredine, or sea borer; and probably thousands on thousands of miles from the place where it grew—on the banks of the Mississippi. In the afternoon of the 9th instant, they passed in sight of the Peak of Pico, one of the Azores, or Western Islands, and on the following day made the northern coast of St. Michael's, belonging to the same group, a high and mountainous island, but exceedingly fertile, and dotted with groves and villas, and rich cultivated fields, which could just be discerned with the glass.

(6.) At daylight on the 16th of September, the tall cliffs, and jagged precipices, of the island of Madeira, were discovered looming up above the wide expanse of waters at the south. The first sight of the island does not produce a favorable impression, but a nearer view discloses scenery remarkably picturesque, and, indeed, beautiful. Bold, embattled cliffs, rising to the height of sixteen hundred feet, the abodes of the ospray and sea-gull, and beneath which is heard the

to have remarked the singular fact disclosed by the examinations of Lieutenant Bache,—who was unfortunately wrecked off Cape Hatteras, while engaged in the Coast Survey, on the 8th of September, 1846,—that the whole current of warm water, to the depth of at least four hundred and eighty fathoms, divides itself into two principal branches, separated by a portion of cold water. The transition from the cold to the warm water, on the inner edge of the stream, is said to be almost as instantaneous, as if the two were separated by a wall, nearly perpendicular, except that it inclines slightly to the east at the top.

ceaseless roar of the ocean surf, stand like giant warders, on
every hand.   The shores are indented by a few small bays,
receiving the waters of the mountain streamlets, at the upper
extremities of which are the little villages whose white walls
glisten like enamel in the beams of the morning sun.

Throughout its whole extent, the island is mountainous,
and the western half is divided by a central ridge, five thousand feet high, upon which is spread out the vast plain of
Paul de Serra, mostly overgrown, and used for breeding
horses and mules.   Deep gorges, with steep precipitous sides,
everywhere intersect the elevated ground.   The intervals,
and the lower slopes of the hills, are highly productive, and
even the mountain tops are clothed with rich verdure, or
groves of heath and broom,—not the stunted varieties of
northern climes, but the luxuriant growth of the tropics.
From the rugged character of the scenery, it might be supposed that but a small portion of the island could be cultivated; yet, what nature has done amiss, or left unfinished, man
has attempted to remedy and complete.   Terraces, supported
by stone walls, girt the acclivities, even to their summits;
and green patches start out, like emeralds, in bold relief, from
the dark red soil that surrounds them.   Within the narrow
compass of this delightful spot, the productions of the torrid
and temperate zones are brought together : on the lower terraces, oranges, citrons, and lemons, may be found ; higher
up, are bananas, figs, and pomegranates ; still higher, apples,
currants, pears, peaches, plums, melons, tomatoes and egg-
plants, greet the sight ; and above all these grows the potato,
solitary and alone.

Before sunset on the 16th, the Vincennes, Porpoise, and
Sea-Gull, cast anchor in the harbor of Funchal, on the southern side of Madeira, the capital of the island.   The Peacock
and Flying-Fish joined them on the following day,—when a
party of officers was made up to go ashore, and pay their respects to the civil governor, Baron de Lordello, and the military commandant, Señor Rebello, who received them very
courteously   During the stay of the squadron, every point

of particular attraction was visited by one or more parties; the inhabitants usually receiving them with the utmost kindness and cordiality.

The Madeira Islands belong to Portugal, and consist of Madeira proper, Porto Santo, and the Desert Isles. The first two, the only ones inhabited, are included in one district, and contain about one hundred and twenty thousand inhabitants, of all sexes and classes. The people are very loyal to their present sovereign, Donna Maria; their taxes are not very heavy; and though beggars are somewhat numerous among them, they may be generally regarded as exceedingly industrious. They are gay and cheerful in their dispositions, and, with rare exceptions, hospitable and generous.

Funchal, the capital of the island of Madeira, is pleasantly situated on the southern shore, surrounded by an amphitheatre of lofty hills, terminating, on one side, in Loo Rock, a bold quadrangular precipice, with a fortification on the summit, which overlooks the harbor in front of the town. It contains some eight or ten thousand inhabitants, most of whom reside in neat whitewashed cottages one story in height, though there are many more imposing structures, provided with verandahs, or light airy colonnades. The streets are narrow, but well-paved, and present quite a cleanly appearance. There are a number of churches and convents, which are always lighted in the early part of the evening. The prisons are well-filled, and extremely filthy. This may be attributed, however, to defective laws, as every offender is required to be sent to Portugal for trial, and sometimes years elapse before he leaves the island.

In addition to Funchal, there are several other pretty towns, among which are Santa Cruz, Porto Delgada, and San Vincenté, on the north side of the island, and Canical and Comancha, on the east side. The principal objects of interest to the tourist, are, the Currál,—a circular gorge, as the name implies, in the midst of the mountains,—the winding pass at Estroza, and the Convent of Our Lady of the Mountain, the highest building on the island.

2*

There are, also, many fine rides in the interior. After ascending the heights in rear of Funchal, you may travel miles
on miles, over hard and well-conditioned roads, or bridle-paths,
bordered with hedges of roses and myrtles; with trellises supporting an infinite variety of gaudy colored creepers, or aromatic shrubs that load the air with perfume; or with stone
walls, literally buried beneath the long trailing vines loaded
down with their rich clusters of grapes. Gardens stocked
with fruit trees, extensive vineyards, and fields of wheat, barley, rye, and maize, arrest the attention on every hand. Neat
cottages are discovered imbosomed amid thickets of tropical
plants; and the humbler habitations of the peasantry, with
their low walls formed of huge blocks of lava, and their tall
thatches of broom, are constantly peeping out from the luxuriant foliage which surrounds them. Through the gorges
of the mountains, glimpses open of almost fathomless depths,
at the bottom of which are labyrinths of sweet-scented shrub-
beries, miniature forests of dahlias, fuchsias, hydrangeas,
geraniums, variegated convolvuli, and Ethiopian lilies. The
spreading plane tree, the majestic palm, the dark and glossy-
leaved banana, and the Madeira walnut,* enlivened, now and
then, by the white tufts of the cotton-wood, abound on the
lower terraces; and the beetling cliffs above are crowned
with mountain heath and laurel, with towering cedars, oaks,
and elms. Over all this bright and glorious scenery, rests an
atmosphere remarkably soft, pure, and transparent.

Travelling is usually performed on the Madeira ponies,—a
tough and hardy race of animals, like the Shetland breed,—
or in sedans. The latter are generally preferred by the ladies.
The hauling of heavy articles is principally done by the small
oxen of the island, on sledges resembling the stone boats in
use among American farmers. These are employed altogether in the seaport towns, for conveying pipes of wine; but
the liquor is brought from the interior, in sheep-skins, sowed
together so as nearly to preserve the form of the animal,
which are slung over the backs of the peasants.

* The Madeira nut is the product of this tree.

The inhabitants of Madeira are of Moorish origin, though free negroes, and descendants of the European race, are frequently to be met with. The men are tall, muscular, and well-built. The women, particularly among the peasantry, are masculine and vigorous, and rarely exhibit any traces of beauty: as they share the labors of their husbands, the softness natural to the sex is very soon destroyed. All are tough and hearty, and capable of enduring great and long-continued fatigue. Among the higher classes, the fashions of Spain and Portugal are imitated or copied; and rustling silks and gay velvets are often seen in the streets. The dress of the peasant is far less expensive, yet quite picturesque: the men wear trowsers descending as low as the knee, and shirts and jackets of the brightest colors; and the women, bodices laced with pretty ribbons, and short gayly-striped petticoats. A conical cap, common to both sexes, completes the costume.

The difference between the imports and exports of Madeira, indicates a high state of prosperity. The former barely exceed one hundred thousand dollars annually, principally consisting of staves, rice, and oil; while more than eight thousand pipes of wine, valued at over one and a half million of dollars, are exported during the same period. Most of the cereal grains, sugar, coffee, and taro, are produced in abundance. Large quantities of fine beef, vegetables, and fruit, are furnished, also, to the vessels that stop at the island. But the great staple is the far-famed Madeira wine, the best qualities of which, the connoisseur need not be told, come from the "south-side." Great care is taken to maintain the reputation of the wine, and the laws are so strict, that even the genuine article, once shipped, cannot be introduced into the island.

The method of manufacturing the wine is certainly very primitive, and differs but little from that in vogue among the nations of the East in olden times. The grapes are deposited in an elevated vat, usually about six feet square and two feet deep, under an open shed covered with a thatch roof. Some half a dozen bare-legged and bare-footed peasants, then spring into the vat, and commence stamping furiously, accompanying their motions with a rude song. After this process has been continued for a sufficient length of time, the legs of the men are scraped, and the pomace set up in the shape of a cone, and bound about with the young cuttings of the vine. A lever, to which a large stone, or rock, is attached by a screw, is now applied, and the juice expressed into tubs,— one gallon being generally obtained from two bushels of grapes. The must is drawn off into casks, in which it ferments ; it is then clarified with gypsum or isinglass, and the necessary spirit imparted to it by the addition of two or three gallons of brandy to a pipe.

(7.) Having completed their repairs, the Exploring Squadron weighed anchor in the afternoon of the 25th of September, and sailed from the harbor of Funchal, in the direction of the Cape de Verdes.   Delightful weather, and cool breezy winds, attended them during the whole time they were at sea.   Passing Bonavista, one of the Cape de Verdes, to which the sailors have given the *sobriquet* of " Bonny-wiskers," without stopping, they came in sight of the island of Mayo, belonging to the same group, which loomed darkly in the distance, at four o'clock in the afternoon of the 6th of October, and shortly before midnight lay to off St. Jago, the principal island.   On the night of the 6th, a most brilliant display of the radiate animalculæ, known as Medusa, or sea-nettles, was witnessed.   The vast expanse of waters seemed paved with innumerable diamonds that out-sparkled the stars which glimmered above them, and wavy floods of phosphorescent light dashed against the vessels, or rolled slowly in towards the shore.   Long trains of glittering light marked the courses of the fish ; and the motion of a rudder, or the disturbance occasioned in the water by anything thrown overboard, produced beautiful flashing coruscations.   A number of experiments were made, from which it was satisfactorily ascertained that the animalculæ did not extend below eighteen fathoms' water.

In the morning of the 7th of October, the fleet turned the

tall bluff upon which stands the flag-staff and a ruined fortification, on the right of the entrance to the harbor, and came
to anchor in the bay of Porto Praya.

The Cape de Verdes were discovered by the Portuguese,
in 1460, and are still subject to the crown of Portugal. The
islands are about twenty in number, and contain seventy-five
thousand inhabitants, thirty thousand of whom reside in St.
Jago. The population is principally composed of mulattoes
and blacks,—there being but few native Portuguese. Some
of the blacks adhere to their vernacular tongue ; but the
common medium of conversation is a horrid jargon com-
pounded of the Negro and Portuguese dialects. Near the
sea, the islands are low, sandy, and barren ; but further inland, there are lofty hills and mountains, which afford pasturage for numerous herds of cattle and goats. On the coast,
the water is brackish ; but it is brought from the interior—
except in St. Jago—of good quality, in goatskins, on the backs
of asses. The islands are only tolerably fertile, and are subject to frequent droughts, probably occasioned by the prevalence of the dry hot winds blowing from the Sahara, or Great
Desert of Africa. In 1832, the inhabitants suffered severely
from a visitation of this character. Their cattle were starved,
and they would themselves have perished, had it not been for
the contributions made for their relief in other countries, particularly in the United States. The generous conduct of the
citizens of the latter government is still remembered among
them with the liveliest emotions of gratitude. The climate
is said to be healthy, though very warm. The rainy season
continues only three months ; it commences about the middle
of July, and terminates about the middle of October, when
everything assumes a livelier, fresher, and more verdant appearance.

The productions of this group of islands are not numerous,
and the inhabitants are dependent on the vessels stopping
there for many articles of comfort and convenience, for which
they exchange their own products. Beef, poultry, eggs, fresh
fish, cabbages, beans, pumpkins, squashes, corn, sweet pota-

toes, yams, bananas, dates, tamarinds, limes, oranges, and the fruit of the cocoanut tree, are usually quite plenty. Sugar and coffee are also raised in small quantities, and an inferior quality of wine, but a small portion of which is exported, is likewise produced. A palatable article of cheese is made from goats' milk. The flour used is imported, principally from the United States; but a very good kind of bread is prepared from the roots of the manihot, or cassada plant, which are also roasted and eaten like potatoes.* The fecula, or starch, obtained by scraping and washing the roots, is called tapioca.

Coarse salt, hides, goatskins, wine, and archil, are the main exports. The salt plantations, as they are called, are situated on the level, alluvial ground, near the coast. The land appropriated to the purpose is plotted into vats, by banks of clay, from one to two feet high, which become baked by the heat of the sun. The salt water is then pumped into the vats from wells, and exposed to evaporation. It is not an unusual sight to see a whole family, men, women, and children, engaged in the "plantation." Considerable attention is paid to neatness, and the walks between the vats are kept scrupulously clean. Archil is a lichen, which grows on the rocks, and is found both in the Canary and Cape de Verde Islands. It yields a rich purple color, which is exceedingly beautiful, but not durable. The blue pigment, litmus, is prepared from it. At the Cape de Verdes, archil is a government monopoly; ninety thousand millreas,—equal to fifty-six thousand, two hundred and fifty dollars, American currency,—being paid by a company, for the annual crop.

The houses of the Cape de Verdians are miserable huts, built of stone, not six feet high, and thatched with salt hay, or palm leaves. Some are circular, some square, and others oblong. Occasionally one may be seen with a shingled roof. As fuel is scarce, the *estiercol* of the ass is used in its stead,

---

* The bread made from the manihot was the principal article of food among the Caribs, when they were first discovered by the Europeans. They called it *Yuca.*

as hunters and travellers on the American prairies use the *bois de vache* of the buffalo. Horses are found here, but the principal beast of burden is the ass, which carries its load in panniers. A long string of the animals, frequently seen dashing at full speed over the sand, is called a *hato*.

White cotton shirts, aprons, and trowsers, are worn by the men, with dark vests, generally purchased at second hand from the crews of the vessels frequenting the islands. Sometimes they wear straw hats on their heads, but oftener nothing. Party-colored turbans and handkerchiefs form the headgear of the women; a shawl fastened about the waist, and another thrown over the bust and tied behind, complete the dress.

The *gobernádor*, or governor, of the islands, resides at Porto Praya, in St. Jago. This island is about sixty miles in circumference, and is the most fertile and productive of the group. The former capital was Ribeira Grande, but Porto Praya now enjoys that distinction. The latter contains between two and three thousand inhabitants, and is situated on an elevated plateau overlooking the bay. Its whitewashed walls and battlements may be descried far out at sea, and betoken a greater degree of cleanliness than is witnessed on landing. Blind beggars and naked children,—pigs, fowls, and monkeys,—cross the path at every step. Black soldiers, with huge muskets generally out of repair, patrol the *entráda* of the *Presidio*, or governor's house; and a squad of dirty recruits going through the manual exercise is usually the most striking object in the *plaza*. Officers, as well as men, including the governor, are black. A market is held daily in the square, when there are any vessels in port.

A rocky ghaut, or pass, leads to the Valley of Dates, half a mile west of the town, which is one of the most attractive features of the island. Here was formerly the public fountain, from which water was obtained for the inhabitants and shipping. They are now supplied by a reservoir, constructed at the expense of the government, and filled with water brought in iron pipes a distance of two miles. The soil of

the valley is a rich loam and the date tree grows luxuriantly.
Lime, orange, banana, cocoanut, tamarind and papaw trees,*
are also scattered through it, together with other tropical
fruits and plants.

(8.) The squadron left Porto Praya on the 7th of October,
and continued their course southward, in search of the shoals,
said to lie in this quarter of the ocean, off the African
coast; but none of particular importance were discovered.
The nights were clear and beautiful till near morning, and
the zodiacal light was once or twice observed. Falling stars,
some of them of unusual brilliancy, were witnessed on the
morning of the 18th of October, and on the nights of the
11th, 12th, and 13th, of November. Large shoals of dolphins, and wide luminous patches of phosphorescent animalculæ, were also seen. About the first of November, they
crossed the Equator, and on the 22d caught sight of the rich
neutral-tints resting, like a halo, over the tall and rugged
summit of Cape Frio, forty miles north of Rio Janeiro.
Favored by a light wind from the southeast, they entered the
broad harbor of Rio, under full press of canvas, on the afternoon of the 23d; having accomplished the passage in
ninety-five days, about twice the time usually required by a
vessel proceeding directly from the United States. The
store-ship Relief took the direct course; but, in consequence
of her slow sailing, she was one hundred days, three of which
were spent at the Cape de Verdes, in making the trip.

---

* The papaw, or papaya, grows to the height of eighteen or twenty feet. It
is nearly naked to the top, where the leaves start out on every side, with long
footstalks. The fruit, about the size of a melon, grows between the leaves, and
is boiled, and eaten with meat, like ordinary vegetables. The juice is pungent
and milky, but this is extracted by the process of boiling.

CHAPTER II.

(1.) COMING from the sea, Rio Janeiro, or more properly,
perhaps, Rio de Janeiro, presents a grand and imposing appearance. The city is built on the southern shore, close to
the entrance, of the bay of the same name. Near it, but
higher up, is the pretty town of San Domingo, and directly
opposite, is Praya Grande. The bay is a fine sheet of water,
one hundred miles in circumference, and sprinkled, here and
there, with small evergreen islands.

On the right, as you pass up to the anchorage, is Fort
Santa Cruz, at the foot of Signal Hill; on the left is Fort
St. Lucia, on an island near the mainland; beyond this, in
the same direction, is Sugar Loaf Hill—an isolated rock one
thousand feet high, around whose lofty crest the white fleecy
clouds forever linger; and further on, are the notched and
uneven peaks of Gavia and Corcovado. In front is the busy
and thriving capital of the Brazilian Empire,—a forest of
tapering masts and spars in the foreground, and richly decorated churches, glittering façades, and massive tiled roofs, in
the rear. Behind these are the blooming environs of the
city, gay gardens, delightful *quintas*, cool shady groves and
verdant forests, stretching far away into the interior,—a constant succession of beautiful objects meeting the eye, till the
view is bounded in the west by the towering pinnacles of the

Organ Mountains, boldly pencilled against the pure azure of a tropical sky.

(2.) St. Christóval, in the suburbs of Rio Janeiro, is the usual residence of the Emperor, Pedro II ; but his principal *levées* are held at the city palace, which he occupies on all great occasions. This is almost the first prominent object that presents itself, after ascending the rickety stairs at the usual place of landing. It stands on the Rua Direita, the broadest street in the city, and is a heavy stone structure in the shape of a parallelogram. It has a front of one hundred and fifty feet, and extends about two hundred feet to the rear. The main centre building is three stories high, and the wings two stories. On one side of the court, in the centre of the palace, is the Senate House, and on the other a splendid church belonging to the Carmelite friars, near which is the Imperial chapel, a pretty little *bijou* of a thing erected by the mother of the Emperor.* The Chamber of Deputies is nearly a mile from the palace, in the Campo de Aclangao.

While the Exploring Squadron was lying in the harbor of Rio, the Emperor made a visit to the city palace, in state, on the occasion of his birth day, which took place on the 2d of December. Escorted by a large body of troops, he entered the city about noon, in a splendid gilt carriage, English built, drawn by eight cream-colored horses guided by grooms in rich liveries. His two sisters, one sixteen, and the other fourteen years of age—the former of whom afterwards married the Prince de Joinville, son of Louis Philippe—rode in the carriage with him. The inhabitants collected everywhere on the line of his route to welcome him. Triumphal arches spanned the streets ; rich satin draperies, intermingled with festoons of natural and artificial flowers, ornamented the fronts of the dwellings ; national flags were displayed on every public building ; and the custom-house was ornamented with a bright collection of standards, conspicuous among which was that of the American Union. The ships in the

---

* The Empress was for a long time childless, and made a vow that she would erect a church when she became a mother, which she religiously fulfilled.

bay were dressed with flags, and at twelve o'clock, meridian, a grand royal salute was fired from the forts, which was returned by the vessels of war. As the Imperial pageant passed on, loud prolonged *vivas* mingled with the clashing of cymbals, and the braying of trumpets. The Emperor was then but a mere lad, only thirteen years of age ; yet he returned the congratulations of his subjects with ease and dignity. Arrived at the great square in front of the palace, which was densely crowded with citizens, and strangers from the four quarters of the globe, a *feu de joie* was fired by the troops, the Emperor exhibited himself in the balconies of the palace, and a *levée*, attended by the foreign ministers and their suites, completed the ceremonies of the day.

(3.) Rio abounds in churches. On the outside, they bear marks of decay, and the steps and vestibules are frequently used by the market people to display their wares. In the interior, however, they are gorgeously decorated, with ornaments of gold and silver, and fine specimens of painting and sculpture. The music is always good, and on important occasions especially attractive. The inhabitants are principally Roman Catholics, but they are fast losing their attachment to the religion of their forefathers. The churches are regularly opened for public worship on the Sabbath, and at other times during the week, but they are slimly attended. As in most Catholic countries, Sunday is a complete gala day. The stores and shops, particularly those where fancy articles are sold, and the *cafés* and coffee saloons, are kept open ; hunting, riding, and fishing, usurp the place of the forms and ceremonies prescribed in the ritual ; the billiard rooms are crowded ; and the performances at the theatres, of which there are three in the city, are witnessed by a far more numerous auditory than may be seen in the Cathedral.

The English and American residents erected a neat Episcopal church, near the public gardens on the bay, in 1820, which is inclosed by an iron railing, and has a yard in front paved with granite. Service is held here with great punctuality ; and there are missionaries belonging to other denominations residing in the city.

(4.) The houses are built of granite, large beds of which have been opened in the vicinity of the capital. The blocks are cemented together with clay, in consequence of the scarcity of lime, which is principally obtained by burning sea-shells. The floors, beams, and rafters, are made of the hard wood for which Brazil is famous. This is susceptible of a high polish, and might be made to add very much to the neatness and beauty of the dwellings ; but wainscoting is scarcely ever seen, and the interior walls and ceilings are usually provided with a rough coating of plaster, though the apartments of the wealthier citizens are often ornamented with stucco work and fresco painting, in rich and fanciful designs, or with silk and damask curtains and tapestries. The outer walls are also plastered, and generally wear a lively look. Most of the houses are two stories in height, though some exceed this. They have tall pyramidal roofs, surmounted with red tiles, which sometimes project fearfully. The doors and windows have heavy lintels and casings ; and jutting balconies, and wide, disproportioned—though, in a hot day, very comfortable—verandas, are regarded as essential requisites to every private habitation.

With one or two exceptions, the streets are long and narrow, and, for the most part, gloomy and sombre in appearance. They are badly paved with rudely-fashioned blocks of granite, and in the middle of them are the gutters, the receptacles of all the filth and abomination of a seaport town. Sidewalks are mainly dispensed with, and those which have been constructed are never in good repair. There can be no just excuse for the want of cleanliness indicated by the condition of the streets. The location is highly favorable ; wheeled vehicles for carrying burdens are comparatively little used, only a few antique coaches, and two-wheeled *calescas*, or calashes, occasionally jolting along over the rough pavements ; and an abundant supply of water is brought in aqueducts, from the Corcovado and Tejuca mountains, six or seven miles distant.

There are numerous fountains, also, scattered over the city, in the plazas, or squares ; and sparkling jets of crystal water may be seen in all directions, diffusing their grateful coolness through the heated and impure atmosphere. Some of the reservoirs have tastefully constructed edifices erected over them, which are alike useful and ornamental. The inhabitants rely, almost entirely, upon the fountains, for water for domestic purposes, which is carried by their slaves, in jars, or buckets, on their heads ; and " from dusky morn till dewy eve," they are surrounded by a motley collection of water-carriers, engaged in filling their vessels, chattering the while like so many magpies, and laughing and jesting gayly with their companions. Near the fountain of Hafariz, the largest in the city, there are two stone basins, fifty feet long and twenty-five wide, which are daily filled with from two to three hundred negro washerwomen, who stand in the water, often half naked, all the day long, constantly drubbing and rinsing their clothes.

(5.) The city of Rio Janeiro contains not far from two hundred and fifty thousand inhabitants, a great part of whom are slaves. In former years, the society was not very good, but latterly there has been a change for the better in this respect, though there is still sufficient room for improvement. Comparatively little attention is paid to education, especially among the female sex. The presence of the foreign ministers and their suites, and of intelligent merchants and travellers, has given a higher tone and polish to society, though the intercourse between the Brazilians and the citizens of other countries is not altogether free from restraint. This may be attributed, partly to the natural jealousy of their dispositions, and partly to the consciousness of their defective education. Females are rarely seen at public assemblages and parties, and the visits which they interchange with each other are rather formal and ceremonious than cheerful and friendly. These impediments and drawbacks to an easy and unrestrained social intercourse are gradually being softened down, and they must soon entirely disappear.

The time cannot be very far distant when Rio will become, what the capital of one of the richest countries on the American Continent ought to be, as celebrated for the taste and refinement of its inhabitants, as for its importance and advantages as a commercial city.

A fondness for meretricious display and ornament is exhibited by both sexes in their dress ; they endeavor to follow the French *mode*, but are such zealous copyists that they very often overdo the original. This is much better, however, than the opposite extreme. It is certainly more desirable that the Brazilian ladies should appear in dresses powdered with jewels, or fringed with silver, or in party-colored robes and ribbons, on the most unsuitable occasions, than that they should be confined to their *boudoirs*—their only knowledge of the world derived from occasional glimpses through their half-opened jalousies, and from the balconies of their apartments—or immured for life in the dark walls of a convent. Ease and suavity of manners will, sooner or later, follow a " reverence for Turkey carpets and *ormolu*."

There is a large public library, and a well-stored museum, in the city. The latter is open twice a week, and both are much frequented by the inhabitants.

One of the most interesting sights to be witnessed in Rio is a funeral, particularly of one of the wealthier classes ; for poverty, here as elsewhere, is rarely troubled with ceremony. The body of the humble laborer or artisan is carried to the Misericordia; a hasty prayer is said, a little lime sprinkled over his decaying remains, and he is thrown into a trench with some half-a-dozen others of the same stamp, and left to his long sleep,—while his neighbor of distinction, is borne to his last resting-place, attended with all the pageantry of woe. His body is wrapped in satin robes, and his coffin is decorated with a scarlet pall ornamented with silver lace and fringe. The latter is placed on a black hearse, overhung with long nodding plumes, and drawn by mules in rich trappings, sometimes covered with silver bells. The driver wears a cocked hat, trimmed with lace, and adorned with a black plume. The hearse is preceded by altar-boys in their church dresses, and surrounded by the black servants of the deceased, all bearing lighted wax candles. Arrived at the church, or chapel, where the services are to be performed, the coffin is temporarily deposited near the altar, and the friends and relatives arrange themselves along the aisles. All the spectators having been furnished with lighted tapers, the priests enter from the sacristy arrayed in their rich sacerdotal vestments. Clouds of odorous smoke are emitted from the swinging gold and silver censers, and mass and the funeral rites are said from splendidly illuminated service-books. This done, the pall is removed, the coffin opened, and holy water thrown over the dead, after which the body is taken to the place of interment.

A favorite burial-place is the Campo Santo, or cemetery, near the Imperial chapel. This is an amphitheatre, with high walls in which the vaults are built, surrounding a flower-garden. The coffins are deposited in niches just large enough for their admission, which are closed up with mason-work.

Notwithstanding their reserve on ordinary occasions, the citizens of Rio Janeiro are fond of amusements. There are three theatres in the city, all of which are well attended. Hunting, riding and fishing, are favorite pastimes. *White-jacket balls*, so called from the fact that the gentlemen who attend them appear in white jackets and trowsers, and the ladies in white dresses, without ornaments or jewelry, are held monthly at Praya Grande; and similar entertainments are frequently given at Gloria Botofogo, and other small towns in the neighborhood of the capital.

(6.) The great excess of the slave over the white population in Rio Janeiro, is soon noticed by the stranger. The former are nearly five times more numerous than the latter. In the city, burdens are carried almost exclusively by slaves, and scores of them may be seen at all hours of the day, bearing their water buckets, or staggering under packages of hides or bags of coffee. They usually go in gangs of from twelve to thirty, sometimes yoked together with heavy necklaces of iron and attended by a driver, and at others headed by a leader, one of their own number, who carries a small tin rattle, filled with stones, with which he keeps time. They move along at a slow trot humming a monotonous refrain, the words of which are often changed, though the sound is rarely varied. Many masters rely solely upon the income derived from the earnings of their slaves, who are required to pay over from twenty-five to fifty cents, according to their ability, every evening. If they are so fortunate as to earn more during the day, the surplus is their own; but if they fail to produce the prescribed amount, they are severely whipped. The females who are not employed as house servants, work at millinery, or other light handicrafts.

Those slaves that carry burdens in the streets, or work in the fields, are poorly fed and scantily clothed, scarcely ever wearing anything more than a slight covering about the loins. Unlike the owners of slaves in most civilized countries, the Brazilians manifest but little feeling for their servants. When they become worn out, or seriously diseased, they are generally turned into the world, without compunction, and left to die unfriended and alone.

In 1830, the slave trade was prohibited; but from seven to ten thousand blacks are now imported, annually, in defiance of the law. Pains are taken, however, to prevent their increase. The two sexes are usually locked up at night in different apartments, and all intercourse between them is prevented as far as possible.

(7.) If within the city of Rio, the eye is pained by the constant recurrence of stone and mortar—very few of the houses having either yards or gardens—ample atonement is made for this defect in the suburbs and environs. Here all is bright and beautiful. A superabundant vegetation, flowers of the gayest colors, gardens filled with fruit trees and choice shrubby plants, and wide-spreading groves of tamarinds, oranges and bananas, extend to the foot of the distant mountains. But the delightful *qui tas*, or country residences, half hidden by thick screens of mangrove bushes, or peeping out from behind hedges of laurels and myrtles, or rows of quaintly clipped arbor vitæ, constitute the chief attraction as you progress towards the interior. There are, likewise, fields of corn and sugar cane in the champaign country, and on the slopes of the hills are the coffee plantations, presenting, in the season, a constant succession of ephemeral white blossoms. Wild roses, tufts of sweet scented marjoram, and different varieties of cacti, spring up by the wayside, and, ever and anon,

> " The white Camella rears
> Its innocent and tranquil eye."

Further on, are bosky dingles and leafy coverts, from whence the shrill chirp of the cicada is heard long after the dense forests that limit the view in the west are overspread with the sober hue of the passing day.

(8.) Pedro Alvares Cabral is generally regarded as the discoverer of Brazil. He visited the country in 1500, when on his way to the East Indies, where he had been sent with a fleet by King Emanuel, of Portugal. Previous to this time, however, a Spanish mariner, by the name of Lepe, had penetrated as far south as the Brazilian strand, and two other Castilian navigators had landed and taken formal possession of the territory for the crown of Castile,—but the claims of Spain were subsequently relinquished by the treaty of Tordesillas. Cabral first gave it the name of Santa Cruz, afterwards changed, by his sovereign, to Brazil, in allusion to the Brazil-wood found in the country, which, in turn, derived its name from the Portuguese *braza*, a live coal or fire, referring to the brilliant red color of this important dyeing material.

For several years after its separation from Portugal, Brazil was subject to internal political dissensions and commotions; but since the abdication of Pedro I, in 1831, it has been tolerably quiet, and has steadily improved in commerce and advanced in refinement. The government is a limited monarchy, with a sovereign styled an Emperor. The legislative power is vested in two houses—the Senate, and the Chamber of Deputies. The people seem to be well satisfied with their form of government, but there exists a very friendly feeling towards the United States and their institutions, which it is for the pecuniary interest of both countries sedulously to cultivate.

Brazil is not wanting in the elements of greatness. She embraces within her boundaries a vast area of territory—over three million square miles—and her soil is highly fertile and productive. Nature has projected almost everything that belongs to her on a magnificent scale: she has four thousand miles of sea coast; her plains and valleys are vast and extensive, and her rivers* and mountains grand and imposing. Her population is computed to be five millions. About one fourth are whites, who chiefly occupy the narrow strip along the Atlantic and the province of Minas Geraës; and the remainder are negroes, mulattoes, and Indians. Many of the savage tribes in the interior, who live remote from the white settlements and mission establishments, are exceedingly ferocious.

Few countries surpass Brazil in the richness of her Flora, and her forests are truly magnificent;—although the second growth is generally thickly matted with the bamboo that furnishes the material for the huts of the half-civilized Indians, which are covered with thatches of palm, in their primeval state they are comparatively free from underbrush; and the unsightly daddocks, which so often mar the beauty of northern scenery, are rarely encountered. Cedars, as stately as those which, in ancient days, shaded the brow of Mount Lebanon, rear their giant limbs towards the sky. Oaks, of various fantastic forms, lofty palms and cæsalpinias, wide spreading mangos and tall and slender cecropias, are mingled with sycamores, myrtles and acacias,—with the

* Steamboats can ascend the Amazon, and its main tributary near its source, the Ucayali, to the mouth of the Rio Tambo, or Apurimac, nearly four thousand miles above Para.

juvia,* the cassada, the mahogany, and the macaw tree. In many sections of the country, and particularly on the upper waters of the Amazon, there are miniature forests, or groves, of cacao, of surpassing beauty.

Besides the rich cabinet and dye-woods found in the Brazilian forests, the finest timber for ship-building is also obtained in abundance. Excellent cordage resisting the action of water, is manufactured of the fibres of the palm tree. From the nuts, or seeds, of the cacao, the preparations known as cocoa and chocolate, are made ; this tree, sometimes called the chocolate-tree, is a species of theobroma, growing about twenty feet high, and bearing oval and pointed pods, in which are the numerous seeds imbedded in a white, pithy substance. The mango produces a fruit as large as an orange, and resembling the egg plant in shape ; it has a thick outer rind, beneath which is the fruit, of a fine golden color, surrounding a pit two inches long, to which it adheres, and possessing the mingled flavor of pine-apple and spruce.

The agave, here called *furcræa*, from its long furcated leaves, attains its highest state of perfection in this climate. Prominent among the other plants and shrubs, are the numerous varieties of the orchis tribe, with their odorous and beautiful flowers, the vochysia and its gorgeous yellow blossoms, the cupheas with their clusters of lilac and purple, the lobelias and their long blue spikes, the towering organum, the anil, or indigo plant, the vanilla, the sarsaparilla, and the coffee-tree. Until of late years, the indigo plant was not very extensively cultivated in Brazil: it is usually planted towards the latter part of March, twelve pounds of seed being allotted to the acre, and if the season is favorable, it will be ready to cut by the first of July. The maturity of the plant is indicated by the bursting forth of the flower-buds, and the expansion of the blossoms. Two croppings are taken during the year. The indigo is extracted by steeping the dried leaves and stems, or by allowing them to ferment when fresh ; the former process being considered the most

* The Brazil nut is the fruit of the Juvia.

advantageous.   A liquor is obtained, by either mode, which is churned or agitated till the dye begins to granulate ; the flakes are then permitted to settle, the remaining liquor is drawn off, and the indigo is drained in bags, and dried in boxes.

One of the chief staples of Brazil is obtained from the coffee-bush.   This shrub, in its natural state, rises to the height of fifteen or twenty feet, but, when cultivated, it is kept down by pruning, to five or six feet, for the greater convenience thus afforded of gathering the fruit.   The main stem is upright, and has a light brown bark ; the branches shoot out horizontally and opposite, crossing each other at every joint, and forming a sort of pyramid ; the flowers, which are of a pure white color, like those of the Spanish jasmine, grow in clusters, at the roots of the leaves, along the branches.   The flowers soon fade, and are replaced by a fruit resembling a cherry, which contains a yellow glairy fluid enveloping two seeds or coffee berries.   The seeds are glued together, and each is surrounded by a peculiar coriaceous membrane.   All along the Atlantic coast of Brazil, there are extensive plantations of coffee, the culture of which is said to be highly profitable.   When the cherry-looking fruit assumes a deep red color, it is gathered, and passed between two wooden revolving rollers, and a third fixed one, from which it falls upon a sieve that separates the pulp from the beans.   The latter are then steeped for a night in water, carefully washed in the morning, and afterwards dried in the sun.   They are now detached from the coriaceous husk surrounding them, by a wooden edge wheel turned vertically by a horse or mule, and the membranes are subsequently separated from the berries by a winnowing machine.   The final process consists in spreading the coffee upon mats or tables, picking it clean, and packing in bags.

Sugar cane grows thriftily in the low grounds and interval lands, and all the tropical fruits are also produced ; in the interior, on the more elevated localities, where the vegetation begins to creep up the sides of the mountains, the shrubs

BRAZILIAN FOREST.

and fruit trees natural to colder climates are met with in great variety.

The markets in the Brazilian towns are plentifully supplied with beef, fish and poultry, and vegetables of all kinds are sold in the streets. The principal articles of food, however, especially in the country, are *cárne seca*, or dried beef, and *farina*, a preparation of the manihot.

It is not only for their valuable timber that the forests of Brazil are celebrated. Numerous species of parasites and creepers abound,—bromelias, bignonias, honeysuckles, and mistletoes,—which, extending their long sprays from tree to tree, from limb to limb, like the cordage of a ship, form leafy coverts that afford a shelter from the oppressive heat of the equatorial sun, to the brute denizens of these vast woodland solitudes. Birds displaying in their plumage all the brilliancy and splendor possible to combine from gold and scarlet, purple and emerald; fierce and ravenous beasts, chattering monkeys, and huge scaly serpents and alligators, frequent these dark and shady retreats. Conspicuous among the birds, is the couroucoo, whose plumage is purple, green, and gold, beautifully blended together; the cephaloptem, which has a singular tuft on its head, like a parasol; the aicurus, whose head is variegated with yellow, red and violet, its body green, the tips of its wings red, and its long tail yellow; the mocking-bird, famous for its unrivalled strains of richest melody; the witwall, or golden oriole, whose swinging nest, depending from the loftiest tree, sways to and fro with every breeze; the gay-coated king fisher; the scarlet macaw; the lustrous jacamar; the guara, of a vivid red color; the cotinga; and the many-tinted paroquet. Among the beasts, are the jaguar, or ounce of Brazil; the puma; the tapir; the cabial; the ant-eater; the paca, which resembles the guinea-pig; and the armadillo, called *taton* by the natives. Of the monkeys there are upwards of twenty different species, varying in color and size, from the acari, or scarlet monkey, to the silky tamarin.

In the interior of Brazil, west of the Araguay river, and

south of the Acaray mountains, there are extensive plains,
wooded near the streams, but elsewhere covered with rank
grass. These grassy plains are called *llaños*, or *pampas;*
countless herds of wild horses and cattle roam over them at
will, unchecked and unpursued, save by the *guachos*, or
herdsmen, who spend most of their time upon horseback,
armed with the knife and lasso. Immense numbers of cattle are annually taken by them and slaughtered, chiefly for
their hides and horns, though the hams, and sometimes other
portions of the carcass, are smoked or jerked. After being
cured, the hides are bound up in packages, for exportation,
one of which is called a *last*, and contains twelve dozen.

(9.) Not more famous were the pearls of Ormuz, or the
diamonds of Golconda, than, in former days, was the mineral wealth of Brazil. This may be said to have been measurably exhausted, yet the annual products of the mines and
diamond washings, at this time, are by no means inconsider-
able. The first discovery of gold was made in 1682, at Ca-
lapreta, in the sands of the Mandi, a tributary of the Rio
Dolce. Since that time it has been found almost everywhere
in the streams and ravines at the foot of the Brazilian Andes,
from the fifth to the thirtieth degree of southern latitude.
The most productive mines are near Villa Rica, in the suburbs of the village of Cocaës : a remarkable example is
here presented, of the existence of this mineral among the
primitive strata, disseminated in small grains, spangles and
crystals ; great quantities of native gold, in spangles, being
obtained from beds of granular quartz, or micaceous specu-
lar iron. There are, also, many valuable mines in the province of Minas Geraës, where the metal is found in veins, in
beds, and in grains, among the alluvial loams ; and there
are washings yielding handsome profits, on the eastern slope
of the Cordilleras, in the upper valley of the Amazon.

From 1790 to 1802, over fifteen thousand pounds, avoirdupois, of gold, were annually taken from Brazil to Europe ;
but the yearly product is now estimated at only two thou-

sand eight hundred pounds, of the value of one million sterling.

The matrix, or original repository, of the diamond of Brazil, is brown iron ore, occurring in beds of slaty quartzose micaceous iron ore, or composed of iron-glance and magnetic iron ore. The diamond mines were originally discovered in 1728, in the district of Serro-do-Frio. The most celebrated mine is that of Mandanga, north of Rio Janeiro, on the Jigitonhonha. The river, which is from three to nine feet deep, is made nearly dry, by drawing the water off with sluices at certain seasons : and the diamond gravel, here called *cascalho*, is removed from the bed of the stream, to be washed elsewhere at leisure. The gravel is always collected in the dry season, and washed during the rainy. For the latter purpose, a stream of water is admitted into a number of boxes containing the *cascalho*, beneath an oblong shed. Attached to each box is a negro washer, and there are inspectors placed at regular distances, on elevated stools. Great precautions are taken to prevent the concealment of the diamonds by the washers, and when one is discovered, the finder is required to rise up and exhibit it. When the negro is so fortunate, which very rarely happens, as to discover a gem weighing seventeen and a half carats,* he recovers his liberty. The earth of the bottom lands on either side is as rich in diamonds as that in the channel of the river. All the diamonds found in the district of Serro-do-Frio, are deposited, monthly, in the treasury at Tejuco. The amount thus delivered, from 1801 to 1806, has been estimated at about eighteen or nineteen thousand carats, annually.

There are fine mines of diamonds on the Rio Pardo, and at Tocaya, in the district of Minas Novas, near the confluence of the Jigitonhonha and the Rio Grande. The largest diamonds, however, obtained in Brazil, are found in the cantons of India and Abaité.

In addition to these great mineral treasures, there are

---

* A diamond of that size is worth £2400 sterling, not far from $10,000, federal currency.

mines of silver and platinum in various parts of the country. In the canton of Abaité, in the province of Minas Geraës, there are rich lead mines, and a fine mine of antimony has been opened near Sabara in the same province. Iron is likewise found in Minas Geraës, at Gaspar-Saärez, and there are extensive iron mines and furnaces in the captainry, or province, of St. Paul.

(10.) The commerce of Brazil is rapidly increasing and extending. Most of her trade, however, is carried on through the vessels of other nations, although she has a very respectable commercial marine. The imports amount to about twenty-five millions of dollars annually, and the exports ordinarily exceed that sum. Coffee is the principal article exported from the central provinces; upwards of one hundred and thirty-five million pounds being shipped every year, principally from Rio Janeiro and its great rival, San Salvador, or Bahia, on the Bay of All Saints. From the northern provinces, sugar, cotton and tobacco, are exported through the ports of Pernambuco,* Maranham, and Para. The best caoutchouc, also, is exported from Para, in large quantities: it is extracted from the *siphonia cahuca*, or *siphonia elastica*, which is found in other parts of South America, as well as in Brazil, although it is nowhere so valuable as in the vicinity of Para. Incisions are made into the tree, through the bark, in several places, from which a milky juice, of a pale yellow color, and having the consistence of cream, is discharged; this is spread upon clay moulds, and dried in the sun, or by the smoke of a fire. The latter process, however, blackens the gum. Of late years, the juice has been extensively exported; but it is generally shipped in a concrete state. It is better known among us by the names of gum elastic, and india rubber, than by its appropriate one of caoutchouc.

Hides, tallow and horns, are the chief products of the

* A large portion of the population of Pernambuco are foreigners, who are not very warmly attached to the government. Frequent *émeutes* and disturbances have taken place—one occurring as late as January, 1849,—which have been with difficulty suppressed by the government troops.

southern provinces of Brazil. The most important seaport town in this section of the Empire, is Rio Grande.

To the United States, the trade of Brazil is of considerable moment, as a ready market is afforded in the latter for a portion of our surplus agricultural products; but it is more than probable that she is the greater gainer of the two,— since our imports from Brazil, during the year ending in June, 1847, amounted to over seven million dollars, while our exports were a little short of three millions.

(11.) In consequence of the unseaworthy condition of the Peacock, and the long time required to fit her for continuing the cruise, the squadron was detained at Rio for several weeks. About the middle of December, the Relief was dispatched to Orange Harbor, to cut wood for the use of the other vessels, and on the 6th of January following, the remainder of the fleet dropped down the harbor of Rio and stood out to sea, directing their course towards the same place of destination.

3*

CHAPTER III.

(1.) SOUTH of the thirtieth degree of north latitude, strong westerly gales prevail for a greater part of the year, which frequently terminate in severe *pamperos*, or hurricanes, the effects of which are often experienced far out at sea. These are supposed to be occasioned by the vast *llaños*, or grassy plains, in the valley of the La Plata, which disturb the equilibrium of the atmosphere. The currents of air here collected, being walled in on the west by the giant barriers of the Andes, and finding little or no resistance on the east, rush forth in the latter direction, either skimming softly and gently over the bosom of the Atlantic, or plunging and dashing on like the frightened courser.

(2.) Favored by propitious, though light, and somewhat variable winds, the Exploring Squadron held on their way to the south. On the 25th of January, 1839, they again approached the coast of South America, at the mouth of the Rio Negro, the southern boundary of Buenos Ayres, or, as it is now called, the Argentine Republic. The coast in the vicinity of the river, is low and barren; consisting of a succession of sand hills and downs covered with a dry and sickly vegetation, where the stunted shrubs that break the monotony of the landscape, rarely rise to the dignity of tree-hood,

" And shrivelled herbs on withering stems decay."

Further inland, there are immense pampas, over which roam

countless herds of horses and cattle.   The inhabitants, who
are principally of mixed Spanish and Indian descent, are
employed, for the most part, in herding, and other occupations incident thereto.   The costume of the *guachos*, or
herdsmen, is strikingly picturesque ; and it is shown to full
advantage, when the wearer is mounted, with the knife in
his girdle and the lasso at his saddle bow, pressing forward
in hot pursuit after the lusty bullock, flying for dear life,
over the broad grassy plain.   It usually consists of a red,
or party-colored shirt, striped or plaided ; white, Cossack
drawers, fringed at the bottom of the leg, which are called
calzoons, or *calzoncillas* ; wide, loose trowsers, of scarlet
cloth ; riding boots, fitting tight to the foot and leg, of untanned horse hide ; a gay sash ; and a conical cap, fiery red,
with a large tassel dangling at the end.   Thus arrayed, with
his swart countenance, dark mustachios, and keen penetrating eyes, the *guacho* is either formidable, or *bizarre*, according to the circumstances under which he makes his first
appearance in the presence of a stranger.

Twenty miles above the mouth of the Rio Negro, on the
northern bank of the stream, is El Carmen, a small town
containing about five hundred inhabitants.   This is a convict
settlement, under the authority of a governor general, and
there are usually two or three hundred soldiers stationed
here.   The *estancias*, or residences, of the better and more
prosperous inhabitants, consist of a dwelling house made of
adobé bricks,* divided into two or three compartments, without floor, ceiling, inner doors, or furniture, except a few
rough benches and stools ; outhouses for the horses and
slaves, also built of *adobés ;* and a *câral* for the cattle—a
circular inclosure surrounded by a palisade fence, constructed
of poles from four to six inches in diameter, and twenty or
thirty feet high.   The converted Indians, who collect around
the white settlements, and are called *Indios Mansos*, live in
rudely fashioned huts, or *toldos*.

Including the population of El Carmen, there are not

---

* Bricks baked in the sun.

far from three thousand inhabitants embraced within the
limits of the settlement on the Rio Negro.   The river is only
one third of a mile wide, but it is navigable for boats to Chi-
cula, two hundred miles from its mouth.

(3.) When Buenos Ayres first achieved her independence,
she was connected with Paraguay and Uruguay, and the
confederation assumed the name of the United Provinces of
South America, afterwards changed to United Provinces
of La Plata.   Difficulties and contentions, artfully promoted
by the government of Brazil, followed the separation from
the mother country; and after a severe and bloody struggle, in
1813, Paraguay became independent of the confederacy, and
established a distinct government.   Shortly after this, Brazil
laid claim to Uruguay ; another fierce and protracted contest
ensued, which was finally terminated, in 1828, by the erection of the disputed territory into an independent state.
Since that time, the remaining portion of the confederacy has
been known as Buenos Ayres, and, latterly, as the Argentine
Republic.*   Harmony and tranquillity, however, have not
generally prevailed in the country.   Internal dissensions
have been fomented by the intrigues of Brazil and the mo-
narchical governments of Europe; and international difficulties have been occasioned by the attempt of Buenos Ayres
to enforce her right to the sole navigation of the La Plata—
a right which would probably have never been invaded, or
questioned, had she been as great and powerful, as she is
weak and humble.   England, France, and Brazil, have
united to oppress her ; and at the time of the visit of the Exploring Squadron, her ports were blockaded by a French fleet.

Buenos Ayres contains about two million inhabitants, scattered over a territory nine hundred thousand square miles
in extent.   Its capital is Buenos Ayres, which contains near
eighty thousand inhabitants, and is pleasantly situated on

* The term Argentine Republic, (silver republic,) was, no doubt, adopted as
being expressive of the mineral character of the soil; but it is hardly more appropriate, and is certainly less beautiful, than the former name of Buenos Ayres,
(pleasant breezes.)

the southern shore of the majestic Rio de la Plata—the river
of silver. The manners and customs of the inhabitants,
and the style of building, do not differ very essentially from
those at Rio Janeiro. In the interior, there are several other
towns of importance. Mendoza, containing twenty thousand
inhabitants, and San Juan, about one third smaller, are situated near the great passes through the Andes. Cordova
and Tucuman are important trading towns, and Salta, on the
Rio Salado is a celebrated market for mules.

The climate of the country is delightful; the heavens are
serene; the atmosphere is soft and refreshing, and remarkable for its transparent purity. In the southern provinces
the air is so dry and pure, at certain seasons, that fresh meat
will keep for a long time without becoming tainted.

Grain, fruit and vegetables, are raised with comparatively
little labor, and the soil is exceedingly fertile, with the exception of a narrow strip of sandy barren land along the coast,
like that near the mouth of the Rio Negro. But the inhabitants seem generally disinclined to till the ground, and their
whole time and attention are directed to raising horses,
mules and cattle. Of these they have the finest breeds in
South America, and the mules exhibited every year at Salta,
are unsurpassed in the world. The prices are quite moderate.
Bullocks are sold at from five to ten dollars per head, according to age; and horses and mules, when broken to the saddle,
at from twelve to fifteen dollars. Buenos Ayres is not deficient in mineral stores; she has valuable mines of gold and
silver on the eastern slopes of the Andes, from which over
four million pounds sterling of the former metal, and twenty-
seven millions of the latter, were obtained, from 1790 to
1830; but, after all, the real, substantial wealth of the
country, consists in the flocks and herds that feed upon the
broad plains irrigated by the tributaries of the La Plata.
Numbers of horses and mules are driven over the mountains
to Chili, and quantities of hides, beef, tallow, horns and
bones, are annually exported.

Salt is also an important product. North of the Colorado,

and between that river and the Rio Negro, there are numerous salt lakes—*lagunas de salinas*—upon which the salt
collects in incrustations. It is obtained in great quantities
after a severe rain, when the soil, which seems to be highly
impregnated, has been the most thoroughly disturbed. The
water soon evaporates, and the white salt, perfectly pure,
and finely crystallized, appears in its stead. It is sold on
the Colorado and Rio Negro, for twenty cents per bushel.

On the right bank of the Paraguay, a small plant is found,
called *matte*, which is used as a substitute for tea. It is
sometimes called Paraguay tea. Sarsaparilla and vanilla
likewise abound in the country.

Most of the animals seen in Brazil exist in Buenos Ayres.
There are deer in abundance, in the neighborhood of the salt
lakes; ostriches are quite common on the prairies; tapirs,
cabials, and other species of the cavy genus, frequent the
grassy hummocks on the banks of the streams; and ducks,
partridges, pheasants, cassowaries, and wild geese, gratify,
alike, the ambition of the sportsman, and the appetite of the
epicure. The guanaco, an animal belonging to the same
genus with the llama, is also frequently seen; and in the
northern section of the country there is a very pretty species
of hare, called tapeti. Porcupines and armadillos a-e found
in every thicket.

(4.) Ever since the first settlement of Buenos Ayres, the
white population have been more or less annoyed by the
savage Indian tribes of the interior,—the off-shoots of the
great Araucanian family, whose descendants still occupy the
southern part of Chili. North of the Colorado are the Ran-
gueles Indians; between that river and the Rio Negro, are
the Pehuenches; and on its southern bank are the Tehuili-
ches, or Patagonians, who are said, though on doubtful authority, to be of gigantic stature, but mild and inoffensive in
their dispositions. The most formidable enemies of the
whites, are the Chileños Indians, who inhabit the mountain
fastnesses separating Chili from the pampas of Buenos
Ayres. The usual weapons of the Indians are a long lance,

and the *bólas*, or balls ; the latter consisting of two leaden
balls attached to either end of a stout strip of hide, four feet
long ; this is grasped in the middle, whirled over the head a
few times, and then thrown with astonishing velocity and
precision. It rarely fails to disable the object aimed at, be it
man or beast.

(5.) Upon the appearance of the Exploring Squadron off
the coast, the inhabitants living on the Rio Negro, fancying
the French fleet was approaching to despoil them, became
much alarmed, and having hastily collected their cattle, fled
with them into the interior. The first party that landed
found the *estancias* deserted, and the fires smoldering on
the rude hearth stones. The mistake was soon discovered,
however, and the people gradually ventured forth from their
places of concealment. Partial observations and surveys
were made, in order to prepare a correct chart of the river—a
work subsequently completed by Lieutenant Alden—and on
the 3d of February the squadron again got under way, and
proceeded on their voyage.

(6.) As they approached the southern extremity of the continent, flocks of speckled haglets, or cape pigeons, and albatrosses, were occasionally seen ; the moon began to wear
round further to the north, and the nights were rendered
gloomy by the lengthening shadows which it cast. On the
12th of February, the barometer fell rapidly, and heavy
squalls of rain, mingled with hail and sleet, followed. When
the day broke on the morning of the 13th, and the dense
mists that curtained the sky had lifted sufficiently to enable
objects to be distinguished, the gray cliffs of Staten Land
were discovered ; and, not long after, the barren rocks, and
snow-clad mountain peaks, of Tierra del Fuego—the land of
fire—loomed above the horizon, dark, bleak and desolate,
and showing no signs of vegetation, except, here and there, a
stunted shrub or tree.

The coast of Tierra del Fuego may well be called iron-
bound. It is composed of huge masses of trap rock,
traversed by red veins, indicating its volcanic origin, which

rise abruptly to the height of one thousand or fifteen hundred feet. Inland, there are mountains, many of them of a conical shape, from four to five thousand feet above the sea level. Tall isolated rocks, detached from the main shore, are scattered along the coast, like giant sentinels on guard. Numerous ravines intersect the wall of rocks behind them, where the fierce blasts of the stormy Atlantic die away in echoes, or howl the requiem of some gallant ship stranded amid its foaming breakers. Even during the midsummer months of this climate—January and February—the mountains do not put off their mantle of snow; but ever wear the same cold and cheerless appearance.

Tierra del Fuego is separated from Patagonia on the north, by the Straits of Magellan, named after the Portuguese navigator who discovered them. Vessels bound to the Pacific can pass through the straits without difficulty, if attended with favorable winds; but, as there is a strong current setting in from the Atlantic, it is hazardous to attempt the passage, from the east, in a square rigged craft, —though with steam vessels, or small fore-and-afters, there is much less danger. Coming from the west, the passage may be made with ease, and it is infinitely less hazardous than to encounter the squalls, "catpaws," and icebergs, which are the common accompaniments of a voyage around the cape.

Between Staten Land and Tierra del Fuego, are the Straits of Le Maire, which are about fifteen miles wide, and something less than that in length. As a general thing, it is always best for a vessel intending to double the cape, to pass through these straits; it shortens the distance considerably, and on all ordinary occasions there is not the least danger. Violent squalls sometimes issue from the ravines, but it is easy to guard against them. Northwest winds prevail off this coast, and with these the straits may be threaded in three or four hours. This was the route taken by the Exploring Squadron; they passed through the straits on the 13th of February, with all their canvas spread. It was a beautiful day, and the weather continued favorable till they reached the cape.

"Be it fair or foul, rain or shine;"—

in all weathers, at all times and seasons, Cape Horn is a terror to the mariner; and many and marvellous are the tales of peril and danger spun in the forecastle, as this dreaded promontory is approached, and the hoarse wail of the beating surf that spends its fury upon its rocky sides, is heard rising over the waters. In favorable weather, vessels sail within a short distance of it, in perfect safety; but when the storm-king "holds high revel there," as wide a berth as possible is given to this formidable breakwater which nature has reared against the fury of the Atlantic.*

The cape is situated in latitude 55° 58' south. It is a conical, jagged peak, of trachytic rock, rising at the southern end of Hermit Island. The latter is two or three miles in length, and behind it there is a line of rocks extending towards the north. Between it and Tierra del Fuego, there are several long, high, and narrow islands, which are covered with snow during the whole year. Cape Horn, however, is not the southernmost land in this quarter. The Diego Ramirez Islands, a small cluster of sea-holms, on one of which is False Cape Horn, are 34' further south.

(7.) On the 16th of February, the Squadron passed the "stormy cape," within a few miles of the shore;—most of the vessels having their studding sails set on both sides— and were soon lifted upon the long rolling swell of the Pacific—"the summer sea." The 17th was cloudy and nearly calm; and the day and night following were spent in beating through the passage between Hermit Island and False Cape Horn, and from thence into Nassau Bay, an

---

* Vessels are often compelled to go as high as the sixtieth degree of southern latitude, in order to double the cape.

indentation of the southern coast of Tierra del Fuego. Early in the morning of the 18th instant, the Squadron came to anchor in Orange Harbor, on the western side of the bay, but separated from it by Burnt Island, where they found the Relief had arrived before them.

CHAPTER IV.

(1.) AFTER leaving Rio de Janeiro, Captain Long proceeded with the Relief to the coast of Patagonia, where, in accordance with his instructions, he commenced running a line of soundings, and making examinations of the shoals said to exist in that quarter.

Like that of Tierra del Fuego, the Patagonian coast is bold and rocky, but indented with frequent small bays or harbors, which are scantily protected, however, against the violence of the winds and waves. The Relief drew in towards the land several times, sufficiently near to discover the herds of guanacoes feeding on the slopes of the hills, and on two occasions came to anchor; but it was deemed hazardous to remain so near the shore, and she accordingly hauled off where she would be sure of a wider berth in the event of a storm.

(2.) Patagonia was discovered by Magellan in 1519. On account of the insecurity of its harbors, and their being so difficult and dangerous of access, no permanent white settlement has yet been formed in the country. About the year 1779, a party of Spaniards established themselves at Port St. Julian, in latitude 49° 10′ S., and longitude 67° 40′ W., but the attempt to colonize this inhospitable region was speedily abandoned. A few expeditions have been undertaken into the interior, yet very little is known, beyond the coast outline, in regard to it. The Andes here consist of but one *cordillera*, the mean height of which is estimated at three thousand feet, although there are many peaks opposite the Archipelago of Chiloë, from five to six thousand feet high. This mountain range divides the country into two unequal parts ; the larger of them, by far, lying on the East. The western coast is extremely abrupt and precipitous, and is skirted with numerous irregularly shaped and rocky islands. On the East, the surface of the country rises from the Atlantic to the Andes, in a succession of terraces, all of which are arid and sterile ; the upper soil being chiefly composed of marine gravelly deposits. On the banks of the rivers, herbage and trees are occasionally found, but with this exception, these terraces produce nothing but a coarse wiry grass, and a small thorny shrub fit only for fuel. The general sterility of East Patagonia is probably occasioned by the westerly winds that prevail throughout most of the year ; the moisture which they bring with them from the Pacific, is condensed and precipitated in the mountains and their immediate vicinity, and they consequently become quite dry. Almost the only moisture, therefore, that is brought to this desert tract, comes with the easterly winds, which are very rare. Near the Andes, however, where the grateful moisture of the westerly winds is precipitated, wheat, maize, beans, lentils, pease, and other similar grains and vegetables, are raised.

The most prevalent mineral formations of East Patagonia, are porphyry, basalt, sandstone, and a friable rock resembling chalk. Organic remains are found of different kinds, and in great numbers. There is an abundance of rodent mammals in the country, but there are few varieties of larger animals. Guanacoes are the most common, and are frequently seen in droves numbering several hundred. The puma, the inveterate enemy of the guanaco, and the fox, are the only other wild quadrupeds worthy of mention. The principal birds are the condor, the cassowary, and the rhea, or South American ostrich.

(3.) Until of late years, it was pretty generally supposed

that the Patagonian Indians were absolute giants. The examinations made by recent navigators have shown this impression to be entirely erroneous* ; yet they are undoubtedly the tallest people of whom we have any account, since the average height of the men is full six feet. Their heads and features are large, but their hands and feet are small, and they have less muscular strength than their size would indicate. Their dress adds much to the bulkiness of their appearance ;—it consists of a large mantle of guanaco skins loosely gathered about the person, which it completely envelopes, hanging from the shoulders to the ankles ; and a kind of drawers, or loose buskins, usually made of the same material. Their complexions are a dark copper color ; their hair is long, black, and coarse, and tied above the temples by a fillet of braided or twisted sinews. Their foreheads are low, and their cheek-bones prominent. They are fond of disfiguring their faces, and other parts of their bodies, with paint ; and those who live remote from the white settlements in Chili and on the Rio Negro, besmear themselves with clay, coal, and soot.

The Patagonians live in tents formed of poles and skins. They lead a nomadic life and subsist mainly on the flesh of wild animals and birds. In the northern part of East Patagonia, the inhabitants procure wild horses on the *pampas*, which, when tamed, are ridden by both men and women. Saddles, bridles, and similar accoutrements, as well as Spanish goods of various kinds, are obtained from Valdivia and other places in South Chili. The arms of the Patagonian are a long tapering lance, a knife, and the *bolas*, which consist among them of two round stones, weighing about a pound each, covered with leather, and attached to the thong or cord. So expert are the natives in the use of this double-headed shot, which, in its use and effects, resembles the ancient sling, that they will hit a mark of the size of an English

---

* This idea originated with the Spaniards and Portuguese who first visited the country, and was probably based on a comparison of their diminutive proportions with the tall and bulky forms of the natives.

shilling, with both stones, at a distance of fifteen yards. It is not customary to strike the guanaco or ostrich with them, but they are thrown in such a manner that the cord is twisted about the legs of the animal or bird, so as to prevent its running away.

As may well be presumed, there is little semblance of law or authority among the Patagonian Indians. They nominally live under various petty chiefs, but the latter in reality possess no power except that of might, and, in point of fact, every individual is his own master.

(4.) In passing through the straits of Le Maire, Captain Long visited most of the harbors, and nearly two days were spent in Good Success Bay, on the coast of Tierra del Fuego, the best and largest of them all. While here, Captain Long, accompanied by several officers, went ashore in three armed boats, to hold communication with a party of natives, who invited them to land by their cries and gestures. The natives appeared friendly, and when the captain and his men landed, they ran towards them, crying out, at the same time,— "*cuchillo! cuchillo!*" As this is the Spanish word for knife, it was thought they were begging to be supplied with that article; but as they seemed to apply the term to everything shown them, or rather continued its repetition almost incessantly, it was found impossible to ascertain its real meaning or application. In their dress and physiognomy they resembled the Patagonians, and were supposed to belong on the other side of the straits of Magellan; they wore guanaco skins over their shoulders, and fillets were bound around their heads. Some members of the party had sandals, also made of the guanaco skin, on one foot. They were provided with bows and arrows,—the latter having flint heads; but they seemed to depend principally on fish for subsistence. All were exceedingly dirty, though well formed, and most of them were troubled with a disease of the eye,— occasioned, perhaps, by the dazzling reflection from the snow during their long winters.

It was evident that they had had intercourse before with

the sailors of civilized nations, as many manufactured articles, which they could have obtained in no other way, were
found in their possession, and the report of fire-arms did not
intimidate them in the least.   The hair on the tops of their
heads was cut short, and their faces were painted with a
kind of clay, like red ochre.   They were particularly well
pleased with a looking glass and a string of glass beads
which were shown them.   Although they attached great
value to their bows and arrows, they were willing to exchange them for a piece of iron hoop or a few rusty nails.

From Good Success Bay the Relief continued her course
towards Orange Harbor.   On the way, she touched at New
Island; no natives were seen here, but there were indications
of their having recently been on the island.   On the 30th of
January, Captain Long cast anchor in Nassau Bay, and subsequently entered Orange Harbor.   Immediately after he got
his anchor down in the bay, a native canoe came alongside,
—in which were three men, one woman, and a child.   Two
of the men came on board without hesitation.   They were
found to differ in many respects from those seen at Good
Success Bay.   They did not speak the same language; they
were not so tall in stature, nor so well-proportioned; and
they were far more filthy and disgusting in their appearance.

(5.) Orange Harbor is decidedly the safest, and the most
spacious and convenient of all the harbors on the Fuegian
coast.   Captain Cook anchored and refitted here previous to
his Antarctic cruise, as did also Captains King and Fitzroy
while engaged in their expeditions.   It is surrounded by lofty
hills, intersected with numerous small inlets or coves, in
which boats can enter and obtain wood and water, which are
both abundant and of excellent quality.

Shortly after the arrival of the squadron at Orange Harbor, they were visited by the natives,—a most abject, ill-
shapen, and miserable race of beings.   On one occasion, a
party consisting of five men and one woman,—the latter old
and ugly, but as strong and muscular as those of the other
sex,—approached one of the vessels in a frail and leaky

canoe which required constant bailing to keep it afloat. But one of the number—a young man not far from nineteen years of age—could be induced to come on board. They brought with them a number of spears, and a necklace of shells, which they exchanged for pieces of cotton and an iron hoop. In dress, language and appearance, they resembled those at Nassau Bay. They were highly delighted with music, and fond of mimicking everything they heard; the flute and guitar were played for their amusement, and they endeavored to imitate the accompanying songs.

(6.) Tierra del Fuego properly includes the group of islands lying off the southern extremity of South America, and separated from it by the straits of Magellan; but the term is usually applied, by way of distinction, to the largest, or main island, formerly called King Charles' South Land. The eastern part of this island is low, with sloping plains like those of Patagonia, though there is really no level land. On the west side it is traversed, from north to south, by a chain of mountains four thousand feet high. The island is all mountainous, and appears to have been partially submerged in the sea by some convulsion of nature,—by which so many inlets and bays are occasioned where valleys would otherwise have been. The surface at the foot of the hills is covered with a thick bed of swampy peat. On the mountain sides, reaching up to an elevation of twelve hundred feet, there are dense forests; the trees rise uniformly to the height of forty or fifty feet, and generally incline towards the northeast, in consequence of the prevailing southwestern winds.

The principal trees are beech, birch and willow. One species of birch, the *betula antarctica*, has a stem from thirty to forty-six inches in diameter. Winter's bark, (*drymis winteri*) first introduced as a medicine in 1579, was originally discovered here. In Tierra del Fuego and the adjacent islands, hornblende is the most common rock, but slate is abundant. Lava and other volcanic products were discovered by Captain King, but nothing of the kind was found during the limited, and necessarily imperfect, reconnaissances of the American Exploring Squadron. The line of perpetual snow descends as low as three thousand feet; yet, notwithstanding the unfriendliness of the climate, the scenery of the island is in many respects grand and imposing. " There is a degree of mysterious grandeur," says Mr. Darwin, in his Journal of a Voyage round the World," in mountain behind mountain, with the deep intervening valleys, all covered by one thick, dusky mass of forest. The atmosphere, likewise, in this climate, where gale succeeds gale, with rain, hail, and sleet, seems blacker than anywhere else. In the Strait of Magellan, looking due southward from Port Famine, the distant channels between the mountains appeared from their gloominess to lead beyond the confines of this world."

(7.) Guanacoes, wolves, foxes and otters, are the only wild animals of importance found in Tierra del Fuego. Fish and seals are quite numerous. Among the birds are the cape pigeon, the petrel, and the albatross. Wild fowl, geese, ducks, and plover, are also plenty. The cape pigeons are of a white and lead color ; they fly in large flocks, and seem much attached to each other ; their flesh is equal to that of the American teal. The albatross resembles a goose, and its feathers, down, and quills, are equally valuable ; its meat is dark-colored but not unpalatable ; by sailors, it is considered as a *rara avis*, indeed, from the fact that it has no gizzard, —and many of them look upon it with the same abhorrence with which the Mussulman regards pork.

(8.) The Fuegians are elevated by only a few degrees above the brute creation. They have small low foreheads, prominent brows, diminutive eyes, large mouths, wide nostrils, thick lips, black lank hair, and long and slender arms. Their bodies are large in comparison with their extremities, but they are rarely over five feet in height. On the eastern coast, the natives wear guanaco skins, and on the western, seal skins. The central tribes have otter skins. Sometimes a small scrap takes the place of a whole skin, and where this is the case, or the skin is too small to protect the whole person, it is laced across the breast by strings, and shifted from

4

side to side, according as the wind blows. It is by no means uncommon, however, to see them entirely naked. They appear stunted in their growth; their dark copper colored skins are filthy and greasy; and their hideous faces are generally bedaubed with ashes or paint. Their voices are discordant, and their gestures, in conversation, animated and even violent.

Their wigwams are sometimes built of the trunks of trees, arranged in a circle and leaning against each other at the top, like a cone; the interstices are chinked in with earth, leaves, and wild grass. Another kind of wigwam is made of boughs or small branches bound together at the top with sedge or twigs; other branches are interlaced with these so as to form wicker-work, and the whole is covered with grass, peat or bark. They subsist almost wholly on fish, seals, sea-eggs, and testacea. A few tasteless berries and fungi are the only productions of the moist soil which they make use of to satisfy hunger. The only habitable land is directly on the coast, and in summer and winter, through the endless mists and storms, parties of them may be seen wandering along the beach in quest of food. Their only mode of conveyance is a canoe drawn through the water by the kelp, or propelled by a rude paddle; it is made of strips of bark sewed together, and is usually about twenty-five feet long and three feet wide. The bottom of the canoe is covered with a layer of clay a foot thick, on which a fire is always kept burning. Sea-eggs are obtained by diving, and small fish are caught by a baited hair-line, without any hook. Larger fish are speared. Shell-fish are picked from the rocks whenever it is low water, be it night or day, in storm or sunshine.

Seasons of famine are frequent among the Fuegians, and at such times they often kill and eat the old women, before they devour their dogs. They are divided into different tribes, and when at war they are also cannibals. It is rarely the case that they object to any kind of food; and if the carcass of a putrid whale is discovered, it is hailed as a special blessing. Traces of superstition exist among them, and each tribe has a conjuring doctor; yet it has been found impossible clearly to ascertain his duties. They exhibit a dread of some mysterious and invisible superior powers, but have no definite idea of a future life. Bows and arrows, spears, and, in the northern part of the island, the *bolas* of the Patagonians, are their only weapons. The arrow and spear heads are made of bone, or iron where it can be procured. The different tribes have no particular head or chief, nor any form of government; but they speak different dialects—all of which have many affinities with the Araucanian—and reside in different districts.

For three hundred years, notwithstanding they have been frequently visited by navigators and the crews of whalers and sealing vessels, the Fuegians have made little or no advance in intelligence. According to Drake, they travelled in the same canoe, and slept in the same wigwam, two hundred and fifty years ago, which they now do. In some respects they are even more sunken and degraded than the Australians, who have generally been considered the lowest in the scale of humanity. Their skill and sagacity are like the instinct of animals, and they manifest still less invention and foresight in providing the means of comfort and subsistence.

(9.) On the 25th of February, Captain Wilkes left Orange Harbor in the brig Porpoise, accompanied by the Sea Gull under Lieutenant Johnson, for a short cruise in the Southern Polar regions. Captain Hudson sailed on the same day with the Peacock and the Flying-Fish—the latter in charge of Lieutenant Walker—in the direction of Cook's Ne Plus Ultra, under instructions to penetrate as far south of that point as the season and other circumstances would permit. Lieutenant Craven remained at Orange Harbor in command of the Vincennes; and the Relief was ordered to the straits of Magellan, for scientific duty—the corps of scientific gentlemen being temporarily transferred to that vessel.

The Sea Gull returned to Orange Harbor on the 22d of March, having separated from her consort during the cruise, and the Porpoise arrived on the 30th. No new discoveries

of importance had been made. The weather had proved unfavorable, and on penetrating as far south as the sixty-sixth
degree of southern latitude, Captain Wilkes found himself
surrounded on all sides by innumerable icebergs and field ice,
and was therefore obliged to retrace his course. While he
was absent from Orange Harbor, he visited the South Shet-
lands and Palmer's Land, but was only able to verify the
discoveries of former navigators.

Captain Hudson encountered the first icebergs on the 11th
of March, in latitude 63° 30′ S. and 80° W. longitude.*
The Flying Fish separated from the Peacock in a gale, in
the early part of the cruise, but fell in with her again before
its termination. Captain Hudson ascended a little above the
sixty-eighth degree of southern latitude, and Lieutenant
Walker went as high as the seventieth degree, where his
further progress was impeded by impassable barriers of ice.
Both vessels came near being hemmed in by these frozen
bulwarks. The Flying Fish was once rescued from a most
perilous position by a fortunate breeze, and the Peacock, after
being enveloped for six days, from the 19th to the 25th of
March, in ice and icebergs, was with great difficulty worked
out into the open sea, through a dense fog, by carrying on all
her canvas. The decks and rigging of the vessels were coated
with ice, and everything was dark, dreary and cheerless. If
there was a pause in the howling of the wind, it seemed to
bellow with increased fury when it again swept above the
wintry waste. If the leaden-colored clouds parted over head,
and the beautiful tints of blue sky were reflected in the water,
they could scarcely be admired, before the heavens were once
more overshadowed by that black and dismal pall which almost shut out the light of day.

As if to compensate for all this dreariness and gloom, several splendid exhibitions of the aurora australis† were wit-

---

* In the South Pacific, the Polar currents being very little interrupted by land,
deviate less from their general course than those in the northern hemisphere,
and, consequently, carry icebergs nearer to the tropics than is usual north of the
Equator.

† The *aurora australis* is the phenomenon in the southern hemisphere corresponding to the *aurora borealis* in the northern.

nessed. The Magellan Clouds, the Zodiacal Light, and the brilliant constellation of the Southern Cross, whose magic beauties have so often been remarked and admired by travellers in the Polar regions, were seen in all their perfection. Other luciform appearances, less striking, perhaps, but full of interest and beauty, were likewise observed.

From these vast southern solitudes, where the sea-lion, the petrel, the albatross and the penguin, are rarely disturbed in their ice-bound retreats, Captain Hudson and Lieutenant Walker gladly turned the heads of their vessels to the north, when they found that the season was so far advanced, that nothing further could be gained by protracting their stay.

(10.) The Flying Fish sailed for Orange Harbor, where she arrived on the 11th of April, and the Peacock shaped her course for Valparaiso. On the 17th of April, orders were issued to the squadron at Orange Harbor to get under way. The Vincennes and Porpoise dropped down to Scapenham Bay in the afternoon, when the wind being light and unfavorable, they came to anchor. A heavy squall coming up, they ran back into Orange Bay for a few hours. At daylight on the 18th, a more propitious breeze finally wafted them from those desolate regions, and launched them upon the broad and comparatively peaceful bosom of the Pacific.* The south east trades are the favorite winds of this ocean, but it was not until the Exploring Squadron had passed the latitude of Chiloë, that they felt the genial influence of these prosperous gales, which wafted them on far more rapidly than before towards the Valley of Paradise.

Early in the morning of the 12th of May, they came in sight of the coast of Chili, and not long after, the grand and majestic peaks of the Andes were seen towering up in the back ground. In a few days, the Vincennes and Porpoise joined the Peacock in the harbor of Valparaiso. The Sea Gull and Flying Fish were left at Orange Harbor to await the return of the Relief from her cruise in the Straits of Ma-

---

* The Pacific received its name from Magellan, in consequence of the prosperous weather with which he was favored while navigating its surface.

gellan. That vessel, however, had been so long delayed that it was thought best to sail direct to Valparaiso, where she arrived in safety. The two schooners left Orange Harbor on the 28th of April, but were separated in a gale, and the Sea Gull probably foundered, as no tidings have ever been heard of the vessel or crew. The Flying Fish reached Valparaiso on the 19th of May.

CHAPTER V.

(1.) Few travellers approach the coast of Chili, or Chile, without turning their eyes in the direction of the lofty crests of the Andes, the giant vertebræ of South America. On entering the harbor of Valparaiso, fine glimpses are obtained, in the northeast, of the peaks of the Great Cordillera ; though the distance—from one hundred to one hundred and fifty miles—at which they are situated, cannot be truly appreciated till you ascend the hills overlooking the beach. These peaks begin to be numerous in latitude 30° S., and increase in number as the cordillera trends away to the south. The principal one is Aconcagua, at least 23,200 feet high—an elevation greater than that of Chimborazo—which is, at intervals, an active volcano.

In pleasant weather,—the general rule, rather than the exception, in Chili,—the sunset view of the Andes, off the coast, is remarkably beautiful and picturesque, probably more so than at any other time of the day :—the soft, transparent atmosphere ; the clear blue heavens ; the light fleecy clouds, glowing with all the colors of the rainbow, sailing along the pure depths of the sky, or floating around the rugged mountain summits ; the purple hue of evening falling in the nooks and crevices, and the golden flush yet lingering on the bolder rocks and precipices, impart to it all the charms of romance and enchantment,—and Fancy roams half bewildered, through lordly castles and fairy palaces, glittering with all the wealth of Ophir, sparkling with gems and precious stones, and crowned with burnished domes supported on pillars of ivory and gold, beneath which hang

> " Pendant by subtle magic, many a row
>   Of starry lamps and blazing cressets, fed
>   With Naphtha and Asphaltus."

But at early dawn, just before the sun peeps above the horizon, when the morning light streams from the east through every cleft and fissure, when Night still enshrouds the bases of the mountains in her sable mantle, and the tops are tinged with the maiden blushes of Aurora, the rough outlines are more clearly distinguished, and, perhaps, a more powerful impression of vastness, magnificence, and sublimity, is made upon the mind of the beholder.

(2.) Were it not for its beautiful and matchless climate, Valparaiso could boast of nothing that would entitle it to the distinction implied by its name.* The country in its vicinity is sterile and monotonous ; along the sea coast there extends a range of steep round-topped hills, from fifteen to sixteen hundred feet high, covered with a bright grayish red soil, worn into numberless gulleys, in consequence of the slight protection afforded by the dry and scorched turf scattered about over it in small patches ; there are few or no trees except half-withered cacti ; and the clumps of low stunted bushes and brambles occasionally seen, do not go very far towards relieving the dreary sameness of the landscape. In the deep valleys, the vegetation is a little more abundant ; and the plants and shrubs,—which possess, as in most dry climates, peculiarly strong and pungent odors, and, when in blossom, present greater liveliness and richness of color than is usually met with,—are considerably more numerous.

Still, the view of the town from the anchorage is quite pretty. It appears to be built in terraces, at the foot of the range of hills flanking the coast. The houses are mostly con-

* The meaning of Valparaiso is—Vale, or Valley, of Paradise.

structed of *adobés*, from one to two stories high, and surmounted with heavy red tiles. They are for the most part erected in a loose and straggling manner. All are plastered on the outside, and whitewashed; and when the level rays of the declining sun are poured full upon the walls, they glisten like burnished silver. A closer examination, however, destroys much of this pleasing and picturesque illusion. On the north, the town stretches out on the level sea shore, in a long double row of houses, called the *Almendral;* towards the south, it rises in the direction of the hills, upon which there are many neat cottages, with tasteful flower gardens. One of these eminences, Mount Alégre, rises abruptly from the centre of the city, and is chiefly occupied by the residences of wealthy foreigners and merchants. The main street is intersected by a number of *quebrádas*, or gorges, running parallel to each other, and leading up which there are narrow and inconvenient thoroughfares, with a few houses built at intervals; these streets are badly lighted, and are very dangerous at night. The southern part of the town is divided by two principal ravines, into three districts, to which sailors have given the names of Fore Top, Main Top, and Mizen Top.

The harbor, or bay of Valparaiso, is open to the north and northwest; but on the south and southwest, it is protected by the small promontory of Púnta de Coronílla, though the shore on this side of the bay is steep and rocky, and the waves dash against the heights with great fury. From the point, the bay sweeps round to the northwest, in the form of a crescent, having a sloping sandy beach which rises gradually towards the hills. In entering the harbor from the south, there is great danger, at times, of drifting upon the point, from the sudden dying away of the wind. The holding ground being of stiff clay, the anchorage is secure, except during the northerly gales, which, though far less frequent than those from the opposite quarter, sometimes blow with terrible violence, and often terminate in severe storms. The bay is protected by three small forts; the most strongly fortified is the castle

4*

of San António, containing about a dozen guns, which stands in the southern inlet of the bay ; el Castíllo del Rosário, which has six guns, is in the northern part of the town, and the remaining fort, mounting five guns, in the southern.

Formerly, there was no facility for landing goods at Valparaiso, except by launches moored to the shore, across which packages were carried on men's shoulders, or by boats ; but a mole has been recently built at the most favorable point for landing. This is considered perfectly safe, except during the prevalence of north winds, when it is exceedingly dangerous to approach it, on account of the violence of the surf. A wooden jetty stretches out into the sea about sixty paces, which is frequently submerged by the waves, and has been several times demolished. The harbor-master's boats, and those belonging to men-of-war, land on the right side of the jetty, and those of merchant vessels on the left. Small boats, usually manned by two Indians, are always to be found near the landing-place, ready to convey passengers to and fro the vessels in the harbor. Whenever a stranger makes his appearance on the *muele*, or mole, he is sure to be greeted with the importunate inquiry—*Vámos abórdo*, señór? (Going aboard, sir ?)—which sometimes gives place to, "Want a boat ?—want a boat ?" in English.

On reaching the shore, almost the first object that attracts the attention is the motley crowd of Choloës, or country people, dressed in their long coarse *ponchos*,* who congregate here for the purpose of disposing of their wares. Passing through the clamoring boatmen and jabbering peasantry, you approach the custom-house, a large and fine building erected on the mole. Near the custom-house is the exchange, a more unpretending structure, but containing a spacious and elegant reading-room well supplied with foreign newspapers. This is the favorite resort of ship-masters and commercial travellers,

---

* The *poncho* is a long blanket, varying in color according to the taste of the wearer, with a hole, or slit, in the middle, through which the head is thrust— thus permitting the ends to hang down behind and before.

great numbers of whom are constantly to be seen at Valparaiso.

The other public buildings are a government house situated on the *pláza*, a small triangular space in one of the *quebradas*. In the vicinity of the *pláza*, are the principal church, and the Dominican and Franciscan chapels; and between it and the castle of San António, is the arsenal, consisting of a number of low buildings and sheds. About the middle of the *Almendral*, are the ruins of the church and convent of La Mercéd, destroyed by the great earthquake of 1822. There are several monasteries in the city, but all wear a gloomy and cheerless look. The churches are unusually plain and simple; they are neither distinguished for architectural ornaments on the outside, nor for their decorations in the interior.

For places of amusement, the inhabitants of Valparaiso have a theatre poorly fitted up, and a *chingáno*, both of which are open, and generally crowded, on Sunday evening. The *chingáno* is a large amphitheatre, surrounded by apartments, or booths, where liquors and refreshments are sold; it is much frequented by both sexes, particularly of the lower classes, and one of its most attractive entertainments is a lascivious dance, termed the *samacuéca*, which is performed by a young man and woman, on a stage, under an open shed.

One of the most remarkable objects in the city, is the moveable prison. This is a large covered wagon, resembling those used for the conveyance of wild beasts. The door, at which a guard is stationed, is at the back end; inside, there are plank bedsteads, like those in guard-houses, large enough to accommodate eight or ten persons; and in front is a small apartment for cooking. A large number of these prisons may be seen in the streets; they are drawn by the prisoners, who are mostly employed in working on the roads and bridges.

There is a great plenty of taverns in Valparaiso, though not much can be said in their favor. The best are kept by Frenchmen, but these are incommodious and expensive.

Want of cleanliness is the chief fault of all. The tables are amply provided from a market, held in the *pláza*, always well supplied with good meat, poultry, fish, bread, fruit, and vegetables.

No one ever visits this town, of late years, without remarking the efficiency of the police established by Diego Portales, formerly Minister of War and the Interior. It consists of two bodies, the *vigilantes*, or police proper, and the *serénos*, or watchmen. The former are armed and uniformed, and patrol the streets on horseback ; the latter are provided with swords alone, and go on foot. Each *seréno* has his particular beat or district, and carries a small whistle, which makes a loud and shrill noise. It is customary to call the hours at night, and announce the state of the weather. At ten o'clock the *seréno* commences with—*Viva Chíle ! víva Chíle !—las diéz han dádo cláro y seréno!* (past ten o'clock and a clear and fine night !) In the morning they say, *Víva Chíle ! víva Chíle !*—Ave María puríssima—las cuátro de la mañána, *y nubládo !* (past four o'clock in the morning, and cloudy !) or,—*la séis de la mañána, y lluvióso!* (past six o'clock in the morning, and rainy !) These calls are uttered in a sort of tune, pitched to a high key, which is rather pleasing than otherwise. If an earthquake takes place, it is announced in the same manner by the *seréno*, as he goes his round. Midnight brawls and murders were formerly quite common, but they are now of very rare occurrence, and are mainly confined to the southern quarter, the most abandoned part of the town.

Valparaiso contains not far from thirty thousand inhabitants,—a large proportion of whom are foreigners, from Germany, England, France, and the United States,—and it is annually increasing in extent and population. The old Spanish families are few in number, but they are remarkable for the combined grace and dignity of their demeanor, the neatness of their personal appearance, and the cleanliness and tidiness of their dwellings. The main dependence of the city is its commerce, and the avocations and tastes of the inhabitants are, consequently, almost exclusively of a mercantile character. They are hospitable and kind to strangers, not more from interest than from impulse. With the influx of so many foreigners, new customs have been introduced, and those of the ancient Spanish residents are gradually disappearing. Their costumes likewise are being supplanted by French styles and fashions. That these changes have taken place without serious disagreement or difficulty, is probably owing to the intermarriage of the foreigners with Spanish ladies. Now and then a genuine Castilian—one of the old *noblesse*—may be found, who looks with mingled emotions of contempt and abhorrence on these innovations; but the great majority have long since learned to regard them, if not with love, at least without hatred. Until quite recently, it was not customary for the ladies of Valparaiso to wear either hats or head-dresses, even in the streets,—their dark glossy ringlets being gathered into two plaits, and suffered to hang down the back, sometimes nearly reaching the ground,—but latterly bonnets have been introduced, and they are becoming quite the fashion.

In point of morals, Valparaiso does not compare favorably with many other South American towns. The higher classes are excessively fond of amusements, and those beneath them in position imitate their example, though manifesting less regard for the decencies of life, and substituting coarser enjoyments for those of a more refined character. A great part of the houses in the southern quarter of the city, are grog-shops, brothels, and kindred places of resort; at every step you discover the wrinkles of cankering care and passion disfiguring the countenance of the *chevalier d' industrie*, who strives, in vain, to conceal his repulsive features under his broad *sombréro*,—or start at the dark flashing eyes of the courtesan, who gathers her gay crimson or green *bayéta** more closely about her half-exposed person, not from any instinct of modesty, but rather to hide the dirty calico dress beneath it.

* The *bayéta* is a coarse baize shawl worn by women of the lower classes.

On a high hill overlooking the town, are the burial grounds. The principal one is divided by mud walls into two compartments, one of which is used by Catholics, and the other is appropriated to heretics. Near by is a charnel house full of skulls and bones. Interments are conducted with very little care or attention. The graves are shallow excavations, in which the dead are laid, with their heads to the west, often without either coffin or shroud. A small quantity of earth is then thrown in and beaten down with a billet of wood; not unfrequently half of this thin covering is blown off by the wind in a few days, and the decaying body exposed, wholly or in part, to the sight. A rudely-fashioned cross placed at the head of the grave, is, usually, the only designation employed. In the Protestant cemetery, which adjoins the former, there are neat marble slabs, and every other indication of the respect paid by the living to the dead.

(3.) Previous to the Spanish conquest, Chili formed a part of the possessions of the Peruvian Incas. In 1535, Almagro invaded the country, under the orders of Pizarro; and in 1540 it was overrun and subjugated, with the exception of Araucania, by Valdivia. The first insurrectionary movement looking towards a separation from the mother country, was made in 1810, and terminated in 1814, when the province was temporarily quieted. From that time till the year 1817, the disaffected inhabitants were overawed by the presence of a large body of royalist forces. But the tocsin of liberty had not been sounded in vain; its echoes continued to reverberate among the fastnesses of the Andes, and to awaken glad responses in the breasts of the true-hearted patriots of Chili. In 1817, the banner of freedom was again flung to the winds, and after a bloody and obstinate engagement on the plains of Chacabúco, in which General Mendoza, at the head of the patriot army of four thousand men, defeated five thousand, the Spanish troops were expelled from the country. The preliminary measures for forming an independent government were being taken, when a new and increased force of royalists appeared in the field, under the command of General Osorio. This force was likewise routed, at Maypú, on the 5th day of April, 1818, by the Chilian troops under San Martin, O'Higgins, and other patriot leaders. Still another effort was made by Spain' to regain her lost dominion, and a fifty-gun frigate, convoying eleven transport ships, with twenty-five hundred men on board, was ordered to Chili. This formidable armament was met at Talcahúano, and captured, by a small squadron commanded by Captain Manuel Blanco, consisting of two armed ships, a corvette and several trading vessels, hastily collected and equipped, after the enemy had reached Cape Horn.

This was the last attempt made by Spain to reconquer the country; and the independence of the latter being now permanently secured, a form of government was established. The first government was dictatorial. General O'Higgins, originally chosen Dictator on the 16th of February, 1816, was continued in office, under the title of Supreme Director of Chili, till the year 1823. He was succeeded by Ramon Freyre, who resigned in 1826. Meanwhile various factions had sprung up, all evidently desirous of securing the advancement of the country in prosperity and greatness. Civil disturbances and dissensions naturally grew out of these political divisions; repeated changes were made in the Executive, but the government does not appear, at any time, to have been administered with sufficient firmness and rigor. In 1828, a republican constitution was proclaimed, and General Pinto was elected president. The latter shortly after resigned, and was succeeded by Ramon Vicuña, then president of the Senate. Vicuña soon became unpopular; and the friends of liberal institutions, under the lead of General Joaquín Priéto, took up arms against him. The civil war ended in the complete overthrow of Vicuña. The brief administrations of Taglé and Oválle followed, and in 1831, General Priéto was elected to the presidency. After holding the office two terms, of five years each, he gave place to his nephew General Bulnés,—the constitution of the republic

prohibiting the election of the same person for a third successive term.

With the accession of Priéto to the Chief Magistracy, a
new era dawned upon Chili. He found everything in confusion and disorder ; the military fast gaining the ascendency ; and a national debt already contracted amounting
to the enormous sum of over eight million piasters.* He
was just the man for the crisis ; and he was warmly and
ably seconded in his efforts to restore the credit and character of the country, by his minister of war and the interior,
Diego Portales. Certain means were taken to develop the
resources of the state ; commerce was fostered, and industry
and enterprise of every kind encouraged ; the government
was administered firmly, but mildly ; the taxes were reduced, and order and economy rigidly enforced in every
branch of the public service. Congress kept pace with the
Executive ; and its legislation was so directed as to secure
the perfect liberty of the citizen, so far as was compatible
with the public safety, and absolute equality under the law
to every man. No titles or special privileges were permitted
to be conferred, and all distinctions between native and
adopted citizens were abolished. One happy result of the
financial measures of Priéto, was the rapid increase of the
revenue—an advance of more than two hundred and fifty
per cent. in the annual receipts being realized in the short
space of twelve years—and, as a necessary consequence, the
speedy extinguishment of the public debt. Ever since the
year 1835, there has been a surplus of the revenue over the
expenditure ; in 1842, the former amounted to three million
eight hundred thousand piasters, and the latter to two million
four hundred thousand,—showing a surplus of nearly fourteen
hundred thousand piasters. In May, 1843, Chilian six per
cents rose to 93, and in 1845 they were quoted at 104. Too
much praise cannot be awarded to Priéto, for his wise, skilful, and successful statesmanship ; the chief merit of accomplishing these splendid results within so brief a period is

* About ten million dollars, federal currency.

certainly due to him, as his successor, Bulnés has but carried
out the principles of political economy introduced under his
auspices.

Chili is what may be called a central republic. The Executive power is vested in a President, who receives an annual
salary of twelve thousand dollars; he is assisted in the discharge of his duties by four ministers, who constitute his
cabinet. There is also an executive council of eight members. The legislature consists of a Senate and a House of
Deputies; the former containing nineteen members, and the
latter eighty-two. The senators are chosen for the term of
five years, in ten provinces; and the deputies for three years,
in thirty-five departments. The administration of justice is
not yet free from the old Spanish forms, but it is expeditious,
and, in the main, impartial and equitable; the judges hold
their offices for life. The army, in time of peace, numbers
about three thousand men.

Within the past ten years, Chili has steadily pursued a
career which promises at no distant day to produce a high
state of national prosperity. The indications of a sound and
healthful progress are everywhere visible. Flourishing towns
and villages, rich farms and plantations, occupy the places of
the miserable huts and haciéndas of former times. Schools,
colleges, and other public institutions, have been established,
and the young people are now generally instructed in the
rudiments of knowledge. The national religion is the Roman
Catholic, but an exceedingly tolerant spirit prevails even
among the clergy. Protestant denominations are allowed
to worship after their own mode, but not to erect churches.

The republic of Chili is bounded on the north by the desert
of Atacama, which separates it from Bolívia and Peru; on
the south by Patagonia; on the east by the Great Cordillera
of the Andes; and on the west by the Pacific. The islands
of Mocha and Juán-Fernández, and the archipelago of
Chiloë, also belong to Chili. Within the limits above mentioned, however, the province of Araucania is embraced,
which, perhaps, may be a subject of dispute, as the warlike

tribes who inhabit it have never yet been subdued, and claim
to be entirely independent. Including the islands, the total
area of Chilian territory is about one hundred and thirty
thousand square miles. Various estimates in regard to the
population have been made; but the most reliable authorities
fix it at one million two hundred thousand. The people are
mostly of Spanish and Indian descent, although there are
some negroes and mulattoes. In the seaport towns, as in
Valparaiso, there are great numbers of foreigners, to whom
the country is much indebted for its present commercial importance.

There are no slaves in Chili, but there exists in the country a condition of servitude, called *péonage*, common to most
of the colonies of Old Spain. After its conquest by the
Spaniards, Chili was divided into three hundred and sixty
portions, which were given to that number of individuals.
These, of course, have been frequently subdivided, but there
are still many large estates, which are generally kept for
grazing purposes. The proprietors usually reside with their
families in the towns; the management of their farms being
entrusted to a *major-domo*, or steward, under whom are a
chief, and a few subordinate herdsmen, or guachos. These
are assisted in taking care of the land, by tenants, who hold
their dwellings under the proprietor, by a sort of feudal
tenure—being obliged to give their services in any kind of
labor required of them, either without pay, or for a small
remuneration—and are termed *péons*. They are for the most
part entirely dependent on their landlord, and sometimes the
most arbitrary exactions and impositions are practiced with
impunity.

One great drawback on the prosperity of Chili, has been
her difficulties with Peru. The latter was essentially aided
in her struggle with Spain by the men and money of the
former, and her independence was finally achieved, in 1821,
by a Chilian army under San Martin; it would, therefore,
have been but reasonable to suppose, that the strongest ties
of gratitude and fraternal feeling would have united the

people of the two countries firmly together. But the disaffected politicians and malcontents of Chili were always welcomed in Peru, and not only allowed, but encouraged, to concoct their plans, and carry on their intrigues, for the overthrow of the government of their own country. The growing commerce of their neighbors had attracted the attention of the Peruvians, and commercial jealousies and rivalships were, doubtless, at the bottom of the inimical feelings which they soon began openly to manifest. The Chilians are resolute, independent, and high-minded, and they took no pains to conceal their displeasure. The animosity thus engendered became more marked and decided, in 1836, when Santa Cruz was elected Supreme Protector of the Peru-Bolívian Republic.

The Protector not only issued a decree nullifying the treaty with Chili then in existence, but he received the disaffected Chilians with open arms, and even went so far as to arm three men-of-war at Callao, which he placed at their disposal in order to effect a revolution. The government of Chili was not idle, however ; an expedition was fitted out, and the vessels captured by a bold and well-executed *coup de main*, the legality of which Peru was ultimately obliged to acknowledge, before they had left the harbor of Callao. The difficulty between the two governments did not end here ; one act of aggression was followed by another ; and at length Santa Cruz procured the passage of a law forbidding all foreign vessels to visit any place on the Pacific coast of South America, without having first entered a Peruvian port, under the penalty of being required to pay additional entrance duties. Chili promptly resented this insult by a declaration of war ; a large military force was immediately raised, and placed under the command of General Bulnés, who invaded Peru, and occupied Lima and other towns with his forces. In January, 1839, a general engagement took place at Yungay, which resulted in the complete defeat of Santa Cruz. The loss of his power followed the loss of his army, and the Protector was subsequently banished to

Europe. A new treaty of peace was now concluded between Chili and Peru, the provisions of which have been
faithfully regarded and observed.

(4.) Sixty four miles from Valparaiso, in a south easterly
direction, is Santiago, the capital of Chili. It is pleasantly
situated on the eastern verge of the broad and fertile plain
of Maypú, at the foot of the Cordilleras.* The city proper
is on the southwestern bank of the Maypocho, a mountain
stream which is generally dry for nine months in the year,
but during the rainy season is swollen into a powerful
torrent. A handsome stone bridge, of five arches, spanning
the river, connects the suburb of La Chimba with the capital. On the southeast side of the latter is its suburb of
Cañadilla, from which it is separated by the Cañada, a
pleasant promenade, fifty yards wide, and planted with pop-
lars. At the southwestern angle of the city is the suburb
of Cuchunco.

At a distance Santiago has a very imposing appearance.
In the outskirts, there are numerous pretty *quíntas*, delightfully embowered amid groves of laurel, myrtle, and poplar.
The approaches to the city are mostly through shady lanes,
or avenues, flanked by high *adobé* walls, inclosing extensive
vineyards, well-stocked orchards and gardens, and finely-
cultivated maize fields. Passing these, you catch sight of
the domes and steeples of the capital towering above the
humbler edifices around them. Like most Spanish towns,
Santiago is divided into *quadras*, or squares, whose sides are
each a little over four hundred feet in length. The streets,
which are generally well-paved, and have good side-walks,
are about thirteen yards wide. In the city and its suburbs,
there are between two and three hundred *quadras*, which
are included in five parishes. As the ground slopes gently
towards the west, the location of the town is peculiarly favorable for supplying the inhabitants with water, and for under
drainage ; in the latter respect, no other city in South Amer-

* Santiago occupies the site of an ancient Indian Settlement. It was founded
by Valdivia, in 1541.

ica can compare with the Chilian capital. The waters of the
Maypocho are also employed for ornamental purposes ; there
being a great number of public fountains and reservoirs scattered through the city. The *Pláza*, occupying an entire
quadra in the centre of the town, contains the largest fountain, furnished with water by a subterraneous aqueduct,
from which the inhabitants principally obtain their supplies
for drinking. The water is conveyed in barrels holding ten
gallons each—two of which are a load for a mule—and sold
for about ten cents per barrel.

A solid brick wall, or rampart, six feet broad, and ten feet
high, extends along the south bank of the Maypocho, as a
protection against inundation during the heavy rains. Between the river and the town is the *Alameda*, which is
planted with willows, and furnished with seats, reservoirs,
and artificial streams of running water ; in pleasant weather,
it is thronged, in the afternoon and evening, with all classes
and sexes, with beggars and hidálgos, rosy-cheeked pádres,
dark-eyed señoritas, and stately caballéros,—and the soft
moonlight that streams down the rugged sides of the Andes,
and falls tremblingly upon the plain of Maypú, rests nowhere
on happier or more picturesque groups, than those which may
be seen in the cool paséos of this favorite promenade of the
citizens of Santiago. At the northeastern angle of the city-
proper, is the hill of Sánta Lucía, the site of the fortress
bearing the same name, intended to command the town ;
there is no other defence, and the artillery in this work
could be easily silenced by guns planted on the neighboring
hills.

In cleanliness, regularity, and salubrity, Santiago greatly
surpasses the other cities of South America ; but it is inferior
to Lima in its public buildings. On the northwest side of
the *pláza*, are the presidential mansion, the palace of government, the prison, and the chamber of justice ; on the south-
west side stands the cathedral, and the old palace of the
bishop, now occupied by the *estádo mayór ;* on the south-
east there is a range of shops with a colonnade in front, and

the remaining side is occupied by private residences. All these buildings, except the cathedral, are built of brick, plastered over and whitewashed, and show more or less marks of the injuries occasioned by the frequent earthquakes. The palace, originally built for the vice-regal government, makes the most pretensions to architectural beauty ; it consists of two stories surrounding a large open quadrangle ; in the lower story are the armory and treasury,—in the upper, the great hall of audience and the ministerial offices.

The cathedral is the only stone edifice in the city ; the material of which it is constructed was quarried in the suburb of La Chimba ; its design is Moorish, and has been executed with considerable taste and skill ; it is a large and extensive building, and contains, inside, an abundance of gold and silver ornaments, paintings, tapestry, and wax figures. The parish churches are comparatively mean structures ; but the conventual establishments, of which there are many, are well built and furnished. The bishop's palace is a heavy, sombre-looking building, fast going to decay. The largest public edifice in Santiago is the mint, which covers a whole square. To most strangers it seems unsightly enough, but the natives really look upon it with admiration. It is of plain brick, and like the other buildings erected for state purposes, was constructed by bricklayers sent out from Spain expressly for this purpose. Its front presents a series of heavy pilasters, supporting a rude cornice and ponderous balustrade, in the centre of which is a massive arched portico. It is still incomplete, and is much dilapidated, principally by reason of the earthquakes. It consists of a variety of offices arranged round three quadrangular courts. Few of the modern improvements have been introduced here, and the operation of coining is still in a rude state. The *Consuládo*, a spacious structure, plastered and whitewashed, in which the commercial *tribunál*, and the national congress, meet, is also worthy of notice. Santiago likewise boasts of a custom-house, a theatre, and a *chingáno*. There is a national college, too, occupying what was formerly one of the Jesuits' convents ;

and another of these edifices is used for the public library and printing-office. The library contains several thousand printed volumes, and a number of curious manuscripts relative to the Indian tribes, who originally occupied the country.

Most of the private dwellings in Santiago are but one story high,—being built in this manner on account of the earth-quakes. They have red tiled roofs projecting so as to form a piazza, or covered-way; and the outside walls, as well as those around the orchards and gardens, are all whitewashed over every year, which gives them a peculiarly neat and lively appearance. The houses occupy considerable ground; many of them take up one sixth part of a *quadra*. They consist of different compartments, or suites of rooms, ranged round three *pátios*, or quadrangular courts; the first, or outer court, is usually paved with pebbles from the bed of the Maypocho; the second is commonly laid out as a parterre, and decorated with shrubs and flowers; and the third is used for domestic purposes. A wide archway opening into the front *pátio*, is open during the day, but closed at night by heavy folding gates. The windows looking into the two outer courts, are protected by ornamental iron gratings; the windows in the rear court are generally small openings in the doors also covered with gratings. The two fronts, on either side of the gateway, and the sides facing the streets, where there are not blank walls, are often divided into rooms separate from the apartments occupied by the family, and rented for shops and fancy stores.

There are three markets in the city, the principal one of which is held in the *Bassorál*, a large open space covering four or five acres, at the foot of the bridge. The area is surrounded by a low building, with a tile roof, supported by columns. Good meat, and fruit and vegetables of all kinds, can be procured here. The other markets are mere moveable stands at either end of the *Cañada*. Meat, kitchen vegetables, fruits, and lucerne, the common fodder for horses, are continually hawked about the streets.

Santiago is famous for its fine horses. Large quantities

of stock are raised on the extensive grazing grounds near the city, and there is scarcely a family in the town but has one or more horses. These animals are generally well broken, and are more docile than those of Buenos Ayres. The average price of a horse is twelve dollars, but when thoroughly trained they command as high prices as in the United States. Beef and mutton, of the finest quality, are both cheap and abundant.

The inhabitants of Santiago are remarkably obliging and courteous; somewhat too fond of their chief national amusements, dancing and music, and, to a certain extent, addicted to their fashionable game of *monté,* yet, withal, orderly and well-disposed. They are sincerely attached to the devotional forms and ceremonies of their religion. No obtrusive exhibition of this feeling is made, but the stranger cannot well avoid noticing it; even though it may be common in most of the cities and towns of South America. It is particularly remarkable, when the bells of the cathedral announce the arrival of the hour for the *oración,* or sunset prayer. The streets are then filled with the gay and lively population, and all is mirthful and joyous. But as the first peal echoes from the cathedral tower, everything is hushed and still, as if some mighty spell had been thrown over the city; the caballéro reins back his steed on his haunches; the laughing señorita hesitates in the midst of her witty repartee; the artisan suffers his hammer to fall silently on his bench; even the gamester pauses in his throw of the dice; and in the pauses of the chimes, the cool plash of the water falling over the marble statutes in the fountain, may be heard many a yard from the *pláza.*

As in Valparaiso, the gentlemen in Santiago follow the European fashions; but the ladies, notwithstanding the French milliners and mantuamakers who have immigrated to Chili, adhere more closely to the customs of olden time,— and a bonnet, thanks to the soft atmosphere and beautiful climate which allows them to dispense with this incumbrance, is almost as great a rarity on the plains of Maypú, as it would be in the Feejee Islands.

Santiago contains about sixty-five thousand inhabitants, and is constantly increasing,—a fact which speaks volumes in favor of Chilian industry and enterprise, since the same cannot be said of another inland capital in South America. Besides Santiago and Valparaiso, there are several other towns in Chili of considerable note. Coquimbo, or La Seréna, in North Chili, has a population amounting to nearly ten thousand ; it is the chief port of the mining country, and its copper is esteemed the best in the world. The town is remarkably clean, and well laid out—the streets intersecting each other at right angles. It has several churches, a public school, and a hospital; the houses are built of sun-dried bricks, with few exceptions, and are one story in height. Numerous gardens of fruit-trees and evergreens, give the place a refreshing and agreeable look. Huasco, still further to the north, is famed for its rich silver mines. Concepçion and Valdivia, in the southern part of the republic, are noted for their fine harbors. The former, was once a flourishing town containing twenty thousand inhabitants, but it has latterly declined in trade and manufactures, and the population does not now exceed eight thousand. It stands on a low neck of land between the river Biobio and the bay of Concepçion ; it is laid out like Coquimbo, and the houses are constructed in the same manner ; previously to 1835, it possessed a large cathedral and several other fine buildings, but, in that year, these, with the greater part of the town, were destroyed by an earthquake. Valdivia is rather an insignificant collection of wooden huts, but it contains five thousand inhabitants, and has the finest, and one of the most strongly fortified harbors, in the South Pacific ; this consists of an estuary, formed by the Valdivia and several smaller rivers, entered by a narrow strait, the shores of which are garnished with batteries, mounting, in all, one hundred and thirty guns; ships of the line ride here in safety—there being from six to seven fathoms of water in the centre of the bay, and five fathoms near the shore. The town is about sixteen miles from the mouth of the Valdivia, and was almost ruined by an earthquake in 1837. It is the capital and market town of the province of Valdivia, and has a large and rapidly increasing trade.

(5.) What has been said in regard to the style of dress prevalent in Valparaiso and Santiago, is applicable to the Chileños generally, and especially so to the inhabitants of the larger towns. Elsewhere, the old Spanish costumes are more frequently met with among the better classes ; but the dress of the common people is a mixture of Spanish and Indian. The latter are fond of bright colors. The males wear a blue or brown *poncho*, over their shirt and trowsers, and a steeple-crowned, small rimmed hat, beneath which is a bright cotton handkerchief, tied on with strings under the chin. In very warm weather the tall hat is laid aside for the broad-leafed sombréro. The women wear gowns of calico or woolen stuff, and mantillas, or *bayétas*, as attractive in color and quality, as the ability of the wearer will permit her to purchase. In the mining districts, a most picturesque dress is worn by those who work in the mines. It consists of a long shirt of dark baize, with a leathern apron fastened around the waist by a bright-colored sash ; very broad trowsers ; and a small cap of scarlet cloth fitting closely to the head.

The Chilians possess fewer vices than the Creoles of the other Spanish colonies in South America, but they are frequently dissipated and profligate in their habits, and, in the towns, much too fond of dress and display. They are moderate in their food, though addicted to drinking to excess. They are less indolent, and more hardy than the Castilian race generally ; more industrious and enterprising, and more of a money-getting and money-loving people. Kindness and courtesy characterize their intercourse with strangers ; yet are they proud-spirited and high-mettled, somewhat jealous in disposition, quick to take affront, and of an unforgiving temper.

As in Valparaiso and Santiago, most of the better class of private dwellings throughout Chili, are built of adobés, one story in height; the habitations of the peasantry, and of the lower classes in towns and cities, are mere huts, usually having but one room, constructed of reeds and mud, and thatched with straw.

Educational improvement, and the introduction of a more refined taste, will, doubtless, produce great changes in the manners and customs of the people of Chili; but, while earthquakes continue to be so frequent, it is questionable whether a finer or more expensive style of building will prevail. Prudence and economy, in neither of which are they lacking, will always give the preference to the safest and cheapest mode.

Most of the Indian population continue to dwell in a state of independence south of the Biobio; but a considerable number live in missions. The former belie, in almost every respect, the highly-wrought and flattering descriptions in the *Araucana* of Ercilla y Zuñiga; they are wild, fierce, and intractable, and but little more advanced in civilization than the rude inhabitants of Patagonia.

(6.) In the northern part of Chili, the country rises from the coast to the Great Cordillera, by a number of successive terraces running parallel to the sea; but, elsewhere, it is a broad expansion of the mountainous Andes, spreading forth its spurs and branches from the central ridge towards the Pacific, which diminish continually, but irregularly, till they reach the ocean. These ramifications of the main Cordillera are generally two thousand feet above the bottom of the valleys that intersect them, and seldom less than one thousand feet. The patches between the ridges constitute the finest portions of middle Chili. Some of the valleys are broad, as is the case with the boasted vale of Aconcagua, one of the most fertile spots on the American continent. North of 30° 30', the Cordillera is divided into separate ranges, inclosing the immense valley of Uspallata, celebrated more particularly for its extensive mineral riches. There are a few small plains along the coast, between the spurs of the mountain chains; but the shores are mostly high, rocky, and precipitous.

The climate of Chili is equable and healthy. In the summer the weather is remarkable fine. Day after day, for weeks and months together, the atmosphere is transparently pure and clear; save, perhaps, the light blue haze which sometimes adds a new, and almost unnecessary charm, to what is all brightness, gayety, and joy. The interior is much warmer than the coast; at Valparaiso, the thermometer ranges, in midsummer, from 64° to 72°; and, at Santiago, the mean summer heat, from December to March, is about 84½° at midday, and 58° at night. During the summer, the wind blows steadily from the southward, and a little off the shore, but at sunset there is almost always a cool and pleasant breeze. No rain falls in the summer; it is abundant, however, through the winter months, from June to September, in the southern provinces. No snow falls along the coast, and frost is very rare. North of Santiago there are only a few occasional showers even in the winter; and in the arid province of Coquimbo, no rain whatever falls, but its place is occasionally supplied by heavy night dews.

Chili abounds in small rivers, which carry off the melted snow from the Andes, but it has none capable of being navigated to any extent, except the Maule and the Biobio.

The high chain of the Andes is chiefly composed of argillaceous schist, and the lower chains and groups, of granite. Sienitic, basaltic, and felspar porphyries, serpentines of various colors, quartz, hornblende and other slates, pudding-stone and gypsum, are found in the Cordillera, and there is fine statuary marble in the department of Copiapo. The soil of the northern provinces is sandy and saline, and probably not one fiftieth part of the north half of the country can ever be cultivated. In the central provinces, some of the valleys are considerably inclined, and admit of irrigation where water can be procured; but the hills and ridges, for the greater part of the year, are dry and parched. South of the Maule, the proportion of arable land is greater, and the soil becomes more

stiff and loamy. At Concepçion, in about 37° southern latitude, the plains and valleys are decked with the brightest
and richest flowers, or clothed with the most luxuriant foliage; while hills and mountains are wooded to their summits
with stately forest trees. In the latitude of Valparaiso, from
one hundred and fifty to two hundred miles further north, it
is only in the cultivation of the interval lands, that the husbandman finds a recompense for his toil. At Coquimbo, the
sickly grass and stunted brushwood which alone redeem the
hills in the neighborhood of Valparaiso from the curse of barrenness, are no longer to be found, and, in their stead, are
seen only a short wiry grass, and a feeble apology for the
prickly-pear. At Guasco, vegetation entirely disappears; the
country is diversified, indeed, with hill and plain, but all is
one vast and dreary Sahara,—the little rivulets, that carry
off the liquefied snows of the Andes, sing their lullaby in vain,
and their moisture is soon evaporated by the dry scorching
heat, that, vampire-like, robs the earth of nourishment and life.

Most of the hard woods abound in the forests of Chili; and
laurels, myrtles, cypresses, and other evergreens, attain to
such a size that they are highly valuable and useful for their
timber. The *mimosa farnesiana,* and the *algarob,* are quite
common; and the *guillai,* from the bark of which a natural
soap is made, is brought to the towns as an article of trade.
The palm and cinnamon tree were formerly met with in
abundance, but they are now rarely seen. Apricots, figs,
plums, pears and cherries, of large size and fine flavor, are
produced in great quantities. Herbaceous plants and flowers
are as various and abundant, as they are rich and beautiful.
The climate and soil of southern and middle Chili are peculiarly well calculated for the culture of the cereal grains.
Wheat is the principal agricultural staple, and is largely exported from the central provinces. Barley is grown to a considerable extent, in the south. Little attention is paid to the
culture of corn. All kinds of pulse and culinary vegetables
are raised, and potatoes are extensively produced.* The vine

* The potato is a native of South Chili.

and olive, where they are properly cultivated, yield an abundance of good fruit; but the manufacture of wine and oil is in a very rude state.

The art of agriculture is greatly behindhand in Chili, and the implements of husbandry are of the most primitive models. The plow consists of the part of a trunk of a tree, with a crooked branch projecting from it which serves as a handle; the forepart of the trunk is wedgeshaped, and has a flattish pointed piece of iron nailed to it which performs the double duty of colter and share. For the harrow, a heap of brushes, weighed down with stones, is substituted; and the blade-bone of a sheep is the principal implement used for weeding the garden. The greater part of the labor at the *haciéndas,* or farms, is performed by oxen; mules being principally employed in carrying burdens, and horses kept for riding and similar purposes. The yoke is fastened not to the shoulders, but to the horns of the cattle, according to the ancient Spanish method. Reaping is done with a rough sickle, and the grain is thrashed, or stamped out, with horses, on a hard dry spot of ground. From eight hundred to a thousand bushels are thrashed at one time. The grain is generally left in the open air till the rainy season begins.

Cattle-breeding, however, is probably the most important branch of agricultural industry. In the middle provinces, from ten to twenty thousand head of cattle are often fed on a single *haciénda,* and the smallest grazing farms support from four to five thousand head. Horses, mules, asses, goats and sheep, are likewise plentiful. Hogs are not so common, and are of an inferior quality.

Llamas and guanacoes, the puma, the jaguar, and other wild animals found in South America, inhabit Chili. There are likewise numerous varieties of the monkey tribe. Foxes are very common. A kind of beaver which frequents the rivers, and the chinchilla abounding in the deserts at the north, are hunted for their furs which are much prized. The country is comparatively free from venomous quadrupeds, and noxious insects and reptiles; the skunk being almost the only really annoying animal to be found there. There are good fishing grounds on the coast, at which whales, dolphins, cod, pilchards, and other small fish, are caught. Now and then a sea-dog is observed, but they are quite rare. Among the birds are the great condor, several species of vultures, the cormorant, the penguin, the cut-water or shear-bill, and the snipe. Flocks of parrots and parroquets are found. Small green parrots, not larger than finches, are caught in the interior, tamed, and sold in the towns. But the most beautiful and majestic bird is the swan, which is often seen sailing in the bay of Valparaiso ; its body is of dazzling white, and its neck and head are black.

(7.) Chili is said to be the only American state, formerly subject to Spain, whose commerce has increased since the separation from the mother country ; and this single fact is, of itself, a high encomium upon the enterprise and industry of its inhabitants. Under the Spaniards, Chili had no intercourse but with Peru and Buenos Ayres; now the vessels of all the principal commercial nations on the globe frequent her harbors. From 1825 to 1829, the annual average receipts from customs were less than nine hundred thousand dollars : in 1834, they amounted to nearly one and a quarter million ; and in 1841, they were but little short of two millions of dollars. Linens are imported from Germany ; silks, paper. leather, wines and brandy, from France ; manufactured goods, hardware and iron, from Great Britain; silks, nankeens, tea and sugar, from China and the East Indies ; tobacco, oil, spermaceti candles, sugar, and manufactured goods, from the United States; and various products from the different countries in South America. The principal exports are bullion, copper, hides, tallow, pulse, wheat, fruits, and drugs. During the year ending the 30th of June, 1847, the imports from, and exports to the United States, amounted to about one million seven hundred dollars ; there being a small balance in favor of Chili.

Valparaiso enjoys the honor of being the chief seaport town, and is commonly called " The Port," by way of distinction.

In 1834, only 450 vessels, aggregating 77,700 tons, entered this harbor, and in 1842 there were 685 vessels, 617 of which were commercial, aggregating 187,453 tons. The transit trade is enormous. On the 21st of May, 1842, there were over seven hundred thousand bales of merchandise, valued at upwards of seven millions of dollars, and coined metals exceeding three millions, at the custom-house of Valparaiso alone.

The internal trade of Chili is not very great; there being no principal towns in the interior except the capital. Besides, there are few accommodations or facilities for travelling. The only passable roads are those leading from Santiago to Valparaiso and Concepçion; bridges are scarce and poorly constructed, and in some places the mountain torrents and ravines are crossed by Indian hanging bridges, made of osiers and thongs of raw hide, which sway to and fro fearfully, with the weight of the person crossing them. Burdens are chiefly carried, over the high ridges separating the valleys, on the backs of mules; on the main roads, heavy merchandise is hauled in ox-carts constructed entirely of wood, strongly framed and pinned together. From two to four yoke of oxen are attached to one cart; the box, or top,—similar in shape to the tilt of a Pennsylvania wagon, but not so large,—is made of wattles covered with stout bull's hide. The vehicle principally used for the convenience of travellers is a sort of double gig, called a *birloche*, carrying two passengers. Three *birlocheros*, or drivers, and from ten to fifteen horses, accompany the carriage. One horse is secured in the shafts, and one on either side, attached to the vehicle by thongs of hide, is ridden by a driver. The horses on duty are relieved by those that run along in the *cabalgada*. These conveyances, like the Irish jaunting-car, are driven at break-neck speed, and the traveller is fortunate if he reaches his journey's end without any injury. The *paisános*, or country people, bring their wares to the market towns in panniers, on the backs of asses or mules, which they delight in scourging with the long poles that they invariably carry. Hay, mainly consisting of lucerne grass, is brought in the same manner,—the owner sitting in the midst of his load, almost out of sight, and his lower extremities completely lost in the brobdignag stirrups, nearly as large as a peck measure, that dangle beneath him.

Connected with the commerce are the manufactures of the country. The Chileños are excellent potters, and make light and strong earthen jars that ring like metal. Hempen cloths, common hemp cordage, soap, leather, wine, brandy, tallow, charcoal, and some rough articles of copper ware, are the chief articles manufactured. Besides the *acida* and *aguardiente*, or wine and brandy, made from the grape, a potation called *chicha** is made by boiling down the clear grape-juice after fermentation.

(8.) Though so large a portion of Chili is not susceptible of cultivation, nevertheless, even there, it contains vast depositories of wealth, which more than compensate for the deficiency. The country is extremely rich in minerals. Silver is found there at a greater elevation than any other metal; it is also met with in the valleys, or bowls, in the lower ranges, but it generally decreases in quantity in proportion to its distance from the Andes. The most valuable silver mine is that of Huasco. Gold occurs altogether in alluvial formations, and most, if not all, the rivers, wash down this valuable mineral. Lead and iron are abundant, but are not much sought after. Zinc, antimony, manganese, arsenic, tin, alum, salt, nitre, and sulphur, so pure as not to require refining, are plentiful. Coal mines, which improve as they are worked, have been opened near Concepçion, and already form a principal article of trade and consumption at Valpa-

---

* This is not the *chica*, or intoxicating beer, found among the aborigines of Chili and Peru. That was produced by fermenting maize or Indian corn, prepared in a most disgusting manner, according to the account given in Acosta's Natural History of the Indies, and Frezier's voyages to the South sea, and the western coast of South America,—the saliva of the females being used for barm in producing the fermentation. The Abbé Molina says it was customary with the aborigines, when burying their dead, to deposit an earthen jar filled with chica in the mound, with the deceased, to subsist him on his journey to the other world.

raiso. From 1790 to 1830, gold to the value of two million, seven hundred thousand pounds sterling, and about half that amount of silver, were produced in Chili. In 1833, the gold coinage at the mint in Santiago amounted to three hundred ninety-two thousand, five hundred dollars, and the silver to ninety-two thousand dollars.

But the copper mines in Coquimbo, at Jajuel, near San Felipe, and other localities, constitute the chief sources of national wealth. The mineral is extracted in different forms, —as native copper, orange oxide of copper, carbonate of copper, and copper pyrites associated with some muriate of copper. In a few mines, masses of native copper, of extraordinary magnitude have been found. In 1834, nearly 42,860 quintals of copper and copper ore, were exported from Coquimbo alone; the total value of the product in all Chili, in the same year, was 75,000 hundred weight. The annual exportation of copper is now worth upwards of two millions of dollars.

Every facility and encouragement in the search for mines, is afforded by the government. The discoverer may work a mine in any ground by paying five shillings sterling; and before paying this, he may try, even in the garden of another man, for the space of twenty days. At the copper mines, the laborers undergo the severest hardships for a trifling remuneration; one pound, sterling, a month, together with food, being the usual compensation. In winter and summer, they begin work at early dawn, and leave off at dark. But little time is allowed for meals. The food furnished to the miners consists of sixteen figs and two small loaves of bread for breakfast, boiled beans for dinner, and broken roasted wheat grain for supper. Once a week, very rarely, but never oftener, they are provided with the hard dried beef of the country, called *charqui*.

There are two classes of laborers,—the *barretéros*, or miners, who work the lode, and the *apirés*, who carry the ore upon their backs to the surface. The latter perform the most difficult and laborious part of the work. According to a general regulation, the *apiré* is not allowed to halt for breath, except the mine is six hundred feet deep. With a lighted candle in a cloven stick grasped in his hand, and over two hundred pounds of ore on his back, twelve times in the day, where the mine is not over eighty yards deep, the *apiré* climbs the notched trees placed in a zig-zag line up the shaft, and during the intervals is employed in breaking and picking ore. Yet, notwithstanding this great tax upon his physical powers, he appears healthy and cheerful. On reaching the surface with his *carpácho* he is nearly overcome, and the perspiration rolls down in streams; but after depositing his burden on the pile of ores, a few seconds serve to revive him, and he again descends the mine at a quick pace, and with a light step.

Two principal persons—the *propriétor*, and the *habilitádor* —are usually concerned in a mine. The *propriétor* is the actual miner; he resides at his *haciénda* near the mine, the working of which he superintends, and supplies his laborers with vegetables and meat from his farm. The *habilitádor* is the capitalist, who resides at one of the seaport towns, and manages the financial affairs of the partnership. The melting-house is generally built on the *haciénda*, and where the mine is distant, the ore is brought from it on the backs of mules.

(9.) The Porpoise sailed from Valparaiso for Callaö on the 26th of May, and the remainder of the squadron got under way on the 6th of June. The Peacock and Flying Fish came to anchor in the harbor of Callaö, under the island of San Lorenzo, on the 18th of June, and the Vincennes joined them on the 20th.

CHAPTER VI.

(1.) SAN LORENZO is a small, long-shaped, barren island,
which protects the southwest side of the bay of Callaö. It
is about fifteen miles in circumference, and is intersected,
throughout its whole length, by a ridge of sharp crested hills,
the highest of which are nearly thirteen hundred feet above
the level of the sea. Few or no signs of vegetation are to be
seen. Seals and sea-otters inhabit the steep rocks on the
southern side of the island, and flocks of water-fowl make
their nests on the desolate shore. On the south, San Lorenzo
is separated by a narrow strait, from a small rocky island
called *El Fronton*, and between it and the coast of the mainland, is an extensive shallow two miles wide, termed the
Camótal. Two centuries ago, the *Camótal* was dry land,
upon which large quantities of *camótes* (sweet potatoes) were
raised, but was completely inundated, either in the great
earthquake of 1687, or in that of 1630. The geölogical appearances presented on the island and along the main coast
indicate a gradual rising of the land since its submersion,
but sufficient facts have not yet been ascertained, to establish any reliable or satisfactory data. The only object of
attraction which San Lorenzo contains, is the burying-ground
of foreign seamen who are not of the Catholic faith. The
graves are covered with white stones, and a white board,

placed at the head of each, contains the name of the person interred beneath, and, in many instances, poetic inscriptions, commemorative, alike, of his virtues, and of the friendship of his surviving comrades.*

The bay of Callaö is one of the largest and calmest on the western coast of South America.   The roadstead is decidedly the best in Peru ; there being good anchorage in from seven to ten fathoms.   In former times, a raft or float, called the *bálsa*, formed of two long skin bags, blown up like bladders, and covered with a light platform, was used to load and unload vessels ; afterwards a rude pier was constructed, behind which vessels of heavy burden could discharge or receive cargoes, in perfect security from the breakers ; and, more recently, a fine mole has been erected, surrounded by an iron railing.   The beach is flat, and for the most part shingly ; about the mouths of the Rimac and the Rio de Chillon, two small rivers that debouch into the bay, it is somewhat marshy. The harbor is, or rather was, well fortified.   Two massive fortresses built in low situations, extending far out into the sea, once commanded the harbor and its entrances, and the plain between Callaö and Lima.†   The northern fortress consists of two castles, the largest of which the Spaniards named

---

* Some of these inscriptions are as quaint as those on the tomb-stones in the old English churchyards.   One of the wooden monuments, erected to the memory of Thomas Hedrick, a lad belonging to the U. S. ship of the line North Carolina, has the following :

> " In vain had youth its flight impeded,
> And hope its passage had delayed ;
> Death's mandate all has superseded,—
> The latest order Tom obeyed."

Another, reared above the remains of one of H. B. M. Royal Marines, says :

> " I 'm here at rest from busy scenes ;
> I once belonged to the Royal Marines;
> I 'm now confined within these borders,
> Remaining here for further orders."

† The principal fortress is now used for custom-house purposes, and tide-waiters and messengers, utterly guiltless of everything like cleanliness, occupy the places once honored by the presence of the brave Rodil and his gallant brethren in arms.

Real Felípe, but since the Revolution it has been called El Castíllo de la Independencia;—it has two round towers, wide, but not high, spacious courtyards, and a deep ditch which can be filled with water from the sea. The southern fortification is called El Castíllo del Sol. Before the War of Independence, the two together mounted four hundred pieces of cannon, many of them of very large calibre; but they are now dismantled and decayed; the armaments have disappeared; the cross and shield of Castile and Leon no longer float above their ruins, and the *galeóns* which once poured an unbroken tide of wealth into the coffers of old Spain have forever vanished. Gloomy witnesses are these relics of the past, of ancient Castilian pride, and power, and wealth—of modern lethargy and retrogradation!

Callaö is comparatively of modern origin. The ancient town bearing the same name stood a little nearer the ocean, and was completely destroyed and submerged by the dreadful earthquake of 1746; it contained, at that time, four thousand inhabitants, barely two hundred of whom escaped. It has often been said that the old town could be seen beneath the waves, on a calm day and with a clear sky; and Captain Wilkes seems to have adopted this opinion, probably without a very careful examination, in his Narrative of the Exploring Expedition.[*]   Dr. Von Tschudi[†] and other intelligent travellers have repeatedly examined the *Mar brava*—the spot designated as the locality of the ruins—but without discovering the least trace of these *châteaux en Espagne.* The story is, doubtless, all a mere fiction, originating like many another marvel, which, though equally unfounded, has not been without believers.

Modern Callaö is situated on the north side of a projecting tongue of land. It contains about five thousand inhabitants, and begins to wear the appearance of a populous town; yet it is damp and dirty in the winter, dry and dusty in the summer, and excessively filthy at all seasons of the year. The

* Vol. I. p. 235.   † Travels in Peru, (Wiley and Putnam's edition,) p. 33.

principal street, parallel with the beach, is paved in a miserable manner; the others, with the exception of that leading to Lima, are mean, narrow lanes. The houses are slightly built, and are usually one story high; the walls are constructed of *adobés*, or of reeds plastered over with loam or red clay; the *azotéas*, or flat roofs, consist of a framework of reeds with straw mats laid upon them. In order to ensure privacy, the windows are generally in thé roof; they are mere trap-doors, with wooden gratings, closed by shutters on the inside. The houses are all whitewashed outside and in, and most of them are furnished with clumsy verandas and flagstaffs.

Very little attention is paid anywhere to comfort and cleanliness. Heaps of offal and rubbish are suffered to accumulate in the streets, around which the dogs and buzzards congregate in droves. Unshorn and unwashed *pádres* jostle each other on the *trottoir*. Groups of lazy, idle soldiers, consisting of Indians, negroes, and mulattoes,—all attired like ragamuffins,—may be seen collected about every dirty and miserable *café*; while their officers, in popinjay costume, saunter along the mole, or lounge at the Custom-house. Fowls and hogs are free commoners in door and out. The orange-women, who sit all day long in front of their houses, beside the rich and luscious fruit that tempts the passer-by, when not engaged with their chaffering customers, are busily occupied in hunting for vermin on their own persons; and the fine ladies over the way, who thrum their guitars, or exhibit their finery on the *paséo*, in the after part of the day, would scarcely be recognized in their slatternly costume in the morning.

Callaö derives most, if not all, its importance, from its excellent harbor, and its proximity to Lima, from which it is about six miles distant; and should the country ever be freed from the misrule of military demagogues, it may yet become one of the most populous and important seaports on the Pacific. A broad, and what was formerly a well paved road, runs, nearly in a straight line, from the Castle of Independence to the Callaö Gate of Lima. Omnibuses built in Newark,

New Jersey, ply regularly between the city and the port. For more than half the distance, the road is flanked on either hand by sandy and uncultivated fields, or low brushwood ; but about one mile from the capital commences the *Alameda del Callaö*, through which the road passes,—a charming promenade, provided with beautiful shade trees, and stone seats for the weary foot-passenger, and bordered with beautiful gardens and luxuriant fruit trees. Less than half a mile from the castle is the small village of Bella Vista ; beyond this are the ruins of an ancient Indian town ; and midway between the harbor and the city are the convent of *la Virgen del Carmen*, a chapel, and a *Tambo*. The *Tambo* is an inn, and, were it among us, would probably be styled " The Half-way-House." Among the Peruvians, however, it is called *La Legua*—The League—which conveys the same idea, as the house is a Spanish league distant from either town.

(2.) Lima is built in an amphitheatre formed by the spurs jutting out from the great chain of the Andes, near the eastern side of a broad plain which slopes gradually down to the Pacific, and is elevated nearly five hundred feet above the level of the sea. It lies on both banks of the river Rimac, from which the modern name of the city was derived by a corrupt pronunciation. The larger part of the town—the city proper—is on the southern bank of the river, and is connected with its suburb of San Lazaro, or the fifth section, on the opposite shore, by an excellent stone bridge of six arches, furnished with recesses and seats, and forming a delightful and favorite promenade. The city is about two miles long from east to west—from the Gate of Maravillas to the Monserrate—and a mile and a quarter broad. The plain on which it stands slopes from the east to the west. Like other Spanish towns in South America, it is laid out with great regularity, in *quádras*, or squares of houses, the sides of which average from 140 to 145 *varas*.* The streets, generally about thirty-four feet wide, intersect each other at

---

* Each *vara* is about thirty-three inches English measure.

right angles, and, in the older and principal part of the city, run from south-east to north-west, so that the walls of the houses cast a shade both in the morning and afternoon. At noon, there can be no shade, as the city is situated in latitude 12° south.

Through the centre of most of the streets in Lima, there runs a stream of water, three feet wide, which is the receptacle of all the garbage, refuse and filth, thrown from the private dwellings; yet, as there are buzzards and dogs, without number, to perform the part of scavengers, the nuisance is not so intolerable as it would otherwise be. The streets generally are paved with round pebbles, and the sidewalks are flagged; but the latter are almost always in bad repair.

Ever since the foundation of the Peruvian capital, by Francisco Pizarro and his fellow adventurers,* it has been celebrated for the beauty, richness, and splendor, of its public edifices; and, in this respect, it has long maintained a position, second only to the proud city reared above the ruins of "the Venice of the Aztecs." In passing through the Periphery, or outer circle of the town, the stranger is not favorably impressed by the groups of old houses, whose dirty and dilapidated walls seem ready to topple down at the first blast of the tempest; but on entering the *Pláza Mayór*, in the centre of the business part of the city, his eye rests with delight

---

* Historical records differ widely, in regard to the year in which Lima was founded; some asserting it to be 1534, and others 1535. Garcilaso of Cuzco, Herrera, Montalvo, and Ulloa, adopt the latter date; and Mr. Prescott, in his Conquest of Peru, (vol. II, p. 24,) does the same, on the authority of Quintaña, and Bernabe Cobo. Dr. Von Tschudi, however, (Travels in Peru, p. 42, *nota*,) says the city was founded in 1534. According to Captain Wilkes, also, (Narrative, vol. I, p. 242,) the title of the book in the city hall of Lima containing the signatures of the viceroys, fixes the date of the organization of the municipality at 1534. There has likewise been considerable dispute in regard to the day of the month; but it is now generally acknowledged to have been the 6th of January, (the day of the Epiphany,) as the original name of the city was *Ciudád de los Reyes*, (City of the Kings;) and in Germany, and other countries on the European Continent, the day of the Epiphany was called "the festival of the three holy Kings." At the time of the foundation, it will be recollected, Charles V, emperor of Germany, was also King of Spain.

on the lofty spires, the swelling domes, and splendid façades, rising everywhere around him, and he then begins really to appreciate the fact, that he is treading on " the silver soil of Peru."

The great square forms a quadrangle, each side of which is 510 feet long. It is unpaved, but the ground is covered with fine sand. From each of the four corners run two handsome streets, at right angles to one another. In the centre of the *Pláza*, is a massive bronze fountain, of three basins, forty feet high, and raised on a level table of masonry forty feet on each side. From the middle basin rises a pillar, surmounted by a figure of Fame, represented in the attitude of spouting the water from her trumpet. In the other basins, the water is thrown from the mouths of four lions. The pillar and figures were cast in 1650, by the order of the then reigning viceroy, Count de Salvatiérra.

On the north side of the square, is the government palace, a mean unsightly structure, formerly the residence of the viceroys, but now appropriated to the courts of justice, and other government offices. It is a square building, and the front facing the *Pláza* is disfigured by a long range of shops, called *La Rivera*, above which is a balcony. On the west side of the square, are the *Cabildo*, or senate-house, and the city jail; and on the south there is a range of private dwellings, with balconies looking upon the *Pláza*. The cathedral and the archbishop's palace occupy the east side of the square. The latter has a fine façade, but the former is, by far, the most imposing edifice in Lima. The foundation stone of the cathedral was laid by Pizarro on the 18th of January, 1534: ninety years elapsed, however, before its completion, and it was finally consecrated, with great pomp and ceremony, on the 19th of October, 1625. The remains of its founder were deposited beneath its walls.

This edifice has a front of 186 feet, and is 320 deep. At either corner, in front, there is an octagonal tower, 200 feet high, resting on a base elevated 40 feet above the ground. **The multitudinous ornaments profusely scattered in and** about the building, detract very much from the effect that so large a structure would naturally produce ; yet they indicate the vastness of the means at the command of its projectors. Says Caldcleugh, in his Travels in South America :* " The riches which have been lavished at various times upon the interior of this edifice, are scarcely to be credited anywhere but in a city which once paved a street with ingots of silver to do honor to a new viceroy. The balustrades surrounding the great altar, and the pipes of the organ, were of silver. It may be mentioned, as a proof of the abundance of silver ornaments, that in 1821, one and a half ton of silver was taken from the churches in Lima without being missed, to meet the exigencies of the state." The columns, or pillars, forming the balustrade, are of Ionic form, twelve feet high and one and a half thick. Above the altar is a massive silver gilt crown. The tabernacle is seven feet and a half high, and composed of wrought gold, set with a profusion of diamonds and emeralds. On either side of the altar there are tall silver candelabra, each weighing over seven hundred pounds. The seats and pulpit in the choir are exquisitely carved. The interior of the cathedral is divided into three naves, and it is paved with large tiles. The roof is richly pannelled and carved, and rests on arches springing from a double row of square stone pillars. On high festival days, the priests wear robes and ornaments embroidered in gold, and set with precious stones, to correspond with the magnificent decorations of the altar at which they minister.

Besides the cathedral, there are upwards of fifty other churches and convents, which cover full one fourth of the area of the city. Conspicuous among the former, are those of San Lazaro, San Francisco, and Sánto Domingo—the last two belonging to convents of the same name. San Lazaro boasts of a tasteful exterior, and its interior is rich, but exceedingly chaste. The Franciscan convent is the largest monastic establishment in the city. It stands near the *Pláza Mayór*, and covers, including all its buildings, two entire

* Vol. II, p. 56.

quádras. Its church, next in size to the cathedral, is decorated with great splendor. The convent of Sánto Domingo is probably the wealthiest in Peru,—its yearly revenue, derived mostly from the ground-rents of houses in Lima, exceeding seventy thousand dollars. The steeple of the church of Sánto Domingo is the loftiest in the city; it is 188 feet high, and is distinctly visible at the distance of three leagues. The interior of the church is gorgeously adorned, and its grand altar is almost as splendid as that of the cathedral.

There are sixteen nunneries in Lima, the largest of which is the Monasterio de la Concepçion : it has an annual revenue of upwards of one hundred thousand dollars, but is more celebrated for its wealth, than for the piety or vestal perfectness of its inmates. There are several establishments, however, in which the conventual rules are rigidly observed.

In addition to the convents and nunneries, there are *beatérios*, which pious women who desire to lead a cloistered life without taking the veil may enter and quit at pleasure; and also, *cásas de exércicio*, into which females retire during Lent, to perform acts of penance. For the other sex, there are cells in the convent of Recoléto.

Lima also possesses eleven public hospitals and two foundling asylums. The two largest hospitals, San Andrés and Sánta Aña, contain nearly four hundred beds each. Attached to San Andrés is a botanic garden, and adjoining it is the medical college of San Fernándo, established in 1809.

The second large square in the city is the public market-place. Before the war of Independence it was known as the *Pláza de la Inquisiçion;* it is now called the *Plazuéla de la Independéncia.* On this square are the Palace of the Inquisition, now occupied as a jail and a store-house for provisions, and the University. The latter was founded under a decree of Charles V, dated in 1551. The exterior of the building is by no means imposing, but it has a spacious quadrangular court, entered by a lofty door, along the sides of which are pillared corridors. On the walls of the corridors there are allegorical paintings in fresco, representing the different branches of science, underneath which are inscribed apposite quotations from classical authors. The lecture rooms open into the corridors ; and in the left angle of the court are great double doors opening into the *Aula*, or principal hall. On the walls of the *Aula* are hung portraits of distinguished scholars. The university is partly supported by congress, and partly by the produce of an annual *bull-bait!* There are only between thirty and fifty students, and most of the professorships are mere sinecures. Besides the university, there are several colleges in the city, one of which (San Carlos) has about one hundred students. There are also good Lancasterian, Latin, and primary schools, and a number of private ones conducted by Europeans. Notwithstanding the many causes, growing out of the social and political condition of the country, which have a tendency to check or hinder intellectual improvement, the cause of education is slowly, perhaps, yet steadily progressing.

In the vicinity of the square of Independence is the Mint, at which from two to two and a half millions of dollars are annually coined. Near the convent of San Pedro, the ancient *Colegio maximo* of the Jesuits, is the National Library, founded in 1821, one of the first fruits of the Revolution. It contains not far from thirty thousand volumes, embracing many valuable theological and historical works, and is open to the public daily, Sundays and Fridays excepted. In the left wing of the library building is the national museum, still in its infancy.

Lima likewise boasts of a theatre, more notorious for the myriads of fleas that infest it, than for the skill and talent displayed in its performances ; a *coliséo de gallos*, or cockpit ; a tennis-court ; and an amphitheatre, *Pláza firme del Acho*, in the suburb of San Lazaro, where bull-fights are held.

With the exception of the suburb of San Lazaro, and a part of the north side of the city proper, Lima is surrounded by a brick wall, between eighteen and twenty feet high, from ten to twelve feet thick at the base, and nine feet at the top.

It was originally built in 1585, and repaired in 1807; but it is now in a state of complete dilapidation, and furnishes another sad commentary on the history of Spanish colonization. Similar mementos of past magnificence, of the faded splendor of the viceroyalty, arrest the attention full often in the streets of Lima. To the philosopher and historian, these decaying memorials of a by-gone age furnish matter for serious thought and reflection.

Nearly a hundred years elapsed, after Pizarro and his companions unfurled the victorious *bandéra* of Castile and Leon, over the ancient palaçes of the Incas of Peru, before the Pilgrim Founders of the Colony of Massachusetts landed on the rock-bound coast of Accomack.* The former found a land blushing in loveliness and beauty, possessing a genial temperature, yielding with scanty labor an abundant product of luscious fruits and valuable grains, and abounding in silver, and gold, and precious stones; countless *galeóns*, freighted with the treasures which they poured into the coffers of the mother country, soon crossed the sea, and seemed to foreshadow a long and prosperous career for those who should come after them. The latter, fleeing from the tyranny and persecution of kingcraft and priestcraft, were welcomed to a bleak and inhospitable clime, by the howling of the wintry wind and the shrill war-whoop of the murderous savage.—Centuries have passed away:—indolence and effeminacy on the one hand, have ended in corruption and anarchy; and industry and enterprise on the other, have terminated in happiness and prosperity. The descendants of the Puritans have not only preserved their patrimonial inheritance unimpaired; they have beautified and improved it to an unexampled degree; they have carried the arts and institutions of their forefathers from the Atlantic to the Pacific. The offspring of the Spanish colonists already begin to experience the evils springing from wealth too easily acquired; enervated by luxury and licentiousness, though still clinging with superstitious

veneration to the shrines of their ancestors, they lack the
spirit to preserve them from the ravages of premature decay;
their peculiar traits and characteristics as a people are fast
disappearing; their trade is in the hands of foreign merchants;
and their government, nominally a republic, is, in fact, the
worst kind of oligarchy.

Formerly, the city wall of Lima had nine gates. But six
of these are now open, the remainder having been walled up.
At each of the gates is stationed a custom-house guard,
mainly to prevent the introduction of unstamped silver. The
wall was also designed for a fortification, and was once put
in a condition to be mounted with artillery. It is now entirely valueless in this respect, and the only work of defence
really worthy the name, is the pretty little castle of Sánta
Catalína, at the eastern side of the city, between the gates
of Cocharcas and Guadelupe, and about two hundred yards
from the wall. The castle is flanked by two bastions, and
its internal arrangements exhibit more of cleanliness and
regularity than are usually met with.

Few of the private houses in Lima are more than one
story high, and those exceeding that have the upper walls of
cane, or wattled reeds, plastered over with clay, and whitewashed or painted. The lower walls are usually built of
adobés. The better class of dwellings correspond with one
another in the style of building. The fronts are mostly quite
plain, but occasionally a house may be seen with a finely
ornamented façade. There are two doors in front: one called
the azagúan, forming the principal entrance, and the other
leading to the cochéra, or coach-house. Above the door to the
cochéra, or on the side of the main door, there is often a small
chamber, with a window, closed by a wooden railing, looking
towards the street. At this window the ladies of the family
frequently place themselves, to see and be seen, and if young
and pretty, to be admired, even if they do not admire in their
turn. Entering the azagúan, you find yourself in a broad
court, called the pátio, on either side of which there are small
rooms. Facing the azagúan is the main dwelling-house,

usually surrounded by a balcony. Two large folding doors
lead into the *sála*, or hall, which is generally carpeted with
straw matting, and furnished with a sofa, a hammock, and
several chairs. From the hall a glazed door opens into the
cuádro, or drawing room; among the wealthier classes this
room is always elegantly furnished. Adjoining the *cuádro*,
are the sleeping rooms, the dining room, and nursery. All
these apartments communicate with the *traspátio*, an inner
court yard laid out as a garden, the walls of which are tastefully adorned with decorative paintings in fresco, some illus-
trating scenes from scripture, others the festival of the Amancaes, and others representing various subjects, according to
the taste of the painter or the fancy of his employer. Beyond
the *traspátio* is the kitchen and stable,—the latter often nothing more than a mere yard, or *corrál*.

The roofs are uniformly flat. The best houses have a large
terrace, called the *azotéa*, over the *sála* and *cuádro*, which is
paved with free stone, or thin baked bricks, and surrounded
by a railing. The *azotéa* serves as a play-ground for the
children, is ornamented with flower pots, and covered with
an awning to shade it from the sun. Where there is an
upper story, the roof is composed of mats and bamboos, covered over with mortar or a light layer of earth. As in Callaö, the windows of some of the rooms are in the roof. The
other windows, generally few in number, are on each side of
the house-door; they are ornamented with casings of carved
work, in stone or wood, and often have richly gilt lattices.

It was once the custom in Lima to bury the dead in graves
dug within the churches, but the heat of the climate forbade
the continuance of this custom, and early in the present century, a general cemetery, styed the *Pantéon*, was established
outside the walls, on the eastern side of the city, on the high
road leading to the Siérra de Tarma. It is a square inclosure, neatly laid out in walks and gardens. The surrounding
walls are filled with niches for the reception of corpses. Burials are not permitted to take place after noon. The bodies
of the rich are deposited in coffins, but those of the poor are

provided with winding sheets only. Unslacked lime is applied to the remains to accelerate their decay, and to prevent contaminating the atmosphere with noxious gases.

Various estimates have been formed in regard to the population of Lima. The wide difference in the accounts that have been published, may, probably, be attributed to the remarkable fluctuations that have taken place since the Revolution. The most reliable statement in regard to the number of inhabitants may be found in the tax register drawn up in 1836, under the protectorate of Sánta Cruz, in which it is said to be a little over fifty-four thousand. It is very evident, however, that the population has diminished, rather than increased, during the last forty years. In 1810 there were said to be nearly ninety thousand inhabitants in the city, and about seventy thousand in 1826. No one familiar with the history of the country, or the scenes which have transpired there, need wonder at this. Earthquakes and epidemic diseases have swept away their thousands; many more have fallen victims to the social and political anarchy which have prevailed, to the bloody war of Independence, and the sanguinary tumults that have since disturbed the peace of the country; and numbers of families belonging to the *ancien régime* have either voluntarily expatriated themselves, or been included in some compulsory decree of banishment.

The present population of the city is made up of white Creoles, the descendants of foreigners, principally Spaniards; Indians, descended from the ancient Peruvians; and people of color, consisting of the offspring of whites and Indians, called *Mestizos,*—of whites and Mulattoes, called *Cuarterons,*—of Indians and Negroes, called *Chinos,*—and of Negroes and Mulattoes, or Mestizos, called *Zambos.* To these are to be added about five thousand slaves, mostly Zambos, and not far from one thousand ecclesiastics, lay and monastic.

(3.) Among the other principal towns in Peru, are Cuzco, the ancient capital of the Incas, Arequípa, Cérro di Pasco, Guamánga, Huácho, Huancavélica, and Truxillo, or Tru-

jillo. Cuzco is about four hundred miles from Lima, in a
southeasterly direction.   It is situated in an extensive valley,
at the foot of some lofty spurs of the Andes, nearly twelve
thousand feet above the level of the ocean.   Its population is
about twenty-five thousand, and consists mostly of Indians.
They are exceedingly industrious, and are celebrated for
their skill in embroidery, painting and sculpture.   Cuzco is
famed for its magnificent ruins, particularly those of the
Temple of the Sun, and for its splendid religious edifices.
The cathedral church and convent of St. Augustine are said
to be the finest in South America.   The Dominican convent
is also an imposing structure, and is raised on walls that
originally formed part of the Temple of the Sun ; the high
altar, according to Ulloa, standing on the very spot occupied
by the golden image of the Peruvian deity.   There are six
other convents in the city, five churches, three monasteries,
four hospitals, a university, and three collegiate schools.
Most of the private dwellings were either constructed before
the conquest of the city by Pizarro, in 1554, or have been
built of the stones that once formed part of the edifices of the
ancient Peruvians.   On a hill north of the town, are the ruins
of a large fortress, principally constructed of the angular Cy-
clopeän stones so frequently found among the ruins of Eastern
cities.   A great part of the town was destroyed, during the
siege shortly after it was taken possession of by Pizarro, but
there is still left much to interest the scholar and antiqua-
rian.

Arequípa has a population of thirty thousand souls.   It
lies at the foot of Mount Omaté, on the road leading from
Lima to the south, thirty miles east of the Pacific, and two
hundred miles southwest from Cuzco.   It was founded by
order of Pizarro, in 1536.   The houses are strongly and neatly
built, though, on account of the prevalence of earthquakes,
but one story in height.   A cathedral, a fine bronze fountain
in the *Pláza Mayór*, a college, and several convents, are the
only objects of particular attraction in the city.   Its foreign
trade is carried on through its port, Mollendo.   Though this

town is elevated upwards of seven thousand feet above the level of the sea, its environs are highly cultivated and remarkably fertile. Beautiful groves and gardens dot the landscape; hedges and fruit trees, trimmed *en espalier*, are occasionally to be seen; and the shrubs and flowers exhibit a luxuriance of foliage, and a gorgeous brilliancy of color, not surpassed in any other locality in Peru.

For more than two centuries, Cérro di Pasco has been famed throughout the world for its rich silver mines. It contains, at times, when the mines yield abundantly, some eighteen thousand inhabitants, and at others not more than five or six thousand. It is situated in an irregular basin-shaped hollow in the table land of Bombon, on the mountain chain of Olachin, and is 13,673 feet above the level of the sea. At a distance, the town presents quite a picturesque appearance, but a nearer approach dissolves the illusion. The streets are filthy, and mere narrow and crooked lanes. Some few of the dwellings are European in style, and well-built; yet in close proximity to them are clusters of miserable adobé huts and hovels, covered with thatch, but nearly destitute of chimneys and windows. The town is so burrowed under, by the numerous adits leading to the main lodes, some of which are almost fathomless and usually half full of water, that a ramble through it, even in broad daylight, is attended with no little danger.

Two hundred and ten miles southeast of Lima, on the road to Cuzco, is Guamánga, formerly called *San Juan de la Victória*, or *de la Frontéra*. It was founded by Pizarro, and stands in the middle of an extensive and beautiful plain. The houses are constructed with neatness and taste, mainly of stone, and have pretty orchards and gardens attached to them. It has several large squares, and the streets are spacious and convenient. The population is said to be fifteen thousand. There is a cathedral in the city, and several other churches and convents. The climate is very fine, and the situation is regarded as being quite healthy. Huácho is a small village, containing some five thousand inhabitants,

which, since the war of Independence, has been dignified
with the title of city. It is situated on the coast north of
Lima. Four fifths of the population are Indians, and the
remainder mestizos. The natives employ their time in fishing, agriculture, and the rearing of poultry. Every Friday,
large caravans of Indian women, mounted on mules, start
for Lima, with fowls, ducks, and turkeys. Two bunches of
fowls, consisting of from fifteen to twenty each, are attached
by every chola to the pommel of her saddle, one hanging
down on either side. About two days and a half are required to perform the journey, and the poor creatures are
kept all the while in this position, except when the caravan
is halted.

Huancavélica lies about midway between Lima and Guamánga. Its population is estimated at about twelve thousand. This town has long been celebrated for its rich quick-
silver mines; they have been worked for almost three hundred years, and are still highly productive. Truxillo is the
principal town in North Peru, and contains not far from ten
thousand inhabitants. It lies on the coast, and was named
after the birth place of the conqueror of Peru, Francisco
Pizarro.

(4.) The handful of Spaniards, commanded by Pizarro
and Almagro, entered Peru in 1532. Availing themselves
of the dissensions among the Indian tribes then occupying
the country, as Hernando Cortés and his warriors had already
done in ancient Azteca, they at first formed an alliance with
Atahualpa, or Atabalipa, the reigning Inca, and afterwards
deprived him of his liberty and put him to death. This deed
of cruelty having been perpetrated, the whole country was
rapidly overrun and reduced to submission. It was afterwards formed into a viceroyalty, and continued subject to the
dominion of Spain until the year 1821. The inhabitants
were long firm in their loyalty, and the royalists were eventually put down, only by a strong Chilian army under San
Martin, in coöperation with the Peruvian patriots. The independence of Peru was proclaimed at Lima, on the 28th of

July, 1821, under the auspices of San Martin, who was declared protector of the new republic and invested with dictatorial power.

In 1823, San Martin retired, and Riva-Aguero was proclaimed president. At the same time, General José La Már was placed at the head of the Peruvian division of the great liberating army under General Bolivar. The Spaniards and royalists had now rallied, and the patriot garrison of Callaö hoisted Spanish colors, in February, 1824. Aided by General Bolivar,—then president of Bolivia, and clothed with supreme military power in Peru, under the title of *Libertador*,—and a strong Colombian force under General Sucré, the republicans firmly maintained their ground. Meanwhile, Riva-Aguero had been driven from the presidency by Bolivar, and a new constitution formed on the model of that of the United States had been adopted, which was not to take effect, however, till the expiration of his dictatorship.

After sustaining a number of reverses, the patriots were finally victorious over their enemies, who were defeated by Bolivar at Junin, on the 6th of August, 1824, and by Generals Sucré and La Már, on the 9th of December following, at Ayacucho. This secured the independence of Peru, although the Spaniards, under General Rodil, remained in possession of the fortress at Callaö till the 22d of January, 1826, when they were forced, by famine, to surrender. During the whole struggle for liberty, the country was in a most wretched condition. Civil war, at all times dreadful, had little here to mitigate its horrors. Life and property were insecure; murders and assassinations were of frequent occurrence; and the most glaring outrages were committed with impunity. Reckless cruelty was exhibited, alike by the general in the field, and the statesman in the cabinet; and the prevailing looseness in private morals was only equalled by the licentiousness openly exhibited in public life. No change for the better took place while Bolivar maintained his authority as dictator.

In January, 1827, the Peruvians revolted, and freed themselves from the presence of the dictator and his armed legions. The constitution established by Bolivar was now abrogated, and that of 1823 restored; and General La Már,—a man not more pure and honest in private life, than just and blameless in his public career,—was then elevated to the presidency by the Peruvian Congress. La Már remained at the head of affairs till June, 1829, when he was deposed by General La Fuénte, in consequence, as was alleged, of the imbecility displayed by the former at the battle of Tarqui, in the month of February previous, at which the Peruvians had been defeated by the Colombians under General Sucré. But, in fact, La Már was too pure-minded to hold the reins of government, in a country where military success was the only passport to public favor, and among a people so easily duped by the demagogues who readily pandered to their vices and ministered to their corrupt tastes and depraved appetites. The deposition was, really, the result of a conspiracy between General Gamarra, through whose treachery or cowardice the battle of Tarqui was lost, General La Fuénte, and General Sánta Cruz, then the President of Bolivia. The conspirators were completely successful in obtaining the control of the government. In August, 1829, Gamarra was elected President, and La Fuénte Vice President, of Peru.

Gamarra remained in office, though much dissatisfaction was evinced in regard to the mode in which he administered the government, till 1833, when he resigned, shortly before the expiration of his constitutional term of service. It was evidently his intention to establish a strong central government and place himself at its head; but his friend and minion, Bermúdez, whom he supported for the presidency as his successor, being himself ineligible for a second consecutive term, was defeated by General Orbejóso. The latter, owing to the distracted state of the country, called in the assistance of Sánta Cruz, who was made Supreme Protector of Peru. He divided the country into two separate republics, North and South Peru, but they were ultimately reünited. The war with Chili ensued; Gamarra was again restored to power at the point of the bayonet, and in 1839 Sánta Cruz was driven into Bolivia. Peru was then involved in a war with Bolivia, which was at length brought to a close, through the mediation of Chili, by the treaty of Puno, concluded on the 7th of June, 1842. Since that date one military chieftain after another has gained the ascendency, and assumed to direct the government. At this time General Castílla exercises the functions of the presidential office.* He belongs to the centralists, but the plan of government they propose to adopt, if honestly and justly administered, is probably the best calculated to secure the internal peace and tranquillity of the country, at least while so great a laxity of morals prevails in public and private life, and the masses seem so unwilling, or so unable, to comprehend the great principles of self-government.

(5.) Different estimates have been made, and different accounts published, in regard to the population of Peru. It cannot vary far from 1,700,000. Full three fourths of the inhabitants are Indians, or of Indian extraction, and the remainder are white Creoles and Negroes. The white Creoles are of moderate stature, yet well-formed, and slender in figure. Their complexions are almost colorless, but usually quite fair; their hair and eyes are black; and their features strongly marked. The men are as feeble in mind as in person; they look prematurely old; they are effeminate, irascible, incapable of long-continued physical or mental exertion, and as impatient of contradiction as a Milesian. Though not entirely destitute of frankness, yet they know how to dissemble. They are just the men for demagogues to excite and inflame; just the men for *émeutes* and conspiracies. Smoking, gaming, and cock-fighting, are the chief occupations of their lives, yet, withal, are they singularly abstinent in the use of intoxicat-

* President Castilla is by no means firmly seated in power. Several conspiracies have recently been formed, through the instrumentality of Generals San Roman and Torrico, both prominent federalists, and noted revolutionists, to overturn the existing state of affairs. One project was set on foot as late as the month of February, 1849, but the conspirators were arrested before they had time to mature their plans.

ing drinks.   The wealthy devote their whole time to idleness
and amusement, and the poor, who are compelled to earn
their own livelihood, pursue some light handicraft, which will
afford them plenty of leisure for gossip and recreation.

But what Nature has denied to the men, she has bestowed,
with a liberal hand, upon the Creole women.   In the streets
of Lima, at almost every hour of the day, you may discover
rich and rare specimens of female loveliness and beauty.   The
fair Limeña can boast of a complexion of velvety softness
white and clear as the purest Parian marble, and beneath
whose polished surface the delicate tracery of each vein and
artery is distinctly visible.   Eye-brows exquisitely pencilled,
and long silken lashes, shade a pair of orbs dark as the moon-
less night, that charm and fascinate, alike when kindling
in anger, or glowing with the fire of an unworthy passion, as
when beaming with the blessed light of an honest and holy
love.   Masses of luxuriant hair, black as the plumage of the
raven, fall in long wavy plaits down the finely arched neck,
and over the nicely rounded bust and shoulders.   Teeth of
pearly whiteness, a form of small but elegant proportions, and
a neatly turned foot and ankle, complete the picture, and
form a *tout ensemble* not often seen in other climes, and,
when once seen, not easily forgotten.

To these personal attractions must be added, a captivating
deportment, ease and grace of manners, amiability of temper,
and, generally speaking, a far greater degree of intelligence
than is found in the other sex.   The glowing breath of the
tropics, indeed, has given to every passion and emotion, a
depth and intensity not common in colder countries, and if
the Peruvian señoríta hates, the feeling is not idly manifested ;
but if she loves, it is with an unselfish *abandon*, a generous
and trustful confidence, and a whole-souled devotion, that
would startle the prudishness of northern dames and belles.
One knowing anything of the national character, would not
be apt to fancy that the Creole women were notable house-
keepers.   In fact, almost everything is left to the domestics,
particularly in Lima ; and but little attention is paid to clean-

liness, in private dwellings, except in the *sála* and *cuádro*, the more public apartments. More regard for personal neatness, however, is exhibited. The Limeña cleans her teeth several times a day, with the *raiz de diéntes* (root for the teeth); considerable time is spent at the toilet; and perfumery is lavishly used. The climate naturally produces indolence; and, while at home, she is fond of reclining on a sofa, or swinging in a hammock, and, at the same time, enjoying a plate of sweetmeats, or smoking a cigar. Visiting, promenading, the theatre, the ball, and the concert, occupy the rest of her time. When she has passed the prime of life, **and** her beauty begins to fade, the missal takes the place of the mirror, and she devotes herself to works of piety and charity.

Travellers in Spain have often remarked upon the fondness of the people for scriptural names. This custom is carried to a greater extent even, in Peru, than in the mother country. *Marias, Concepçions, Asunçions, Natividads,* and *Joséfas,* are quite common. A girl born on Candlemas-day is called *Candelária.* If a child's birth day is the first day of the year, it is called *Jesus,* or *Jesusito,* if a male, and *Jesusita* if a female. A married woman does not assume the surname of her husband, except as an addition to her own family name; as for instance, if Dóña Maria Dolóres Castílla should marry Don Lafuénte, she would style herself *Dóña Maria Dolóres Castílla de Lafuénte.*

Little more can be said of the mixed races, than that they resemble similar classes the world over. The bad qualities of their progenitors are more frequently copied than their good qualities; their vices are pretty sure to be inherited, but their virtues generally prove a lapsed legacy. In the remote districts, descendants of the ancient Indian tribes may occasionally be found, who preserve unimpaired the nobler and better traits and characteristics of their ancestors, but it is oftener the case that they exhibit the demoralization and corruption consequent on their intercourse with the whites. The mestizos constitute the most active and enterprising

6*

part of the population, but the zambos are lazy, sensual, and vicious.

The divers shades of blood, and the peculiar and distinct characteristics, found among the different races composing the population of Peru, have tended in a great measure to produce the disaffection and turbulence which have so long prevailed in the country. For many years, it has been everywhere known as

"The field of freedom, faction, fame, and blood;"

and it will, doubtless, continue to remain so, till the prejudice of birth and caste is done away. Something has been already gained in this respect, and we have much to hope for, so far as regards the future, in the prevailing religion. The Catholicism of Rome is a sad leveller of distinctions, out of the pale of the church; and its worship teaches—nowhere more forcibly than in Peru—the important truth, that there is a power before which the hereditary taskmaster and the hereditary bondsman are alike equal.* In Lima, when the great bell of the cathedral announces the raising of the host, during the performance of high mass, business and conversation of all kinds are suspended; every sound is hushed; the humble tire-woman uncovers her head, and kneels beside the proud *señóra* whom she serves—and the old decrepit beggar utters the same prayer with the haughty cavalier who bears a prince's ransom on his shoulders. A similar effect is witnessed, at evening, as the church bells sound for the *oraçion;* and when the prayers are ended, each one makes the sign of the cross, and salutes his nearest neighbor,—whether he be slave or freeman, rich or poor,—with the kindly greeting, " *Buénas nóches!*"†

Until quite recently, the prevailing style of dress in Peru was Spanish, blended, in the interior, and among the lower

---

* The charter of Independence says that "no man is born a slave in Peru;" but the National Congress have, practically, legislated to the contrary. There are between four and five thousand negro slaves in Lima alone.

† Good night!

classes throughout the country, with an occasional imitation of Indian costume; but latterly, according to Lieutenant Revere, " English tailors have transmogrified the men, and French milliners have played the deuce with the women."*
The *cholo* still adheres to his *poncho*, and his embroidered jerkin, or *zamárra;* the Indian woman does not lay aside her gay-colored *bayéta;* the mestizo continues to display his vest and breeches of shining velvet, decked with bright fili-gree buttons; but the prevailing fashions, among the upper classes, are French and English, and these are fast extend-ing to every rank and condition.

At Lima and Truxillo, a singular dress, peculiar to those two cities, is worn by the ladies, at church, in religious pro-cessions, in their promenades, and sometimes during a morn-ing call; but it is never seen in a ball room or theatre. This dress consists of the *Sáya y Mánto,*—literally, a petticoat and veil. There are two kinds of *sáyas*—the *sáya ajustáda,* and the *sáya culéça,* or *sáya desplegáda.* The former is a skirt, or petticoat, of thick silk, either of a brown or some other dark color, which is plaited at the top and bottom, in small fluted folds, drawn close together at the waist, but widening as they descend. It fits tightly to the form, and nothing could be better devised to display the symmetry of the wearer's limbs, unless it were complete male attire. It, of course, prevents any rapid movement in walking, though it does not reach quite as low as the ankle,—the inventor, probably, not caring entirely to hide the tasteful *chaussure.* This garment, however, is rapidly going out of date,—few really modest females making use of it,—and the *sáya desple-gáda* is taking its place. The latter is plaited close at the waist, but from thence downwards, it presents the appear-ance of a hooped petticoat.

The *mánto* is a veil of thick black silk, fastened at the back of the waist, where it joins the *sáya,* by a narrow band. It is thence brought over the shoulders and head, and drawn over the face, so as to leave a small triangular space, in

---

* Tour of Duty in California, p. 11.

which glistens the eye of the wearer, like a diamond set in jets. Sometimes a rich shawl is thrown over the shoulders, beneath the *mánto*. The folds of the veil are confined by a small hand, always neatly gloved; in the other hand is carried a richly embroidered handkerchief, or a pretty nosegay.

Those who wear this strange costume are called *tapádas*. Its original design, it is said, was to secure privacy and prevent intrusion; but, of late, it has been sadly perverted, and is now a convenient shield and cover for the demirep and *intrigant*. Many are the tales related, in the gay capital of Peru, of jealous lovers and husbands outwitted,—and of frail friars, and frailer nuns, forgetting the solemn vows which they had taken, and soiling forever the vestal purity and perfectness of their high calling.

All classes in Peru are passionately fond of amusements of every kind,—of dancing, theatrical performances, and musical entertainments. Religious processions may likewise be classed in the same category, as many seem to regard them in that light. The festivals of Corpus Chrísti, Sánto Domingo, and San Francisco, are celebrated, in the cities, with great pomp and ceremony; and from the highest to the lowest, the brilliant pageant is enjoyed with unusual zest. On St. John's day, (24th of June,) a grand festival is held by the lower classes in Lima—and not, as Captain Wilkes, perhaps hastily, conjectured, by the population generally*—in the valley, or plain, of Amancaes, which is about half a mile northwest of the city, and derives its name from a beautiful yellow lily, whose blossoms are liberally sprinkled over its surface at the time of the *fête*. It is merely a drunken bout, however; drinking, gaming, gormandism, and dancing the obscene *samacuéca*, constituting the principal attractions of this Peruvian Floralia.

As has heretofore been stated, the white Creole in Peru, is not much addicted to the use of intoxicating drinks. When he takes wine, it is usually some sweet and light kind, and is partaken of sparingly. But the mixed races, and the peo-

* Narrative of the Exploring Expedition, Vol. I, p. 244.

ple generally in the interior of the country, are not so abstemious as those who reside in the cities and along the coast. The mestizo loves his *aguardiénte*, and the cholo his *chica*. Smoking is an almost universal practice among all classes and sexes. Among the other stimulants made use of, is *coca*. This is a shrub extensively cultivated in the mountainous districts of Peru, the leaves of which, when dried, are mixed with burnt lime. It forms a powerful stimulating narcotic, which is used as a masticatory. Like opium, it brings on an apathy to surrounding objects, but its effects are more pernicious, and a confirmed coca-chewer, or *coquéro*, is with difficulty reclaimed.*

The private habitations of the Peruvians, in the interior, resemble those in Chili. Those of the better class are built of *adobés*, one story high, with thatched roofs; but the Indians, and the poorer inhabitants, live in miserable hovels constructed of cane and mud, which are dirty and filthy in the extreme. In the northern part of the country, among the sandy *lómas*, or hills, which are so common in that section, houses may often be seen that are erected on posts, from eight to ten feet high, in order to render them cool and airy, and to protect the occupants from the sand-flies. The material used in their construction is a species of reed, and the roofs are thatched with leaves.

Mules and llamas are the principal carriers of burdens in Peru, and travelling is performed, either on horseback, or, where the roads will admit, in antique coaches of Spanish patterns, or in the *calésa*, a small chaise. Since the introduction of steam navigation, there have been steamers to accommodate those persons wishing to go from one port on the coast to another. In Lima, omnibuses have become quite common, and they have almost superseded the other modes of riding in the city, and between it and Callaö.

(6.) Two great mountain chains, running parallel with each other and the coast, intersect Peru, and divide it into

---

* The annual value of the *coca* prepared in Peru and Bolivia, is estimated at two and a half millions of dollars.

three regions. These two ranges are called the Cordillera and the Andes. Strictly speaking, the Cordillera is the chain nearest the coast, and the Andes the eastern chain; but the terms are now used indiscriminately. The strip between the coast and the first chain, is from sixty to seventy miles wide; some portions of it are covered with dry, barren sand; others are less arid; and, here and there, are small oases, like that in which Lima is built, which are exceedingly fertile. The space inclosed between the two mountain ridges, is called the *Siérra*. This tract is partly occupied by the cross ranges intersecting the two principal chains, and by huge naked rocks; partly by wide-spread table lands, known as the *Puna*, or *Despobládo*, which are mostly uninhabited, and scantily covered with sickly looking yellow grass, stunted *quinuä* trees, and large patches of the Ratanhia shrub; and partly by expansive valleys, which make a suitable return for the labor of the husbandman.* But little is known of the third region, along the base of the eastern mountain chain, although the old inhabitants chiefly dwelt there, and obtained from the mines the metal which they manufactured into the curious forms and shapes that aroused the cupidity of Pizarro and his followers.

The Peruvian coast is rugged and lofty, throughout its whole extent, except in the northern provinces, where some miles of a loose sandy desert occasionally intervene between the high lands and the Pacific. There are but few secure harbors in the whole sixteen hundred miles of sea coast. Those of Callaö, Payta, Sechúra, Salína, Písco, Islay, and Iquiqua, are esteemed the best. At Truxillo and Lambaqeque, there are mere open roadsteads, which, in rough weather, are extremely insecure. On account of the great depth of the water, vessels are generally obliged to anchor within a quarter of a mile of the shore. Where there are no moles, or piers, the operation of landing, usually effected by means of the *bálsa*, is very dangerous, in consequence of the heavy surf occa-

---

* It is very evident from the appearance of these valleys, that they once sustained a much larger population than they now do.

sioned by the mighty swell almost constantly rolling in upon the shore.

Peru cannot boast of any great rivers. The Rimac merely carries off the melted snow of the mountains; it has not sufficient force to break through the sand-bar at its mouth, and its waters percolate through it in the most lazy manner imaginable. But the largest tributaries of the Amazon, the Tunguragúa, the Huallága, and the Ucayalé, have their origin here. The Tunguragúa has its source in the small lake, Llauricocha, lying north of Cérro di Pasco. There is another lake, the Titicaca, the largest and most elevated in South America, situated partly in Peru and partly in Bolivia, which abounds in fish, but its navigation is not free from danger, as it is liable to sudden squalls and storms; and there are several smaller lakes in different parts of the country. The sources of the Amazon are considerable streams, and if the occasional obstructions were removed, they could be navigated for some distance, by steam-vessels of light draught.

In most of the provinces of Peru, the climate is said to be proverbially fine, but the bills of mortality indicate that this must be taken with some reservations and exceptions, though, upon the whole, it may be pronounced salubrious. There are two seasons during the year—the wet and the dry. From April till October, the coast lands are covered during the morning, and often throughout the day, by a dense fog or mist, which serves to moisten the ground, instead of the rain which nature has denied to it. Towards the north the fogs grow lighter, and in the extreme northern province rain sometimes falls; and when this blessing is vouchsafed, the *arenáles*, or arid sands, are soon covered with an exuberant vegetation. In October and November, the mists begin to rise, and, by a gradual transition, the dry season, which commences in December and terminates in March, is at length introduced. During the summer on the coast, heavy rains, often accompanied with thunder, fall among the *montañas*, or mountains, in the interior. The rivers and smaller streams now rush down to the ocean swollen far beyond their customary size, and thus furnish abundant means for irrigation.

Notwithstanding its proximity to the equator, the temperature in the coast region is not so high as would naturally be supposed. The prevailing winds are from the southwest, and are very cooling. West winds are not common, but they sometimes blow with terrific violence, and when they break against the mountains, often form dangerous whirlwinds. The northern winds, or, rather, currents of air,—for they can hardly be called winds,—are very sultry and oppressive. At night, the land breezes take the place of the sea breezes that blow during the day. The mean temperature of the year in Lima is about 70°, but there are villages in its immediate vicinity, subject to the same atmospherical influences, where it is still higher. The great humidity of the atmosphere upon the coast gives rise to severe fevers, and the change from the damp to the dry season frequently produces violent attacks of dysentery. Colics, bilious and inflammatory diseases, and small-pox, are also very common.

The most agreeable climate in Peru is probably to be found in the extensive elevated valleys, between the Cordillera and Andes, and the *parámos*, or ranges connecting the two great ridges. The valley of Cuzco has long been admired for its fine climate, though it is ten thousand feet above the level of the sea. Earthquakes are of frequent occurrence in the country, and have repeatedly been attended with the most disastrous consequences. The entire town of Callaö, and the greater part of Lima, were destroyed by an earthquake, in 1746. Shocks are felt—more or less powerful—every year. Since 1746, there have been two destructive earthquakes, in 1806 and 1828, and another is confidently predicted as being soon to take place, by those persons in Lima and Callaö who are fond of relating marvels, and divining signs and wonders.

Were Peru deprived of all beside, she would still have much to boast of, in the vast mineral wealth concealed beneath the frowning buttresses of the Andes. For centuries she has poured forth an almost unbroken current of gold and

silver, but the supply is not yet exhausted. Stories bordering upon the marvellous have long been told in regard to
these precious deposits, but though they have not, and will
not be realized, they are not wholly fictitious."*

Silver has always been the principal mineral obtained in
Peru. The most productive mines of this metal now wrought,
are at Cérro di Pasco. These were accidentally discovered
in 1630, by an Indian shepherd, who was tending his flocks
on a small pámpa southeast of the lake of Llauricocha. Having wandered one day further from his hut than usual, he
found himself, towards evening, in the vicinity of the Cérro
de Sántiestevan. After building a fire to protect him against
the cold, he lay down to sleep. On awaking the following
morning, he discovered that the stone underneath his fire had
melted and turned to silver. The discovery was immediately
made known to his master, who forthwith commenced active
preparations for working the mines. Since that time they
have been constantly worked by a greater or less number of
persons. One class of speculators has been eagerly followed
by another class; but few of them, however, owing to the
want of thrift and proper management, have amassed any
very considerable wealth.

All the mine laborers are Indians. They consist of two
classes,—one working in the mines the year round, and receiving regular wages from the proprietors of the mines,—
and the other making only temporary visits to Cérro di Pasco,
when an unusual supply of the metal is procured. In the
mines, also, the laborers are divided into two classes; the
barretéros, who break the ore,—and the *apirés*, who bring
up the ore from the shaft. From fifty to seventy-five pounds
of metal is the usual load of the *apiré;* this he carries up
the shaft in an untanned hide, called a *carpácho*. When the

* At the commencement of the present century, the annual value of the gold
and silver produced in Peru, was upwards of six millions of dollars. It is now
between three and four millions. But about one thirtieth part of this amount is
gold. Great quantities of gold and silver are smuggled out of the country,—
the latter in the shape of *plăta piña*, or native silver.

mines yield abundantly, the laborers receive a share of the ore instead of wages; but at other times, the *barretéro* is paid six reals per day, and the *apiré* four.

Mining at Cérro di Pasco, as well as at the other mines in Peru, is not managed with as little difficulty as in other countries, where improvements in science and the arts are so quickly employed to diminish labor and expense. One advantage is possessed at the former place, by which a great saving is made : the mines are near a large coal bed which has recently been opened.

Besides the mines at Cérro di Pasco, there are other rich mining districts in the provinces of Pátaz, Huamanchúco, Caxamárca, and Hualgayoc. The mines of Cérro de San Fernando, in Hualgayoc, were discovered in 1771, and there are now more than fourteen hundred *bocaminas;* the veins of metal intersect each other in every direction; they are easily worked, and are very productive. The mines of Huantajáya, on the coast near Iquiqua, were at one time considered quite valuable, as they yielded, annually, about fifty-two thousand pounds of silver. The metal obtained was nearly pure, but it was soon exhausted.* In southern Peru, there are some rich mines, among which are those of San António de Esquiláche, Tamáyos, Picotáni, Cancharáni, Chupícos, and Salcédo.

Gold is obtained in Tarma, from the mines of Pátaz and Huilies, and in the washings on the banks of the upper Amazon. At Huancavélica there is one of the richest quicksilver mines in the world. Between 1570 and 1800, they yielded 537,000 quintals of the metal, and the annual product is now estimated at 18,000 quintals. Most of it is used for the purposes of amalgamation, at the silver mines.

Besides the precious metals, Peru produces iron, copper, tin, coal, and saltpetre.

(7.) Agriculture has never been in a prosperous state in Peru, and it is now languishing more than ever. None of

---

* Two masses of native silver were found at Huantajáya,—one weighing 225 pounds, and the other 890.

the inhabitants appear fond of moiling in the earth, and, in most cases, where the maize fields or gardens, exhibit more than ordinary luxuriance of vegetation, it must be attributed to the kindness of Nature, rather than to the industry of man. The implements of husbandry are rude enough. The plough is slightly made, has but one handle, and is constructed of wood, without a mould-board. The ploughshare is a thick iron blade, or piece of hard iron-wood, tied, when in use, to the point of the plough, by a strip of leather. There are no harrows; but large, clumsy rakes, are used in place of them; and, sometimes, a green bough with heavy stones laid upon it, is dragged over the sown ground, in the same manner as in Chili. Cane plantations are ploughed and cross-ploughed eight or ten times, and the earth is then broken down with the heel of a short handled hoe. The Indians use, for the same purpose, a flat round stone, with a long handle inserted in a hole perforated through the centre.

Instead of the scythe, the sickle is used for cutting grass and grain; and among the large planters, two or three persons are kept constantly employed in cutting lucern, or *alfálfa*, for the cattle and working oxen which are confined at night in pens, or *corráls*. Potato grounds are turned up with long narrow spades. The same instrument is used for preparing the soil on the hillsides, for the reception of maize. The seed is planted in holes made by a sharp-pointed stick.

The fields and gardens in Peru are principally inclosed within *tapias*, or mud fences, and hedges of maguey and the Indian fig. Considerable attention is paid to irrigation, without which a great portion of the land now yielding abundantly, would be wholly unproductive. Manure, however, is not deemed of much consequence. Quantities of guano are brought every year from the adjacent islands in the Pacific, but this is applied rather to horticultural, than to general agricultural purposes.

Cotton, sugar cane, maize, and camotes, or sweet potatoes, are the principal products along the coast. The sweet potatoes are of two kinds,—the yellow and the violet; they do

not grow beyond the height of 3500 feet above the level of
the sea.   Cotton and maize are grown in almost every part of
the country.   The former ranks next to the Sea Island and
Egyptian, in the English market, and, except in the province
of Piura, is all short-stapled.   Maize has formed, from time
immemorial, the chief farinaceous food of the Peruvians.
There are three sorts of this grain : the *máis morócho* has
small bright yellow or reddish brown kernels ; the *máis amarillo* is large, shaped like a heart, solid and opaque ; and the
third species, the *máis amarillo de chançay*, resembles the
second variety, but is a square-shaped grain, semi-transparent,
and having an elongated head.   The maize stalks are from
eight to nine feet high and bear very large ears.

The sugar plantations lie on the sea-coast or along the
banks of rivers, below the altitude of 4500 feet above the sea
level, on the western declivity of the Andes, and extending as
high as 6000 feet on the eastern declivity.   In former times,
the creole, or West India cane, was the species most cultivated ; but, latterly, the Otaheitan cane has been introduced,
and the product is both more abundant in quantity, and much
better in quality.   The sugar mills are very rude structures.
In the valley of Huanuco, which contains the largest and
finest plantations, the cane is passed through wooden presses
with brass rollers.   These clumsy machines are called *trapi-
chés* or *igénios ;* they are mostly worked by oxen or mules ;
though, upon the largest plantations, water power is sometimes employed, and steam-engines have recently, in a few
instances, been put up.   A portion of the expressed cane juice
is distilled into rum, or used for making a liquor called *guá-
rapo ;* the remainder is boiled down into sirup, or simmered
till it forms cakes (*chancácas*) of brown sugar.   From the
latter, loaves of white sugar are made, by purification, which
usually weigh about two *arróbas.**   The Peruvian sugar
exceeds the Havana in sweetness, but its color is not so pure,
nor is its grain as fine.

* The *arróba* in Spanish America, as in old Spain, contains twenty-five pounds
avoirdupois.

Maize is likewise produced abundantly in the fertile mountain valleys, on the warm slopes of the Andes, and in the elevated Siérra. Wheat and other European cerealia are little cultivated, though they succeed admirably in the high lying sections of the country. Potatoes do not thrive very well near the coast, where both the climate and soil are unfavorable to their growth; but on the high ridges and in the elevated valleys, from seven to ten thousand feet above the level of the sea, they constitute a profitable and productive crop.

A most agreeable and nutritive tuberous vegetable, called the *aracácha*, grows in abundance on the coast. It resembles celery in flavor, and is either boiled or made into a soup. In favorable districts, two crops are obtained within the year. The *yucca*, or *jatropha manihot*, is another fine vegetable found almost everywhere below the elevation of 3000 feet. The stalks of this plant grow to the height of five or six feet, and are about the size of a finger. The roots, which are the edible parts, are from one to two feet long, and shaped like a turnip; the external skin is tough, but internally they are pure white. In taste they resemble chestnuts. They are boiled in water and then laid in hot ashes, when they become quite mealy. Flour is prepared from them by the Indians, out of which the finest bread and biscuits are made. The yucca is propagated by cuttings from the stalk, which are placed obliquely in the earth. The roots are fit for use in five or six months.

Nearly all the different kinds of pulse are raised on the coast, but beans flourish best in the hilly country. Cabbages and salads of every variety, tomatoes, and peppers, are produced in all parts of Peru except in the very coldest sections. Rice is also grown to a considerable extent. Of culinary vegetables there is a generous supply, as well in kind as in quality, throughout the year. The vine is cultivated in some quarters to great advantage; the grapes are exceedingly well-flavored, but the wine made from them is rather insipid. In the southern coastwise provinces, the olive tree

is found. Its früit resembles that of the Spanish olive, though
the oil is by no means as good, probably on account of the defective manner of expressing it. The olives are permitted to
ripen thoroughly on the tree; they are then gathered, subjected to a slight pressure, dried, and packed in small earthen
jars. They are served at table with pieces of tomato and *aji*
(Spanish pepper) laid upon them. Sometimes they are preserved in salt water, when they remain plump and green,
instead of becoming shrivelled and black, as in the other process. The castor-oil plant grows wild in Peru, and is cultivated also on many plantations; the oil, however, is not
purified, but is used for the street lamps in Lima, and for
greasing machinery. Another oil plant is the piñoncillo tree,
which produces a fruit shaped like a bean, and, when roasted,
having an agreeable flavor.

One of the most nutritious, and one of the most important
articles of food, in the Siérra, is the quinuä, or quinoä. Its
leaves, when green, are eaten like spinach; but the most
valuable parts of the plant are the seeds. These are boiled
in milk or in broth, and are sometimes cooked with cheese
and Spanish pepper. They are highly prized by the Peruvians, and most travellers commend their agreeable flavor.
The dried stems of the quinuä are also made use of as fuel.
Besides the potato, there are three other tuberous plants cultivated with success in the Siérra. These are the *ullúco*, the
óca, and the *mashúa*. The ullúco is much smaller than the
potato, and varies in its form, being either round or oblong,
straight or curved. The skin is thin and of a reddish yellow
color; the inside is green. When boiled, its flavor is nearly
the same as that of the potato, yet it is much more savory
when cooked as a *piquante*. In addition to the root, that
part of the plant above the ground furnishes an agreeable
and wholesome vegetable, something like the bean; three
crops of this green portion of the ullúco may be gathered in
the same season.*

* The *ullúco* has been cultivated with success in the gardens of the Luxem-
bourg palace, and is regarded as a very good substitute for the potato.

The óca is an oval-shaped root; the outer skin is a most delicate red, and inside it is white. It is watery when cooked, but has a sweetish taste. The mashúa resembles the óca in this respect, though it is somewhat more insipid; it is of a flat pyramidal shape, however, and its lower end terminates in a fibrous point.

Lucern, or alfálfa, as it is called by the natives, is the great article used for fodder. From the "sea-beat shore" of the Pacific, across the sunny slopes of the *tiérra caliénte*, up the luxuriant valleys and gloomy *quebrádas* of the interior, to the rocky heights of the Siérra, eleven thousand feet above the level of the ocean, it is scattered lavishly around. It is cut from three to five times during the year, and, as may readily be presumed, furnishes an almost inexhaustible supply of provender. The hot weather of the coast, in February and March, and the keen frosts of the mountainous districts, occasionally dry it up, and the *maisillo* is then used in its stead.

The most fastidious epicure would be delighted with the fruits which ripen in the fine climate, and on the rich soil, of Peru. Besides the vine and olive, the succulent pomegranate, famed for its "pleasant sweetness," the luscious plantain, the grateful and nutritious banana, and the juicy guava,* are found here in profusion. Apples and pears grow but indifferently; and cherries, plums, and chestnuts, are likewise as inferior as they are rare. The absence of these productions of temperate climes is more than made up, however, by the extensive groves of oranges, lemons, limes, nectarines, and granadillas, which occupy the warm mountain valleys even as high as ten thousand feet above the sea. Peaches and apricots, too, of the finest and most agreeable flavor, are abundant. In the months of April and May, excursions to the *duraználes*, or apricot-gardens, are all the rage. Melons

---

* The fruit of the guava is yellow and smooth, and a little larger than a hen's egg. The pulp is flesh colored, and has a very agreeable aromatic taste. It is used at the dessert and made into a preserve. The jelly prepared from it is one of the finest conserves.

of every variety are raised on the coast, and in the woody districts.

Of figs there are two kinds,—the *higos* and the *brévas.* The pulp of the former is red, and that of the latter white. Fig-trees grow wild in every section of the country. No one thinks of drying the fruit, as the almost perpetual summer furnishes a constant succession of figs. The mulberry tree also flourishes without cultivation, but its fruit is so little esteemed in comparison with others more tempting to the appetite, that the birds are left to enjoy it with impunity. Quinces are rare on the coast, but are plentiful in the *que-brádas.* Among the other fruits are the patta, resembling the pear in shape, which dissolves like butter on the tongue, and has a not unpleasant bitter taste ; the tuna, the product of different varieties of cactus, which is almost the only indigenous fruit in the Siérra ; the pacay, a white, soft and flaky substance, contained in the seed pods of the *prosopis dulcis,* which is extremely sweet; the lucuma, a dry, fibrous, yellow-colored fruit, inclosed with its kernel in a gray-brown husk ; the pepino, or Peruvian cucumber, a fruit produced by a small plant grown in the fields, the pulp of which is solid, juicy, and highly-flavored ; and the mani, or earth almond, an oily kernel contained in a shrivelled husk, which is roasted and crushed, and then eaten with sugar.

Pine-apples are not much cultivated on the coast. They were formerly brought to Lima, in considerable abundance, from the Montaña de Vitoc; but since the era of steam navigation on the Pacific coast, they have been brought, in much less time, from Guayaquil, and, consequently, they are generally allowed to ripen before being cut. Cocoa palms are tolerably abundant in the northern provinces, and the date palm grows excellently well about Yca at the south.

But the just pride and boast of the Peruvian, is the chirimoya ; beyond question excelling all other tropical fruits in the delicacy of its flavor. The tree which produces this rich fruit is from fifteen to twenty feet high, and has a broad flat top. Its foliage is of a pale green color. In Lima and its vicinity, the fruit is small, being scarcely larger than an orange; but in Huanuco and other districts, where it is indigenous, it attains to the greatest perfection, and often weighs sixteen pounds and upwards. It is of a roundish pyramidal or heart-shaped form, and unites with the stem at its broadest base. Externally it is green, and is covered with scaly knobs, and black marks resembling network. When it becomes perfectly ripe, black spots appear on the surface. The skin is thick and tough, but, underneath this, there is a juicy, snowy-white fruit, containing a number of seeds, which is prized above all other delicacies by those who have once tasted it. Both the fruit and the flowers emit a fine fragrant odor that fairly intoxicates the senses.

Cedar, ebony, mahogany, and walnut, are the most valuable forest trees. Numerous medicinal plants are obtained in the country, and the bark of the *cinchona lancifolia*, so well known under the name of Peruvian bark, forms an important article of export. The various species of cinchona grow spontaneously in the forests of Peru. The tree resembles the cherry in appearance, and bears large clusters of red flowers. Its medical properties were discovered by the natives, and brought into use by the Jesuits, for which reason it was originally called Jesuits' bark. It takes its botanical name from the Countess del Chincon, the wife of a Spanish viceroy, who was cured by it. The natives collect the bark from May till November. The trees are felled close to the roots, and then cut up. After the sticks have dried three or four days, the bark is peeled off in broad strips, which are immediately exposed to the heat of the sun. This causes them to roll up in a cylindrical form,—the folds or coils being sometimes so close that there is no cavity in the centre. The value of the bark depends mainly on the rapidity with which it is dried. The drying process being completed, it is packed in bales, each containing four or five *arróbas*, and exported in chests carefully inclosed in skins.*

---

* It is comparatively but a few years since the French chemists, Messrs. Pelletier and Caventou, made the discovery, that the medical properties of Peruvian

Balsam of Peru is an important product, chiefly valued for the benzoic acid it contains, and also employed as a perfume. It is extracted from the *myroxylon peruiferum*, sometimes by incision, and sometimes by evaporating the decoction of the bark and branches of the tree. The first kind is very rare, and is exported in cocoa husks, from whence it is called balsam *en coque;* it is of a brown color, of the consistence of thick turpentine, and has an agreeable smell, but an acrid and bitter taste. The second kind is called the black balsam, and is quite common. It is of a deep reddish brown color, and is much more acrid and bitter, and has a stronger smell, than the other sort. The balsam of Peru always commands a high price, and is, therefore, frequently adulterated.

A species of red thorn apple, (the *datura sanguineä*) is found in the Siérra, from which a powerful narcotic drink, called *tonga*, is prepared by the Peruvian Indians. It produces a heavy stupor, during the continuance of which the natives who make use of it fancy they can hold communication with the spirits of their forefathers, and obtain from them a clew to the rich treasures said to be concealed in their graves, or *huácas*. From this superstitious belief, the thornapple has obtained the name of *huáca-cachu*, or grave-plant, among the Indians.

In the Puna there are large patches of ground covered with the ratanhia shrub (*krameria triandria*.) This is used by the Indians for fuel, and for roofing their huts. It is also a favorite remedy among them, for spitting blood and dysentery. The extract was formerly prepared in Peru, and exported in large quantities to Europe, but latterly very little has been shipped.

Warmed by a tropical sun, and blessed with a genial climate, Peru exhibits a most magnificent flora during the greater part of the year. Blossoms and flowers constantly

---

bark depended upon the presence of the valuable alkaloid known in pharmacy as quinine. It is said that the use of 90,000 ounces of the sulphate of quinine, produced in France in a single year, obviated the necessity of swallowing at least 10,000,000 ounces of the bark.

alternate with each other.　The great and mysterious agents of decay and reproduction are incessantly at work.　If, at one moment, Nature seems to sicken and die, at the next, borrowing, as it were, renewed beauty, life and loveliness, from death itself, she springs forth again, like the Phenix from its funeral pyre.　The fertile oases of ,the coast country are liberally sprinkled with tropical flowers, not more rich in color than agreeable in fragrance ; and even in the Siérra, amidst rushes, and mosses, and syngenesia, may be seen the purple gentian, the brown calceolaria, the echino and ananas cactus.　The different varieties of cacti can scarcely be enumerated ; their Proteän shapes and divers hues excite the wonder and admiration of the traveller ; and in many instances, where the vegetation is otherwise scant and sickly, they clothe the landscape in rare and beautiful apparelling.

(8.) Peru not only carries on her own commerce through her seaports, but she is the great entrepôt of the adjacent state of Bolivia.*　The total value of Peruvian and Bolivian produce shipped through the ports of Peru, in 1837, amounted to near seven and a half millions of dollars.　The principal articles of export were bark, bullion and copper ore, hides, seal skins, and vicuña, alpa'ca, and sheeps' wool.　The imports for the same period were also about seven and a half millions.　Two thirds of the imports, and rather more than that proportion of the exports, belong to Peru alone.　For the past ten years the foreign commerce has increased but slowly, and in some years has sensibly declined.　Great Britain enjoys by far the better part of the Peruvian trade ; the United States, in 1847, exported goods only to the amount of $227,537, and imported from Peru $396,223.

Internal commerce languishes under the numerous disadvantages which have long obstructed its successful prosecution.　In the days of the Incas, anterior to the Spanish conquest, there were several great roads traversing the country,

* Boliva has but one small seaport,—that of Cobija, or La Mär.

which, aside from the bridges constructed of osiers, would compare favorably with the *viâs* of ancient Rome, that

" Time, and Goth, and Turk, have spared."

In addition to these important and extensive thoroughfares,— the remains of which, grand and imposing though in ruins, are still visible,—various passes were cut in the steep *pará-mos*, or mountain ridges, of the Andes. But the deplorable effects of the same want of spirit and energy, that, elsewhere in Peru, have suffered her morning splendor to be prematurely dimmed and overshadowed, may be witnessed here. The roads built by the rude and unlettered aborigines have fallen to decay under the auspices of their European masters ; and the passes excavated with so much labor and care, have disappeared beneath the *débris* washed down from the Cordilleras. With a few exceptions in the neighborhood of the large cities, the roads laid out by the Spaniards are mere bridle tracks for horses or mules, and the gulleys and streams that cannot be crossed or forded, are passed by means of hanging bridges, in nine cases out of ten a very unsafe mode of transportation. Quite recently, laudable efforts have been made for the improvement of the roads, but the want of suitable means of communication constitutes the chief drawback on internal commerce, and is a great obstacle in the way of social and commercial progress.

But little can be said in commendation of the manufacturing industry of a country whose pedigree dates back so many hundred years. Lima can boast only of her mint, some smelting houses, and a glass house lately established. At Cuzco, cotton, linen, and woolen stuffs, and leather and parchment, are manufactured, in which considerable trade is carried on with the neighboring provinces. There are flourishing manufactures of woolens and cottons, and gold and silver cloths, at Arequípa ; and at Guamánga is made the fine filigree silver work for which inland Peru is celebrated. Coarse straw hats, and mats called *petátes*, are manufactured at Huácho, and brought into Lima for sale. In Piura, cordage for packing is prepared from the maguey, and at Tarma, loose cloaks, or *ponchos*, are made, of great beauty and firmness. In the Siérra, coarser and heavier blankets and *ponchos* are manufactured by the Indians. In the lower districts, goat skins are made into cordovans; cow hides into saddlebags, and travelling cases for beds and bedding; and rushes into mats and carpets.

(9.) The bay of Callaö abounds with the finest water-fowl. Humboldt's penguin, and the common gray penguin, are the most remarkable. There is another small species, called by the Peruvians the *paxáro niño*, or child-bird; it is easily tamed, and follows its master like a dog, waddling along after him on its short legs and balancing itself with its wings. Among the other marine birds, are the banded cormorant; the iris, which changes throughout the whole circle in regular square spots of the most delicate white and sea-green; and the spotted gannet, and the inca tern.

Of the land birds, the turkey, or red-headed vulture, is, perhaps, the most commonly seen on the coast, and in the interior the black gallinazo takes its place. There are some beautiful gold-feathered colibri in the country. A small bird about the size of the starling, of a deep blue color, and with a short curved bill, is called the horse-protector; it is extremely fond of perching on the back of the horse or ass and catching the flies and insects—a kind of amusement which both the animal and bird enjoy with equal zest. The principal singing birds are the crowned fly-king, the red-bellied picho, the black chivillo, and the cuculi; the picho and chivillo are of the starling species, and the cuculi is a pigeon.

The most extravagant notions once prevailed respecting the size and strength of the condor, the king of Peruvian birds. A full grown condor measures from twelve to thirteen feet, from the tip of one wing to that of the other, and about five feet from the point of its beak to the extremity of its tail. It feeds chiefly on carrion. When hungry it is sometimes extremely fierce, and will seize and carry off lambs

and the young of the llama and vicuña.   It is unable, however, to sustain a greater weight, when flying, than eight or
ten pounds, and it is absurd to suppose, as has been frequently
stated, that sheep and calves could be carried off by it.   The
Indians of the Siérra relate numerous instances of its attacking children, but their stories must be received with a great
deal of allowance.   The plumage of the condor is strong and
thick, and forms a very good protection against fire-arms.
It is usually caught by the natives, in traps or by the lasso;
or killed by the *bólas*, or by stones thrown from slings.

Among the wild animals are the puma, or American lion,
the ounce, a kind of tiger cat called the uturuncu, the tapir,
and the hucumari, a black bear that inhabits the mountains.
The *anas*, or skunk, and a singular kind of guinea pig, are
found in the bushes.   The red deer, the wild boar, and the
tarush, or Puna stag, are the favorite objects of the chase.
Armadillos, rock rabbits, chinchillos, and the *venádo*, a species of roe, are also caught in large quantities by the hunters.
Of the amphibia, the iguana, the land agama, and the fresh
water tortoise, are the most numerous.   Alligators infest the
streams, but noxious reptiles and insects, though occasionally
found, are not as frequently met with as in many other countries.   Monkeys are abundant in the forests.

Of far greater importance than the other native animals of
Peru, are the llama, or South American camel, the alpaca,
the guanaco, and the vicuña.   Both the llama and alpaca
are domesticated, and previously to the Spanish invasion
they were the principal beasts of burden among the Peruvians.   The young llama is left with its dam for about a
year, after which it is removed and placed with flocks.   When
four years old, the males and females are separated; the latter being kept for breeding, and the former trained to carry
burdens, principally in the silver mines of North Peru.   They
are usually made to carry about one hundred pounds each,—
as they are only capable of sustaining one hundred and twenty-
five without injury,—and if overloaded they will lie down,
and utterly refuse to rise again till some part of the load is

removed.   These animals will rapidly and safely ascend, or descend, the steep mountain sides, where the ass, or mule, cannot maintain its footing.   They cannot well travel more than three or four leagues during the day, as they will not graze at night.   The Indian drivers, or *arriéros*, are very fond of them, and often attach bows of ribbons to their ears, and hang bells round their necks.   The llama is not used for riding or draught; the Indian lads sometimes mount them, but this is very rare.   The price of one of these animals, when full-grown, is from three to four dollars; but in Cuzco and Ayacúcho, where they most abound, they may be purchased in flocks for one and a half or two dollars per head. The flesh of the llama is spongy and of a disagreeable flavor. Its wool is used for making coarse cloths.

The alpaca, or paco, whose wool enters into so many fabrics now commonly worn, is smaller than the llama, and but little larger than the common sheep, which it resembles in form. Its neck is longer than that of the sheep, and its head is much better proportioned.   The fleece is from four to five inches long, and is beautifully soft.   Its color is commonly white or black, but it is occasionally speckled.   These animals are kept in flocks, in the elevated pastures, and are driven to the Indian huts or villages, only at shearing time.   The wool is made into blankets and *ponchos*, and always commands a good price for exportation.   They are very shy, but equally obstinate.   It is almost impossible to separate one from the flock; if the attempt is made, the alpaca will cast itself upon the ground, and neither punishment nor entreaty will avail in the least.   If separated from its species when very young, it may be reared; otherwise it soon dies, where it cannot escape to its companions.

The guanaco is the largest of the family to which all these animals belong.   It measures five feet from the bottom of the hoof to the top of the head, and resembles the llama very nearly in form, though its color is different, and its wool is shorter and coarser.   Its neck, back, and thighs, are reddish-brown, and the under part of the body and breast, and the inner sides of the limbs, are of a dusky white. The face is of a dark gray color, and the lips of a pure white. The guanacos live in herds, from five to seven in number. If taken young they may easily be tamed, but it is with great difficulty that they are trained to carry burdens.

Still more beautiful than either of the animals of which it is the co-genera, is the vicuña. In size it is between the llama and alpaca, but it has a longer and more slender neck than either. The crown of its head, the upper part of the neck, and the back and thighs, are of a reddish-yellow color, possessing so peculiar a hue that it is called by the natives *color de vicuña*. The lower part of the neck, and the inner parts of the limbs, are of a bright ochre, and the breast and belly are white. While the rainy season continues, the vicuña inhabits the ridges of the Cordillera, but does not venture up the rocky acclivities, as its hoofs are soft and tender, and better adapted to turfy ground. Like the guanaco, it lives in herds, consisting of from six to fifteen females and one male; the latter is the leader and protector of the herd, and is as jealous of his companions as the Grand Turk of the beauties in his harem. Unlike the latter, however, the female vicuñas exhibit the utmost fidelity and affection to their lord and master; and if he be wounded, when pursued by the hunters, they will gather about him in a circle, uttering their shrill tones of lamentation, and suffer themselves to be captured rather than desert him. This animal is principally caught in what the Indians call a *chacu;* this consists of a circular inclosure surrounded by stakes connected by ropes or cords. The vicuñas are driven into the *chacu* through an opening left for the purpose, and are prevented from leaping over the ropes by the fluttering of colored rags which the Indian women hang upon them. Thus secured, the animals are easily dispatched by the *bólas*.

The flesh of the vicuña is more tender and better flavored than that of the llama. After a hunt the meat is divided among those engaged in it, and the skins are always set apart for the church. The price of a skin is four reals.

Fine cloth and hats are made of the wool, which is soft, delicate, and curly. The vicuñas can be tamed when young; but when old they are intractable and malicious.

Most of the domestic quadrupeds now used by the Peruvians are descended from foreign stock. This is the case with the horse, the mule, the famous black cattle of the Siérra, the sheep and goats. The sheep were the easiest acclimated, and have succeeded the best. On the great commons or pastures of the Puna, flocks may be seen containing many thousands, which are mostly coarse wooled. Few sheep are raised on the coast, and the markets of Lima and the seaport towns are mainly supplied with mutton from the interior. The fecundity of the sheep in Peru is remarkable. The farmer usually calculates on obtaining one hundred and fifty lambs from one hundred ewes, at a single yeaning. The ewes bear twice a year, also, generally in June and December.

Goats are common in Peru, and the province of Piura is especially famous for them. Great numbers of pigs are likewise fattened for the markets; when from ten to sixteen months old, they sell readily at from six to nine dollars per head, if of a good breed.

The cattle of Peru are, upon an average, as large as the generality of English, American, or Spanish breeds. The horses and mules are particularly fine. The former far excel their Andalusian progenitors in grace and elegance of form, and in the rapidity and precision of their movements. The saddle horses trained for the Lima market are practiced in every art of the *manége*, and are highly esteemed by all competent judges. Ordinary horses and mules bring from forty to fifty dollars; but the best mules raised in Piura, which is noted for its excellent breed, will often command two hundred and fifty dollars each.

(10.) After spending about a month in making the necessary repairs, furnishing their outfits, and taking in stores, the Exploring Squadron completed its preparations for the projected western cruise, on the 13th of July. At five o'clock

in the afternoon of that day, the flag ship of the Expedition
stood out to sea, having the whole squadron in company,
with all canvas spread.   The Relief directed her course towards the Sandwich Islands, under orders to proceed thence
to the United States, by way of the port of Sydney ; but the
other vessels steered nearly due west from Callaö.

CHAPTER VII.

(1.) Skirting the Southern Oriental Ocean on the west, between the tenth degree of southern latitude and the Tropic of Capricorn, is a group of low coral islands, sixty-five in number, which, though comparatively little known, form one of the most striking features of Polynesia, " the region," as the name imports, " of many islands."   Different navigators visited this group previous to the Expedition under Captain Wilkes; but their observations and reconnoîssances were directed rather for hydrographical purposes, than with a view of making valuable contributions to physical geography and ethnology.   There is another reason why the information obtained in regard to these islands has been so limited; which is, that the crews of whalers have repeatedly stopped here, and so grossly maltreated the poor and inoffensive inhabitants, that it is with great difficulty they can be brought to have the least intercourse with the whites.

This cluster was formerly designated on maps and charts, as the Low Archipelago; but it is now known as the Paumotu Group, or Cloud of Islands,—the term applied to it by the natives themselves, and by the inhabitants of the Society Islands.

(2.) It was with considerable reluctance that the officers and men of the Exploring Squadron bade adieu to the glorious climate and fertile soil of Peru; yet the prospect of visiting the fairy islands towards which they were fast wend-ing their way, soon compensated them for the absence of the beautiful scenes they had witnessed, and they had not been out many days, ere they began anxiously to cast their eyes over the western waters, and to fancy they already felt the

" gentle airs which breathed,
Or seemed to breathe, fresh fragrance from the shore."

On the afternoon of the 13th of August, they caught sight of the feathery shrubs cresting the surface of Clermont de Tonnèrre, or Minerva Island.—English navigators have given the latter name to this island, but the former, by which it is at this time more generally known, was bestowed upon it in 1823, by Captain Duperrey, of the French navy, in honor of his countryman, Count Clermont de Tonnèrre, who fell a victim to his opposition to the Jacobins, in 1793. On approaching the island, the boats were lowered, and some of the officers and scientific corps started to reconnoître. Though obliged to swim through the strong surf, they succeeded in reaching the shore, and obtained a number of specimens of shells, plants, and coral. Several natives were discovered, but could not be induced to approach near enough to have any conversation with them. A second attempt to hold communication with the islanders, which proved equally fruitless, was made on the 14th instant, by means of one of the crew of the Vincennes, a New Zealander by birth, who spoke the Tahitian language. It being evident that further efforts, even if successful, would most likely lead to collisions with the natives, the island was surveyed, by stationing the vessels at intervals around it, and measuring base lines by means of guns fired at each station in quick succession, and noting the lapse of time between the flash and the report; and the commander then issued orders for the squadron to get under way.

From Clermont de Tonnèrre, the squadron proceeded to Serle Island, further to the west and north, which was surveyed in like manner. They then continued on their northwesterly course, and on the 19th of August made Hennake, or Honden Island. On the 23rd instant, they reached the

Disappointment Islands, (Wytoohee and Otooho,) so named by Commodore Byron, who discovered them in 1765. The natives of these two islands appeared far more friendly than those seen at Clermont de Tonnèrre; yet they did not seem over anxious to cultivate an acquaintance with their visitors; they were shy and timid, and manifested great fear lest their women, whom they had concealed, would be taken from them by violence. These islands having been surveyed, the squadron bore away for Raraka, one of the principal islands belonging to the group.

On the 29th instant, a small island, named King's Island, after the man at the mast-head, who first saw it, was discovered in latitude 15° 42' 25'' S., and longitude 144° 38' 45'' W. This is a small island,—being only about four or five miles in circumference, and averaging one mile in width. The highest point on the island is not over twenty feet above the level of the sea. Springs of fresh water were found here; cocoa-nuts were abundant; and the soil appeared to be highly productive. No natives were seen, but there were indications that the island had been recently visited by persons engaged in the pearl-fishery.

Early in the morning of the 30th of August, they came up with Raraka Island, the inhabitants of which, though few in number, exhibited every feeling of kindness and friendship. The influence of the missionaries at the Society Islands has been extended hither, and a native missionary from Tahiti was found among them. Every opportunity was afforded to the commander of the American Expedition and his officers, to obtain the information they desired; a few presents distributed among the natives permanently secured their good will; and a couple of sheep given to them by the purser, Mr. Waldron, elicited the warmest expressions of gratitude.

Leaving Raraka towards sunset on the 31st of August, the squadron proceeded to Vincennes Island, called by the natives Kawahe, and from thence to Aratica, or Carlshoff Island, where they arrived in the morning of the 3rd of September. Hogs and fowls were found on Aratica. There were large quantities of fish seen also in the lagoon. Cocoa-nuts and bread-fruit likewise appeared to be abundant. A large supply of very good water was procured by the squadron, from a deep pool near the lagoon; after obtaining which, the vessels again got under way, with the intention of making King George's Group, to the northeast. This being found to be impracticable, without great loss of time, the tender was dispatched to survey the group, with directions to follow the squadron to Tahiti. Previous to this time, on the 1st of September, the Porpoise had parted company with the other vessels; she coasted along the south side of Raraka Island, and then proceeded to Tahiti, the appointed place of rendezvous, where she arrived on the 9th instant, having taken, in her way, the islands of Katiu, or Sacken, Makima, Aratica, and Nairsa.

The Vincennes and Peacock now bore further westward, and on the 5th instant made the island of Manhii—the Waterlandt of Schouten and Le Maire, so named by the former of those navigators, in allusion to a large pool of fresh water on the southwest side of the island. Having surveyed this island, they proceeded to Ahii Island, still further to the west, which was found to be uninhabited. The two vessels then separated; the Peacock proceeding to Aratua Island, and thence around the southern side of Nairsa, or Dean's Island, the largest of the Paumotu Group, and the Vincennes steering directly for Nairsa, and then continuing her southerly course, by way of Metia Island, to Tahiti.

(3.) All the islands visited by the squadron at this time were carefully examined and surveyed. Subsequently, in the winter of 1840-1, the Porpoise, in command of Lieutenant-Commandant Ringgold, was again dispatched to this quarter, from the Sandwich Islands. She visited the principal islands which had been missed on the former occasion; and while engaged in surveying, a small party, under Lieutenant Johnson, landed on Aratica Island with boring instruments, in order to ascertain, if possible, with some precision, the geölogical character of this extensive group. But the rainy sea-

son having already come on, the soil was found to be so
saturated with water, that very little progress could be made
in boring, after attaining a depth of twenty feet, and the
project was abandoned without arriving at any satisfactory
results.

(4.) A remarkable peculiarity of the Paumotu Group, is
the existence of large and deep tunnel-shaped lagoons, containing salt water, in the centre of most of the islands. Sometimes these are entirely isolated from the surrounding ocean,
and, at others, its waves break over the broken ramparts of
coral which appear here and there above the surface of the
water. Such of them as have their pretty little lakes completely insulated, present a singularly picturesque appearance
when viewed from the mast-head of a vessel. In the centre
is the lagoon,—" deeply, beautifully blue,"—neither disturbed
by the tempest whose sullen roar is heard amidst the neighboring breakers, nor ruffled by the tossing surge rolled lazily
in upon the shore by the soft winds of the summer; immediately around this, is a strip of earth,—in some cases but a
few, and in others several hundred yards, in width,—covered
with a vegetation varying with the character of the island,
and either sparse or luxuriant, according to the nature and
depth of the soil; and further beyond, extending to the brink
of the ocean, is a belt of white sand glistening like silver in the
perpendicular rays of the tropical sun. Within is the blue
turquoise, looking up to the bright heavens reflected from its
polished surface; about it, is a gorgeous setting of emeralds;
and the latter is, in turn, encircled by a rich chasing of
argent.

Most of the islands are of a curvilinear form, and, with the
exception of Metia, which is a coral island uplifted, and surrounded by a bold coralline shelf, rarely exceed twenty or
thirty feet in height. They are composed, at least near the
surface, of corallites, conglomerates, and limestone, above
which are coral *débris*, decayed vegetable matter, and guano,
with coral blocks occasionally cropping-out. The bottoms
and sides of the lagoons are lined with coral, and the shores,

which are generally shelving, are likewise of the same formation.

(5.) Various theories have been advanced in relation to the geölogy of this group. Some have supposed that the islands were entirely the work of the lithophyte; but the better opinion seems to be, that they are the crests of submarine volcanoes, the ruins and bottoms of whose craters are overgrown with coral.* Captain Wilkes has based a very pretty theory on the result of his examinations, which has certainly the merit of originality, if not of ingenuity. He supposes that the coral islands of the Pacific originally composed a vast continent, the several portions of which have been separated from each other ; and that the borders of the islands, being less compact in some places than in others, have been torn asunder, the underlying strata carried off by the influx and efflux of the sea, and thus undermined, the central portions have caved in and formed the lagoons.† In support of this view, he lays great stress upon the facts, that the islands are evidently in a state of dissolution, produced, in the main, by the constant abrasion of the sea, and that there are comparatively few living polyps to be found.‡

But assuming his own premises, and taking his own facts, although they may tend strongly to show that the islands could not be the work of zoöphytes, they clearly do not prove the existence of a continent; on the contrary, the theory which he advances, appears to be left very much in the situation of the central portions of the islands, without any underlying strata to support it. It requires far less stretch of the imagination, to suppose these islets to have been thrown up separately, by volcanic agency, than that a whole continent was upheaved, with its superincumbent load of corallites. The position of the Paumotu Group, also, with regard to the currents of the Pacific, the conical form of the islands, and ,the existence of coral, in a living, or decomposing state, all

* Lyell's Geölogy, Vol. III, p.226, et seq.
† Narrative of the Exploring Expedition, Vol. IV, p. 268, et seq.
‡ Narrative, ut suprà.

around them, and in the basins of the lagoons, show, conclusively, that the coralline substances must have been deposited, either by the animals themselves, or by the sea, since
the upheaving of these submarine mountains. If this be so,
why put the fancy to so severe a test, when a much sim-
pler, more probable, and more rational explanation, is at
hand ?

(6.) The productions of these islands are not numerous.
A species of short wiry grass, and low tropical shrubs, cover
many of them, but on others there are trees from fifty to sixty
feet high. Endogenous plants are the most frequently met
with. The cocoa-nut (*cocos nucifera*), the bread-fruit, and
the *pandanus odoratissimus*, are the most valuable trees.
On the island of Anaä, the cocoa-nut is exceedingly abundant.
Like the other palms, this tree is tall and straight, and from
thirty to sixty feet in height. It has leaves only at the top,
under which the nuts hang in bunches. Fresh blossoms appear every four or five weeks, and there are generally ripe
fruit, and newly opened flowers, on the tree at the same time.
One tree will sometimes produce a hundred nuts within the
year. There are few trees which furnish more useful products to the islander. Besides the milk and kernel of the
nut, whose nutritive qualities are so well known, the woody
shell of the trunk, when old enough to be tough and durable,
is employed in building huts and canoes ; the leaves are used
for thatching and ceiling houses, and for making baskets and
wicker-work ; and of the fibres of the nut, twine and sennit,
and even strong ropes and cables, are twisted, which last
longer in salt water than those made of hemp.

Pisonias, tournefortias, euphorbias, and apapas, are found
on the islands. *Hibiscus tiliacus*, bamboo, and wild cane,
are likewise common. Among the principal roots are the
taro, (*arum esculentum*,) and the sweet potato,—the latter
probably introduced by the Spaniards. The leaves of the
taro resemble those of the water-lily : the roots, which are
large, thick, and oblong, are baked and eaten by the natives,
and a favorite paste, called *poë*, is also made of them. Mel-

ons, yams, and tobacco, are more rare than other products, but they thrive excellently well where they have been introduced.

(7.) Pigs and fowls are the only domesticated birds or animals, except the sheep recently introduced, on which the inhabitants rely for food; and these are alone found upon those islands to which the influence of the Tahitian missionaries has extended. Fish are plentiful in the lagoons, and are principally caught in pens into which they are driven; latterly, however, nets woven of cocoa-nut fibres have been used for the purpose of taking them. Cetaceous animals of all kinds abound in the vicinity of the islands. Aquatic birds of almost every species are equally numerous, and some of the uninhabited islets are perfect rookeries. Among the sea-fowl, the frigate and the tropic bird, the gannet, and the sooty tern, are the most important.

Crabs and snakes—to the former of which the natives are especially partial—exist in great numbers. The pearl oyster is tolerably abundant in the lagoons, and the fishery promises at no distant day to be quite valuable. Quantities of *biche de mer*, or the sea-slug, are also obtained on the rocks; and this may, in like manner, ultimately prove an important article of commerce.

(8.) It is difficult to form any precise estimate of the population of the Paumotu Group. It can scarcely exceed ten thousand, and very likely may not be over eight. Full one half of this number live on the island of Anaä; one fourth on Gambier Island; and the remainder are scattered about among the different islands,—some containing from one to five hundred, and others not exceeding twenty or thirty inhabitants.

Since the first discovery of these islands, and since the establishment of the missionaries at Tahiti, the character of the population, particularly on those members of the group west of 144° W. longitude, has changed materially for the better. The inhabitants of the easternmost islands are now, or were recently, cannibals; but on the western islands, there are already many native missionaries, and a degree of comfort and prosperity is witnessed among the people, which compares favorably with the loathsome wretchedness exhibited further to the east.

In regard to the physical character of the inhabitants, there is a wide field for speculation. The distinctive features of the Malay and the aboriginal American, are presented in a blended form, and now and then some peculiar characteristic of the Papuan negro is observed, which threatens to overturn all the carefully-constructed theories of the ethnologist. It is by no means improbable that these islands were originally peopled by American aborigines and Asiatics, or by the descendants of those races found intermingled on the other islands of the Pacific; and, perhaps, some of the Papuan stock inhabiting the Admiralty Islands, New Ireland, New Britain, New Hebrides, etc., may have found their way hither. Trees of American and Asiatic growth, have been often carried to this part of the ocean, by the winds and currents; and Indians in their canoes, and Japanese in their junks, who had strayed too far out to sea, have been picked up by European and American vessels, in the middle of the Pacific. Junks, boats, or canoes, might easily pass in the variable winds, without the tropics, from the Asiatic coast and the neighboring islands, till meeting with the trades, they would naturally be driven towards the Sandwich or the Society islands; and they might also be blown in that direction, by strong westerly winds prevailing for a long time.*

The dress of the females usually consists of a dirty piece of *tapa*, swathed about the form like a petticoat; but among

---

* Lyell well remarks in his Principles of Geölogy, (vol. ii. p. 121,) that if the whole of mankind, with the exception of a single family occupying either of the two great continents, or Australia, or even one of the coral islets of the Pacific, were cut off, " we should expect their descendants, though they should never become more enlightened than the South Sea Islanders or Esquimaux, to spread, in the course of ages, over the whole earth, diffused partly by the tendency of population to increase beyond the means of subsistence in a limited district, and partly by the accidental drifting of canoes by tides and currents to distant shores."

the more intelligent and civilized natives, mantles of delicate matting, made from the bark of the hibiscus, are worn over the shoulders, and a *pareu*, or robe of cotton cloth, is wound round the body.   The *maro*, or covering for the loins, and a mat of pandanus leaves, are the principal articles of clothing for the men.   The children are allowed to go entirely naked. Upon a gala day, however, the Paumotuan costume exhibits a droll *mélange*, representing, in some feature, that of every nation on the globe.   These holiday dresses consist of articles obtained by barter from the crews of vessels touching at the islands, and are in general highly prized.

Among the inhabitants of the eastern islands, whose extreme squalidity and wretchedness so pointedly contradict the assertion of Locke, that "a person is a thinking, intelligent being," it is customary to bedaub the face with cocoa-nut oil and ashes.   The beauties of these cosmetics are never so well appreciated by the European or American, as when going through with the process of salutation.   When they wish to welcome a stranger, they approach him with a purring noise, like that of a cat, clasp the right arm about his neck, and rub their noses across his, backward and forward, three times; and when the ceremony is ended, it will not surprise him to find that, in color at least, they are all birds of a feather.   On the other islands a little more refinement is exhibited at the toilet, and cocoa-nut oil and turmeric* are used to give a bright shining polish, and an orange tint, to the complexion.

(9.) As great a difference exists among the Paumotuans, in the mode of constructing their habitations, as in their dress.   On some of the islands, they are mere huts, consisting of four or five poles stuck into the ground at both ends, with strips of cocoa-nut wood, or bamboos, laid upon them horizontally, and tied down, over which grass and pandanus leaves, or mats, are spread: they are from six to eight feet

---

* The turmeric dye of the East Indies, and of the Pacific islands, is obtained from the *curcuma longa*, a very different plant from the blood-root (*sanguinaria canadensis*) of America, to which the name is sometimes applied.

long, four feet high in the centre, and five feet wide. In the other parts of the group neat and tasteful houses are constructed of stakes of the bread-fruit tree driven into the ground,—the framework of the walls being composed of bamboo or hibiscus rods; they are thatched with pandanus leaves, and mats are hung against the sides when the state of the weather requires it. Some of these framed huts are mere temporary structures, and may be taken up, and removed from place to place, like the tents of a nomad.

The canoes of the natives are made of the excavated trunks of the pisonia and other trees, or of strips of cocoa-nut wood sewed together over a framework. In navigating from one island to another, double canoes, which are two single ones lashed side and side, are mainly used. Across these is laid a platform, above which is sometimes spread an awning of plaited cocoa leaves. Moveable masts are inserted, with vines for stays. The sails are made of matting of the pandanus leaf, and the oars and paddles of hibiscus wood. Outriggers are also common, especially among the vessels belonging to the inhabitants of Anaä, or Chain Island.

CHAPTER VIII.

(1.) TAHITI well deserves the appellation which has been
bestowed upon it, of "the brightest gem of the Pacific."
When its tall pinnacled cliffs and rugged peaks are first
descried, far out at sea, but little promise is afforded of the
luxuriant beauty and magnificence which a nearer view presents. The object that soonest attracts the attention, is the
fringe of snow-white surf, wreathing itself, as if instinct with
life, about the coral reef that encircles the island. Within
this is a girdle of quiet water,—deep, calm, and placid,—
sheltered from the ocean-storm by the line of breakers, and
rarely disturbed, save by the soft invigorating breezes wafted
from the shore,

> "where the pale citrons blow,
> And golden fruits through dark green foliage glow."

In the centre of the circle is the island itself,—the coast
irregular in outline, and indented with numerous bays, but
having a decidedly pleasing effect; beyond it, extend a succession of undulating slopes and pleasant valleys, carpeted
with rich verdure or enamelled with flowers, interspersed
among embowering groves and noble forests, conspicuous in
which, are the leafy canopies overshadowing, like the *pana-
ché* of the Peruvian warrior, the branchless trunks of the
stately cocoa; and in the midst of these Hesperian gardens,

rise the lofty mountains of Aorai and Orohena—the former seven, and the latter nearly nine thousand feet, above the level of the sea—with their rough sides decked with the vines and parasitic plants, creeping up over the escarped rocks to their summits, around which hover clouds of white mist, like guardian angels from the spirit-land.

Contrasting finely with the bright mantle of vegetation spread over the lower portions of the island, are the little streams and rivulets coursing down the mountain ravines, and winding their way, like threads of silver, between thick banks of foliage preserving ever its perennial bloom, hither and thither, till they mingle their crystal waters with those of the dark green sea. The landscape is dotted, too, with clustering hamlets, composed of the sombre huts of the natives, or the more modern and more tasteful cottages of the foreign residents. In the harbors there is always more or less shipping, either men of war, or merchant vessels, visiting the island for purposes of traffic, or to obtain supplies. Gay flags and streamers float from their mastheads, and numberless canoes may be seen plying between them and the shore, reminding the beholder how vast has been the change since the pennant of the gallant but unfortunate Cook first appeared in these waters. The flowers are not more bright, perhaps,—the grove and the forest not more beautiful,—but the air is no longer filled with scents of slaughter, nor the sky darkened with the smoke of human sacrifices; the songs of David are borne on the evening wind instead of the wild notes of the savage, and the dark and bloody rites of paganism have given place to the solemn and impressive worship of the Christian!

(2.) The group now known as the Society Islands, of which Tahiti, or Otaheite, as it was formerly called, is the largest and most important member, was first discovered by Captain Cook, in 1769. It consists of eight large islands, and several smaller ones. The names of the principal islands are, Tahiti and Eimeö,—sometimes distinguished from the others under the name of the Georgian Group,—Raiatéa,

Huahine, Tahaä, Borabora, Tubai and Maurua. The first two, with some small islands, form one cluster, and the others compose a separate cluster, over one hundred miles to the northwest; but all lie between latitude 16° and 18° S., and longitude 149° and 152° W.

Tahiti, the largest and most populous, is one hundred and eight miles in circumference, and contains seven thousand inhabitants, supposed to be not far from one half of the population of the whole group. This island rises gradually from the sea, and in the interior is mountainous; extensive and fertile valleys open on every side towards the ocean; and from the water's edge to its topmost heights, it is clothed with an abundant vegetation constantly renewing the freshness and vigor of its appearance. Eimeö, ten miles west of Tahiti, is about forty miles in circumference; it is still more wild and mountainous, and has an abrupt coast, rising in some places precipitously to the height of twenty-five hundred feet; it derives its chief importance from the fact that it is the central station of the missionaries, where a separate school for the education of their children, and a printing office—the latter on a limited scale—have been established.

Ulietéa, or Raiatéa, one hundred and thirty miles northwest of Tahiti, is sixty miles in circumference; it is encircled by a reef of coral, bordered by numerous small islets, and has a bold, mountainous, and highly picturesque appearance. Huahine, fifteen miles east of Raiatéa, is nearly as large; this, as well as the other islands, partake of the same general features of those which have been described. All consist of basalt and other igneous formations. Their rounded summits, and the character and composition of the soil, clearly indicate their volcanic origin. Iron is so abundant on some of the hills that the magnet cannot be used, and the sand on the sea-coast is more or less impregnated with it. Olivine and pyroxene are plentifully distributed through the rocks, and lava everywhere abounds.

(3.) From the small size of these islands, it could not be expected that they would contain any considerable rivers or lakes. There are a number of mountain torrents, however, dignified with the name of rivers, which are swollen to such an extent during the rainy season that it is really dangerous to attempt to ford them. The principal of these on the island of Tahiti, are the Pappino on the north, and the Ooaigarra on the south side, both rapid streams, but narrow, and usually only a few feet deep. Tahiti also has a pretty lake, seventeen hundred feet above the level of the sea, called Lake Waiheréa; it is of an oval shape, ninety-six feet deep, half a mile long, and one third of a mile in width; and is bordered with a beautiful fringe of woody plants. The lake has no visible outlet, but the natives say that if a bread-fruit be thrown in, it will appear after a while in a spring, whose waters gush forth from the hill-side, at a distance of nearly three miles.

The excellence of the harbors of Tahiti and her sister islands, is well known to navigators. Deeply embayed between lofty hills, which have a sheer descent to the water, and often many hundred feet below, or faced by perpendicular piers of coral, and protected in front from the waves of the ocean, by the massive breakwaters reared by the same skilful engineer, they afford ample and perfect security against both wind and tide. Papiéti, on the north side of Tahiti, is the most capacious and the first in importance. Fronting a deep recess in the island, is a reef of coral trending away for several miles to the east, but broken just on the right of the fiorde, by a stream of fresh water putting in, which, it is said, always interrupts the labors of the polyp. Tall hills rise on either side of the recess, and between these and the reef, is the harbor, or bay, of Papiéti. It is about one mile in length, and half a mile in width. It affords a deep and secure anchorage,—large vessels being safely moored within a stone's throw of the shore,—and is capacious enough to accommodate a hundred sail.

As you pass through the opening in the reef, and enter the circular and land-locked harbor, the beautiful little coral island of Moto-utu starts up on the left, like Aphrodité, from the frothy sea, with its cool, verdant groves, and its old, dilapidated fortress, over which waves the red flag of Tahiti.* Across the fine sheet of smooth water spreading out before you, along the middle of the curvature of the hot sandy beach, lies the town of Papiéti, backed by pinnacle-shaped mountains, and half-hidden beneath the dark green foliage of the bread-fruit,—beneath the round-leaved myrtle, the luxuriant palm, and the noble cocoa. The white cottages of the foreign residents, with their thatched roofs and green blinds, and the light-built and sombre-looking huts, of the natives, are scattered along the shore, or peep out, here and there, from the thickets of limes and oranges in which they are imbosomed.

Papiéti is the largest town on the island, or in the group. It is difficult to form any estimate in regard to the population. The habits of the Tahitian are extremely migratory; his wants are easily and quickly supplied, and a few hours' work will provide him with a comfortable habitation. When there are a number of foreign vessels in port, and on other great occasions, the village is overrun with inhabitants, who flock thither in crowds, but soon betake themselves again to other parts of the island. This is the ordinary residence of the queen and the foreign consuls. It boasts a wharf and a warehouse, and the harbor is probably the best and safest in the Pacific; it is frequently visited by whalers, and is now second only, in commercial importance, to Honolulu.

Five miles east of Papiéti is the town of Matavai, which has a fine harbor. Vessels pass up to it from Papiéti, inside the reef. It is situated on lower ground; but its location, nevertheless, is quite pleasant. Point Venus, on Matavai Bay, is chiefly celebrated, and, indeed, derives its name, from the fact, that Captain Cook observed the transit of Venus over the sun's disk from this place. Papoä and Toä-noä, also on the northern side of the island, have good harbors. On the south side is Otapuna, next in size and importance to Papiéti; it is built on a low point of land, and the pearl

* The Tahitian flag consists of two red horizontal stripes, with a white one between them.

fishery of the Paumotu Group centres here. Papara and
Panaweä, both of which have convenient harbors, are on the
same side of the island.

Taloö is the principal town and harbor on Eimeö. The
anchorage ground is an inlet three miles in depth, inclosed
between walls of precipitous mountains; it is deep and spacious, and, though exposed to the western winds, they do not
often blow hard enough to injure shipping. At its head is a
broad flat of alluvion, well adapted for the cultivation of the
sugar-cane. Papoä, also on the northern side of the island,
and Afareaitu on the south side, are safe and excellent harbors.

(4.) Europeans became earlier acquainted with the Society
Islands than with any of the other groups in the Pacific; and
the language of Tahiti was the first Polynesian language reduced to writing by the English missionaries. As early as
1797, there were eighteen missionaries settled on the island
of Tahiti; and, in 1814, there were about fifty adult natives
who had embraced Christianity. Although the number of
converts was so few, a general and visible improvement followed the introduction of Christianity; many useful arts
were introduced; schools were founded; the meliorating influences of the law of kindness and love daily became more
manifest; and the change was finally marked by the establishment of comparative order and tranquillity, and the adoption of a form of government, modelled, under the auspices
of the English missionaries, after the British Constitution.

The present constitution was originally framed by the missionaries in 1823, and was revised in 1826. The form of
government, like that of England, is a limited monarchy.
The crown is hereditary in the male or female line. The
sovereign appoints all the principal officers of state, the governors of the different islands, and the chiefs of districts; and
has an unqualified veto on all legislative enactments, though
a bill which has failed to receive the royal signature may
subsequently be revised and modified. The legislature is
composed of two members from each district, who are trien-

nially elected ; annual sessions are held for the general purposes of legislation, and extra sessions may at any time be
convened. Each district has a court of its own, and there is
also a general supreme court consisting of seven judges, five
of whom reside at Tahiti, and two at Eimeö. All the Society Islands, and some of the Paumotu Group, acknowledge
the authority of the sovereign ; but the more remote islands
are little known or civilized, and are not represented in the
national assembly.

Aimata, or Pomare IV, the present queen, is the grand-
daughter of king Pomare I, so well known in the early history of Tahiti. She is now (1849) about thirty-nine years
of age, is a good-looking, though not a pretty woman, and has
a clear olive complexion, dark intelligent eyes, and black
hair. She is not above the medium height, and is somewhat
inclined to corpulency. The queen has been twice married.
She was divorced from her first husband. Her second is
called *Pomare-taui*, or " Pomare's-man," equivalent, probably, to " king-consort," in the more refined courts of Europe.
He is nine years younger than the queen, and is a gay, easy-
humored man, comparing favorably with the other young
men of Tahiti in personal appearance, but rather too much
given to the use of intoxicating drinks. Matrimonial squab-
bles are not wanting, it is said, to disturb the harmony of the
royal *ménage*. When her consort was a mere lad, Pomare
exercised quite a motherly sort of authority over him, and,
if reports be true, frequently applied the rod of correction.
But as soon as he reached man's estate, the tables were
turned ; although she could rate him soundly as ever with
her tongue, she was no match for him in physical strength,
and he repaid the inflictions of his august spouse, in kind, with
something added, too, in the shape of interest. Happily, perhaps, for the safety of the state, both parties seem to have
been benefited by this reciprocal chastisement, and jog along
together, without seriously disturbing the peace of the island.

Both their majesties are fond of state and display. There
are sentinels constantly parading in front of the royal resi-

MISSIONARY PREACHING BEFORE QUEEN POMARE.

dence, and when the queen attends church, or shows herself to her loving subjects, she is accompanied by a body-guard, as an escort, consisting of about one hundred men, commanded by officers who can hardly be called martinets in discipline. The uniform of this corps is a blue coat with white pantaloons. The former is made after various patterns, and worn in different ways—sometimes being buttoned, sometimes hooked, and sometimes sewed about the person of the wearer. The guard have muskets; but, on Sundays, they are only allowed to carry their ramrods. When the queen and her husband issue forth, the royal standards are borne before them, and the soldiers follow, two by two, with the rabble at their heels. If an aquatic excursion is the order of the day, a whaleboat, dignified as the royal barge, receives the *cortége*.

Although royalty is so often exhibited in caricature, at Tahiti, it is probable that the people of this, and the other islands belonging to the group, are as well-governed, and that as great a degree of order is observed as in those countries where there is more real brilliancy and show. Generally speaking, the statesmen and politicians of the Society Islands are well-informed, reasonable, and sagacious. They always appear willing to redress grievances, and anxious to promote the welfare and prosperity of their fellow-citizens. As in more enlightened countries, there are two opposing parties, one of which is headed by the queen and the missionaries, and the other, by Paöfai, chief judge of the supreme court, and Hitoti and Taua, two prominent chiefs. The former are constantly proposing new innovations in laws and customs, and the latter, though by no means unfriendly to reform, have resisted, with more or less earnestness, their adoption. Sometimes the queen and her advisers have pushed their favorite measures with too great zeal and severity, and their opponents, by appealing to the national feeling and spirit, or threatening resistance, have achieved a temporary success; but the queen usually manages, in one way or another, eventually to secure everything she wishes.

She rarely fails, also, in maintaining the dignity of her queenly state, though once in a while, as in the difficulty with France in 1842–3, obliged to yield to the force of circumstances, or compelled to humor the caprices of *Pomare-taui*, who, at the dictation of the foreign residents, occasionally interferes in questions of state, and, for the most part, successfully.

The police regulations, especially on the island of Tahiti, are excellent, though some might term them severe. At eight o'clock in the evening a gun is fired, followed by another at an interval of fifteen minutes, after which all stragglers found in the streets are carried to the guard-house by the patrol. The members of the police, with few exceptions, are faithful and efficient, and do not leave much cause to regret the abolition of the ancient custom of *taboo.**

(5.) In enterprise, industry, and intelligence, this people are, doubtless, far behind the inhabitants of the Sandwich Islands; yet, one who has read the accounts of the old navigators, can hardly fail to be struck with the vast change effected by the missionaries. The natives of this group, though indolent by nature, were originally wild and turbulent, when aroused, and fierce and vindictive. Long and bloody wars desolated the islands; parental affection, love, and tenderness, were almost entirely unknown; woman was sunk in the lowest state of degradation; polygamy was common; a species of marriage was in vogue, but not esteemed sacred; female virtue was prized as a thing of little worth; depravity and licentiousness abounded; sexual indulgences and infanticide were encouraged by a singular institution called the *Areoï;†* all the finer feelings of humanity were nearly obliterated, and

> " hardened mothers in the grave could lay
> Their living babes with no compunctious tear."

---

* This custom, formerly prevailing throughout Polynesia, but now nearly done away, may be regarded as something like a police regulation in a rude and barbarous state of society, and, no doubt, was highly beneficial, in curbing the passions, and controlling the lawlessness, of the savages, even though it may sometimes have been the instrument of wrong and oppression.

† The baneful influence of this society once extended over the whole Pacific.

There was, indeed, little to encourage the missionary in such a condition of society, and the light of civilization struggled long before it was able to penetrate the Cimmerian darkness which overspread the Pacific like a pall.   But the Christian soldier, clad in the robes of righteousness, and brandishing a weapon from the arsenal of Jehovah, fought and toiled, long and manfully, till his labors were ultimately crowned with success; and, though he may have achieved less than what he might once have anticipated, the good seed has been planted, and he can console himself with the hope, that in God's own time it will yield an abundant harvest.

True enough, there is great room for improvement; the influence of the foreign traders, like their interests, has been adverse to that of the missionaries; outbreaks and disturbances, fomented by them, are sometimes witnessed; and the chastity of the female sex has not been proof against the temptations offered to their vanity by the introduction of European finery.   But these things were to have been expected, for civilization has its vices as well as its virtues; and we need not despair, when we see wise enactments enforced, instead of ancient laws and customs, a written constitution adopted, and order steadily rising out of chaos and confusion.   Though the *morais* described by Cook, within whose sacred inclosures human sacrifices were offered up, are still visible, they are pointed out by the natives only as relics of a by-gone age.

The inhabitants may be said to be constitutionally indolent. The influence of the climate is decidedly enervating, although, owing to their small extent, the islands have the temperature of the ocean, and, on the west, are favored by the prevailing

Its members were not prohibited from marrying, but if they had children, they were obliged to put them to death.   It is computed by the missionaries, that at least two thirds of the children born were murdered; but though the number was undoubtedly large, the correctness of this estimate is doubted, simply, perhaps, for the reason, that it seems too revolting for belief.   It is certain, however, that the fact, that the islands are far less populous now than they were at the period of their discovery, may be attributed to the prevalence of infanticide, and the bloody and desolating wars.

winds. The heat is not often really oppressive, as there is a constant succession of light sea and land breezes, but it soon produces, if one is disposed to yield to its seductions, a soft dreamy languor and lassitude that cannot easily be resisted. A considerable variety of character is presented here. Generally, the people are light-hearted, merry, frank, honest and well-behaved, kind and affable in disposition. Exceptions are not uncommon. Some are deceitful and thievish, and addicted to the use of ardent spirits, though drunkenness and rioting are not common save when provoked or incited by the whites. Chastity is not the chief virtue of the female sex, but licentiousness is not near as prevalent as in former years.

All are excitable, fond of music, dancing, social enjoyments and amusements, of which the missionaries, perhaps unwisely, have endeavored, in some respects, to deprive them. Their fondness for music is natural, and they frequently assemble in parties to sing in the open air in the evening. Their voices have a slight nasal twang, but chord unusually in harmony. They will quickly imitate a new tune, and readily adapt symphonious parts to it. The native music is now rarely heard, and its place is supplied by the songs which they have learned from the sailors, and the familiar tunes of " God save the King," " Cambridge," and " Old Hundred."

They are attentive at worship—the elderly people particularly so—and pay due respect to the authority of the law. Of pride they have not much to boast; and the highest ministers of state, and the officers of the queen's body-guard, may often be seen swimming out to a vessel newly arrived, with nothing on but the *maro*, to solicit the honor of washing clothes. From the ease of procuring food, clothing, and lodgings, they are as improvident as they are indolent, though there are many who keep more than one eye on the main chance. Both men and women arrive at maturity at an early age; the latter look older at thirteen than American females at twenty-three. Their mode of salutation is very friendly; the parties shake hands, as with us, and say "*ia ora na oe!*"—"peace be with you!"

Scrofulous complaints, which are attributed to drinking the water of the rills descending from the mountains, are quite prevalent. Syphilitic diseases, and elephantiasis, are also common. Intoxication often produces, or aggravates, many of the prevailing complaints, and the inhabitants suffer a great deal for the want of suitable medical attendance.

They are of good stature, tall and well-made. Their complexions are a light olive, or reddish brown. They have regular, open, and prepossessing features, with a facial angle as perpendicular as in the European head; full, jet-black, and brilliant eyes—those of the women "half languor and half fire;" finely-arched eye-brows; straight or aquiline noses; well-formed mouths; coarse, but not wiry hair, either black or brown. They are lithe and supple of limb, but not inclined to exertion. There are few very ugly women; most of them are good-looking, and some are really handsome, with their long dark tresses hanging gracefully over their shoulders, and interwoven with roses and jasmine blossoms.

Tattooing is not practiced as much now as formerly. Attempts were made a few years ago to abolish it in Tahiti, but they were not entirely successful. It is often performed at the age of eight or ten. A great deal of taste is displayed in this barbarous custom of deforming the person. The bodies of those who have been tattooed are sometimes completely covered over with beautiful figures exhibiting every variety of curve—with animals, flowers, and the sprigs and branches of trees.

There is a close analogy between the dialects spoken here and those observed in other parts of Polynesia. The language is similar to the Hawaiian, and many words are precisely the same, though the two groups are twenty-three hundred miles apart. Some words resemble the Malay, some the Indian, and some every language spoken on the shores of the two great continents from which these islands were, directly or indirectly, peopled. The inhabitants of the

8*

Sandwich, Marquesas, and Society Islands, communicate with each other without difficulty, after a few days' practice, and the Tahitian and New Zealander readily understand each other.*

A translation of the scriptures into the Tahitian tongue has been made by the missionaries, and printed at Eimeö. Other books, too, have been published, and the cause of education is progressing, more slowly than might be desired, but still progressing. The schools are tolerably well attended; more pains are taken to instruct the rising generation; and a greater degree of interest in their improvement has recently been manifested.

(6.) So many new fashions and customs have been introduced by Europeans, that it is difficult to say what constitutes the national dress. The queen usually appears in public, in a dress of satin or figured silk, made after the European style, with slippers and gloves of corresponding color, a white satin hat, open and flattened on the upper rim, and surmounted with ostrich feathers. So fastidious is she, that she will not appear at church in the afternoon, in the same dress she wore in the morning; and it is needless to say that others follow her example. The king-consort displays himself in a brilliant crimson uniform, decorated with gold epaulettes, a sword, and a chapeau ornamented with the plumes of the ostrich. The princesses wear white frocks, shoes and stockings, and flaring chip, or straw bonnets, which last are all the rage in Tahiti. The chiefs and higher dignitaries also appear in the European dress, on all public occasions, though their coats and trowsers are of all colors and fashions,—the half worn costume of the sailor generally having the preference.

The ordinary costume of the natives consists of a kind of mantle covering the upper part of the person, and reaching down to the *pareu.* The latter is about two yards long, is wound around the waist, and extends just below the knees. Some of the men have *pareus* made of blue cotton cloth, and

* Cook's Voyages, Vol. I, book i, chap. 8; Moerenhout, Vol. I, p. 395, et seq.

red check, or calico shirts, of gaudy colors; others wear duck trowsers and sailors' round-jackets, and use the *pareu* as a mantle. A full loose dress, resembling a night gown, buttoned at the wrists, but not confined at the neck or waist, is worn by the better class of females, but those who are unable to indulge in this luxury appear in the *pareu* alone, which merely conceals the lower part of the body, and leaves the bosom and shoulders bare. Shoes are rarely seen, and stockings may be classed among the prerogatives of royalty. Straw hats are worn by both sexes, though it is more common to go bareheaded; and black felt hats, some high and some low crowned, some with broad and some with narrow brims, are possessed by a very few, whom their countrymen esteem as fortune's especial favorites.

Naked Tahitians, with the *maro* only, are scarcely ever seen. Clothing of some kind or other is deemed essential, no matter how odd or fantastical it may be.

Formerly, *tapa* was the principal article used in the manufacture of clothing, but cotton cloths and calicoes are now much more common at Tahiti and Eimeö. The men appear singular enough in their calico *pareus*, and a stranger coming among them, ignorant of their manners and customs, would be very apt to suppose he had introduced himself into one of the most approved gyneöcracies of the modern school of philosophers. On the other islands, the original dress of the natives is the most frequently worn.

A love of flowers is characteristic of the Tahitian female, and her sisters on the other islands of the group, though far less civilized, are not a whit behind her in this womanly trait. They are fond of wearing flowers stuck in their hair, and through the lobes of their ears. Sometimes they decorate their heads with wreaths of the most fragrant and beautiful flowers, and they have also an ornament called a *hau*, which consists of a rim of braided pandanus leaves, projecting on either side of the head like a chapeau.

Though the inhabitants of the Society Islands are not overmuch attached to labor, contenting themselves, in the main, with the cultivation of a few bananas, and a small patch of yams and sweet potatoes, they are always ready for any kind of amusement. Fishing is one of their chief sports, and every fine night the romantic scenery of the numerous bays and inlets is illuminated by the glare of their torches, and the coral rocks echo back their cheery songs and joyous shouts. They fish mostly with the spear, in the use of which they are very expert.

(7.) There are few trees or plants usually found in the tropics, which are not indigenous to, or have not been acclimated in, this group. The soil made by the decomposing rocks and decayed vegetable matter, is of great fertility, yet agriculture is in a languishing state ; and there are acres of the most fruitful ground, to which, were it not for the spontaneous growth of its products, the expressive phrase of *part du diable*, used in designating the fallow corners of the ploughed fields of Finistèrre, might well be applied. There is, indeed, no very powerful inducement to labor, where the means of subsistence are so easily obtained.

On the hills and uplands there are forests of stately trees, and the mountain sides are variegated with shrubbery, and richly embroidered with the parasitic plants that grow in every rift and cranny. Ornamental shrubs and aromatic plants are common. Yellow, orange, red, and party-colored acacias, enliven the scene with their gorgeous dyes. The laughing sunlight rests lovingly on the rich yellow fruit of the lime and orange, and the soft breezes of the ocean delight to linger amid the bright green foliage of the banana, the broad leaves of the bread-fruit, and the waving tufts of the cocoa.

Of the *apapa* and *faifai*—the latter the more valuable of the two—the canoes of the natives are made ; and the *tamanu* and *hibiscus* of the plains, are used for the same purpose, and also for making furniture. The mape (*inocarpus edulis*) furnishes excellent timber for small vessels, but only a limited supply can be obtained. The wood of the bread-fruit tree is used in various ways, in house and ship building.

Besides the fruits which have been mentioned—the cocoa, bread-fruit, orange, lime, banana, yam, and sweet potato— pine-apples, shaddocks, citrons, plantains, papayas, lemons, vi-apples, taro, figs, guavas, and cape mulberries, are found in great abundance. Pumpkins, melons, turnips, onions, beans and cabbages, would flourish with proper care and til- lage, but the ground is scarcely ever turned up, except with an iron-shod stick, and little can be expected from such husbandry. From the ti-root (*dracona terminalis*) an infe- rior spirit, called *ava*, is made ; this was once drank by all classes, to excess, but the introduction of foreign spirits has banished it from use, unless it be among the poorer people. A native chestnut, the rata, (*tuscarpus edulis*,) has a sweet nut, and is an agreeable substitute for the bread-fruit. On the south side of Tahiti, the grape thrives luxuriantly ; the coffee shrub has been tried and succeeds well ; tobacco is grown in small quantities ; and sugar cane, cotton, and in- digo, may be raised with little effort. The Otaheitan cane produces four crops, while the common variety, requiring a better soil, yields only three ; its cultivation is yet in its in- fancy, but there are a number of fine plantations at Tahiti and Eimeö, which promise in the future to be highly pro- ductive.* The tuitui tree, the nut of which is used in tattoo- ing, is a native of the group ; so is, also, the tacca, from which arrow-root is prepared.

The pine-apples raised here are excellent, and the oranges delicious. The latter are sold at fifty cents per hundred ; they are often prepared so as to keep for a long time, by selecting them with care, and drying them in the sun, dur- ing which process the moisture of the rind evaporates, but the juice of the pulp is not impaired. Lemons are unusually large, and limes are so abundant that it is quite a traffic to supply ships with the juice, prepared by fermenting the fruit with chalk, which is highly valued for its anti-scorbutic properties. Citrons are plenty, but are hardly equal to those obtained in the East Indies. The vi-apple resembles the

* The cane is often seen growing wild, in tufts, in the interior of Tahiti.

egg plum, and is the product of a rough tree like the oak. Of the banana and plantain there are numerous varieties; they are sometimes preserved by cutting them in slices, and exposing them to the heat of the sun, by which they are dried, and at the same time covered with a rich saccharine matter.

A species of banana, called *fei*, or *fayee*, by the natives, is found wild on the mountains and highlands. Unlike the other varieties, which it resembles in shape, its spikes of fruit rise up from the stalks instead of depending down. Internally, the fruit is of a bright chrome yellow; it has no seeds, and is covered with a rind of a brilliant red tint. In taste it resembles the parsnep. There are two kinds of the taro, one of which is the denizen of wet, marshy places, and the other of higher and dryer ground. The guava is wonderfully prolific, and threatens eventually to overrun the islands, if serious attempts are not made to exterminate it, or confine it in proper limits. It here attains the height of from six to twelve feet; its fruit is like that of the quince bush in shape and size, pulpy and rich in flavor like the strawberry, of a deep crimson color in the interior, and covered with a yellow skin shaded with a tinge of carmine. So abundant is this fruit, that the swine are allowed to go at large, in order that they may feed upon it.

The natives pluck the cocoa when it is still quite green, and do not wait for

> " Th' imbrowning of the fruit, that tells
> How rich within the soul of sweetness dwells."

When in this unripe state, the kernel is pulpy and the shell soft; it can then be eaten with a spoon, and, if a little Madeira wine and lime juice be added, it is really excellent. At this time the nut contains from a pint to a quart of a slightly acidulous, but fine beverage. The mode of obtaining the cocoas is peculiar. A boy with a long line in his hand, and his feet fettered by a short rope so that they are from ten to twelve inches apart, ascends the tree by pressing his feet against the shaggy trunk, and clasping it with his

arms.   He vaults up with astonishing rapidity—his body
swinging clear from the tree at every spring—and lowers
down the nuts with the long rope.   The cocoas are so productive that the nuts are often sold at one dollar per hundred.

Valuable and important as are the productions which have
been described, the bread-fruit, after all, is the vegetable
Corypheus of the Society Islands.   The tree grows to the
size of a middling oak, is umbrageous, and has its broad
leaves deeply notched, like those of the fig.   The trunk rises
to the height of ten or twelve feet without a branch, and has
a rough light-colored bark.   The foliage is a dark green, rich
and glossy.   Its fruit is circular or oval, from eight to nine
inches long, and averaging about six inches in diameter ; it
is covered with hexagonal warts, and grows in clusters of
five or six ; at first it is of a pea-green color, subsequently
changing to brown, and, when fully ripe, assuming a yellowish tinge.   The pulp is white and soft, partly farinaceous and
partly fibrous, and in its ripe state is yellow and juicy.   Inside of the pulp there is a hard core extending from the stalk
to the crown, about which there are a few imperfect seeds.
The fruit is gathered before it is entirely ripe, for it soon decays; it continues in season above eight months in the year,
and is so prolific that two or three trees will yield a sufficiency
for the yearly support of one person.*

This delightful esculent is boiled or baked, or roasted under
ground, after the true native fashion.   The second rind is
scraped off, and the interior is eaten in the same manner as
bread.   It has a pure white, mealy appearance, resembling
potatoes, and an agreeable sweet taste, between that of wheat

* There are, in fact, two species of bread-fruit—the *artocarpus integrifolia*,
and the *artocarpus incisa*.   The leaves of the former are not sinuated ; it grows
chiefly on the continent of Asia, and is called *jaca* by the inhabitants ; the fruit
is very large, often exceeding thirty pounds in weight.   The latter is the proper
bread-fruit of the South Sea, originally discovered in the Ladrónes.   Through
the exertions of Captain Bligh,—who had just left Tahiti, while on an errand
of this kind, when the crew of the Bounty mutinied,—and at the expense of
the English government, plants of the bread-fruit were introduced into the West
Indies.   It is easily cultivated there, but does not excel the banana.

bread and roasted chestnuts. Sometimes it is beaten up with cocoa-nut and milk. It is highly nutritive, but must be eaten new, as it becomes harsh and unpalatable in twenty-four hours after being cooked. As it is impossible to keep this fruit in a crude state, it is often buried in pits, when it ferments, and forms a substance called *mahi*, that may be preserved for a long time, and is resorted to out of the bearing season.

Since the abolition of the custom of *taboo*, it is usual for the owner of a private grove, if he wishes to protect it from strangers, to tie girdles of leaves about the trees. This signal is always respected, and the most tempting fruits remain unmolested, without any other guard or protection. The people of other countries, who boast of their intellectual advancement, and moral perfectness, might well profit by this example.

Having such an abundance, and so great a variety, of the finest and most luscious fruits, the people of these islands are bounteously provided for in respect to food. They live principally on vegetables ; though pigs, fowls, and fish, are considerably eaten. Bread-fruit, taro, and pig, is the standing dish. All are fond of *poë*, particularly the children. They prepare a delicious hotchpot, of taro, cocoa-nut, and bread-fruit, called *poë-poë*, and another, equally good, called *poë-maia*, of feis, taro, bread-fruit, and cocoa-nut. They eat no salt, but, instead thereof, use a sop, or compound, made of sea-water, cocoa-nut milk, and the nut of the *ti ;* taro or bread-fruit is dipped in this, and sucked, before being eaten.

(8.) The albatross, tropic bird, petrel, heron, wild duck, woodpecker, and turtle dove, are the principal birds found in the islands. Pigeons and swallows are common, as is, also, the trichoclossus, a species of parroquet. Horses, asses, cattle, hogs, goats and sheep, have been introduced, and thrive well. The horses are quite numerous ; they are never shod, as they are used exclusively for the saddle. The cattle roam at pleasure through the fine pasture grounds, and the leaves of the bread-fruit form excellent fodder for them. Large numbers of hogs are reared, and they are fast supplanting the wild ones, belonging to an entirely distinct breed, that once abounded in the mountainous regions of Tahiti and Eimeö. Dogs and cats are domesticated; and rats, musquitoes, and horse-flies, are plenty enough to be regarded as great pests.

Fish are abundant. The best of them are the albicore, bonito, ray and shark, all of which are eaten. Fine rock fish are caught in the small streams, and salmon and eels in the rivers. As has been stated, fishing is a favorite employment of the natives. Besides the spear, they use nets made of the twisted bark of the hibiscus. They are likewise fond of taking the molluscous crabs and turtles, numbers of which are obtained on the coral rocks and reefs.

(9.) The queen's residence at Papiéti is the most conspicuous house there. It is one story in height, and has a peaked roof of thatch, and a wide piazza extending completely across the front. The church at the same place is a large and convenient edifice; the rafters and frame work supporting the roof are concealed, in part, by ornamental matting reaching up ten or fifteen feet from the wall. The residences of the foreigners are light wooden structures, painted white, with green blinds and thatched roofs. The " palace," and some few other houses, have glazed windows. The rafters are generally left uncovered, on the inner side. Some dwellings are divided off into separate rooms, by board partitions, though, in general, there is but a single room.

Most of the timber used in house-building, and in making the heavier articles of furniture, is obtained from the breadfruit; but the tamanu (*calophyllum*) is sometimes employed as a substitute. The wood of the former tree is of the color of mahogany, and is exceedingly durable: it is hewn into posts, or sawed into boards, as may be required.

The natives, ordinarily, build their habitations, however, very differently from the more modern style just represented. They are a single story high, and of an oblong shape, resembling more closely, at a distance, a Dutch hay-stack, than

anything beside. They consist of posts or stakes, at the
corners, and at intervals between them, driven firmly into
the ground. The walls are built of bamboo interlaced, or of
strips of hibiscus. Where there are floors, they are made of
planks from the bread-fruit. There is not often more than
one apartment; but, occasionally, a separate shed is employed
for cooking. Frequently a part of the hut is railed off, for
the use of a sow and her litter.

Some of the houses, on Tahiti and Eimeö, have neat inclosed gardens for vegetables and flowers. The queen's
palace is surrounded by a fine lawn well stocked with shade
and fruit trees.

Of furniture there is but little. The principal articles are
a few mats and low wooden stools; a trough and stone for
preparing *poë*; and a number of cups and eating vessels made
of cocoa-nut shells. A log of wood is used for a pillow, and
a mat for a bed; in the better class of dwellings, they have
pillows stuffed with cotton or aromatic herbs. An old musket and several fishing spears, extended on rude hooks, and
some bunches of fruit depending from the rafters, are the
customary ornaments witnessed in the native houses.

(10.) Though they make no long voyages, the Society
Islanders are essentially a maritime people. Their commercial resources are limited, however; and most of their trade,
which is carried on exclusively by foreigners, principally
French and English, is with New South Wales, whose ports
are opened to their vessels on the same footing as the English.
They export thither, sugar, cocoa-nut oil, and arrow-root, to
an amount exceeding thirty-five thousand dollars annually,
and receive in return, hardware, calicoes, and other manufactured goods. In the course of a year, perhaps one hundred whalers visit the islands to barter, whose trade amounts
to nearly fifty dollars for each vessel. The American property annually visiting the group is estimated to be worth at
least five million dollars. About ten thousand dollars' worth
of pearls are annually obtained from the Paumotu Group,
most of which are sent to France.

Double canoes are the only large vessels belonging to the natives. Recently, small schooners of one hundred tons burden have been built at Tahiti, under the superintendence of Americans, which are employed in the trade to New South Wales. The large timbers of the schooners are made of mape, and the smaller ones of hibiscus. The native canoes are of various sizes and shapes, either double or single, and are decidedly superior to those found elsewhere in the Pacific. Some of them are seventy feet long and but two feet wide, with high stems and sterns, ornamented with grotesque carved work. The war canoes are from forty to sixty feet long, well-modelled and firmly built, and fancifully ornamented with carving, and decorated with gay flags and streamers. The canoes built for trading with vessels anchored in the harbors, or for fishing on the reefs, are always single, and rarely hold more than two persons. Mape and hibiscus furnish the principal materials used in the construction of canoes. The cordage is made of grape-vines, or the fibres of the bread-fruit. The sails, usually of a half oval shape, are made of matting of pandanus leaves; they are very large, and one would suppose that the canoes might be easily upset in a squall, but the native sailors are expert and skilful, and, at such times, they get far out on the outriggers, and thus keep their frail barks in an upright position, while they dash forward with the utmost velocity.

There is little or no internal traffic. Almost every one raises what food he needs for himself and family, and the poorer class of natives manufacture their own clothing, from that never-failing source of supply, the bread-fruit tree. Vehicles for carrying burdens are not much used, although there is a fine road, called the Broom Road, extending completely around Tahiti near the beach, and finely arched with trees, among them many cocoas, termed the queen's, the fruit of which is free to strangers and travellers. The mode of carrying articles, in general use, is the same with that observed in the East Indies, and throughout the islands of the Pacific: —a stout stick, from four to five feet long, is extended horizontally over the shoulder, and a portion of the burden attached to either end.

Sugar, cocoa-nut oil and arrow-root, are the chief articles of commerce, which require to be manufactured before being fit for market. Much larger quantities of these might be produced, were the natives more industrious. The annual product of sugar, probably the most important of all, is steadily increasing. Nearly two hundred tons are raised on the plantations of Tahiti, and half that quantity on those of Eimeö, in the space of a year. One hundred tons of cocoa-nut oil were once annually exported, but, in consequence of some unwise restrictive measures of the government, there is much less obtained. The oil is extracted in a very simple manner :—the kernel is chopped up in fine pieces, and placed in a trough, so inclined, that when the oil is expelled by the heat of the sun it will trickle down into a reservoir placed beneath ; it is preserved in pieces of bamboo cut off at the joints, and is used for lubricating machinery and making soap, and, when perfumed, is burnt in lamps. The value of the arrow-root annually prepared, is about five thousand dollars. As in other countries, the root is washed and beaten into a pulp, and the fecula separated from the fibrous matter by elutriation through sieves.

Attempts have been made by the missionaries to introduce cotton spinning and weaving, at Tahiti, but with little or no success ; and a carpet factory established at Eimeö, has failed. Yet the natives are not deficient in mechanical ingenuity. In former times, skill in the manufacture of *tapa* was esteemed an important female accomplishment, and, as such, highly prized. All the labor in preparing this native cloth is performed by women, and those who continue to make it are as proud of their stores, as were our Dutch grandmothers of their rolls of kersey and heaps of linen. The *tapa* is made of the inner fibres of the bark from the branches of the bread-fruit tree. These fibres are macerated, and then beaten on a long spring-board, slightly convex, with a small grooved mallet, under which process, while in a moist

state, they become interlaced with each other, and assume
the appearance of woven cloth. Bales of it are sometimes
made, two hundred yards long, and four yards in width. Its
color, in an unbleached state, is a darkish brown ; and it is
customary either to bleach it, or to color it with vegetable
dyes. Since the introduction of European cloth, there has
been a great deal less made, especially on Tahiti and Eimeö,
and it is now chiefly worn by females, children, and the
poorer classes.

(11.) There is some contrariety of opinion in regard to the
general influence exerted by the missionaries in the Society
Islands. No doubt, the condition of the inhabitants is very
different from what it would naturally have been, had they
remained enveloped in the mists and darkness of heathenish
superstition,—but might it not have been still better ? The
missionaries were unquestionably right in theory, yet they
lacked practical tact. They discouraged the fondness for
flowers which characterized the natives, because it was connected with ancient customs and a dark and cruel faith, instead of teaching the poor benighted pagan to love them better, from a higher and nobler impulse—from adoration for
their Creator, whose matchless handiwork is nowhere more
strikingly or beautifully exhibited, than upon the islands of
the Pacific. They endeavored to check, or prohibit altogether,
some of their favorite amusements—among others, those of
singing and dancing—forgetting, meanwhile, that amusements are far more necessary to an excitable people, though
they may be indolent by nature, than to those who are cold
and phlegmatic in disposition. Though he failed to profit
by it in the end, Louis Philippe understood better the character of his subjects—of course more refined and enlightened
than the Society Islanders, but, like them, volatile, gay-
hearted, and mercurial in temperament—when he enriched
the collections, and added new beauties, to the noble *Jardin
des Plantes*, and filled the lofty halls and corridors, the
vaulted chambers and saloons, of Versailles, with all the

glories of France.*   True, the one labored to establish a
temporal power on a firm foundation, while the others were
employed on a divine mission ; but the laws of nature, of
man's physical constitution, can never be disregarded with
impunity.   As the love of flowers might have been made to
subserve a happy purpose, so might the amusements of the
natives, by rendering them harmless, or substituting others
in their stead, if that were impossible, have produced a happiness, and contentedness of feeling, under the influence of
which they would have been less likely to fall into the vices,
and become victims to the temptations, introduced, or placed
before them, by some of the foreign residents.

The traders and merchants who followed the missionaries,
have undoubtedly done much to counteract their efforts ; but
the influence exerted by their own children has been equally
pernicious, and the establishment of a separate school for
them, looks so much like exclusiveness, like an aristocratic
barrier, that its tendency cannot be otherwise than prejudicial.   Until quite recently, very little pains have been taken
to instruct the natives in any useful arts, or to present inducements for them to be active and industrious.   Had they
been taught some light and easy employments, particularly
the females, and been allowed to indulge their native tastes
and customs, where they were not decidedly immoral, it is
but reasonable to suppose that they would have been a happier, more virtuous, and better contented people.

* "*A toutes les gloires de la France,*" is the inscription on the portico of the
palace of Versailles.

CHAPTER IX.

(1.) At sunset on the 10th of September, the Vincennes anchored in Matavai Bay, where she found the Porpoise,—the latter having arrived in Papiéti Harbor the day previous. The Peacock arrived on the 12th, and the Flying Fish on the 14th instant. Immediately after the arrival of the Squadron, the instruments were landed, and observations made, on Point Venus,—a convenient and airy house having been kindly offered for this purpose by Queen Pomare. While the Americans remained at the island, their intercourse with the civil authorities, the missionaries, and the natives, was of the most friendly character; they experienced the most hospitable and generous treatment on every hand; and during their stay, a number of grievances complained of by the American consul, were promptly redressed, through the intervention of the commander of the expedition.

All the harbors of Tahiti and Eimeö were carefully surveyed, and correct charts made, by one or other of the vessels of the Squadron. On the 20th of September, the Vincennes put to sea for a short cruise in the Paumotu Group, with instructions to join the flag ship, at Rose Island, the easternmost of the Samoän, or Navigators' Group, between the 1st and 5th of October. The Vincennes moved to Papiéti Harbor on the 22d of September, and was joined, on the 24th instant, by the other vessels belonging to the Squadron. On the 25th, she sailed to Eimeö, and on the 29th pursued her course to the west. Passing Bellinghausen's Island on her route, where she stopped to make some magnetic experiments, she hove in sight of Rose Island on the 7th of October, two days later than the appointed time, where she found the Porpoise awaiting her arrival. The Flying Fish was detained at Papiéti, for repairs, till the 10th of October—the Peacock remaining to bear her company—on which day both vessels sailed for the place of rendezvous.

(2.) The Samoän Group—formerly called Navigators' Islands—is situated between latitude 13° 30' and 14° 30' S., and longitude 168° and 173° W. These islands were discovered in 1768, by the distinguished French navigator, Count de Bougainville, who gave them the name which they have heretofore usually borne. There are eight of the islands inhabited, viz.—Manuä, Oloosinga, Ofoo, Tutuila, Upolu, Manono, Apolima, and Savaii—and there are several smaller and uninhabited islands, among which is Rose Island, a low circular coral islet, with a lagoon in the centre, nearly inundated in high water, and covered to the very rim with tall and graceful pisonias. The other small islands resemble this in general formation and appearance, and are mainly situated within the shore reefs of the larger islands.

Manuä is the first island west of Rose Island. It is about sixteen miles in circumference, and upwards of twenty-five hundred feet above the level of the sea. Its shores are high and bold,—rising, in most places, precipitately, to the height of three or four hundred feet. Above this the ground swells gracefully, upward and inward, till it attains its greatest elevation, like a vast dome reared above some mighty citadel. It is well-wooded, and covered with rich verdure to its summit. Four miles northwest of Manuä is Oloosinga, which consists of a narrow ledge of rocks, three miles long, rising abruptly from the water. The only portion of it that is productive, is a narrow strip running lengthwise of the island, and overspread with the most luxuriant vegetation. Ofoo

lies west of Oloosinga, from which it is separated by a channel
for boats, one quarter of a mile in width. It is of but little
importance, and contains but few inhabitants, most of them
having been cut off during the bloody wars that have more
than decimated the population of the islands.

Fifteen miles west of Ofoo and Oloosinga, from which it is
visible in fine weather, is Tutuila, the most central island,
and one of the most important of the group. It is nearly
fifty miles in circumference ; its shores are precipitous ; and
it has, generally, a broken and rugged appearance, occasioned
by the numerous sharp spurs and ridges that vary its surface,
—though its scenery is highly romantic, and its unevenness
is more than half concealed by the dense forests of cocoas and
bread-fruits, whose thickly-matted foliage, interlaced with
innumerable vines and creepers, covers the island as with a
carpet, which, when disturbed by the summer wind, rises
and falls, in wavy undulations, like the billows of the ocean.
The highest peak on Tutuila is Matafoä, upwards of twenty-
three hundred feet above the ocean. It contains a large population, who are chiefly congregated in the valleys and plains
sloping down to the sea. Lofty and impassable hills separate
the island into two parts, the only communication between
which is by the sea shore,—the one, on the northeast, exceedingly rough and uneven ; and the other, on the south-
west, lower, more level, and more easy of cultivation.—
Tutuila was visited by the unfortunate La Pérouse, in December, 1788, and derives something of its importance from
the fact, that M. de Langlè, the captain of the Astrolabe,
and the naturalist of the Expedition, with ten other persons,
lost their lives on the island, in a collision with the natives.

Upolu, thirty-six miles west of Tutuila, is seventy miles
in circumference. It is not so lofty, nor so much broken, as
the other islands of the group, and in population, beauty and
fertility, far exceeds either of them. The land rises gradually, for some distance from the shore, and then breaks into a
succession of mountainous ridges, clothed to the top with
verdure of the richest green. Wide tracts of table land lie

9

along the coast; and there are broad valleys between the ridges, carpeted with the finest tropical flowers, and sprinkled with clumps and groves, of bread-fruit, pandanus, and cocoa-nut. The steep hill-sides are fringed with the white foliage of the candle-nut, with the long waving fronds of arborescent ferns and the graceful plumes of the mountain palm. The clustering hamlets of the natives are scattered here and there; and the tasteful cottage of the missionary, and the neat chapel, peep out, once in a while, from the deeply-shaded bowers that overhang them. The beautiful and the wild, the pretty and the picturesque, are exhibited in striking contrast. On one side, there is all the dreamy softness of an Italian landscape; on the other, the sublime grandeur of Alpine scenery. Tiny brooklets, singing ever so many a joyous lullaby, course down the upper slopes, and anon, widening into miniature rivers, leap in cascades of milky foam over precipices seven hundred feet above the level of the ocean. Wild glades and glens there are, within whose sylvan recesses the spirit of romance might forever love to linger, and where

> " Gentle gales,
> Fanning their odoriferous wings, dispense
> Native perfumes, and whisper whence they stole
> Their balmy spoils."

Within the sea reef of Upolu, and near its western extremity, is the island of Manono, but four miles in circumference, yet containing eleven hundred inhabitants and a missionary station. Connected with Upolu and Manono by a line of soundings, is Apolima—in former days the *olo* (citadel), or place of refuge, of the inhabitants of Manono in time of war and danger. This is a small castellated island, the crater of an extinct volcano, surrounded by perpendicular cliffs almost five hundred feet high, which are unbroken and inaccessible save at one point, where there is a slight indentation, forming a bay, with an entrance large enough to admit the passage of one small boat at a time, and therefore quite easy to be defended against a much superior enemy. On the elevated tableau there is sufficient depth of soil to support the cocoa, bread-fruit, and banana; and taro and yams are cultivated by the inhabitants, who do not exceed five hundred in number.

Savaii, the farthest west, and the largest of the group, is also connected with Apolima by a line of soundings. It is not as populous or as important as Upolu, and its coast outline is much less beautiful. It is over one hundred miles in circumference, and is protected, on the north and east, from the violence of the surf, by reefs of coral; but, on the opposite sides, the breakers dash unchecked against its rocky bulwarks. Except on the south and west, the shores are low, and there is a gradual ascent to the centre of the island, where many abrupt volcanic craters are seen, whose fires were long since silenced, above which towers a single peak, four thousand five hundred feet high, almost always enveloped in clouds, and in a clear day visible at a distance of fifty or sixty miles.

Mountain streamlets, sometimes forming quite respectable rivers, frequently intersect the larger islands, with the exception of Savaii, which has no permanent streams, though possessing an abundance of copious springs. There are likewise numerous lakes and waterfalls,—the latter of which may one day be serviceable for mills or machinery. On Upolu there is a pretty lake, called Laüto, occupying the basin of a crater, twenty-four hundred and fifty feet above the sea, with nine and a half fathoms of water in its deepest part, and a subterranean outlet.

Like the Society Islands, the members of this group are generally surrounded by coral reefs, with occasional channels, or openings, dividing them, through which vessels may pass, and appear to be of volcanic origin. The general structure of the islands is conglomerate, of a drab color, lying in horizontal strata. The mural walls and precipices upon which, as it were, the upper stratum, or productive soil, rests, are of basaltic rock. There is an abundance of scoria; currents of lava are visible; and it is also found in large blocks full of vesicles. The rocks of basaltic lava contain augite, olivine, common feldspar and albite. All the higher hills and mountain peaks are crateriform. The beaches consist of a light-colored sand, composed of a mixture of coral and shells. Coral *débris* is found on the smaller islands, and along the shores of the larger ones. The soil is principally formed of decomposed volcanic rocks and vegetable mould.

The climate is mild and agreeable, and the mean temperature about 80°. It is more moist than at Tahiti, and the vegetation is more thrifty. Nearly one third of the days in a year are rainy. From April to November, the season is fine, —the winds being light, and affording merely a pleasant variety to the long-continued calms. During the remainder of the year high winds prevail, principally from the southward and eastward. Destructive hurricanes sometimes occur, and earthquakes are not infrequent. The latter are not usually violent, but produce a slight wavy motion, like that of a vessel in an ordinary sea.

(3.) On the northwest side of Manuä, there is a small settlement, and anchorage ground for vessels of light draught, with a pretty little cove to land in, in pleasant weather. Near the village are a number of irregularly-shaped stone walls, the object of the erection of which is not known, but they are supposed to have been intended for defence.

Pago-pago, on the south side of the island of Tutuila, is the largest, and in many respects the most important harbor, in the group. It is deep and land-locked—penetrating so far into the interior as to cut the island nearly in two, and lined on both sides by steep inaccessible precipices, from eight hundred to a thousand feet high. The coast, on either hand of the entrance, which is about one third of a mile in width, is bold and rugged. Opposite the opening, at some three miles distance from the shore, is a coral bank on which the sea breaks in stormy weather. Except during a strong southerly gale, vessels of almost any class may run into the harbor in safety. If the wind be unfavorable, it requires considerable tacking to get in or out, but the place boasts a white pilot, who has established himself there. and is always ready to come off when the proper signal is given. The village of Pago-pago contains but about forty dwellings, a council-house, (*fale-tele*), and a neat church. Supplies can be obtained here in abundance.

On the southern coast of Tutuila, there are, also, two other small villages, called Faigatuä and Leone, belonging to the "devil's men," as the heathen, or unconverted natives, are styled by the christian party. There are, likewise, desirable ports, or bays, on the north side of the island, at which vessels can procure water and supplies. Among them are Fungasar and Massacre Bay,—the latter the scene of the murder of M. de Langlè and his party.

Apia, on Upolu, is a safe and spacious harbor, less difficult of access than Pago-pago. It faces the north, and ordinarily admits of easy ingress and egress. The bottom is sandy, and at twenty-five yards distance from the shore, there are five fathoms of water. As a river empties into the bay which forms the harbor, fresh water is easily obtained. The town of Apia is about the same size as Pago-pago, and contains a large *fale-tele*, and a pretty white stone church, constructed under the direction of the missionaries. Twenty miles west of Apia, is Fasetootai, having a small harbor within the reef; and between the two places is Sagana, a neat settlement containing six hundred inhabitants, and a missionary school. It is situated on a peninsula, and is surrounded by cultivated grounds, intersected by broad walks and paths, the fruits and crops growing on which are protected from the ravages of the swine by a stone wall extending across the isthmus.

Savaii has numerous inlets, but they are either too shallow to float large vessels, or only large enough to admit the entrance of small boats. Mataätuä Bay, on the north point of the island, is an exception, however, and affords good anchorage except when northwesterly winds prevail. Paluale on the eastern end of the island, and Felialupo on the northwestern point, are small but pleasantly located villages.

(4.) Formerly, the population of the Navigator Group was supposed to be one hundred thousand, but it is now estimated by the missionaries at only sixty thousand. Infanticide has never been practiced here, as at the Society Islands; but severe and bloody wars have been frequent, sometimes whole districts being depopulated by them. It is not improbable, therefore, though by no means certain, that the number of inhabitants is not so large as at the time of the first discovery of the islands.

In complexion, the Samoän is, perhaps, a shade darker than the Society Islander, but in their features there is a strong resemblance. The first is taller and better formed, and altogether of more commanding presence, than any of the other Polynesians, except, it may be, the Tongese. Generally speaking, the inhabitants of the Navigators' Islands have frank and open, intelligent and pleasing countenances; their eyes are black; their teeth good and white; and their hair dark, coarse, and straight, though sometimes curled, or frizzled. The men are strong and muscular, fierce and warlike, active and energetic in disposition. There is a wide difference, however, between the chiefs and the *kanakas*, or common people, in regard to personal appearance. The former are more athletic, better made, and superior in physical strength and dignity of deportment.*

When young, the Samoän women are tolerably handsome; but as they advance in years, they become too stout and corpulent to be called even good-looking. But this change is not produced, as might be supposed, by hard labor or ill-usage. On the contrary, woman is here treated with a respect not usual among the savage islanders; she enjoys nearly the same privileges as the man; the affections are strongly manifested, and the ties between husband and wife,

---

* This fact has been remarked almost everywhere in the Pacific, and has led many travellers and scientific men to suppose, not without reason, that the Polynesian chiefs belong to a distinct race who reduced the former occupants of the islands to subjection.—See Ellis' Polynesian Researches, Vol. I, p. 78, et seq.; and Moerenhout, Vol. II, p. 247, et seq.

parent and child, in the main sacredly regarded. All the hard work, even that of cooking, is performed by the men, while their wives and daughters are engaged in beating *tapa*, or some other light employment. The women are reserved in their manners, and particularly cautious in their intercourse with foreigners : though chastity is a rare virtue in the Pacific, where they have not been corrupted by the whites, they possess a great deal of that native modesty, which, like the element of fire, can never change its nature,

> " But burns as brightly in a gipsy camp,
>   As in a palace hall."

Adultery is not common, even among the " devil's men ;" and wherever the missionary influence has extended, it is regarded as a high offence, and is severely punished. Polygamy is still practiced to some extent, but it is nearly abolished ; and a great many have been forced to yield to public opinion on this subject, who, wedded to ancient customs, look back to the days when that abomination was generally tolerated, with regret. The husband may repudiate his wife, however, if he is so inclined ; but the wife cannot separate herself from her husband without his consent.

The Samoäns are thrifty and industrious, though, as their wants are so easily supplied, there is little inducement to labor. They are cunning and inquisitive, yet generally honest and well-behaved. On public occasions, in the church or council-house, they are sedate in manner, but they have kind and social dispositions, and are extremely fond of visiting. They can conduct themselves with great propriety, whenever it is necessary, for they are not deficient in self-respect ; but their hearts are naturally as light as the soft atmosphere that rests over their verdant hills and lovely valleys. They are fond of receiving presents, and often liberal in tendering them, in return, though not offended when they are declined. Hospitality is one of their chief virtues ; still they always expect pay for any services they may render, not so much out of selfishness, as because they have always been accustomed to receive gifts, by way of remuneration or otherwise, from the whites, ever since the first discovery of the group. Their minds are susceptible of cultivation, and a thirst for obtaining information pervades all classes. They are a poetic people, and have numerous beautiful legends, which they are fond of repeating. They have some considerable musical talent, too, and the males have clear and fine voices; their singing is monotonous, but correct in harmony.

Pride of character is not wanting among them; their chiefs know very well how to maintain their dignity, and, while thus solicitous on their own account, they hold the memory and reputation of their ancestors, in great veneration and esteem. A calm and dignified mien is thought to be the most fitting at their public assemblages, except where amusement is the order of the day; the utmost decorum is preserved; no one stands in the presence of his superior; and all conversation is carried on in a whisper. In respect to talent, they are far above mediocrity, as those will bear witness who have observed the shrewdness, tact, and ability, displayed by the speakers at the native councils.

Cleanliness in their personal habits is another characteristic of this people. The first thing the Samoän does in the morning, after he rises from his rude couch, and before going to his daily occupation, is to bathe thoroughly; and then he anoints his body with cocoa-nut oil and turmeric,—both for the sake of the shining appearance thereby communicated, which they esteem an ornament, and, as they allege, to preserve their suppleness and elasticity of limb. The females bathe daily, and anoint their bodies, as well as the men. All, of every age and sex, practice frequent bathing, not merely as a cleanly habit, but as an amusement; and they have become so much attached to it, that the missionaries have felt constrained to prohibit it altogether on the Sabbath. Excessive eating, bordering on gluttony, is a common vice, but they drink sparingly of wine and liquors, unless it be among the inhabitants of the "devil's towns," where greater latitude is claimed and allowed.

There are, of course, exceptions to these general remarks in regard to the traits and characteristics of the people of the Navigator Group. A striking difference is observable between the towns belonging to the "devil's men," and those of the other party ; and a similar difference may be remarked in the conduct of their respective inhabitants. But their natural dispositions are the same, whether they be christian or heathen, only the better qualities which all possess, are more conspicuous in the former than in the latter. The heathen are more wild, blood-thirsty, and vindictive than the christians ; but, though living side by side, there are comparatively few broils and contentions between the two parties. The "devil's men" are equally hospitable with their neighbors, when the fit is on them, but they are sometimes sullen and surly, though it is said that strangers may travel through their towns and districts, entirely unarmed, without being molested. Fondness for *ava* was once a national failing, and the heathen continue to drink it to excess ; they are also great gormands, and frequently have large feasts, at which they devour numbers of hogs, and quantities of other eatables, till their literally swinish appetites become completely satiated. The heathen women are bashful and reserved to some extent,—more so, indeed, than might be expected,—yet they lack the remarkable *naïveté* of the christian damsel.

For some reason or other, also, the people of Savaii differ slightly in physiognomy, and in their manners and appearance, from the inhabitants of the other islands ; their features are more regular, and the women more gracefully formed. Their spears and war-clubs, too, are not exactly of the same fashion, and they are more neatly made.

A fondness for traffic is common to them all ; they are ever ready to exchange their fruit, fowls, and hogs, for tools, cloth, powder, tobacco, and trinkets, though the christians care but little for the last two. They are quite shrewd at a

9*

bargain, and the people of Savaii would do no discredit, in this respect, to the land of wooden nutmegs and cucumber seeds.

Fevers and syphilitic complaints are very rare on these islands. The diseases to which the inhabitants are subject, are generally of a sporadic character. The most prevalent are dysentery, caries, catarrh, and bronchial disorders. Ophthalmia is often produced by the heat of the sun reflected from the sand. Elephantiasis,—which is here attributed to eating food without salt, drinking cocoa-nut water, exposure at night, and want of exercise,—is also quite common. Children are very liable to an eruptive complaint, called *ilumea*, which breaks out on their heads. The only remedy which the natives had for disease, besides bathing, was shampooing; but since the missionaries appeared among them, they have been supplied with proper medicines as far as was possible, and have received better medical attendance.

It has been well doubted whether any living language could be properly regarded as the parent stock of the Polynesian.* The language of the Samoän Group is, doubtless, a branch of the Malay; but it has so many features analogous to other tongues and dialects, that it would require all the credulity of Lord Kingsborough to reconcile them. It is constructed like the Tahitian, though it is smoother, softer, more flexible, and not so easily spoken. It is the only Polynesian language in which the sound of *s* is heard. Notwithstanding the resemblance, in its construction, to that of the Society Islands, the inhabitants of that group and the Samoäns cannot understand each other.

The *maro* was, originally, almost the only article of clothing worn by the natives; and it is now the ordinary dress of the common people, being well adapted for active exercise, not cumbersome, light, easily made, and easily renewed. It is constructed of the leaves of the ti, (*dracœna*,) which are sometimes slit, and thus form a short petticoat. It is worn about the loins and between the thighs, so as to conceal the

---

* Crawfurd's Indian Archipelago, Vol. II, p. 80, et seq.

pubes. A dress, called the *titi*, made of the same materials, is also worn in the heathen villages, particularly by the females : it is merely an apron or girdle extending round the body, and reaching from the loins half way down the thighs or to the knees. The *titi* is much cooler than the *maro*, but like the latter requires frequent changing, as the leaves soon wilt and decay. *Tapa* mantles are worn by the chiefs and their attendants, whenever they appear in public. Beautiful shaggy mats made of the fibres of the hibiscus, fastened at the neck and hanging down to the feet, are worn by the wives and daughters of chiefs.

Latterly, the missionaries have introduced the *siapo* from the Friendly Islands. This garment resembles the Tahitian *pareu*, and is either made of cotton cloth, or of ti or pandanus leaves. They have also brought the *tiputa*,—the ancient dress of the women in the Society Islands, and like the South American *poncho* in shape and form,—into partial use, among the Samoän women.

Articles of European costume are occasionally seen. Some of the chiefs are the owners of white striped cotton shirts, white vests, sailors' blue cloth round jackets and pantaloons, fur hats and coarse brogans, in which they appear on extraordinary occasions ; and their wives and daughters are equally fortunate in the possession of calico or gingham frocks, waist ribbons, flaring straw bonnets, and morocco shoes.

Of ornaments but few are worn. After taking her daily bath, and anointing her person, the Samoän girl sometimes arranges her hair in ringlets, entwined with flowers : but this practice is fast going out of date, as it is now the custom to crop the hair close in the christian towns, and it is often filled with fine coral sand, lime, or ashes, to destroy the vermin. The missionaries, too, have interdicted the use of flowers. The native men wear a shell suspended from the neck by a string, as an amulet. Tattooing is regarded as the emblem of manhood ; it is performed, at from fourteen to eighteen years of age, and is very expensive. The males have their whole bodies, from their breasts to their knees, covered with the ornaments ; but the females have only a few lines around their hands, arms, and legs. The young women in the heathen villages also paint a spot on each breast, from the size of a dollar to that of a small plate, of a reddish brown color.

In the christian towns the hair is shaven close, but among the heathen it is suffered to grow, and gathered in a knot at the back of the head, which adds very much to their wild and ferocious appearance.

Having few wants, the Ṣamoän has few cares. A house, a taro and yam patch, a visiting canoe, a half dozen pigs, several bread-fruit and cocoa-nut trees, and a neat, well-form-ed woman, for a wife, will satisfy the ambition of any man. But though all these are easily acquired, the converted Sa-moän is not improvident, though eating, bathing, sleeping, and dancing, are the chief employments and occupations of his heathen neighbor. In the christian villages the men assist in cooking, cultivate and weed their taro and yam patches, repair their fences, build houses and canoes, and make sennit The women do the light household work, beat tapa, and weave mats and other similar articles. The boys and girls in a family either wait upon their parents, or spend their time in playing. Both young and old occupy a great many of their leisure hours in reading and study, of which they are very fond ; and there are now between ten and twelve thou-sand persons in the group who can read with great facility.

Fishing and bird-catching are favorite amusements of all classes ; and it is needless to say that a great deal of skill and expertness is exhibited in their prosecution. Of boxing and wrestling they were likewise once fond, but these sports are much less common now. Singing and dancing are not so much in vogue as formerly, except in the heathen towns. The chief dance is called *siva ;* it is lascivious and ungrace-ful, and the christian girl cannot easily be induced to exhibit in it. This dance consists in throwing the legs, arms, and bodies, into divers graceless and wanton postures ; and is per-formed at the *fale-teles* in the heathen towns, by the native girls, for the entertainment of guests and visitors. The men likewise have their dances, which are not so indecorous, and which they perform in parties, advancing and retreating, clapping their hands, and stamping with their feet.

Their principal musical instruments are the drum and flute. The first is long and narrow, and is made of a part of a tree hollowed out. The flute is of bamboo, usually about one inch in diameter and sixteen inches long. They also make pipes of the bamboo, and have a rude sort of guitar formed of a loose slat fitted into a piece of board, upon which they beat with two sticks.

They have a number of games. Among them is that of *lafe*, which resembles shuffle board, and is played by the chiefs only, on a mat, with cocoa-nut shells finely carved and ornamented. *Tuaë-fuä* consists in keeping balls in the air, like the Chinese jugglers; and *litia*, in throwing light spears of hibiscus rods. *Lupe* is played by two persons; the one strikes the back of his closed fist on a table, and then holds up, instantly, one or more fingers; if his opponent fails to hold up the same fingers immediately, he loses one point, and there are ten in the game.

In each village there is a *fale-tele*, or council house, where the *fonos*, or public meetings, are held. In the heathen towns, also, strangers are entertained in them with feasts and dances.

When the Samoän salutes a friend, or visitor, he takes his hand, and rubs the back of it against his own nose.

As in most savage, or unenlightened nations, wives are obtained by making presents to the parents, usually to the father. Marriages take place early. Girls are betrothed without regard to age, and are *saä*, or *taboo*, till they become marriageable. After the betrothal, the parties commence the preparations for housekeeping; a house is built, and a supply of mats and *tapas* made. Two days previous to the marriage are taken up with feasts and amusements; and on the third day, the bride is produced before the guests, the Jewish ceremony customary on such occasions is performed, the marriage is consummated, and the day ends, among the heathen, in riotous feasting and dancing.

Parturition takes place without danger, difficulty, or ceremony. After delivery, the mother takes the infant to the nearest spring, bathes it, and returns to her ordinary occupations, just as if nothing had happened. Names are given to males and females indiscriminately, previous to the birth. Children are usually suckled till they are six years old, and some women have been known to suckle two or three of their offspring of different ages, at the same time.

They are not very ceremonious in regard to burials, but it is customary to feast those who are present.

In the preparation of food, their customs are similar to those which prevail throughout the Pacific islands. Their stove is the well-known Polynesian one—a hollow in the earth lined with heated stones, and another layer over the articles to be cooked, with a thin covering of earth and leaves above. They have no fixed time for taking their meals, but eat when they are hungry. Pork, fowls, birds, fish, bread-fruit, cocoanuts, bananas, taro and yams, are their chief articles of food. Rata, the native chestnut, is also much eaten. The sour paste, called *mahi*, made from the bread-fruit, is used when the trees are not in a bearing state. Pig, taro and bread-fruit, are served up for visitors on banana leaves ; and sometimes cooked bread-fruit, or the delicious cocoa-nut pudding (*faiai*), is handed round in wooden trays. When eaten, the bread-fruit is dipped in salt water, or cocoa-nut oil. Their drinking vessels are made of cocoa-nut shells.

As has been before mentioned, the heathen are exceeding great gluttons. They eat hogs, biche de mer, echina, holithuria, and wood-maggots, entrails and all, with unusual *goût*.

They have a fine beverage in the cocoa-nut milk, which they heat in shells ; but they are far more attached, especially the " devil's men," to their stimulating *ava*. This is prepared in a most disgusting way. The ava plant, (*piper mythisticum*,) is chewed by the women, and then thrown into a large bowl—the saliva of the females, as in the manufacture of *chica* among the Indians of Chili, being supposed to produce the necessary fermentation ; water is then added, after which the delectable compound is strained through the leaves of the plant.   Being now fit for use, it is guzzled down by the Samoän toper, in copious draughts, stinted neither in number nor quantity.

(5.) There is no general sovereign head in these islands, and the Executive power is claimed, and in most cases really possessed, by the principal chiefs.   There are what may be termed four different estates—the principal chiefs, the alii, or minor chiefs, the *tulafales*, or landholders, and the common people.   The islands are divided into districts, each of which has a principal chief, though some are of superior rank to others, and a distinct government.   The *fonos*, or public meetings, are attended by the *alii* and *tulafales*, who decide what is to be done.   The most influential chiefs generally carry everything before them.   The *tulu-fono*, or decision of the council, is always held in respect, and must be obeyed.

Upolu and Savaii, though divided into districts, and Manono, which, with Apolima, constitutes a district by itself, are united together in a sort of compact ; that is, on occasions affecting the general welfare, the principal chiefs of the different districts meet together in council, and act in concert in carrying their determinations into effect.   Tutuila is divided into several districts, the head chiefs of which frequently hold similar councils.   Manuä, Ofoo, and Oloosinga, have what is called, by way of courtesy, a king, who resides sometimes on one island and sometimes on another ; but he is little more than a chief of the highest rank, and his authority is treated with very little respect.

Few crimes are committed ; and the state of society is fully as good, and personal rights are as much respected, as could reasonably be looked for, considering how short a time has elapsed since the light of civilization and christianity first dawned upon these islands.   Among the christians, the ten commandments constitute their common law ; and any infringement of them is punished, usually with promptitude, by expelling the offender from the church and forbidding his attendance on public worship. Deep disgrace always attaches to those who have been thus dealt with. In the heathen towns, crimes are punished by expulsion from the particular village or community to which the offending person belongs, by exposure of the body to the heat of the sun, by flogging, by cutting off the ears, by confiscation of property, or by being compelled to eat noxious herbs. A murder is avenged by the friends and relatives of the deceased, by putting to death the murderer and his family, if they are within reach. A compensation, however, is sometimes made, in property, for a murder; and there are places of refuge, such as the tombs of great chiefs, which are deemed sacred, and those who escape to them are free from molestation.

Numerous divinities are worshipped by the heathen, and were formerly held in reverence and esteem by all the inhabitants of the group. They have one chief, or principal god; three war gods; a god of earthquakes; a god who supports the earth; gods of lightning, wind, and rain; and a great number of inferior deities, called *aitus*. Each chief has his *aitu*, or familiar spirit, who adheres to him through life, like the Demon of the ancient Greek, and whose commands he is bound to obey. Some of the chiefs, whose vanity and self-esteem are pretty prominent, believe that after death they become *aitus*, and, in turn, exercise the office of spiritual guide and protector. These *aitus* are adopted arbitrarily, and, in general, are birds, animals, or reptiles. After their conversion, the christian chiefs treated them with little ceremony; and it is said of one, whose *aitu* was fresh water eels, that the first thing he did was to kill and eat them.

It is now but about thirty years since the missionaries of the British Board began their labors in the Samoän Group. Relying solely upon moral suasion, preaching, in truth, a gospel of peace, and discarding entirely the use of forcible means, they have obtained an influence which is felt, and that beneficially, everywhere throughout the islands.*   A few abandoned white men, in connection with the heathen chiefs, have endeavored to counteract their efforts ; but they have never been injured or insulted.   The results of their ministry are before the world.

Old customs, some of which,—the use of flowers, for instance,—might, we think, have been retained without prejudice, have been done away, and newer and better ones introduced.   One third of the whole population are professed christians.   The schools established in the different towns are attended by over twelve thousand pupils, children and adults.   Ordinarily, it is as still and quiet on the Sabbath as in a New England village.   Great attention is paid to religious duties ; frequent exercises are held during the week ; and grace before meals, and morning and evening prayers, are said.   There are about a dozen missionaries, who are assisted by one hundred and fifty native teachers, on the different islands.   They have a printing press at Upolu ; and nearly all the Bible has been translated and printed by them, and read by the natives.

(6.) The houses of the natives are of an elliptical form, and from twenty to forty feet in length.   They are generally built amidst groves of bread-fruit trees, which afford their inmates a shelter from the storm, and a protection against the rays of the sun.   Sometimes they are erected on the bare earth, and sometimes on flagged terraces of stone raised from two to four feet above the ground.   In the former case, it is usual to cover the floors with a layer of small stones, in order to keep them dry.   In the centre of one of these houses, there are several upright posts, varying in number with the size of the building, from twelve to fifteen feet high, upon which a ridge pole is laid and firmly secured by lashings of sennit.

---

* One of the most efficient and successful of the missionaries on the Navigators' Islands, was the Rev. John Williams, author of " Missionary Enterprises," and " The Missionary's Farewell," who fell a victim to the cause in which he was so zealously engaged, shortly after the squadron sailed from the group,— being murdered by the natives of the New Hebrides, whither he had gone to propagate the gospel.

Rafters, fastened in the same manner, reach from this pole down to the outer circle of posts, about four feet in height, upon which are extended long sticks or plates. The rafters are connected with centre posts, nearly half way down, by a network of cross beams and braces. The roof is thatched, beginning at the top and working downwards, and projects from twelve to eighteen inches, like eaves. Bamboo, hibiscus rods, and the small branches of other trees, wattled together, form the siding.

Great ingenuity is displayed in building their houses, though in their shape they have probably imitated those of the Friendly Islanders. The wood of the bread-fruit is principally used for all the main timbers and posts. The rafters are made of hibiscus. All the fastenings are of sennit. Their *fale-teles*, or council houses, are of the same general fashion, though larger and more firmly built.

The floors of the houses are covered with coarse mats, and in the better class, finer ones are spread over these, on all occasions of ceremony. A few rough-hewn stools and benches are the seats commonly seen; but in the houses of the wealthier chiefs, a raised dais extends round the inside of the outer wall. They sleep on the coarse mats used for carpeting, with a piece of bamboo, or tamanu wood, supported on sticks, for a pillow; and sometimes a piece of colored *tapa* is hung above their place of repose, to protect them against the musquitoes. Baskets, mats, and cocoa-nut shells for eating and drinking, of which they usually have an abundance, are scattered about in every part of the dwelling, and conspicuous among the articles of furniture, is the vessel in which *ava* is prepared—the wassail bowl of the Samoän. Now and then an old musket may be observed; and in the houses of the "devil's men" there is always a formidable array of clubs and spears, made of the iron wood (*casuarina*,) and of bows and arrows. At night, a lamp, consisting of a cocoa shell, filled with the oil of the nut, and having a piece of vine stalk for a wick, is kept burning till daylight, near one of the main centre posts, where the hearth for the fire is situated.

(7.) Next to the inhabitants of the Caroline Islands, the Samoäns, or Navigators, are the most skilful sailors and fishermen in all Polynesia ; and they received their name from De Bougainville, because of the superior construction of their canoes, and their surprising dexterity in the water. Abundant supplies of water and provisions may be obtained by vessels on these islands, but there are few articles adapted for foreign commerce ; still they may eventually become of some importance in this respect, especially as their situation in the Great Archipelago is so central, and they have such fine harbors. Tamanu wood for furniture, the casuarina for its rich dye, and other trees for their valuable gums, may yet be profitable articles of exportation. The inhabitants now have considerably more cocoa-nut oil and arrow-root, than can be used by themselves and their ordinary visitors. Tortoise shell can also be obtained in great plenty at Savaii. In exchange for what they are willing to dispose of, they mainly desire useful articles,—such as cotton cloths, writing paper, hardware, needles and tools.

Springs, lakes, and streams, abound in the islands, and machinery might be worked advantageously in many places. The natives have shown that they did not lack ingenuity, by their discovery of the uses to which the wood of their forest and fruit trees might be applied, and the construction of so many articles of necessity and comfort, with their miserable adzes and other tools, made of stone, shell, or bone. Since they have been able to procure iron instruments, they have executed their work much more neatly and handily. Cocoa-nut oil is made in the same manner as in the Society Islands. They likewise prepare a very good article of lampblack from the candle-nut, by burning large quantities of it in a curiously constructed oven. This is used in painting their canoes, idols and drums, and ornamenting their garments with various devices.

Tapa is not made as good here as at the Society Islands. The mallet used is larger, and the board is not springy. Some of their mats, however, are very beautiful, and are as smooth and soft as nankeen cotton. But few of this quality are now made, as a single one requires nearly a year's labor. A species of cloth, of which *pareus*, *siapos*, and *tiputas*, are made, is manufactured, by the women, of course, of the inner bark of the Chinese paper mulberry (*morus papyrifera*); and the tree is now cultivated for this purpose in nurseries. The stems, or branches, are cut when small, and the gum separated from the bark by washing. The bark is then beaten like *tapa*. Both the mulberry cloth and *tapa* are varnished with the gum obtained from the tuitui tree, or dyed in fanciful colors with other materials.

The largest canoes of the natives are from thirty to forty feet long, and will hold twenty or twenty-five persons. Some are built of a single log, having pieces fastened upon it, to raise it as high as is desired. Others are formed of several pieces of bread-fruit planks, rudely dovetailed together, and secured with sennit. They are covered in at both ends,— thus presenting decks forward and aft. The former is the post of honor, where the chiefs usually sit crosslegged on a platform, underneath an awning made of pandanus leaves. For cement, they use pitch manufactured from the gum of the bread-fruit tree. The paddles are long, narrow, and elegantly shaped; and they are used with great dexterity. Double canoes are made by lashing two single ones side by side. Both are very swift, and are managed with a skill almost unparalleled. The sail, usually of a half oval shape, serves the purpose of an outrigger, and is used to windward or leeward, as may be necessary. On the opposite side a boom projects, to steady the craft, which is secured to the top of the mast with guys.

Recently, several small vessels, of from twenty-five to forty tons burden, have been built by foreigners, to trade between the different islands, and with the neighboring groups.

(8.) Pigs and fowl in great numbers are found here. The natives are fond of the former, but they prefer selling to eating them. There are no native quadrupeds—the hog having been imported; and the only mammal observed, is the bat, which is very destructive to the bread-fruit. Cattle have been introduced by the missionaries, and have increased so rapidly that vessels can now be supplied with fresh beef. There are but few horses in the group; yet these are highly prized. There are no venomous reptiles; but eels, and land and water snakes, are seen. Turtles are also quite common.

Frigate birds, boobies and noddies, abound. Tern breed in great numbers in the thickets on the smaller islands. Sixty or seventy different kinds of pigeons are found, some of which are held sacred and kept as playthings. The principal singing bird is the philomel; but the woods and groves are filled with countless warblers, prominent among which is the *poë*, that make them vocal with their " wordless melody."

The most common fish are the mullet and the *lou*—the latter much smaller than the other. They are caught in casting nets, seines, and fishing weirs. Women also catch them by placing baskets near the holes in the reefs, where they take shelter. They are likewise speared by torchlight, and taken in deep water with a hook.

(9.) Being favored with a soil so fertile, and a climate so propitious, the productions of the Samoän Group are hardly excelled anywhere within the tropics. The thick tufts of the cocoa, and the long branching sprays of the tree-fern, probably cause the vegetation to appear more abundant than it really is; but if these were removed, a wilderness of choice fruits and rich blossoms would be revealed, to please the eye and gratify the appetite. But a small portion of the land is under cultivation, and there are thousands of acres untilled, where the coffee bush, the sugar cane, and the cotton plant, would thrive luxuriantly.

The cultivated trees and plants are the bread-fruit, cocoanut, banana, plantain, ti, paper-mulberry, tacca, sugar cane, coffee, ava plant, sweet potato, pine apple, melon, papaya, yam, taro, lemon, sweet orange and lime. The manufacture of sugar from the cane is yet in its infancy,—the natives having hitherto been accustomed to use the saccharine matter resembling molasses, obtained by baking ti-root in an oven and subjecting it to a heavy pressure. Arrow-root of a superior quality is made in limited quantities from the tacca. The yam, which is propagated like the potato—the vines running up trees, and when they die indicating that the roots are fit to eat—was formerly cultivated a great deal ; but it is now giving way, in a measure, to the taro, which is thought to be preferable by the natives.

Innumerable varieties of medicinal herbs spring up spontaneously in the valleys and on the mountain sides. Wild oranges are so abundant in some sections that the forest-paths are literally strewn with them. The cerbera, from which caoutchouc might be made, wild nutmeg, wild ginger, and the iris, abound. The trees are of great beauty and variety, and are often hidden beneath dense masses of ferns, convolvuli, and other vines—the rich drapery whose web and woof are supplied by Nature's own hand. They are remarkable not only for their size, but also for the beauty and fragrance of their flowers, and the lusciousness of their tempting fruits. Evergreens are quite numerous. Indeed, there are but two or three deciduous trees in the group. The new leaves push out the old ; and buds and blossoms, the young fruit and the ripe, appear together throughout the year.

Among the trees are the tamanu, hibiscus, pandanus, rata, pisonia, apapa, amai, or miro, tou (*cordia*), toi, toa (*casuarina*), candle-nut (*aleurites triloba*), ohwa, or native banyan, leafless acacia, bread-fruit and cocoa-nut. The most valuable of these for timber, are the tamanu, amai, tou, toi, toa, and bread-fruit. The tamanu attains a vast size, and is often five feet in diameter. It has a beautiful veiny grain, and will take a high polish. Canoes, stools, pillows, bowls, and other articles, are wrought from it with great labor. It would be extremely useful in ship building, as it is very durable, and holds a nail with great tenacity : iron likewise lasts better in it than in any other wood.—The wood of the amai is of a close firm texture, and of a dark brown color. It is but little variegated, but will receive a fine polish. It is worked without difficulty, and makes beautiful furniture. Its leaves were formerly used in religious ceremonies, and embassadors invariably carried a branch of it as an emblem of authority and of peace, like the vervain of the Roman *fecialis.*

The tou is a low umbrageous tree, and is generally planted near the dwellings of chiefs. It is not so hard as rosewood, but resembles it in grain. Rich looking furniture is manufactured from it; and the natives also use it in making wooden drums, which give a more sonorous and mellow sound than those made from the wood of other trees.—The toi is of medium size and height. In the vicinity of the heart, the wood is of a blood red color, but the outer parts are lighter and beautifully waved. It is like satin wood, and is susceptible of a high polish.—The toa, or iron wood, is a large tree, and bears a heavy canopy of graceful foliage. The wood is exceedingly hard and durable, and of a reddish brown color. The richly carved clubs and spears of the natives are made from it; and the missionaries have tried, and proved it to be valuable, for the sheaves of blocks, and for the cogs in their sugar mills and other similar articles. A fine and rich red dye may also be obtained from the wood of the toa.

Probably the bread-fruit is the most abundant of all the trees found in this group. Besides the numerous uses to which it is applied in the Society Islands, a thick cream is here obtained from it, by puncturing, which hardens when exposed to the sun, and, after being boiled, is a good substitute for pitch.

The candle-nut tree is plentifully distributed throughout the mountainous districts, where its white shining leaves contrast finely with the dark glossy foliage of the banana and bread-fruit. This tree bears an oily nut of the size of a walnut, of which domestic candles are made. A number of the nuts, having their husks stripped off, are strung on a rib of the cocoa-nut leaf, which is lighted when required for use. Lampblack is likewise prepared from this nut, as has been mentioned. A gum, of which a good varnish is made, is also obtained from the tree; and from the inner bark, a juice is procured, which is used instead of paint oil, and when mixed with lampblack, or with the dye of the casuarina, becomes so permanent that it cannot be washed off,—differing, in this respect, from the oil of the cocoa-nut, which, when joined with paint, does not dry.

(10.) Immediately after the arrival of the Squadron in the Samoän group, the different islands were divided among the vessels, for surveys and examinations.   An observatory was established on Tutuila, and the head-quarters of the commander of the Expedition temporarily fixed on that island. The Peacock and Flying Fish joined the Vincennes at Pagopago, on the 18th of October, and were at once ordered to proceed to Upolu.

While the Squadron remained at these islands, a *fono*, or council, was held by the chiefs of Upolu, Manono and Savaii, at the request of Captain Wilkes, in which rules and regulations were agreed upon and adopted, for the security and protection of American whalers.   A son of the Rev. Mr. Williams was likewise appointed Consul of the United States, and recognized as such by the Council.   But little dependence, however, is to be placed upon the agreement entered into at that time by the Samoän chiefs, as they have since shown, on more than one occasion, an undue readiness to violate their most solemn pledges.   During the stay of the American Expedition, also, a native was tried by a council of chiefs, for murdering an American citizen twelve months previous, and found guilty.   He was in the first instance sentenced to be executed, and preparations were made to carry the sentence into effect; but at the suggestion of Captains Wilkes and Hudson, his punishment was commuted to banishment for life, and he was afterwards conveyed to Wallis Island, on board one of the vessels of the Squadron, in their subsequent passage to Sydney.

All the islands, with their harbors, having been surveyed, —with the exception of the south side of Upolu, which was finished by the Porpoise, during another visit to the group,

in September, 1840,—the whole Squadron assembled at
Apia early on the 10th of November.   At eleven o'clock in
the forenoon, the signal was made to get under way ; and in
a short time thereafter, all sails were spread to catch the soft
breezes of the Pacific.   On the 18th instant, they entered the
Eastern Hemisphere, when they corrected their time,—one
day having been lost in doubling Cape Horn, as is always
the case.   Passing round the Feejee Islands, and between
them and the New Hebrides, they approached the coast of
New Holland on the 29th of November, and at sunset made
the light house on the headland of Port Jackson bay.   Having a fair wind, though the night was dark, they ran up to
Sydney, seven miles from the mouth of the inlet, without a
pilot.   On the following morning, the people of the town, and
the garrison in particular, were very much chagrined, when
they caught sight of the stripes and stars waving over the
flotilla which had entered their harbor with so little ceremony,
unheralded and unannounced.

10

CHAPTER X.

(1.) NEW HOLLAND—now more properly called the Continent of Australia*—was facetiously termed by Sydney
Smith, " the fifth or pickpocket quarter of the globe." Notwithstanding there is full as much truth as wit, in this designation of the late reverend canon of St. Paul's, the great
extent of this portion of the world, the peculiarities of its soil
and climate, the riches of its vegetable and botanical kingdom, and the character of the colonial establishments founded
here by Great Britain, surround it, as it were, with a deep
and absorbing interest.

The continent lies between latitude 10° 39′ and 39° 11′
S., and longitude 113° 5′ and 153° 16′ E. Its coast line is
estimated at 7750 miles, within which is an area of three
million square miles. Its greatest length, from east to west,
between Sandy Cape and Dirk Hartog's point, is twenty-four
hundred miles ; and its greatest width, from north to south,
is a little short of two thousand miles.

* *Australia* should not be confounded with *Australasia*. The former name
(*Terra Australis*) was originally given by the early navigators, to what they
supposed to be the vast Antarctic Continent, of which the different islands, and
points of land, they had discovered in the southern ocean, formed parts ; but it
is now applied to the continent heretofore known as New Holland,—whereas
Australasia embraces Australia, Tasmania, or Van Diemen's Land, New Cale-
donia, New Hebrides, Queen Charlotte's Islands, Solomon's Archipelago, the
Louisiades, New Britain, New Guinea, and New Zealand.

As early as 1526, a few accidental discoveries on the Australian coast were made by the Spaniards; but the first accurate information was obtained by the Dutch yacht Duyfhen, in 1606, which, while engaged in exploring the coast of New Guinea, discovered that portion of Australia extending south of Endeavor Straits, and gave it the name of New Holland. A few months later, Louis de Torres, a Spanish navigator, passed through the straits which bear his name, and made the northeastern point of Australia, an account of which was given to the world on his return. From 1616 to 1628, various discoveries, of greater or less extent, were made by the Dutch navigators, Hartog, Zeachem, Dewitt, and Carpenter; in 1627, Van Nuyt sailed along the southern coast of Australia, from Cape Leeuwin to Spencer's Gulf, to which his name has been given; and between the years 1642 and 1644, Tasman completed the discovery of a great part of the Australian coast line, and the island of Van Diemen's Land.

The result of these discoveries by the Dutch was, that about one half of the coast outline of the continent was surveyed; but the information which they had obtained was deemed of little consequence, and attracted so little attention, that it was soon more than half forgotten. At length, the English navigators entered with zeal and spirit upon the career of discovery. Between 1684 and 1690, Dampier explored a part of the west and northwest coasts, and subsequently extended his surveys to the neighboring islands. From 1763 to 1766, Wallis and Carteret were engaged on a similar errand, in the same quarter of the world. But it was reserved for the talented, and indefatigable Cook, to accomplish more, in a far briefer period, than the united labors of all those who had preceded him: he surveyed, in 1770, the whole eastern coast of Australia, and was the first to make known the important fact, that this *terra incognita* was a vast island-continent.

Shortly after the return of Cook, a number of expeditions were set on foot for exploring the newly discovered country; and in 1788 the first colony arrived there from England. In

1789, after the mutiny of the crew of the Bounty, Captain Bligh ran for a considerable distance along the north-eastern coast, and made some valuable observations. From 1791 to 1793, a series of discoveries on the northern coast were made by Edwards, Bligh, Portlock, Bampton, and Alt. In 1798, Flinders and Bass sailed round Van Diemen's Land, and made extensive surveys of the Australian coast, mostly in open boats. Grant, in the following year, explored that portion of the southern coast which bears his name. During the five ensuing years, Flinders was actively engaged in prosecuting his surveys and examinations along the eastern and southern coasts and the gulf of Carpentaria, till, unfortunately coming into collision with Baudin, the commander of the French expedition employed on the same coast and Van Diemen's Land, he was forcibly taken to the island of Mauritius and detained there for six years. His discoveries in regard to the coast outlines, and general geographical features of the new continent, were of great value, and were made use of by the French authorities without acknowledgment. Since his time, Captain King, and other officers of the British navy, have succeeded in exploring the whole northern coast.

In its coast outline, particularly on the south and west, Australia is iron-bound, and almost unbroken. It has numerous large and small harbors and inlets, on the eastern and northern shores; Port Phillip on the south, and Van Diemen's gulf on the west, are spacious harbors; Hervey's bay on the east, and Shark's bay on the west, are from forty to fifty miles in width and depth; but the only two great indentations are the Gulf of Carpentaria on the north, and Spencer's Gulf on the south.

From Cape Leeuwin to Spencer's Gulf, a distance of over thirteen hundred miles, the southern coast, generally, is low, sandy and barren, with only here and there an occasional eminence. The northern coast resembles the southern in this respect; but on the east and west coasts, there are parallel ridges or ranges of steep and precipitous mountains, extending northwardly from the southern extremity of the continent.

In regard to the interior but little was known for many years after the establishment of colonies on the island, and there is probably much yet to be learned.   A most remarkable feature in the coast outline, observed by all the navigators who examined it, was the absence of any outlets for large rivers; and the want of the facilities which they would have afforded, long retarded, and has always obstructed, inland discovery. In spite, however, of the numerous obstacles to the exploration of the interior—sustained by a patience that was inexhaustible, and animated by a spirit of perseverance that no danger or difficulty could intimidate—different parties have penetrated into the country from different points, and examined, for the most part satisfactorily, nearly one-fifth part of the whole continent.

Near the southern coast, in the neighborhood of Portland Bay, commences a dark and rugged mass of mountain land, called the Australian Grampians, which runs due north as far as latitude 36° 12′ S., where a range of grassy hills, diverging to the north-east, connects it with the Warragongs, or Australian Alps, whose lofty peaks, rising to the height of fifteen thousand feet above the level of the sea, are covered with eternal snow.   The Warragongs are the highest mountains in Australia,—the loftiest peak of the Grampians, Mount William, being but four thousand five hundred feet high, and that of the Liverpool range, from six to seven thousand feet: they run in a north-easterly direction, from the southern termination of the continent, near Cape Wilson, as low as 35° 20′ S.   In latitude 36° S., a chain called the Blue Mountains, which, in the early history of the colony, was long deemed impassable, branches off from the Warragongs, and following generally the direction of the eastern coast, forms the watershed between the eastern and western streams, and is finally lost in the more elevated Liverpool range, on the thirty-second parallel of southern latitude. Mount York, the highest peak of the Blue Mountains, is a little less than thirty-three hundred feet high.   The Liverpool range at first runs due east, for sixty or seventy miles;

but it then inclines again to the north, and may be traced as far as latitude 26° S.

At the western extremity of the continent, there are three parallel mountain ranges, all running northerly across the continent. The easternmost range is not continuous, but consists of two detached parallel chains extending longitudinally, near the 118th meridian, and separated from each other by a broad plain: they are comparatively unimportant, and in no case attain a greater elevation than one thousand feet. The second, called the Darling range, rises at Cape Chatham, and runs in a direct course to the northern coast, opposite Dampier's Archipelago: these mountains are from thirty to forty miles in width, and their highest altitude is about two thousand feet. The western chain runs close to the shore from Cape Leeuwin, and is called Koikyennuruff by the natives; one of its peaks, Toolbrunup, is three thousand feet high, and is supposed to be the loftiest in West Australia.

In latitude 33° S., a series of irregular mountain spurs or ranges branch off to the west, from the Blue mountains, which soon divide into detached groups; and the interior of the country, as far as has been explored, appears to be studded with isolated hills and mountains. Some of these are only of moderate elevation, but others are of great height. The Canobolas, for example, one of the detached groups branching off from the Blue mountains, are between four and five thousand feet high.

It was for a long time supposed that the interior of the continent was one vast desert; and this supposition was strengthened by the fact, that the wind which blew from that quarter was often as hot, dry, and scorching in its effects, as the African Harmattan. But after the repeated attempts to cross over the rugged and abrupt wall of mountains bordering upon the coast country, had at length proved successful, and the remarkable parallelism of the different ranges was made known, it was thought a broad expanse of table-land lay spread out between them. This opinion had scarcely been entertained, when the continued discoveries which were made, disclosed the existence of numerous rivers and streams, whose courses seemed to tend towards some great internal sea. All these ideas, however, are now known to be erroneous. Although, as remarked by Mr. Oxley, in the narrative of his adventurous tour,* " the whole form, character, and composition of this country, is so singular, that a conjecture is hardly hazarded before it is overturned,"—still, it seems but reasonable to infer, that Australia, so far as it respects the interior, is in an inchoäte or imperfect state, or, in other words, yet in process of formation. All the masses of mountain land, and the detached peaks, between the great ranges at either extremity of the continent, are separated by monotonous levels, or dead flats, singularly deficient in vegetation, which wear every appearance of having been recently submerged beneath the waters of the ocean.

Plutonic rocks are tolerably abundant in the principal ranges, yet the interior, though exhibiting so much that is anomalous in character, is apparently of Neptunian formation. The isolated peaks are composed of sandstone, and the soil of the flats is loose and porous, and strongly impregnated with salt. Small salt-lakes, or brine-pits, are very common in the dead levels. These low grounds are subject to inundations; but they are by no means regular, and are usually succeeded by long periods of drought. Box trees, polygonum, reeds, kangaroo grass, and other marsh plants, and trees and shrubs that delight in excessive moisture, taking root in the soil formed of the *débris* washed down from the high lands, spring up in the low wet places after each overflow, live their brief life, and wither and die. Other plants, to which the fertilizing slime and decomposing vegetation, though lacking humidity, afford sustenance enough, now make their appearance; stately rows of yarra trees, like files of soldiers, line the channels of the rivers, and the bights are crowded with dense thickets of eucalypti; yet all these are, in their turn, destroyed by the constant exposure

* Page 81.

to too much water. But remote from the streams and marshes, the country is, at all times and seasons, an arid desert—barren, dreary, and desolate.

The mountainous districts, on the contrary, are exceedingly rich and picturesque. Deep and impassable gulleys, generally the beds of rivers, sometimes three thousand feet deep,—on either hand precipice rising above precipice, rocks piled on rocks, Ossa upon Pelion,—intersect the ranges, and probably form the avenues by which the waters confined in lakes, in the elevated basins, originally escaped through their rocky barriers to the ocean. Plains and valleys are scattered everywhere amid the mountains, and grassy hills and undulations, slopes and terraces, lie spread out on their flanks, whose abundant fertility presents a strong contrast to the barrenness of the low country. Golden glades interspersed among the green holts, mark the progress of the settler; and the flocks and herds clambering up the mountain sides, indicate the certain rewards of industry and enterprise.

In all ordinary seasons, the high-lying plains and valleys are well-watered; but it is a remarkable fact, that the streams, which, when they leave the mountains, are rushing and impetuous torrents, at their embouchures are scarcely larger than mere burns or brooks. Near the bases of the ranges, they have high bergs, that protect the plains bordering upon them from the extremes of drought and flood, and the banks are being gradually extended by the process of formation constantly going on; but when the waters reach the low sandy levels, they spread over the surface, forming in the marshes dank pools, or tarns, which are connected together like the links of a chain. Evaporation, under the vertical sun, soon diminishes their volume; the thirsty and porous soil drinks up another large portion; and the remainder, after divers meanderings, at length reaches the ocean. This is especially true of the rivers and streamlets of the interior, whose systems are not yet developed, nor their courses permanently established.

If any reliance may be placed upon the appearances which

indicate the recent origin of the continent, the theory, or explanation, of its geological formation, may be this:—The mountain ranges and peaks were originally islands, and the spaces or intervals between them have been filled up by the wash of their streams. This process may now be witnessed in the flats of the interior; and, if we may so speak, we must wait for the complete development of the country, until these are covered to a still greater depth, by the decayed vegetable matter, and the deposits of the mountain torrents—and until the latter, as rivers, have established for themselves permanent channels. There is, indeed, much to be done. While Bathurst plains, lying on the west of the Blue mountains, are nearly two thousand feet above the level of the sea, the country sinks so rapidly as you advance to the westward, that, at a distance of eighty miles, the altitude is only six hundred feet. Ages may elapse, therefore, before the work will be accomplished; but Nature is never idle in her laboratory, and the designs of the Great Architect must, sooner or later, be fulfilled.

(2.) From what has been said in regard to the coast outline of Australia, it will readily be inferred, that there are few large harbors. It would, perhaps, be improper to place among these the Gulf of Carpentaria and Spencer's Gulf, since vessels are as liable to disasters within their headlands as upon the ocean itself, and sometimes even more so. Hervey's Bay on the eastern coast, and Shark's Bay on the western, are capacious natural harbors, being from forty to fifty miles in width and length, and have deep soundings. Van Diemen's Gulf, also on the western coast, and Port Phillip on the south, may likewise be ranked among those of the largest class. Encounter Bay, at the mouth of Murray river, King George's Sound, Western Port, and Corner Inlet, are likewise good harbors on the southern coast. But the harbors on the north and east are by far the most numerous. On the former coast are Exmouth Gulf, King's Sound, Brunswick Bay, Admiralty Gulf, Cambridge Gulf, Raffle's Bay, and Port Essington. On the east are Twofold Bay, Jervis Bay, Botany Bay, and Port

10*

Jackson. The last is, in a commercial point of view, of much greater importance than any of the other harbors that have been mentioned. This magnificent bay, or inlet, is of irregular form, and stretches about fifteen miles into the country. It is completely land-locked, and protected from every wind. The anchorage is excellent, its soundings being more than sufficient for the largest ships; and the whole British navy could safely ride within it. Its shores are indented by numerous small bays and coves, which also afford shelter from the wind, and have, in many cases, good anchoring grounds. Two gigantic cliffs, not quite two miles apart, and from two hundred and fifty to three hundred feet high, rise on either side of the main entrance; upon the most southerly of which is a lighthouse, whose lantern is elevated sixty-seven feet above the ground, and consequently, near three hundred and fifty feet above the sea. The bay is navigable for ships of any burden seven miles above Sydney.

Besides these more important harbors, there are a great number of smaller inlets, and estuaries at the mouths of the rivers, which are easy of access, safe and spacious, and may one day become serviceable.

Owing to the vicinage of the great dividing ranges to the eastern and western coasts, large rivers cannot accumulate; but as they mostly run through parallel valleys, the streams which are found at these two extremities of the continent, have longer courses than might be supposed. The rivers on the western coast are neither numerous, nor important; although burns of excellent water, many of which issue to the sea by noble estuaries, are abundant. The chief streams are the Swan and Canning rivers, which unite in Melville water, near the parallel of 32° southern latitude. The most important rivers that rise in the Blue mountains, on the east, are the Murroo, Clyde, Shoalhaven, Hawkesbury, Hunter, Hastings, and Brisbane, which have their outlets between the parallels of 27° and 36° S. The Boyne, a rapid mountain stream, falls into Port Curtis, in latitude 23° 56′ 30″ S., and the Pumice-stone into Moreton Bay, in 26° 54′ 30″. Endeavor river, celebrated as the place where Captain Cook repaired his ship after it had lain for twenty-eight hours on a coral reef, is in latitude 15° 27′ 12″ S. : it has a wide mouth, easy of entrance, but, at a short distance inland, will not float the smallest boat. The Brisbane is undoubtedly the largest river on the eastern coast. The Shoalhaven and Hawkesbury have fine large bays at their mouths, but like all the other rivers mentioned, their currents are so tortuous that they possess few facilities for internal navigation. The Hawkesbury carries off much the greater share of the rain that falls on the eastern face of the Blue mountains; its two most important tributaries, the Grose and Cox, issue directly from this range, through ravines in the sand-stone rocks,* of from one to thirty-four hundred feet in depth; and the Nepeän, the only other principal affluent, runs along the base of the same chain from fifty to sixty miles. The current of this stream is laggard, not usually exceeding two miles per hour, and it is subject to inundations. Its banks are near thirty feet high; but the water, in a freshet, sometimes rises as high as ninety feet, and spreads over a great extent of country. The floods occur as often, upon an average, as once in three years, frequently in the midst of harvest, when houses and barns, crops and herds, are suddenly swept to destruction by the rushing waters.

The Paramatta river, which enters Port Jackson, is but a small stream, and is navigable for steamers, only, sixteen miles above Sydney, where the tide ceases to flow.

Between longitude 124° 53′ E. and the 135th meridian, on the northern coast, are the Prince Regent, Roe, Hunter, Alligator, and Liverpool rivers. The first three flow between rocky and precipitous hills, from three to four hundred feet high; and the others wind their way lazily through muddy flats, and sandy and monotonous levels. All are full and wide streams, and enter the ocean by vast estuaries, in which

---

* It is computed that a mass of rock equal to 134 cubic miles, must have been displaced by the Cox, and nearly the same quantity by the Grose, in opening their way to the ocean.

the tide often rises to the height of thirty feet; but the largest of them, the Prince Regent, is not navigable for boats more than fifty miles from its mouth, including all its tortuosities. On the southern coast are the Blackwood, which falls into Flinder's Bay near the 115th meridian, and the Kalgan, or French river, about one hundred and fifty miles further east, which debouches into Oyster Harbor, the north part of King George's Sound. About sixteen miles east of Cape Northumberland, is the mouth of the Glenelg, one of the largest coast rivers in Australia: its source is in the Grampians, seventy miles from the sea; it has numerous affluents, and, counting its windings, is upwards of one hundred and thirty miles in length; it presents a narrow outlet to the sea, the entrance of which is choked up by sand-bars, but it soon expands, and, with this exception, is a wide and deep stream throughout its whole course.

There is no other river of importance on the southern coast, except the Murray, which rises in the Warragongs, and empties into Encounter Bay, in longitude 139° E. At its mouth it appears to be an insignificant stream, but, in fact, it includes within its basin an area of more than four hundred thousand square miles, and carries off the surplus waters of a great number of the rivers of the interior, whose systems, as has been before remarked, are yet undeveloped. Its principal tributaries are the Macquarrie, Lachlan, Morrumbidgee, and Darling. The first two are formed by the torrents descending the western face of the Blue mountains, and, in their progress to the interior, diverge, near the 149th meridian,—the Lachlan stretching to the north-west, and the Macquarrie pursuing a more northerly course. Both are large rivers,—the Macquarrie being sometimes capable of floating a ship of the line, within one hundred miles of its source. The Lachlan is more than twelve hundred miles in length, and the Macquarrie from seven to eight hundred. The Morrumbidgee rises in the Warragongs, and after running a tortuous westerly course, for not less than one thousand miles, joins the Murray in latitude 34° 45′ S. and longitude 143° 23′ E., having previously received the waters of the Lachlan. The Darling is a most singular stream; its waters being in some places brackish, then becoming sweet, and, still further below, again impregnated with salt: it is formed by the Gwydir, Dumaresq, and Castlereagh, all large streams, and other affluents of considerable size, whose sources are north of the Liverpool range; it describes, in its course, a curved line, upwards of one thousand miles long, inclosing all the country west of the Blue mountains; and, being joined by the Macquarrie, finally unites with the Murray near the 142d meridian, in latitude 34° 7′ S.

After receiving the Darling, the Murray, which has already traversed over fifteen hundred miles from its remote source in the Warragongs, continues on to Lake Alexandrina, which communicates by a narrow outlet with Encounter Bay,—a further distance, inclusive of the numerous windings, of fifteen hundred miles. Notwithstanding it has so many tributary streams, this river loses so much of its waters, like its affluents, by absorption and evaporation, that it is neither wide enough nor deep enough to admit of navigation; and, in addition, its mouth is defended by a double line of breakers, whose foam extends from one end of the bay to the other.

Lakes are abundant in Australia, but no very large ones have so far been discovered. Lake Alexandrina is the largest, and is fifty miles long and forty wide; yet, it is so shallow, in many places, that it cannot float even a boat. In 1828, there was a fine sheet of water, called Lake George, seventeen miles long and seven miles wide, in 35° 5′ southern latitude, and longitude 149° 15′ E.; but, in 1836, its site was a grassy plain. All the lakes of the interior are subject to the same variation. They abound, however, along the courses of the rivers. The waters of some are sweet, of others brackish. None of them have any outlet: a very few are entirely isolated; but the most are reservoirs for the reception of the surplus waters of the neighboring streams, with which they communicate.

(3.) Fertility is mainly confined to the higher parts of rivers, and not, as in other countries, to their lower valleys. The mountain plains and elevated terraces, and the sides and summits of the hills, near the great ranges, are covered with a highly productive, dry, vegetable soil. The desolate levels of the interior are either composed of a red tenacious clay, or of a dark hazel-colored loam, rotten and full of holes. In the coast country the soil is a black mould, mixed with a clean white sand. The latter is so plentiful that it affects the vegetation in dry weather, and large quantities of it are imported from Sydney to England, for the manufacture of glass.

The connected ranges are mainly composed of granite, with a thick overlying stratum of ferruginous sandstone. In the Blue mountains the former is rarely seen, except in the valleys and beds of streams, when it has cracked the upper stratum. Limestone is not often met with in Australia : it has been found in a district west of the Blue mountains, and in some other parts of the continent, but in no case presents any conclusive appearance of stratification. Trap occurs quite often, though its location, with reference to that of other rocks, cannot be assigned. Vesicular lava is abundant in the neighborhood of Mount Napier, an extinct volcano lying between the Grampians and the southern coast, called by the natives, Murcoä.* In a low range called Wingen, a little south of the Liverpool range, there is a bituminous burning hill, composed of a great variety of rocks : this contains, in close proximity, clay, shale, argillaceous sandstone, feldspar, basalt, ironstone, trap, and hornblende, while the adjacent peaks are chiefly porphyritic.

From what has been said, it will be perceived, that, although all the usual formations are found in this remarkable country, they occur without order, and in defiance of the established laws of geology. It is not safe, therefore, amid so many anomalies, to affirm, that the mountainous strata are not metallifferous ; yet the indications strongly warrant the

* This is the only volcano which has so far been discovered in Australia.

presumption, that they are destitute of the more precious metals. Copper has been found in the Blue mountains and the Darling range ; and traces of lead, occasionally mixed with silver and arsenic, have been observed in the same localities. Alum and plumbago are likewise tolerably plentiful. Of gems, only rock crystals, topazes, garnets, and agates, have yet been met with. But iron and coal,—the former, in many respects, the most valuable of metals, and the latter the most useful of fossils,—exist in profuse abundance. Iron is spread over the whole continent, and the oxide is so abundant on the northern coast, that several of the mountains violently affect the magnetic needle. Coal-fields of immense extent lie beneath the barren sandstone, and in the Blue mountains and the Darling range, which occur in nearly horizontal strata, and are rarely more than eighteen fathoms below the surface.

Not far from one-third of the Australian continent is in the torrid zone. The climate of the southern, or extra-tropical portion, is said to assimilate very closely to that of the lower half of the Italian peninsula ; but the average heat is less, and the extremes of temperature greater. The atmosphere, also, is considerably more arid, and the thermometer falls with much greater rapidity as you ascend the mountains. The mean temperature of the year is rather above 65° at Sydney, about 63° at Paramatta, 67½° at Perth, and 60¼° at King George's Sound. The seasons are distinctly marked. The mean heat during the summer months, (December, January, and February,) is about 80° at noon, on the southern coast ; but this is tempered by the sea breeze, which blows freshly, from nine o'clock in the morning till about sunset. During the three autumn months, (March, April, and May,) the thermometer ranges from 55° at midnight to 75° at noon. In the coast districts, during the winter months, (June, July, and August,) the mean temperature at daylight is from 40° to 50°, and at noon from 55° to 60°. Frost occurs here but rarely, and though snow sometimes falls, it never lies upon the ground ; yet the mornings and evenings are chilly, and the nights comparatively cold. Further inland, the cold is more excessive; hoar frosts are frequent and severe; heavy falls of snow are common, and the upper flats and downs often remain covered for several days. In the spring months, (September, October, and November,) the thermometer varies from 60° to 70°.

But there is little to relieve the aridity of the climate in the interior, where the heat is insupportable, alike in seasons of flood as in those of drought; and there is nothing peculiar in the climatic phenomena of this desert region, unless it be, that when the coast country is inundated with rain, it is invariably the season of dry weather here,—and that the converse is also true. On the coast, May is the wet season; but in the interior, the rains fall between September and February.

Tropical Australia is by no means so well known as the southern portion of the continent; but sufficient facts have been ascertained to render it quite certain, that its climate does not differ essentially from that of other parts of the world similarly situated. Running water is scarce, and a large share of the country is burned up with the intense heat. On the northern coast, the temperature is sometimes suddenly raised by the scorching winds from the interior. These hot fiery blasts are, fortunately, not of frequent occurrence. The average temperature at Melville Island is 83°; the extreme average being 75° in July, and 87° in December. The coolest part of the day is about six o'clock in the morning. The Indian monsoons are irregular in their recurrence, often varying more than a month. The north-western, or summer monsoon, usually sets in early in November; and the south-eastern about the first of April. During the prevalence of the summer monsoon, there are heavy falls of rain, yet these seldom continue above two or three hours at a time, and rarely interrupt out-door labor. From June to September, there is no rain, but this is the healthiest part of the year. While the dry monsoon prevails, the atmosphere is exceedingly moist; so much so, that iron articles are with difficulty kept from rusting; and the exposed surfaces of the rocks along the coast are coated over with the oxide of iron.

Periods, or cycles, of ten or twelve years duration, distinctly mark the division of the Australian climate into wet and dry. In the course of each cycle, there is ordinarily one year of unmitigated drought, during which no rain falls, whose effects are visible, as well in the mountains and fells of the elevated regions, as in the boggy marshes and desert flats of the interior—as well in the sandy plains along the southern coast, as in the jungles of tropical Australia. This dry season is followed by a year of freshets and floods: the rains are then incessant, but they diminish in number and quantity, in each succeeding year, until the dry epoch again recurs. It is only in the years intervening between these two extremes, that the regular transitions from one season to another, before hinted at, are observable.

Dews are abundant at all seasons, and especially so in the summer, and during the long droughts. Earthquakes are not common except on the northern coast, where they are occasionally felt. Hail storms often occur, and thunder and lightning are likewise frequent. Sometimes a brilliant display of the most vivid electricity may be witnessed for a succession of days,—flash following close upon flash, with but brief intermissions, and unaccompanied by either thunder or rain. In the sandy districts a singular phenomenon is often witnessed. Tall columns of dust, or whirlwinds, twenty feet broad, and from seventy to one hundred feet high, may be seen moving along in stately procession, striding majestically, like giant spirits, over brook and plain, with the speed of a race horse. At Sydney, these dust winds, or "brick-fielders," as they are called, are a great source of annoyance; and though doors and windows are always carefully closed when they are seen approaching, everything in the house is sure to be covered with the thick, fine powder, which penetrates through the smallest crevice.

Were this not a country of singularities, the inference fairly deducible from the facts which have been detailed, would be, that the climate of Australia was prejudicial to the human constitution; but it is, in reality, highly favorable, for the reason, probably, that as the vegetation is so scanty, the atmosphere is but little tainted by the miasma formed by its decomposition.   Deaths from disease are very rare; and all disorders, even the worst cases of syphilis, soon yield to the simplest remedies.   Endemic diseases are not at all common; and small-pox, measles, and hooping-cough, are almost unknown.   Dysentery is the most prevalent complaint.   Children suffer considerably from the presence of the teres, or round worm.   Ophthalmia is often produced at the south by the hot dusty winds from the interior.   It may be said to be unhealthy within the tropics, but it is certainly less so than in other countries lying in the same latitude.   Typhus and acute fevers prevail there during the wet monsoons; and in the season of the variable winds, pectolapia, or moon-blindness, supersedes ophthalmia.   Scurvy also appears to be endemic on the northern coast, and manifests itself with peculiar virulence where the tropical heat is exercised full upon the damp soil.   But even in these warm latitudes, though disease is far from being a stranger, it generally puts on a mild form, and is easily subdued.

(4.) Peculiar as are the geölogy and climate of Australia, it might be expected that the vegetable creation would present appearances equally wonderful.   Nature seems here to have escaped from her leading strings, and displayed the powers of a giant.   Discarding the customary shapes in which she appears in the old world, she develops herself in new and unwonted forms.   The humble grasses that carpet our plains and valleys, here collect in tall clumps and tussocks, as if too proud to spread themselves over the earth, for man or beast to tread upon with impunity; and the pretty honeysuckle that shelters or conceals the prairie home of the American settler, or twines its graceful tendrils around the porch of the peasant's cottage in merry England, rears itself in stately majesty among the other denizens of the Australian forests, and disdains either to give protection, or to ask it in return.

The fruits, too, are singular, as well in form as in their attributes ; and what are simple shrubs in other climes, attain a
wondrous growth ; while the monarchs of the wood are Titans in stature, and of gigantic girth.   But, what is stranger
still, all the trees, with a single exception, possess one of the
gifts of perpetual youth, and rejoice in a foliage that never
fades or perishes, but is always green.

Botany Bay, it will be remembered, received its name from
the abundant vegetation discovered on its shores, by Captain
Cook and Sir Joseph Banks.   After their return, and the publication of their animated descriptions of the floral beauties
they had witnessed, general attention was instantly attracted
to the country, and the most extravagant expectations were
formed in regard to its productiveness.   Those who subsequently visited it, for purposes of colonization, and from scientific motives, saw much to charm and interest ; but a careful examination disclosed comparatively little of what was
really useful and beneficial.   The copses of palm, the jungle
patches and mangrove thickets, of tropical Australia, and the
wide reaches of scrub along the southern coast, afforded a picturesque and pleasing contrast to the dark waves of magnificent vegetation creeping up the sides of the Blue Mountains
and the Warragongs, and mingling their rich emerald dyes
with the brilliant azure of the o'erarching heavens ; yet something more than mere beauty of scenery was requisite, as was
well remarked by Governor Phillip, in his account of the first
attempt at colonization, " in a place where the permanent
residence of multitudes was to be established."

There is a remarkable peculiarity in the arrangement of
the primary orders of plants in Australia.   Of the crypto-
gamia, there are about seven hundred species, less than one-
third of which are common to this and other countries.
There are nearly twelve hundred monocotyledons, only forty
of which are found in other regions ; and out of almost four
thousand different species of dicotyledonous plants, there are
but twenty which are not peculiar to Australia.   It will
thus be seen, that Australia contains, as peculiar to herself,

not quite one-fifth part of all the species of plants in the known world; and if their utility only equalled their variety, she would, indeed, be a paradise. But so far from this being the case, there is, in reality, a deficiency of native fruits and vegetables, adapted for human food, without parallel on the globe.

Of the cerealia there is not a single species indigenous to the country; the only substitute for them being a kind of reed, which the early settlers found to make very light and palatable cakes. But since its colonization, every species of grain—wheat, rye, Indian corn, barley and oats—has been introduced into Australia, and is now cultivated with success, though the crops are far more liable to fail here than they are in more equable climates. The yield of wheat ranges from ten to forty bushels per acre,—the greatest quantity being obtained on the low grounds. The kernel is large and plump, and the average weight of a bushel of the best quality is sixty-two pounds.

Grasses of all kinds are abundant and highly nutritious; but these, like the numerous ferns and nettles, and many varieties of flowers, have the form and habits of trees, and grow in detached clumps, and not in a continuous sward. The only native fruits are raspberries, currants, a species of cherry, one or two tasteless fruits, and a nut deservedly held in small estimation. The currants are much like cranberries in form and appearance; but the Australian cherry is a most singular monstrosity. It grows on a large bush; the fruit consisting of a spongy pulp, that shrinks a good deal when fully ripe, on the outside of which, contrary to the usual order of things, and firmly adhering to it, is the stone or pit. Of the tasteless fruits, the wooden pear is one of the most remarkable: it is the product of a low shrub, and, in outward appearance, resembles the rich fruit of the same name which we prize so highly; but, within, it is as hard as lignum vitæ. When this plant was first discovered, it occasioned the remark concerning Australia, that it was a strange country, indeed, since the leaves and fruit of its trees were of wood, and the wood itself like stone.

Among the natural productions are flax, tares, indigo, chicory, trefoil, and burnet,—the last a first-rate substitute for tea; and nearly all the useful fruits and vegetables of other lands have now been acclimatized. Of the foreign fruits, the orange, lemon, citron, date, pomegranate, almond, filbert, nectarine, apricot, peach, plum, English cherry, fig, mulberry, olive, quince, granadilla, banana, guava, pine-apple, water and musk-melon, strawberry, grape, and chiri-moya, are quite plentiful in the older and more thickly popu-lated districts. Except in tropical Australia, the oranges, citrons, and lemons, are not so large or luscious as in their native climates; the trees present a scraggy appearance, and the velvety green of the foliage is changed into a pale sickly yellow by the dry cutting winds. The stone fruits thrive well, but they are not very rich in flavor. Peaches and apri-cots are so abundant in New South Wales that hogs are fat-tened on them; and a quart of green gages, or a pound of delicious grapes, is often sold, in the season, for an English penny.

All the most valuable vegetables,—such as potatoes, car-rots, turnips, beets, parsneps, pumpkins, squashes, cabbages, broccoli, cauliflower, tomatoes, celery, lettuce, capsicum, (Guinea pepper), asparagus, spinach, egg-plant, capers, arti-chokes, radishes, and pulse,—are likewise very common in the settlements.

Tobacco is a native production, but it is extremely liable to be nipped by the frequent frosts. In other respects it suc-ceeds admirably, and with good culture yields a profitable crop.

Great attention, of late years, has been paid to the culti-vation of the grape, for which the climate is decidedly favor-able. Numerous varieties of foreign grapes have been intro-duced, and liberal premiums have been offered by the Agri-cultural Society of New South Wales, for the best specimens of native wines.

Attempts have been made in New South Wales, and other
districts in southern Australia, to cultivate the cotton plant,
but without much success.   The soil and climate of the
Cobourg peninsula, on the north, and the tropical portion of
Australia generally, are well adapted, however, to its growth.
Indeed, no other description of produce promises so well in
this section of the continent: if the seed is sown at the
proper season, the plants come forward rapidly, and arrive at
maturity just after the close of the rainy season, when the
long period of dry weather which ensues, affords ample time
and opportunity for gathering the crop without any liability
to be injured by moisture.

The coffee bush has been tried in northern Australia, but
the attempt to cultivate it proved a decided failure.   This
plant delights in a volcanic soil, and will not flourish elsewhere.   Yet it is remarked, that the peculiar aspect of Australian vegetation disappears, in some measure, in that portion
of the continent within the tropics ; the greater number of
those plants common to other countries are found here ; and
the trees and shrubs assimilate more nearly to those seen in
India.   Chili pepper has been tried with success, and the
round pepper would, undoubtedly, thrive equally as well.
Spices, too, when planted under the shade of the forest trees,
like the nutmeg bush at Banda, grow vigorously, and bear
an abundant product.   The sugar-cane, and almost all other
tropical productions, would, in like manner, thrive in the
lower latitudes of the north ; and when this portion of the
country becomes more thickly settled than it now is, its hitherto untried capabilities will be shown fully to equal the expectations of those who may test them, if any reliance whatsoever may be placed on the appearance of the soil, and the
character of the climate.

One who is familiar with the forest scenery of Brazil will
not fail to be struck with the marked resemblance of the
Australian woods.   Here, also, there is an almost entire
absence of underbrush, and the trees are rarely set so close
as to impede travelling, either on horseback or in a carriage ;

though, strangely enough, they are usually the most abundant on inferior soils.   Except in the tropical districts, however, there are few or no woody vines, or parasitic plants;
but where they are found, their growth is most luxuriant.
Scandent pipers, wild bignonias and passion-flowers, and
vines whose foliage and blossoms are of various hues, are
trailed along the mangrove bushes, and cling to the tall
palms of northern Australia, whose fan-like branches seem
to incline downwards, as if rejoicing to lift them up into the
bright sunshine that smiles above them.   Tree-ferns, of different varieties, are scattered all over the country ; and the
grass tree (*xanthorrhœa hastilis*), presenting when in flower
a most gorgeous sight, is frequently seen.   Flowering and
aromatic plants, of great beauty and powerful odor, are found
in abundance.   On the sandy soils grow numerous prickly
shrubs, which bind them down, and prevent their drifting.
The lily, the tulip, and the honeysuckle exist here, but they
are standard trees of enormous size, and incomparable beauty.
Of acacias there is no end, either in number or variety ; but
the palms are limited to the north and east of the continent.

Nearly all the timber is of the hard-wood kind.   It is generally of greater specific gravity than water, but is liable to
rot at the heart, and is so contractile that it has been known
to shrink upwards of two inches within a week ; consequently, its usefulness to the architect is very much impaired.   All the varieties of eucalyptus and casuarina grow
here, together with different species of rose-wood, sandal-
wood, mountain ash, apple, sallow, turpentine wood, cedar,
and pine.   Most of the eucalypti are called gum trees,—
there being the blue gum, gray gum, iron, flooded gum, and
black-butted gum ; but in some instances this is a misnomer ;
for the exudations of many of the trees are not properly
gums, but resins, and are insoluble in water.   Some of them,
too, yield a fine and pure manna, and others the very best
gum Arabic.   The foliage possesses powerful aromatic properties, and resembles that of the camphor tree in taste.
Boards and plank are made from these trees, and some of the

varieties are used in fencing and ship-building. The pine is equal to maple, and is used for cabinet work. The white cedar (*melia cozedarach*) is the only deciduous tree yet known: it attains a vast size, and is used for making shingles and cabinet work. The she-oak, and swamp oak, are applied to the same purposes, and the turpentine wood is made use of in boat-building. There is another valuable tree, called the miniosa, or black wattle, the bark of which is exported to England for tanning.

Of the medicinal trees, the peppermint, sassafras, and castor-oil tree, are the most conspicuous. The timber of the first two is also held in considerable estimation. There is also a tree called the tea-tree, the leaves of which are used instead of those of the Chinese plant, and make a very potable beverage.

An unusually large growth is characteristic of all the Australian trees, except in the deserts of the interior, where clumps of stunted bushes are sometimes seen, and the occasional tracts in the coast country, which are covered with dwarf shrubs, known among the colonists by the name of "scrub."

A stranger, on entering an Australian forest for the first time, is forcibly impressed with its grandeur and sublimity. He seems to have crossed the hallowed precincts of some Druid shrine, or entered the mighty portals of some ancient temple—a relic of ages long since numbered with the past. The huge bolls of the trees appear like pillars supporting the fretted dome above, and each step along the dim aisles,

"Brown with o'erarching shades,"

conducts him nearer the high altar to which they lead. And if, perchance, the babbling of the fountain, or the soft murmurs of the shaded rivulet, are heard in the distance, their strains sound like choral symphonies, and the illusion is complete.

Sometimes, also, feelings of melancholy are produced. These are naturally inspired by the dark and sombre hue of the foliage of the evergreens, and the peculiar appearance of the leaves of many of the gum trees. These are often seen,— for Nature here is delighted with showing her perverseness,— inverted in position, or set edgewise, the margin being directed towards the stem, and the two surfaces resembling each other.

In regard to the state of agriculture in Australia, but little can be said. The extensive plains on the terraces of that part of the country lying in the temperate zone, afford such excellent facilities for pasturage, that the prejudice of the colonists is strongly in favor of that branch of husbandry   Among the grains produced in this section, wheat predominates; its cultivation, like that of the other cerealia, is carried on much in the same manner as in England. The Illawarra district, south of Sydney, is especially famous for the large crops of fine grain which it produces. In the tropical regions, but little attention is paid to raising edible productions, as sago is obtained in abundance from different species of palm, and there are several varieties of arum much used for food.

Agricultural and horticultural exhibitions are frequently held at Sydney, which exert a highly beneficial influence. In all the large towns, a great deal of taste is displayed in ornamental gardening. Bowers and trellises, loaded with choice grapes, or flowering vines; elegant fuchsias, twenty feet high; geraniums, of such thrifty growth, that they are twined into hedgerows; passion-flowers concealing the entire fronts of pretty little cottages; and American aloes, of prodigious size, attract the notice of the passer-by. In the country there are beautiful orchards and gardens, separated by neat hawthorn hedges, and well stocked with fruits and vegetables. And even in the new settlements, you will often see a cleared patch of ground, amid the stumps, surrounded by a ring fence to keep out the cattle and pigs, abounding with the choicest esculents and the freshest flowers, and

"With tulips, like the ruddy evening, streak'd."

(5.) If anomalies and peculiarities mark the botany of

11

Australia, the same is equally true of animal existence in this singular region. There are three hundred and sixteen different species of birds, but twenty-seven of which are common to this and other countries; yet there is no order of birds without its representative, and there are only two, the Australian species of which are wholly peculiar. Of the common species, the most numerous are the birds of prey, eagle-haws, crows, shrikes, pies, and others of similar character. The most remarkable of the rapacious birds is a white eagle, which was at one time supposed to be an albino of some other species, or a hawk, but has since been proven to be a true eagle. The usual singing birds are wanting. There is a bird, called the superb warbler, having the habits of the redbreast, and a number of variegated thrushes, which are very beautiful, yet, notwithstanding their names, they are said to be songless. The mountain pheasant, however, and the Australian magpie, are birds of song.

A species of thrush, called the thunder bird, has received from the colonists the name of the "laughing jackass," from its peculiarly shrill and discordant cry. Swallows, goatsuckers, crows, magpies, and larks, are quite numerous. The lark is a poor imitation of the European bird, and the swallow is much smaller. Birds of paradise, and the various species of the epimachi, whose beautiful plumage has so often called forth the encomiums of the poet, are confined to the northern part of Australia. The sacred kingfisher and the variegated bee eater are likewise famous for the brilliancy and beauty of their covering. The parrots, parroquets, and cockatoos, are numerous, and are peculiar to the country. Of the bustard there are several species, two of which have been often mistaken for wild turkeys: the emu, or Australian cassowary, belongs to the same order. It resembles the ostrich very much in appearance, but its legs are thicker, and it is more stoutly built. It runs with great rapidity, and will outstrip the swiftest racer. It has small wings, which are nearly hidden beneath the thick tufts of feathers that lie above them, and its head is protected by a helmet consisting of a horny substance disposed in plates or scales, one above another.

Curlews, blue plumaged herons, avosets, and rails, belonging to the same order with the bustard and emu, are also abundant. Ducks, petrels, albatrosses, penguins, and pelicans, are numerous ; and boobies are so plentiful that they have given name to an island on the northern coast. Australia can also boast of producing, in considerable numbers, the black swan—neither brown or umber, but genuine coal black—the *rara avis in terris* of the Sulmian bard.

Geese, turkeys, ducks, and fowls, were introduced by the first colonists, over sixty years ago : and since that time they have increased so rapidly that the country is liberally supplied with them.

Of the mammalia, there are fifty-eight known species, only twelve of which are found in other regions ; and of these twelve, five are whales and four are seals. Thus, there are, in reality, but three terrestrial mammals common to Australia and other countries ; one of which is the large, strong-winged " Flying Fox," or " Great Bat" of Madagascar ; another is a rodent, a co-genera of the American and Asiatic jerboas ; and the third is that well known cosmopolite—the dog.* Thirty-three of the whole number of Australian mammalia belong to the order marsupialia, and of these more than one half are limited to the continent and the adjacent islands. The most prominent peculiarity of this order of animals is the birth of the young in an immature state : at the time of their birth, the fœti are destitute of limbs and other external organs, and remain attached to the teats of the mother, which enlarge so as to fill the mouth, inclosed in a pouch, or second matrix, formed by the skin of the. abdomen, that constitutes the distinctive mark of the order ; and when fully developed,

* It is doubted by Mr. Ogilby, (Linnæan Transactions, vol. xviii., p. 121, et seq.) whether the Australian dingo, or wild dog, is a native of the continent, and he supposes it may have been carried there by the first primitive settlers. It was certainly unknown in Van Diemen's Land, previous to the settlement of the British colonists on the island.

they fall from the teats, and are for the first time ushered into
the world. But for a long time after this takes place, the
dam carries her young in her pouch, even when they can walk,
and on the approach of danger, they always conceal themselves in this secure retreat. When Australia was first discovered, these animals were very numerous, but they are now
fast disappearing.

First in importance, and the largest in size, of the animals
belonging to this order, is the kangaroo, which, in some of
the species, has the proportions of a large calf. Its head, neck,
and shoulders, are small, but it increases disproportionately towards the hind quarters. Its fore legs are short, and are of
no service in walking, but are only used in burrowing in the
ground, or in conveying food to the mouth. The hind legs are
long and powerful, and are highly useful in locomotion, which
the animal effects by a succession of springs or leaps, sometimes jumping thirty feet at a single bound, in which it is
materially assisted by its strong prehensile tail. The color
is generally gray, varying in different shades, though there is
one species which is red and white. Except when feeding, or
lying down, its attitude is erect; squatting on its hams and
tail, like a South Sea islander. Its habits are herbiverous
and gregarious, and it is exceedingly shy and timid. Hunting the kangaroo, affords great amusement to the colonists.
Its flesh is edible, and is esteemed quite a luxury by the natives.

Besides the kangaroo, there are seven other genera of the
marsupialia—the dasyuri, the phalangers, the petaurista, the
parameles, the phascolarctos, the phascolomys, and the potorvus
—the different species of which vary in size, from that of a rat
to that of a dog. The dasyuri found in Australia, resemble
the weasel tribe in size and appearance, though there are
larger species on Van Diemen's Land: all the species are
carnivorous. The phalangers are not all distinguished by
united toes, as the name implies: some of them approach
the quadrumana in the formation of their extremities; and
one of the latter class, the vulpine phalanger, is a pretty

and graceful animal. This genera is insectivorous. The petaurista are a sub-genus of the phalangers, and are sometimes called flying phalangers, from a kind of parachute, formed by an extension of the skin of the side, which distinguishes them : the squirrel opossum (*didelphis sciurus*) belongs to this genus, and has so much the appearance of a squirrel that it is not easy to detect the difference; it skips from tree to tree in the same manner as the squirrel, and is hunted on moonlight nights, like the American opossum. The parameles are commonly called pouched badgers, from their resemblance in form and habits to the common badger : unlike the other genera their tails are very weak. Of the phascolarctos, or koala, as it is generally termed, there is but one species; which has a clumsy body, like that of a moderate sized dog, with short legs armed with claws, adapted for climbing or burrowing : its motions are very slow, and on this account is often called the New Holland sloth; it possesses cutting teeth, but is destitute of canines; the female carries her young for some time, on her shoulders, and not in her pouch, as is customary in this order. There is, also, but one species of the phascolomys, which is called the wombat by the colonists : it is a plantigrade animal, like the bear, a true rodent, and in size approaches the badger. The wombat lives in holes, and when roasted, its flesh is said to be as delicate as that of a young pig. The potorvus, or wallaby, likewise consists of but one species : it is the most diminutive of the kangaroo family, and is sometimes called the kangaroo rat.

There are four species of the edentata : these are all toothless, or so near it, that the term applied to them is not inapplicable. There are two genera of this order, the echidni, or porcupines, and the ornithorhynchi, both of which are destitute of teats, and do not suckle their young. Of the porcupines there are two species : one is entirely covered with closely serried spines, and the other has a coat of shaggy hair which half conceals the spines. The ornithorhynchi are, probably, the most singular animals found in Australia.

There are two species of the genera,—the ornithorhynchus paradoxus, and the ornithorhynchus fuscus : they have the body and habits of a mole, the feet and bill of a duck, and the internal formation of a reptile, though they are not cold blooded ; they lead a burrowing life, in the mud of rivers and swamps, and are so extremely shy, that their mode of reproduction has not yet been discovered.

The rodentia consist of two species of hydromys, called muskrats, uniting the peculiarities of the dormouse, common rat, and beaver ; a rat (*conilurus constructor*), bearing a general resemblance to the rabbit, and remarkable for the formidable defences of earth which it constructs against the dingo and birds of prey ; two peculiar species of mice ; a red shrew mouse ; and the Australian jerboa.

When the first colonists went out from England, in the spring of 1787, they took with them one stallion, three brood mares, three colts, forty-nine hogs, twenty-five pigs, two bulls, five cows, twenty-nine sheep, nineteen goats, and five rabbits. The last two have not thriven remarkably well, but the other species of stock have increased with great rapidity. During the first twenty-five years, frequent importations were made, and in 1797, through the exertions of Captain M'Arthur, a number of fine wooled sheep were imported from the Cape of Good Hope, the original breed of which had been brought from Holland, in order to improve the coarse-wooled varieties then in the country. So favorable is the climate of Australia to the domestic animals, and such abundant pasturage is afforded them on the unlimited plains and terraces among the mountains, that they thrive unusually well. The ratio of increase of horses has been about eleven per cent. yearly : in 1817 there were not far from three thousand, and there are now over forty thousand. The horned cattle have multiplied so fast, that many of them have escaped from the distant stations ; and there are now large herds in the interior, numbering from eight to fifteen hundred, in a completely wild state. In 1821, there were about 120,000 sheep in the country, and in 1838, the number was computed at 5,000,000. The average annual increase is not far from forty per cent. The wool obtained is of the best quality; the finer varieties being equal to the best Spanish, and averaging two and a half pounds to each animal. Sheep are apt to stray, as well as the horned cattle, though they are kept in flocks, and watched by shepherds, either natives or convicts; but they do not return to a wild state, as they are soon cut off by the ferocious dingo, or native dog.

Reptiles are abundant. There are twenty-three known genera, twenty-one of which are peculiar to this country. There are two or three varieties of turtles, and about the same number of alligators. Lizards and snakes are numerous, and some of them are exceedingly venomous. The land lizards, or guanas, and the crimson-sided snake, are of extraordinary beauty, but their bite is deadly. The black, the diamond, and the whip snake, and the deaf adder, are also poisonous; and as it is not easy to distinguish them when curled up amid the tufts of grass, it is sometimes dangerous to frequent the places where they abound, on foot. Sand-leeches, or blood-suckers, are quite common, and are much dreaded on account of their bite, as the wound always ulcerates, and is very painful.

The bays and inlets along the Australian coast, and the adjacent islands, are favorite places of resort for cetaceous animals; and the whale fishery is annually increasing in importance. All the surrounding waters and the rivers abound in fish. The largest of the edible varieties is said to be the river perch, or rock, specimens of which have been taken in the Murray and Morrumbidgee rivers, weighing from one hundred to one hundred and twenty pounds. Besides this species, there are barracoota, native salmon, flat-head, trumpeter, crawfish, rock oysters, muscles, and cockles, all in great plenty. Sharks, of different varieties, are numerous along the shores, and are frequently found a great distance up the rivers. The smallest of the species is called Watts' shark, and is remarkable for having the mouth near the extremity of the head, and not underneath, as is the case with the other varieties.

Insects are also found in considerable numbers, yet they do not differ essentially from those found in other countries similarly situated. Flies, spiders, cockroaches, chintz, and musquitoes, abound. Of ants, there are many varieties, and of different colors and sizes. Some of them are as large as wasps, and have visible stings; and nearly all the kinds are said to be poisonous.

(6.) Mr. Crawfurd insists that the East insular negro is a distinct, and decidedly inferior variety of the human race;[*] and so far as the native Australian is concerned, his many peculiarities afford strong reasons for separating him from the African Ethiop, whom he resembles more nearly than any other species. He is by nature stupid, and puny and weak in person. Both in his physical character, and in his moral and intellectual attainments, he bears the impress of inferiority. His average stature barely exceeds five feet. He has a higher forehead, and a thicker skull than the African negro, and his nose is not so much depressed; but his jaws advance still more boldly, and his buttocks are considerably lower. His chest and shoulders are slenderly built, yet the abdomen is quite prominent. The muscles are not very powerfully developed, though he is remarkable for his agility.

The complexion of the aborigines is chocolate colored, or a tint between the sooty black of the African, and the clear olive of the Malay. Their lips are not unusually thick, and their teeth are white and even. Their eyes are small, black, and deep set. Their hair is long and black, generally straight, but sometimes slightly curled: it is commonly cropped short, but almost always matted and filthy, though without grease, and free from vermin. The beards of the males are thick and bushy, but are not suffered to grow long. They besmear their bodies with fat or oil, when it can be procured,

* History of the Indian Archipelago, Vol. I. p. 24.

and red ochre, black paint, or soot. Sometimes, also, they scarify their breasts and shoulders, which gives them an extremely unpleasant appearance. Their voices sound like the cackling of geese; and they jabber away so rapidly, and in such a confused lurry, that it is almost impossible to distinguish words, or articulations, so as to comprehend their meaning. They have various dialects among them, which differ from any other language in the world, though approximating the most nearly to that of the Indians of South America.

In regard to character, they are said to be treacherous and deceitful, though naturally proud and independent. They are timid, and silent and reserved in disposition. Being almost entirely ignorant of the distinction between *meum* and *tuum*, they are consequently arrant thieves. Of agriculture, or arts, or manufactures, except the construction of rude huts, and a few arms and implements, they are utterly ignorant. Placed by their Creator in an inhospitable climate, and on an unfriendly soil, they seem to have no desire to better their condition. To care they are strangers, and their wants are but few. If the necessities of to-day are supplied, they are content, and leave to-morrow to take care of itself. Since the settlement of the country by the English colonists, great pains have been taken to ameliorate their situation; missionaries have been sent among them, and other means liberally employed, but the results have not been very flattering. Some of their habits have been changed, and, perhaps, they are not as ferocious and murderously inclined as they once were; yet their minds do not seem to be susceptible of improvement; and no excitement can remove the natural sluggishness of their temperaments, and the inertness of their faculties. Latterly, too, they have contracted many of the pernicious habits and appetites of the whites, and have become much addicted to the use of intoxicating drinks. It is not strange, therefore, that they are dwindling away as a people; for, like the North American Indian, it seems to be their destiny, to

11*

give place to the fairer, and more highly gifted races, who are gradually supplanting them.*

(7.) The native huts are of the simplest and rudest character, consisting merely of a few pieces of bark, inclined against a pole laid horizontally across a couple of forked sticks, which are driven into the ground. They sleep on dried herbs or grass, and cover themselves with kangaroo skins. In the warmer latitudes, it is not often that they construct a hut, or provide any protection against the weather. Originally, they went entirely naked, but since their intercourse with the Europeans, many of them clothe themselves with kangaroo skins, and wear caps made of the bark of trees. Those in the immediate vicinity of the settlements array their persons in the cast-off clothing of the whites.

Considerable skill is displayed in the construction of their implements and weapons. They make hooks, and spears, the latter usually three pronged, for fishing; and they have, also, stone hatchets. Their weapons consist of a spear, or javelin, ten feet long, made of cane or other wood; a club, called nulla-nulla, made of ti wood, and about three feet in length; the dundumel, or tomahawk; the bundi; and the boomereng. They have likewise shields, made of the thick bark of the eucalypti, which, though small, with their agility and quickness of eye, are sufficient to protect the whole body against the missiles of an enemy. Their spears are slender, and taper gradually to the barbed point: they are thrown with the wammera, a straight flat stick, three feet long, with a socket of bone or hide at the extremity, in which the heel of the spear is placed. The wammera is firmly grasped by three fingers of the right hand, and the spear steadied between the forefinger and the thumb, till the thrower is prepared to hurl it. Such is their dexterity in the use of this weapon, that a native is a dangerous neighbor, particularly if he cherishes

---

* The number of native inhabitants of Australia was computed, at the time of its discovery, to be about 200,000; but it is now rated at 60,000, and this is supposed to be an over estimate. It is certain, however, that the aboriginal population is diminishing.

any enmity : he will crawl through the tall grass like an American savage, and his aim is deadly, and his spear strikes far.

The boomereng is the most singular offensive implement in use among the Australians. It is made of tough and hard wood, about three feet long, two inches wide, and three quarters of an inch thick. It is curved or crooked at the centre, so as to form an obtuse angle, and sharpened at the ends. When hurled by a skilful hand, it rises with a rotatory motion in the air, strikes at a great distance, and then returns to within a few feet of the thrower ; or if thrown upon the ground, it rebounds in a straight line, and ricochets along till it reaches the thing aimed at. It is useful in hitting one object concealed behind another, and it may also be thrown with the back of the thrower turned towards the mark. It is employed by the natives in hunting, as well as in war.

Rude canoes, fourteen feet long, and three feet wide, are made by the natives from the bark of the gum tree. For this purpose the tree is girdled, and a piece of bark, of the proper size and dimensions, is stripped off ; this is folded in at either end, and fastened together with cords made of the fibres of the bark, or wooden pins. The canoe is then completed, and though not very strong, answers their purpose in coasting along the shores within the surf, or ferrying across the creeks and rivers. It is customary among them, as with the Fuégians, to build fires in the bottom of their canoes, on layers of earth or clay.

They are not great eaters, nor are they fastidious in their diet. Hunger is appeased by the spontaneous products of the soil, such as roots and berries, and the shell fish found on the sea shore, with reptiles, insects, and their larvæ. They sometimes kill a bird or kangaroo, or find one dead ; in either case it is greedily devoured. The latter has become so scarce, that young men are forbidden to eat it. The great quantities of wild cattle now roaming at large over the plains and through the valleys of Australia, might afford a great deal of sustenance to the natives, and contribute much to their comfort; but they seem wholly unable to profit by this streak of good fortune.

Of government they have little or no knowledge. They have chiefs among them, but the distinction is merely nominal, and the respect paid to them is only personal. Their habits are gregarious, rather than social. They live together in families, or tribes, holding everything in common except their women, and rove about from one place to another, usually confining themselves to a circuit of fifty or sixty miles in extent. Frequent conflicts take place between the rival tribes, and encounters between individuals are not of rare occurrence. The former are not very bloody; neither are the latter, except when the feelings of the parties are very much embittered, or the injury sought to be avenged is esteemed of a very grave character. They have a sort of duel, frequently resorted to for the redress of personal affronts, which, though not in accordance with the code of honor, is certainly less harmless than pistols at ten paces :—The challenged party offers his head, with the crown uppermost, to the challenger, who strikes him a blow with a waddy, sufficient to drive in the skull of a white man. The other party then returns the compliment, and thus they continue alternately striking each other, till one or the other is satisfied.

Women are considered and treated in the same manner as goods and chattels. They are sold or given away by their friends, without consulting their inclinations or wishes. The natural consequence is, that all the finer affections are blunted, and parental tenderness, and filial love, are almost unknown among them. Polygamy is commonly practiced; but the men are exceedingly jealous, and infidelity is punished with great severity.

When the boys arrive at the age of puberty, they are " made into young men," as the settlers say, after a strange fashion. An evening or two previous to the time appointed for the ceremony, a dismal wailing cry is heard in the woods, proceeding from some of the old men of the tribe or family, which the lads are told is the voice of the Bùlù, or spirit that watches over the destinies of young men, calling upon them. They then proceed with their elders to some secluded spot, where each one has a front tooth knocked out, and is obliged to submit to other inflictions calculated to test his courage, fortitude, and powers of endurance. The ceremony differs among the different tribes, and in the interior it is said that the teeth are not knocked out. After their initiation, the now young men are restricted in their diet, and are never allowed to speak to or approach a female till their marriage.

Though reserved in their dispositions, the natives have their amusements, the principal one of which is the corrobory, a sort of dance, in which the performers bedaub themselves with pipe clay, and go through a series of saltatory motions, neither very easy or graceful, round a large fire, with a monotonous accompaniment chanted by themselves, and beaten by the spectators upon their shields.

They bury their dead in mounds, constructed with great skill and taste, which resemble the barrows of the ancient Celts. Like that people, too, the corpse is disposed with the head towards the east; though the limbs are doubled back, so that the soles of the feet touch the crown of the head.

Comparatively little is known in regard to the superstitions of the natives. Either from their natural timidity, or from a fear that it would be improper to communicate the information sought, they appear unwilling to talk on the subject of their religion. No adults have yet embraced christianity; consequently, that means of obtaining intelligence, has not been possessed by the missionaries, and others who have directed their attention to this subject. None of the tribes appear to have a just idea of God; and when his character and attributes are explained to them, they seem unable to comprehend what is said. They have some indistinct notions of a Deity, or Supreme Being, called *Bai-a-mai*, whom, with his son *Burambin*, they regard as the creator of all things. According to their superstitious belief, *Bai-a-mai* resides on an island beyond the sea, and lives upon fish, which come up out of the water at his call. *Balumbals* are white angels, who live a great way off, on a high mountain to the south-west, and feed on honey. They also believe in an evil spirit, or devil, called *Wandong*, or *Metagong*.

They have no definite idea concerning a future state of rewards and punishments. After death, they suppose the spirit, or *goor-de-mit*, is conveyed through the bosom of the ocean to some distant land, in which it then takes up its residence. As he is obliged to pass through so much water, the deceased person, as they suppose, is washed white : hence, they deem the whites the returned spirits of their ancestors and friends. The Malays and Lascars are also regarded as returned spirits, but on account of their bad conduct they have been left black.

The night-bird, or cuckoo, which the natives call *pogo-mit*, is considered by them as the cause of boils and erup-tions, which it produces by piercing them, when asleep, with its beak. They have, also, a great dread of sharks ; and a fabulous aquatic monster, termed *waugal*, which they represent as having long arms, long teeth, and large eyes, and inhabiting the depths of the ocean, is regarded with simi-lar emotions. Certain round stones found along the coast they believe to be the eggs of the *waugal*, and when they discover one of them, they always stop, and make a bed for it, of leaves ; believing that by thus treating them with care and veneration, they will be spared by the monster, which is said sometimes to devour great numbers of the inhabitants.

In sorcery and enchantment they are firm believers, and there are persons among them, who are supposed to possess the power of curing many of the ills that flesh is heir to, of healing wounds and sores, and of dooming or devoting those who fall under their displeasure to sudden death. If a fire be lighted at night, or stirred with a crooked stick, it is thought that some young child will immediately die. It is considered ominous of ill, to burn the blood of a wounded person ; to eat the flower of the honeysuckle too soon ; or to sleep on the spot where the blood of a relative has been shed, until a victim has been sacrificed to appease the shade of the deceased.

There are some hills, to pass over which, as they fancy, is certain death. They have quite a beautiful superstition in regard to sleep : when a person is in a slumber, they say he is away "over the water,"—meaning thereby, that his spirit or mind has returned to the country from which he came, to revisit the scenes of his nativity. With respect to their own origin, they suppose that their earliest progenitors either sprung from emus, or were brought to the country they now inhabit, on the backs of crows. Of conception they have a singular idea ; believing that the infant is conveyed into the mother's womb, by a secret and unknown agency, from some place across the sea.

(8.) In May, 1787, the first British colony, for the establishment of a proposed penal settlement in Australia, was sent out from England, under Captain Phillip, the person selected for the office of governor. The Expedition consisted of eleven vessels, conveying, besides their complement of seamen, two hundred marines, and seven hundred and seventy-six convicts. They first landed at Botany Bay ; but becoming satisfied that the adjacent country was barren and unprofitable, the governor sailed for Port Jackson, and on the 26th of January, 1788, laid the foundation of Sydney, the future capital of New South Wales.

For the first twenty-five years after its establishment, the colony was nothing more than a work-house or penitentiary, constructed on an isolated spot, in a defective and costly manner, and altogether too remote from the supervision of the home government. Subordinate settlements were soon attempted at Paramatta and Norfolk Island. The former was eventually successful, but the latter failed, though the attempt has been since renewed, under more favorable auspices, with complete success. A number of voluntary immigrants now arrived, but they were of dissolute habits, and, with the discharged convicts, formed a population not very well calculated to build up a new colony. At length a

regiment of troops destined for service in New South Wales,
was raised in England, and subsequently recruited from
there. The officers' commissions were sold to dissipated
adventurers, and the men placed under their command were
little better than convicts in character and habits. Governor
Phillip had hitherto manfully contended against numerous
difficulties; but on the arrival of this regiment, in 1791, the
embarrassments of his position were increased in a tenfold
degree. The officers set at defiance the civil authority, and
organized a separate faction; and having secured the monopoly of the trade in Sydney, they encouraged the use of
ardent spirits, and in that way exercised a most pernicious
influence.

Utterly despairing of accomplishing any good by remaining at his post, the governor resigned his office in 1792.
He was succeeded by Governor Hunter in 1795, who founded
Castlehill, Bankstown, and Windsor. He, too, was unable,
with the powers at his command, to repress the disorders and
excesses in the colony, which daily grew more outrageous,
wherefore he also resigned. Captain King was then appointed to succeed him, in 1800. He likewise soon resigned, and
was followed, in 1806, by Captain Bligh, who first attempted
to resist the military; but a rebellion ensuing, headed by
Captain M'Arthur, he was seized by the insurgents, and
sent as a prisoner to Europe. Governor Macquarrie was
then sent out, in 1810, and continued at the head of affairs
till 1822. During his administration, the refractory and
turbulent leaders of the military combination were effectually put down, and law and order in great part restored.
Settlements were established on every side; roads were constructed between the principal towns; and measures taken
to develop the resources of the country, and ensure its continued advance in prosperity. Under the administrations of
the subsequent governors, Brisbane, Darling, Bourke, and
Gipps, the affairs of the colonies in Australia have grown
more and more promising, till now nothing short of a miracle
could retard them in their successful career.

The establishment of the colony of New South Wales, was neither easily nor cheaply effected. From 1788 to 1815, inclusive, the expenses of the colony were nearly three and a half million pounds sterling. The annual cost of maintaining each convict, during the same period, was upwards of thirty pounds, while his earnings did not exceed twenty. The cost of transporting the convicts, from England to the colony, was about thirty-seven pounds sterling per head, and it was computed that nearly one-tenth died on the passage out. Various propositions of reform in these particulars were suggested; and, after some delay, improvements were introduced into the system, which secured the better health of the convicts, and greater economy in the administration of the fiscal affairs of the colonies.

The increase of population, too, did not keep pace with the expectations of English legislators, and vessels were freighted with abandoned females, fresh from the purlieus of St. Giles, designed as wives for the male convicts. Of course, every cargo was taken up as soon as landed: all were promptly secured, for better or worse, and pretty surely the latter. It could hardly have been expected that a career of lewdness and vice would have fitted them for being chaste wives, and affectionate mothers; inasmuch as personal vanity, and the rum and gin shops of Sydney, were ready to allure them back to their old habits. Doubts have, therefore, been entertained, whether this step operated beneficially so far as regards the morals of the colonists. Still there are as many arguments on one side as the other. The convicts were, no doubt, better contented; and some of them, with their wives, became thrifty and industrious, and made quite decent members of society.

Encouragement was also offered to the emigration of persons of respectable character and standing. A large tract of land was given, gratis, to every man going to New South Wales with his family : after his arrival, he was allowed as many servants as he might require, from among the convicts, at a very low rate of wages; and he and his family were

victualled for six months, at the expense of government,—
all points, said Sydney Smith, worthy of serious attention,
to those who were " shedding their country."

In 1839 and 1840, there was a great deal of speculation
in the government lands in Australia, and the sales in New
South Wales exceeded, for the two years, three hundred and
forty thousand acres.   When the reäction took place, a general depression of business followed ; the sales for 1841 were
less than sixteen thousand acres ; and a check was therefore
given to emigration.   The whole number of immigrants that
arrived in the Australian colonies in 1841, was 28,721 ; and
in 1842 there were only 5,740.   Since that time, however,
business has revived ; and every year witnesses the arrival
of great numbers of immigrants, who locate themselves on
the unoccupied lands, of which there are still immense tracts,
in the interior.

A penal colony was established on Van Diemen's Land in
1803, which is subordinate to that of New South Wales,
and is under the charge of a lieutenant governor.   Until
1813, it continued to be merely a place of transportation
from the mother colony, but since that time it has gradually
taken the place of the latter as a penal settlement, and convicts are now sent thither direct from England.   This settlement, though requiring an enormous outlay for its establishment, has advanced more rapidly in prosperity than New
South Wales, and is destined to become of great importance.

The other settlements on the main continent, besides New
South Wales, were formed by voluntary immigrants, and
not by convicts.   The proximity of northern, or tropical
Australia, to China and the Indian Archipelago, pointed it out
as a proper site for a colony many years ago ; and attempts
were made, with that object in view, as early as 1824.   But
the difficulties encountered led to the abandonment of the
project, and in 1829 the foundation of a colony on the Swan
river, at the foot of the Darling range, now known as West
Australia, was laid, by commencing the construction of three
towns—Guilford, Freemantle, and Perth—the last of which

was made the seat of government. In 1834, a settlement was formed on Vincent's Gulf, called South Australia, under the patronage of a joint stock association constituted in England, to whom the management of the affairs of the colony was intrusted. The association had the power of disposing of the unappropriated lands within the colonial limits, on condition that the proceeds should be devoted, in the first instance, to replacing the outlay incurred on the original establishment of the colony, and then to be applied for the common benefit of the inhabitants. It was further stipulated, that the colony should remain under the immediate superintendence of the crown,—the governor appointed by whom was also to be the agent of the company,—till the population should reach fifty thousand, when a representative legislature might be organized. This colony enjoyed a large share of prosperity for several years; the price of land, in March, 1836, rose as high as a pound sterling per acre; and by the 1st of January, 1838, 64,358 acres had been sold. But a period of severe financial embarrassment now followed; in 1841, the land sales amounted to only three hundred and twenty acres; and in 1842, there were less than one hundred and fifty immigrants arrived. Still, this colony possesses many of the elements of wealth; it contains some of the finest pasture lands in Australia, and there are nearly half a million of sheep, many of which are merinos, now owned by its inhabitants.

In 1838, a new colony was established to the south-east of New South Wales, to which it was annexed, and received the name of Port Phillip. This settlement lies in the region known as Australia Felix, one of the most delightful and productive tracts of country, as may be inferred from the appellation bestowed upon it, in all Australia. In the course of the previous year, it was, by some means, understood, that the French government were preparing an expedition to form a settlement in northern Australia. They were anticipated, however, by the English authorities; who, in 1838, dispatched a number of persons, and an armed force, to establish a colony and military post, at Port Essington, on the Coburg peninsula. The situation fixed upon for the settlement is a favorable one in a military aspect, and well located for a commercial emporium, though there is not, in its immediate neighborhood, a sufficient extent of soil for an agricultural or pastoral colony.

According to a census taken in 1841, the population of New South Wales, including Port Phillip, amounted to 87,298 males, and 43,558 females, making, in all, 130,856, double the number seven years previous. In this computation were included 26,977 convicts. The population of West Australia, at that time, was supposed to be about three thousand, and the white settlers of the two other colonies probably amounted to about fifteen thousand.

The executive power in the colony of New South Wales resides in a governor, who is assisted by a council consisting of the highest officers of government. He also shares the legislative power with a council, composed of private individuals appointed from among the principal settlers and merchants, and persons elected as representatives by the people, constituting altogether a sort of colonial assembly. Both councils are appointed by the king. Every new law is proposed by the governor, who, after submitting it to the chief justice, to obtain his opinion whether or not it contains anything contrary to the law of England, lays it before the legislative assembly. If they approve of the bill, it must be transmitted to the home government and laid before the British Parliament within six months. The sovereign may interpose his, or her veto, at any time within three years. This tedious process of legislation has naturally created discontent, and elicited frequent murmurs among a people unusually firm in their loyalty, and devoted in their attachment to the "fast-anchored isle." They are now making strenuous exertions to obtain a colonial parliament, and it is to be hoped their wishes will be regarded ; for when we consider the immense distance, about twelve thousand miles, that separates them from the home government, it seems as unjust as it is absurd, to continue their present state of dependence on a power so remote.

The judicial power of the colony is vested in a chief justice, and two assistant judges, who try all cases, both criminal and civil. In criminal actions, which mostly arise among the convicts, a jury consisting of seven naval and military officers, selected by the governor, is associated with one of the judges. The party on trial has the right of challenge, however, and the judge decides all questions that may arise in relation thereto. Civil causes are tried before one of the judges, and two assessors, who must be magistrates of the colony, unless the parties mutually consent to have a jury of twelve men, when the proceedings are conducted pretty much in the same manner as in the English courts. An appeal lies to the governor, in all cases where the amount in controversy exceeds five hundred pounds, and, where a judgment has been reversed, or the amount in litigation exceeds two thousand pounds, to the king in council.

Similar powers are possessed by the executive officers in the other colonies, and the legislative and judicial departments are constituted in like manner, and exercise their functions in nearly the same way.

An Englishman may well be pardoned for being proud of these colonial establishments of his country. They are stupendous monuments, more enduring than marble or brass, of the greatness and power of his native land. The penal settlements, founded at such an enormous outlay, afford unmistakable evidences of her wealth; and the prosperous condition of the colonists, declares, in eloquent terms, the all-conquering industry and indomitable perseverance of the race to which they belong. There is, in all this, much to excite feelings of pride; and he who manifests them, does but justice to the nature God has planted within him.

(9.) Colonial life is the same in Australia as in the other possessions of England, of a similar character. In the towns situate in those colonies which are not penal, there are no peculiarities observable, that seem to require particular mention;

and were it not for the presence of the convicts, the same might be said of those in the penal settlements. At Sydney, and other places in New South Wales, the government officers, and the wealthier inhabitants who have never been convicts, constitute the aristocracy, and are called exclusionists; the commonalty is composed of the liberated convicts, or emancipationists; and lowest in the scale, are the convicts themselves, on whom rests heavily the ban of social outlawry. Each class looks with contempt on that beneath it; and each, in turn, although there may be some little friendliness of feeling between the emancipationists and convicts, regard with hatred that which is placed above it. The aristocracy are as exclusive in the bestowal of their favor and preference as the lady patronesses of Almack's; and the liberated convicts and their families are not admitted into their society, even though the wealth of Crœsus may be theirs,—the sins of the fathers being literally visited on the children, even to the third and fourth generations. The native born sons and daughters of the emancipationists, too, are very reluctant to associate with, or marry, liberated convicts.

In the interior, there is, of necessity, a more intimate fusion of the mixed classes composing the society, and, consequently, the prejudice of caste is not so great, nor so strongly marked. The Australian farmer, or grazier, resembles his prototype in the old country, and grumbles as incessantly, over his glass of poor gin or rum, about the bad weather, the bad crops, and the bad government, as does the other, over his pot of brown stout or humming ale.

Balls, fêtes, and dinner parties, are, of course, of frequent occurrence at Sydney, and the other large towns. All those who possess the necessary means, ape the manners of Bond street; and the fashions are mere copies, with an interval of twelve months, of those of the Rue St. Honoré and Piccadilly. Some articles of dress, however, are more in accordance with tropical fashions; and broad-leafed Panamá hats, and white linen jackets and trowsers, are commonly worn in warm weather.

A most commendable interest is manifested in the establishment of schools, colleges, and literary and benevolent societies; and government has liberally extended to them her
fostering care and patronage.   As early as 1817, one eighth
of the revenue of the colony was set apart for educational
purposes.   Large tracts of land were also given to female orphan schools, and a portion, consisting of fifty or a hundred
acres, allotted to each orphan.   Schools were likewise founded
for the civilization and education of the natives, and funds
provided for sending missionaries among them.   In 1838,
the number of scholars attending the public schools in New
South Wales, to the support of which government contributed
over twelve thousand pounds, was nearly four thousand ; and
there were upwards of eighteen hundred scholars attending
private schools.   There were three collegiate institutions, at
the same time, which were well attended ; King's School at
Paramatta, and Sydney College, and Australian College, at
Sydney.

In the towns, the mode of building is similar to that witnessed in European and American cities, except that everything looks much fresher and newer than in the antiquated
capitals of the old world.   Some of the cottages, or country
seats, are very neat and attractive, particularly when embo-
somed amid the luxuriant foliage with which they are often
surrounded.   They are usually of one story, constructed either
of stone or wood, and have high sloping roofs, attic rooms and
dormer windows, with a portico in front and sometimes in the
rear, and are flanked by wings whose roofs descend at right angles to those of the main building.   The dwellings of the settlers are rude buildings, consisting of slabs driven into the
ground, or attached to frames, with puncheon floors, roofs of
straw thatch or bark, glazed windows, perhaps, and chimneys
of stone or mud, erected on the outside, after the Dutch fashion.
Occasionally a little more taste will be exhibited, and balconies may be seen running along the fronts of the houses, supported by rough trunks of trees, and decorated by vines and
creepers.   In the adjoining gardens, too, there will most likely

be trellises made of rough slats or twigs, covered with climbing plants, the fragrance of whose blossoms load the air with
perfume.

(10.) Much has been written in regard to the misery,
wretchedness, and depravity, of the convicts in New South
Wales, and Van Diemen's Land. Some of these accounts
have, no doubt, been somewhat too highly colored; but the
unvarnished truth possesses dark and repulsive features in
abundance. Vice and licentiousness, in every form and
shape, may be witnessed among the convicts in the penal
settlements, and with these odious characteristics, drunkenness, of the most bestial character, pretty surely goes hand
in hand.

Criminals of the worst description are either confined in
prisons, or sent to the penitentiary on Norfolk Island. The
mode of discipline practiced here is what is called the social
system : the convict is first placed in solitary confinement
for a certain time, and then put at hard labor, in company
with his fellows. During the latter period, he is supplied
with books, and allowed numerous privileges and recreations,
which, unless he is beyond the reach of moral influences, are
calculated to bring him back to a correct way of life. All
the public work in Sydney and other towns in New South
Wales, is performed by convicts, and a strong body of
mounted police, and a large military force, are required to
keep them in subjection. They are driven through the
streets in gangs, accompanied by guards and sentinels, and
work chained together in pairs. Their dress consists of a
coarse canvas jacket and trowsers, of a peculiar fashion,
with "chain-gang" conspicuously marked on the back of the
former, and a jockey cap.

Those convicts whose crimes are of an inferior grade, are
assigned to the settlers, on their application, who put them
to such labor as they please, and are at the expense of their
maintenance alone. Those who behave well, for, perhaps,
half their term, often have their sentences mitigated, and are
furnished with tickets of leave. They are then called ticket-

of-leave men, and are allowed to hire themselves out, their employers stipulating to keep a strict watch over their conduct. Most of the female convicts are also assigned, and the refractory and turbulent ones are sent to the factory at Paramatta, where they are employed in making clothing, picking oakum, and plaiting straw.

Sometimes a convict takes to the bush, as it is termed; that is, makes his escape to the woods in the interior, where he leads a roving, depredatory life, and is called a bushranger. The natives generally stand in great awe of the fugitive convicts, who terrify them by feigning to be "native devils;" yet they frequently render important services to the government officers in recapturing them.

Recently, in compliance with the earnest importunities of the free settlers, New South Wales has been discontinued as a penal colony, and Chatham Island, in 43° 52' southern latitude, and longitude 179° 14' W., has been selected as a convict settlement. The foregoing remarks, therefore, will be taken as applying to the former condition of the convicts, except as to those who are still left there to serve out their terms of service. Since this change was made, and no more convicts are sent to the colony, those who had not been fortunate enough to secure such as they needed for servants, have been forced to employ free laborers, at an average rate of thirty pounds sterling per year, in addition to rations. It was to be expected, therefore, that some considerable inconvenience should be at first felt; but the colony has already recovered from the shock, and is steadily pursuing her career of prosperity.

A few, and but a few, in comparison with the whole number of convicts, become good citizens. Many of them engage in trade, and amass great wealth. A large proportion of the shopkeepers in Sydney are liberated convicts; and ticket-of-leave men often follow similar pursuits, with the consent and patronage of their nominal employers.

(11.) Tasmania, or Van Diemen's Land, has long been associated, in idea, with New Holland, and it should be mentioned in connection therewith. This island was originally discovered in 1642, by the Dutch navigator, Tasman; but it received the name of Van Diemen's Land, which is now justly giving place to that in honor of its first discoverer, after a governor of the Dutch East Indies. It was visited, and partially explored, by Cook, Furneaux, and other navigators, but was not known to be an island till 1798, when Bass sailed through the straits to which his name has been given.

The island is shaped like a heart, and lies between latitude 41° 20′ and 43° 40′ S., and longitude 144° 40′ and 148° 20′ E. It contains about twenty-seven thousand square miles. The population, in 1838, numbered 45,846, of whom 18,133 were convicts. What has been previously said in regard to the free colonists and convicts of New South Wales will apply, with some trifling and unimportant exceptions, to those of Tasmania.

Geölogical appearances seem to lead to the conclusion that this island, and the main continent of Australia, were once united, though they are now separated by a deep sea, averaging one hundred and forty miles in width. Tasmania is much smaller, it is true, and, therefore, there is scarcely room for the same variety of scenery observed in Australia; yet its outlines, form and appearance, are very different. The shores are bolder and more picturesque; and the mountains rise, not in continuous ranges, as on the Australian Continent, but in isolated peaks, often abruptly, to the height of from three to four thousand feet,—their rough sides deeply indented with furrows, and the jutting crags, and tall cliffs of basalt, on their cloud-capt summits, frowning gloomily on the valleys at their feet. The surface of the country is broken and uneven, consisting of elevated table lands, and fertile valleys, disposed alternately, most of which are fit either for cultivation or pasturage. Sandstone, limestone, and basalt, are the principal rocks. Coal, copper, lead, zinc, and manganese, exist; and iron ore has been obtained, yielding eighty per cent. of metal, in considerable quantities.

The upper soil is a rich vegetable mould, or sandy, or argillaceous. A large portion of the island is adapted to cultivation: there are immense tracts of the finest land lying along the coast; and in the interior, there are extensive reaches of prairie, covered with thrifty herbage, and already fitted by Nature for the plough.

Lands were at first granted to the voluntary settlers,—the average price per acre ranging from five to six shillings, English currency. Subsequently they were sold at auction. Great quantities were thus disposed of, yet it is estimated that there are full eleven millions of acres on the island still ungranted.

Europeans are much sooner acclimatized in Tasmania, than in New South Wales. The climate is more healthy, and the changes of temperature more regular in their recurrence; happily, too, the extremes of drought and flood so common in Australia, are not witnessed here. The winters are colder, and the summers more mild, than in the neighborhood of Sydney.

Vegetation is much the same as in Southern Australia. The same trees, plants, and flowers, with few exceptions, are found in tolerable profusion. The most valuable timber trees are the Huon and Adventure bay pines, and the black wood, which last is peculiar to the island. Apples, currants, plums, and gooseberries, attain maturity, but the peaches and grapes are quite inferior. Citrons, oranges, and pomegranates, are not raised. Agriculture is yet in a backward state, rather on account of the improper or deficient culture, than the inferiority of the soil. The latter is probably better calculated for grazing than cropping, and the climate is altogether too cold for maize. Wool is the staple product of the colony, and the amount sheared is said to double every ten years. The stock of horses and cattle is also very large, and goats are quite numerous.

The animal kingdom is likewise similar to that of Australia. Kangaroos are more plenty, however; but there is no native dog. Still, his place is well filled by the forester, a species of panther, which commits great havoc among the sheep. All the different genera of the marsupialia are found, and there are two species of dasyuri peculiar to the island ; these are the dog-faced dasyurus, and the dasyurus ursinus. The former resembles an ill-made dog, but is marked with stripes like the zebra. The latter is an ugly and disgusting animal in appearance, whence the colonists have called him the " devil."

Numerous excellent harbors are furnished in the frequent indentations of the coast, and at the mouths of the rivers there are some of the finest roadsteads in the world. The two principal streams are the Derwent and the Tamar. The latter is formed by the North Esk and the South Esk. All these rivers rise near the centre of the island. The Derwent pursues a south-easterly course, and the others run to the north. The harbor, or roadstead, at the mouth of the Derwent, is forty-three miles in length : it is completely landlocked, and varies in breadth from two to eight miles ; the water is from thirty to forty fathoms deep, and good anchorage is afforded for vessels of the largest class, twenty-three miles above the mouth of the river ; vessels of fifty tons burden can proceed twenty miles higher up, where the navigation is interrupted by an abrupt ridge of rocks. The Tamar, which, perhaps, should more properly be considered as an inlet of the sea, is navigable for vessels of three hundred tons burden, forty miles from its mouth. There is a dangerous bar, however, at the mouth of the river, and the passage up, unless aided by steam, is rather intricate.

There are several lakes of large size in the interior ; one of which, near the centre of the island, is said to be about sixty miles in circumference, to abound with fine fish, and to be surrounded with a profusion of tall funereal pines, and cedars, and eucalypti, whose dark and gloomy shadows are reflected in its clear still waters. Profound silence, broken only by the dismal wailings of the forester, or the shrill cries of the wild fowl that flit slowly over the solitary scene, reigns everywhere around.

Nominally, the government of Van Diemen's Land is subordinate to that of New South Wales ; but, in fact, the local government is administered, independent of the parent colony, by the lieutenant governor, with the assistance of the executive and legislative councils. The former is composed of the lieutenant governor, chief justice, colonial secretary, treasurer, and the officer commanding the forces on the island; and the latter consists of the members of the executive council, *ex officio*, and ten or fifteen other persons appointed by the sovereign. Special acts may be passed by the governor and council ; but the common law of England, and the acts of the British parliament, are supreme. In other respects, the civil affairs of the colony are administered in a similar manner with those of New South Wales. The administration of justice, and the mode of discipline adopted with the convicts, are also similar.

The public revenue, mainly derived from the sales of the public lands, amounted, in 1840, to upwards of one hundred and eighty-five thousand pounds sterling : its annual increase being about forty per cent. The annual expenditure, including over ten thousand pounds appropriated to the support of public schools, fell a little short of that amount.

In 1838, the number of natives on the island was only one hundred and thirty. The aboriginal race had been gradually disappearing; but frequent bloody encounters having taken place between the few that were still left and the settlers, they were nearly all caught and sent to Flinders' Island, in Bass' Straits, where they are maintained at the expense of the colonial government. They are, probably, an off-shoot of the Papuan race of the Eastern Archipelago, and are sunk in the lowest depths of degradation, being at the very bottom of the scale of civilization, and seeming almost to defy the efforts of the missionaries to cultivate their minds or Christianize their hearts   Their habits, modes of life, and superstitions, are similar to those of the Australians.

Hobarton, or Hobart Town, on the south-east, and Launceston, on the northern shore, are the only important towns on the island. The former is the seat of government, and is situated on the Derwent, about twenty miles from its mouth. Its fine harbor, which has been described, affords it great commercial advantages, and it is rapidly increasing in wealth, population, and importance. In 1838 its tonnage already amounted to 6079 tons; and the number of its inhabitants was 14,382, over thirty-five hundred of whom were convicts. Its position is highly picturesque. It lies on the declivities of two hills, sloping gently upwards, on either hand, from the valley of a small stream that intersects them, and is surrounded by delightful villas and country residences, tastefully disposed amid groves, and orchards, and gardens, of surpassing luxuriance and beauty. In the rear of the town, on the west, tower up the rough and rocky walls, and the battlemented heights, of Table Mountain, to an elevation of four thousand feet above the sea. The streets are wide, and for the most part intersect each other at right angles. It is regularly and neatly built, and possesses, among its architectural attractions, a spacious and handsome government house, a pretty church, constructed of brick, and a jail. It has, also, a large and convenient quay, at which vessels of the heaviest burden can load or unload.

Launceston lies on the Tamar, about forty miles from its mouth, and, in 1838, contained about six thousand inhabitants. It is pleasantly and agreeably situated, and is laid out with uniformity and regularity. Most of the houses are of two stories in height, and it contains some very good public buildings. Georgetown, at the mouth of the Tamar, is a pretty little village, to which the inhabitants of Launceston resort for sea-bathing, and to enjoy the fine breezes.

(12.) Sydney, however, the capital and seat of government of New South Wales, is the chief mart of the Australian colonies, and the commercial entrepôt and emporium of all the settlements in its vicinity. It is likewise a favorite place of resort, to refit or to obtain supplies, of the whalers that frequent the " middle ground" between New Zealand and Australia. This town contained a population of about thirty thousand, in 1841, including over two thousand convicts, and has increased with considerable rapidity since that time. It occupies two hilly necks of land, bounding, on the east and west, a cove on the south side of Port Jackson, and a broad extent of interval ground lying between them. In the old town, called 'The Rocks,' occupying the eastern peninsula, the streets are narrow and irregular, lined with grog shops and brothels, and everywhere presenting scenes of vice and depravity, painful to the sight, and that sicken the heart. The new town, separated from the former by George street, the principal thoroughfare, and lying on the left side of the cove, and towards the south part of the interval, is laid out more uniformly, and contains many handsome dwellings, rising in successive terraces, and agreeably adorned with the rich foliage of the Australian forest trees.

The old town, though the best adapted for the erection of wharfs and warehouses, is occupied, in great part, by the government domain. The government house is a new building, standing near the road leading to the south head of Port Jackson, and having in its front a fine range of English oaks and Cape pines, where the inhabitants usually go for a drive or promenade. The other public buildings are the barracks, occupying one side of the principal square; the convict hospital, a spacious stone building, with open verandas; the military hospital; the convict barracks; the court-house, jail, and custom-house. There are some fine church edifices; among them, two Episcopal churches, a Roman Catholic cathedral, built in the Gothic style, and several chapels belonging to various dissenting denominations.

Most of the houses are built of a light drab colored sandstone, or of red brick; and many of the private residences are only one story in height, and almost concealed by the masses of dark foliage in the surrounding gardens. House rent is high. Building land on George street has been sold for twenty thousand pounds per acre. There are extensive auction rooms and commercial establishments in the town; hotels and inns in abundance; a number of steam mills; and

a good theatre.   As the soil in the neighborhood of Sydney
is so sandy, and as there is a total absence of springs, the
inhabitants suffered under great disadvantage, in former
years, for the want of water during the long droughts.   In
order to remedy this evil, and to provide for a permanent
supply, Governor Gipps adopted the expedient of damming
up all the small water courses, and then distributing the
water, when required, from these reservoirs, through the
town.

Banking is, perhaps, the chief business carried on in Sydney.   There have been several joint stock associations established, the oldest of which, called the bank of New South
Wales, was founded in 1816.   A savings bank has likewise
been founded, and auction, insurance, gas, and steam companies, formed.

Among the literary institutions are the Australian college
and Sydney college ; a normal institution ; several denomina-
tional schools ; and numerous boarding schools, and private
seminaries of learning.   There are a number of newspapers
published in Sydney, which are conducted with some ability :
but the licentiousness of the press is a subject of universal
complaint.   Every facility for the printing and publication of
books is afforded here, and those which have appeared are decidedly creditable to the taste and skill of those concerned in
their issue.   A museum, rich in Australian curiosities, and a
botanical garden, occupying a part of the public grounds on
the east side of the town, complete the list of attractions.

Paramatta, fifteen miles above Sydney, and one below the
head of steam navigation on Paramatta river, is a small town,
built in a straggling manner, but containing many fine country residences.   Among its public buildings, are the government house, which the governor occupies during the summer
months, the female penitentiary or factory, the barracks, the
court-house, and several churches.   Most of these edifices are
constructed of stone.   Woolongong, the principal port in the
Illawarra district,—which has a good artificial harbor formed
by a massive stone breakwater, the material for the construc-

tion of which was taken from the basin it protects,—and Bathurst, beyond the Blue Mountains, on the river Macquarrie, are the only other important towns in New South Wales.

Adelaide, the capital of South Australia, lies on the east side of the Gulf of St. Vincent. Its construction was commenced in 1837, and, in 1841, it contained about six hundred houses, and four thousand inhabitants. It has a bank, with an extensive circulation, and dealing in exchange on Europe, India, and Cape Town. It has, also, two newspapers, and is quite a thriving business place. Port Lincoln, founded in 1838, on the west side of Spencer's Gulf, is said to possess still better natural advantages, and to be increasing with equal, if not greater, rapidity. Perth, on Swan river, and Albany, on the southern coast, in West Australia, are small towns; and the same is true of Victoria, in North Australia.

(13.) The commerce of the Australian colonies has made wonderful strides. Nine tenths of the trade is probably carried on through the ports of New South Wales. The imports into this colony, principally consisting of liquor, grain, provisions, and manufactured goods, amounted to over two and half million pounds sterling in the year 1840. The exports for the same year fell a little short of two millions. Wool is the great article of export: the amount sent out of the country, in 1840, was 7,668,960 pounds, valued at fifteen pence, sterling currency, per pound. Next in importance is oil; about two thousand tons of sperm, valued at eighty-five pounds per ton, and over four thousand of black whale oil, valued at eighteen pounds per ton, were exported in the same year. There were two hundred and fifty tons of whale bone, worth one hundred pounds per ton, also exported. The exports of Van Diemen's Land, amounted, in 1840, to nearly one million pounds sterling, of which wool was the principal article; and the imports exceeded eight hundred and fifty thousand pounds. Timber is also an important article of export, particularly to the mother country, from all her Austra-

12*

lian possessions, though of less pecuniary value than the others which have been mentioned.

But little attention has, so far, been paid to manufactures; and the enterprise and industry of the population are displayed more prominently, in their pastoral and agricultural pursuits. Water power is scarce, and not very permanent where it can be obtained. As a substitute, steam has been introduced in Sydney and other towns. Flour and saw mills, the machinery of which is propelled by this agent, have been constructed in considerable numbers. In the saw mills, large quantities of timber are prepared for exportation. Red and white wines, resembling hock and claret, are manufactured to some extent, and the cultivation of the grape is constantly growing in favor. There are extensive saltworks at Newington, near Paramatta, where the water is drawn from the river into ponds, and the salt obtained by evaporation. Salt may likewise be procured from many of the springs and streams in the interior; and in the low places impregnated with this substance, it is sometimes only necessary to cut a small hole, or tank, in the ground, when a convenient pickling pan is at once furnished.

CHAPTER XI.

(1.) THE American Exploring Squadron was detained at
Sydney for a long time, in making the necessary repairs, and
completing the outfits, requisite for the service of the vessels
in the high southern latitudes whither they were bound.
And even when orders were finally issued to get ready for
sea, much remained undone that might have promoted the
health and comfort of the crews, and rendered the expedition
more productive in results. In truth, the vessels belonging
to the squadron were not originally calculated for a cruise in
the Antarctic regions, and they were not strong enough of
build, nor sufficiently fortified, to make their way in safety
through the ice-packs which they were expected to encounter. They were poorly supplied, too, with anti-scorbutics,
and other necessaries and conveniences, the want of which
was seriously felt during the whole voyage. The officers in
command were well aware of the deficiency in their preparations, yet the season was now far advanced; from one cause
or another they had been behind time ever since they left
home; and further delay, at this juncture, was entirely out
of the question. Wisely, therefore, and from the most commendable motives, they determined that no trifling difficul-

ties or embarrassments should balk them in the execution of the enterprise which they had so much at heart.

All the preparations that were possible having been made, sails were set and anchors hove up, and on the 26th of December the entire squadron stood out to sea. The scientific corps were left at Sydney, with orders, after completing their researches in New South Wales, to proceed to the Bay of Islands, in New Zealand, which was fixed upon as the rendezvous for the squadron, on their return from the Antarctic.*

For several days after leaving Sydney, the weather was very fine; the sea was remarkably phosphorescent; the temperature of the air was mild; and the favoring wind, that came in gentle puffs, and distended the bellying sails just enough to display the beauty of their graceful outlines, seemed to speak of a softer and balmier atmosphere than that of the bleak and frozen solitudes to which the vessels were rapidly hurrying, like birds on the wing. Availing themselves of the opportunity thus afforded, all hands on board were actively employed in building hurricane houses around the hatches, and calking and chinsing the seams and openings, so as to keep the cabins warm and dry; it being designed to maintain an even temperature of about 50°, inside the vessels, throughout the cruise.

On the night of the 1st of January, 1840, the wind freshened, and the weather came on thick and misty. Before morning, the tender separated from the rest of the squadron, and was unable to come up with them again. She cruised about for upwards of a month, visiting meanwhile Macquarrie and Emerald islands, and on the 5th of February commenced her return voyage to the Bay of Islands, where she arrived on the 9th of March.

---

* Before the departure of the squadron from Sydney, the scientific corps requested permission of Captain Wilkes to charter a small vessel, in which, during his absence, they might survey and examine some of the interesting and important islands in the vicinity. For some reason, which, as the commander vouchsafed no explanation, seems to have been both arbitrarily and unwisely adopted, no notice was taken of their communication.

After the 1st of January, there were comparatively few pleasant days. Dense fogs, and heavy snow squalls and storms, alternated with the open and favorable weather. On the 3d instant, the Peacock separated from the Vincennes and Porpoise, and on discovering this, Captain Hudson steered for Macquarrie Island, which he found to be a lonesome and dreary spot, destitute of either trees or shrubs, its only verdure consisting of long tufted grass, and tenanted by myriads of penguins, (*eudyptes chrysocome*).—This bird, in respect to size, is an inferior variety of the species. It is from sixteen to twenty inches in height, when standing erect. Its plumage is white on the breast, black on the back, and elsewhere of a dark dove color, except on the head, which is adorned with four or five beautiful yellow feathers. Leaving Macquarrie Island, Captain Hudson proceeded to the southward, and again fell in with the Vincennes and Porpoise. The three vessels were now rapidly approaching the great object they hoped to discover, though all on board were fearful that the solution of the mystery would disappoint their half-formed expectations.

(2.) Ever since Cook penetrated to the southward, in January, 1774, on the 107th meridian, west longitude, till his further progress was stopped by a mighty wall of icy mountains, which he was unable to approach sufficiently near for a careful or satisfactory examination, the existence of a vast antarctic continent has been a reasonable supposition with navigators and geographers, although never positively asserted. Captain Wilkes, indeed, asks, in a tone bordering closely upon assurance—" Who was there prior to 1840, either in this country or in Europe, that had the least idea that any large body of land existed to the south of New Holland ?"* It is not necessary to impute to him a desire to magnify his discoveries beyond their real importance ; this, perhaps, natural and excusable feeling, may have prompted his inquiry ; but, however that may be, it is quite certain that he is mistaken. Dumont d'Urville, in the account of

* Narrative of the Exploring Expedition, Vol. II. p. 282.

his expedition to the south pole, does not even affect anywhere to conceal his expectations of the discovery of large
bodies of land.* Captain Balleny was expressly sent, by his
principals, in search of land ;† and the instructions of the
Board of Admiralty to Captain Ross, clearly show that land
of great extent was supposed to exist in the neighborhood of
the south pole.‡

Icebergs were first encountered by the American squadron,
in latitude 61° 08′ S., and longitude 162° 32′ E. Expectation
was all the while on the *qui vive ;* and on the 13th of January,
Lieutenant Ringgold, in command of the Porpoise, then in latitude 65° 08′ S., and longitude 163° E., from the great number
of sea-elephants that were visible, the discoloration of the water,
the dark earth-colored veins and dusty appearance of the icebergs, and the hoarse cry of innumerable penguins distinctly
heard above the roar of the ocean, fancied he had discovered land,
and thought he saw something like distant mountains to the
south-east. Soundings of one hundred fathoms, however,
gave no bottom, and the dense masses of floe-ice prevented
any nearer approach. This was undoubtedly a mere decep-
tion, and the objects seen must have been clouds of condensed
vapor—not an unusual appearance in these high latitudes—
hovering over the margin of the ice, and unable to ascend
beyond a certain height in the clear cold space above. In
confirmation of this supposition, it may be mentioned, that
on the 6th of March, 1841, Captain Ross sailed directly over
and through the mass of mountain land, which Lieutenant
Ringgold, no doubt sincerely, believed he had discovered.§

But on the 16th of January, appearances of land, much

---

* Expédition au Pôle Austral, *passim.*

† Account of Balleny's Discovery, Atheneum (London), November, 1839.

‡ Voyage of Discovery and Research in the Southern and Antarctic Regions,
Vol. I. (Introduction) p. 25.

§ After his return from the Antarctic regions—in April, 1840—Captain Wilkes
addressed a letter to Captain Ross, detailing his experience, and accompanied
with a copy of a chart, showing the discoveries of the American squadron.
The supposed land of Lieutenant Ringgold was also included, and not distinguished from the other discoveries, though marked as Balleny's land on the

darker and altogether different from ice-islands, were discovered from all three vessels. They then continued in a
westerly course, coasting along the icy barriers that shut
them out from the frozen regions of which they caught frequent glimpses. Repeated but vain attempts were made to
effect a landing; their progress either being stopped by impassable fields of ice, or the massive icebergs gathering round and
threatening to embay them. Wearied with cold and fatigue,
and worn out with excitement, both officers and men still
persisted in their efforts. On the 24th and 25th of January
the Peacock lost her rudder in the ice, her bulwarks were
partially torn off, and she was otherwise so seriously disabled,
that her commander decided to return to Sydney forthwith,
where he arrived with his vessel, in a shattered and sinking
condition, on the 21st of February. The Vincennes and Porpoise' kept on to the west, and on the 30th of January the
former discovered Piner's Bay, so called by Captain Wilkes,
in latitude 66° 45′ S., and longitude 140° 02′ 30″ E. The
name of Antarctic Continent was now first given to the newly
found land. On the 14th of February, the greatest extent of

---

original. Hence, Captain Ross was led to regard it as an original discovery, for
he could not consider it as a verification of Balleny, inasmuch as the land seen
by him was more than seventy miles distant. When, therefore, the non-exist-
ence of the land was practically demonstrated by Captain Ross, a certain degree of discredit naturally, yet unjustly, attached to the other discoveries of the
American expedition. This was heightened, too, by the ill-temper manifested
by Captain Wilkes, in his explanations. In the narrative of the latter, Captain
Ross was charged with a want of courtesy in not acknowledging the reception
of his letter; whereas the British navigator, in the account of his voyage,
thanked Captain Wilkes in the kindest terms, for his friendly attentions, though
complaining, at the same time, that both he and d'Urville had occupied the very
ground which they both knew, in advance, the British expedition was designed
to visit. Captain Ross' work was not published till long after Wilkes' narrative,
yet it is to be regretted that the American commander should have anticipated
a want of courtesy, where none in reality existed; and that when he had in-
cautiously committed an error, he should exhibit so much bitterness and passion
in offering the easy and simple explanation it was in his power to make.—See
Wilkes' Narrative, vol. ii. p. 282, and App. No. 24; Synopsis of the Cruise of
the Exploring Expedition, p. 21, et seq.; Defence of Captain Wilkes before the
Court-Martial, p. 48, et seq.; Ross' Voyage, vol. i. pp. 115, 116—p. 285, et seq.—
and the appendix.

coast in sight at any one time, computed to be about seventy-
five miles in length, and its highest land attaining an elevation of three thousand feet, was discovered in latitude 65° 59'
40'' S., and longitude 106° 18' 42''. On the same day, the
progress of the Porpoise was checked by an immense wall
of ice trending far to the north, and she then commenced her
return, arriving at the Bay of Islands on the 26th of March.
The Vincennes was stopped by the same barrier on the 17th
instant, whereupon her head was turned towards Van Diemen's
Land. Unfavorable winds cut her off from Hobarton, and she
proceeded to Sydney, where she joined the Peacock on the 11th
of March.

During this cruise, a line of coast, plainly visible, except
at occasional intervals, was discovered, between the 104th and
159th meridians, eastern longitude, and the parallels of 64°
and 67°. The furthest point south which the vessels were
able to reach was Disappointment Bay, in latitude 67° 04'
30'' S., and longitude 147° 30' E. A very near approach was
made to the magnetic pole, which, according to the observations obtained, was supposed to be in about latitude 70° S.,
and longitude 140° E.

(3.) Other discoveries by different navigators, prior or subsequent to the explorations of the American squadron, have
verified what they saw, and contributed additional information ; yet the merit of having made the first discovery of a
large body of land, supposed, though not absolutely proven,
to be an extensive continent, is clearly their due. Captain
Biscoe, the discoverer of Enderby Land, believed that he
saw detached portions of the same land in 1831, when in the
brig Tula. In July, 1838, Captain Balleny was sent out from
London, with two small vessels, owned by the Messrs. Enderby
and other merchants, under special instructions to push as
far south as possible, in search of land. In obedience thereto,
Captain Balleny proceeded along the 172d meridian, east longitude, as high as latitude 69° S. Then turning westward,
he discovered a group of islands, five in number, on the 9th
of February, 1839, in latitude 66° 44' S., and longitude

163° 11' E. He also thought he saw appearances of land in the direction of the American discoveries. But the examinations of Biscoe and Balleny were merely cursory, and there is no reliable evidence that they were not deceived by ice-blinks or fog-banks, except the naked fact that a continent was subsequently discovered in this quarter by the exploring squadron under the command of Captain Wilkes.

Another claimant to the original discovery appeared in the French admiral, Dumont d'Urville, so deservedly held in high estimation, while living, for his numerous important discoveries, and his great scientific acquirements, and whose melancholy fate elicited such general expressions of regret.* This eminent navigator left France, in 1837, with two corvettes—*l'Astrolabe* and *la Zélée*—on a voyage of discovery in the Antarctic seas. After visiting the southern Pacific, and discovering Louis Philippe Land, he proceeded to Hobarton to refit his vessels for another cruise. He sailed again from that port, on the 1st of January, 1840. On the evening of the 19th instant he discovered land on the 142d meridian, east longitude, and near 66° southern latitude.† Attempts to reach the main shore were vainly made, but on the 21st instant, some of the officers of the expedition succeeded in gaining a small islet within a short distance of the coast, and obtained a number of specimens of the granitic rock of which it was composed. The land was then traced in a continuous line for a distance of one hundred and fifty miles, between the longitudes of 136° and 142° E., and in about the latitude of the Antarctic circle. It appeared to be entirely covered

---

* M. d'Urville was one of the victims of the fire that destroyed the cars on the railroad between Paris and Versailles, on the 8th day of May, 1842.

† Voyage au Pôle Sud, ect, ect, tom. viii., p. 170 et seq.—Land was first discovered by the American squadron, as has been stated, on the 16th of January, some distance further to the east than the Terre Adélie of d'Urville, although Captain Wilkes and his officers were not fully convinced on the subject till the 19th instant, the very day of the French discovery. This fact, and that of the Americans necessarily following in the track of d'Urville, after they reached, in their progress to the westward, the meridian where he was on the 19th instant, though they went far beyond him, are the only really plausible arguments upon which the French base their claim to the prior discovery.

with perennial snow, destitute of vegetation, and averaging about thirteen hundred feet in general height. The name of *Terre Adélie* was now given to it by the French commander, and he continued his way to the west. In a few days he discovered, and sailed for about sixty miles along, a solid wall of ice one hundred and fifty feet high—probably near the Piner's Bay of Captain Wilkes—which he believed to be the crust or covering of a solid body of land, and named *Côte Clairée*. The discovery was soon after made that the line of coast trended to the southward, and as his crews were in an enfeebled condition, and the vessels, which, like those of the American expedition, were illy adapted for such service, had suffered considerable damage, Admiral d'Urville issued orders on the 1st of February to bear away for the north, and on the 17th of the month he once more anchored in the Derwent. Having repaired his vessels he set sail for France, where he arrived in safety, having performed, as it eventually proved, his last voyage. The magnetic observations of the French vessels corresponded very nearly with those of the American squadron, and indicated that the magnetic pole was not far from Terre Adélie.

(4.) But by far the most important, and the greatest amount of information in regard to the Antarctic Continent, was obtained by Captain Sir James Clark Ross, of the British navy, and the discoverer of the northern magnetic pole, in three successive voyages, made between the years 1840 and 1843. The principal objects had in view in fitting out his expedition were the improvement of the science of magnetism, and the determination of the position of the southern magnetic pole. He left England with two vessels, the Erebus and Terror, in September 1839, and arrived at Hobarton on the 16th of August, 1840. Unlike those of the French and Americans, his vessels were amply provided with suitable stores and necessaries, and so strongly fortified to penetrate the ice, that he at one time forced them through a thick belt two hundred miles across, which would have completely destroyed any other craft, into the open sea beyond.

Having been apprised of the discoveries of the American and French squadrons, and learning that they had failed to get beyond 67° southern latitude in the quarter he had selected for his own operations, Captain Ross determined to deviate from his original plan. He left Hobarton, therefore, on the 12th of November, 1840 ; and entering the Antarctic regions still further to the east, he found himself, early in January, 1841, amid immense fields of ice. The first land seen was discovered on the 11th instant, and consisted of a mountainous range, from seven to nine thousand feet high, whose summits were covered with snow and the intervening valleys filled with glaciers, with the bare rocks peeping out here and there through their wintry coverings, reaching away, far beyond the view, in a southeasterly direction. In front of the main coast, at a distance of thirty miles, loomed up a tall mountain, like some hoary sentinel, called Mount Sabine, which was estimated to be from seven to ten thousand feet above the level of the sea. Not far distant was Possession Island, as it was christened, in latitude 71° 56′ S., and longitude 171° 07′ E., approachable only on the northern side, and covered with a deep bed of guano that emitted an intolerable stench.

The 28th of January, 1841, was signalized by the discovery of two lofty mountains—one of which, called Mount Erebus, was 12,400 feet high, and an active volcano, and the other, called Mount Terror, was an extinct volcano having an elevation of 10,900 feet. Mount Erebus is in about latitude 76° 06′ S., and longitude 168° 11′ E., and Mount Terror lies a little further to the east and south. The former is connected with the main land, and is described as presenting a most grand and imposing spectacle. The officers fancied they saw the streams of red-hot lava ploughing their way through the snows of ages, down its corrugated sides ; and they plainly witnessed the dark gyres and tall columns of smoke hurled into the air, to the height of fifteen hundred or two thousand feet above the mouth of the crater, where glowed unceasingly the forked flames, whose meteor glare illuminates the profound darkness that broods over this dreary clime in the long nights of winter, and literally and truly sheds its light upon the physical construction of the globe. Captain Ross might well congratulate himself upon the discovery of this beacon-fire, standing, as it were, at the very outposts of the world.

Pursuing their westerly course still further, the English vessels reached the highest point of southern latitude, in 78° 04′, where they found the way blocked by a perpendicular wall or cliff of ice, over one thousand feet thick, from one hundred and fifty to two hundred feet high, and four hundred and fifty miles in length, along whose base were scattered wide fields of blocks and bergs of ice, which rose and fell with the restless waves that spent their fury in vain against the frozen bulwarks that confined them. For many a weary mile, the Erebus and her consort coasted along this ice-bound shore, to which Captain Ross gave the name of Victoria Land, inside the ice-pack through which they forced their way. Sixty-three days were spent to the south of the Antarctic circle, and the approach of the winter season—Captain Ross having in vain sought for a place where he might remain till the ensuing spring—alone compelled them to return to a warmer climate. On the 28th of February, they caught the last glimpse of Victoria Land as they bore away to the north. In their subsequent route, they crossed over the land supposed to have been seen from the Porpoise, and the tracks of the American vessels, and on the 6th of August following, came to anchor within the head lands of the Derwent.

Two voyages were subsequently made by Captain Ross in these regions. In the winter of 1841–42, he penetrated as far south as 78° 10′, but was less successful than on the former occasion. At an early period he was entangled in an ice-pack through which he pushed his vessels, and from which he never emerged for a thousand miles. The barrier of ice was traced ten degrees further to the east, when the winter again set in. In 1842–3 the third and last attempt was made to reach the pole, but this was attended with still less success; and the persevering and undaunted navigator was obliged to abandon the ambitious hope he had cherished, of completing the coronal of his fame by the discovery he longed to achieve. He penetrated to latitude 71° 30′ S., between 10° and 20° of west longitude, and from the extensive and minute magnetic observations he had taken, assigned the position of the southern magnetic pole in 75° 05′ S., and longitude 154° 08′ E. Forced to content himself with this, as his officers and men were well nigh exhausted, he relinquished all further efforts in this quarter, and returned to England.

In the winter of 1844–45, Lieutenant Moore proceeded to the Antarctic regions, from Cape Town, on a scientific expedition, in the barque Pagoda, hired for that purpose by the British government. He made a little further southing, between the meridian of Greenwich and 120° east longitude, than any other vessel had previously done, but was unable to reach the magnetic pole, in consequence of the pack ice and bergs he encountered. He completed the observations, however, left unfinished by Captain Ross, and confirmed the existence of the Antarctic continent discovered by Captain Wilkes, of which Victoria Land is probably a continuation.

(5.) As one of the results of these various expeditions to the Antarctic seas, we have the discovery of the vast feeding grounds of innumerable whales, who will probably soon become accustomed to be disturbed in their icy retreats. Navigation in these bleak latitudes, where the thermometer ranges at 12° during the warmest summer month, and at noon rises only to 14°,—and where the waves that break over the vessels frequenting their waters freeze as they fall on the decks and rigging,—must always be difficult and dangerous; yet whalemen are proverbial for their fearlessness in encountering the perils of the deep. Appalling, therefore, as these obstacles may be, if possible to be surmounted, they will both defy and overcome them.

But of primary importance, in a scientific aspect, are the magnetic observations obtained, and the geological discoveries that have been made. The true position of the southern magnetic pole has been pretty nearly ascertained, and a very correct knowledge gained in regard to the dip of the whole southern hemisphere, and the courses of the variation lines, and of the intersecting lines where they approach their respective poles—all indispensable to the establishment of a complete and reliable theory of terrestrial magnetism.

(6.) It is quite evident, from the comparatively few well authenticated facts so far established, that the Antarctic Continent is of a volcanic character, and mainly composed of lava and basalt. Large masses of earth have been seen on the bergs near the main shore, and boulders of granite, and fragments of sand and gravel, found firmly imbedded in the ice. Soundings obtained by the Peacock, too, in five and eight hundred fathoms, brought up granite, red clay, and dead coral. The coast outline is exceedingly bold. Bluff capes and promontories jut out into the ocean, behind which the land rises precipitately, peak above peak, in stupendous mountain ranges, whose steep escarpments present vast icy masses of crystallization, or are enveloped in perpetual snow.

Along the coast there is a belt of field ice, with occasionally an ice-pack, averaging about fifty miles in width. In this there is but little change. Masses of ice are constantly being disrupted, in the winter, by the difference in temperature between the air and the water, and the outer bergs are sometimes driven away by the prevailing southerly winds into warmer regions, where they gradually disappear. But the stationary ice can scarcely be said to thaw, and congelation is constantly taking place to supply any deficiency. Large pools of fresh water, probably rain, in sufficient abundance to supply a navy, are often found on the tops of icebergs, covered over with a thin crust of ice.

(7.) When the icebergs are first disrupted, they are commonly of a tabular formation ; but after they have been for a long time exposed to the action of the waters and the occasional heat of the sun, they present greater irregularities, and frequently assume the most fanciful appearances.* Wide

* Icebergs one-third of a mile in length, and from one hundred and fifty to two hundred feet high, are frequently seen, in the high southern latitudes.

holes are worn into their fluted sides, over which depend
gigantic icicles ; and as the shadows appear and disappear in
the crevices, with the wavy motion of the sea, it requires
but little stretch of fancy on the part of the beholder, to regard them as fairy habitations, or Gothic shrines,—or he may
be reminded of that Neptunian palace which the genius of
Scott has hallowed—

> " That wondrous dome,
> Where, as to shame the temples deck'd
> By skill of earthly architect,
> Nature herself, it seem'd, would raise
> A minster to her Maker's praise !"

When the sky is unobscured by the dense mists, and the
heavy cumulous clouds, whose deep shadows are so commonly thrown over this chosen abode of the gloomy winter,
and the glorious rays of the sun are permitted to dart forth
in perfect freedom, they seem to run riot with gladness, and
the whole atmosphere, the sky, the ice, and the ocean, fairly
flicker with their splendor. And when the long twilight
comes on, everything is adorned with their rich tintings of
puce and salmon color, till the entire landscape glows with
their parting effulgence.

The Aurora Australis is also represented as appearing like
some vision of enchantment. It is so brilliant at night that
the smallest print is distinctly legible. The upper points of
the rays are often more beautifully attenuated than those of
the Aurora Borealis. Sometimes there is no exhibition of
color, and at others the aurora is of a yellow color, with
edges of the purest pink or green. The coruscations are
usually most brilliant. Vivid flashes of a bright pink dart
upward continually, and tall streamers float along the sky,
from the cloud to the zenith, having a tremulous lateral
motion, and presenting a most brilliant display of all the
prismatic colors.

(8) All traces of vegetation, unless exhibiting itself in new
forms hitherto unknown, disappear on entering this region of
eternal frost and snow. The cabbage (*pringlea anti-scor-*

butica) of Kerguelen's Land, is, perhaps, the only plant that flourishes, with even tolerable vigor or luxuriance, as high as 50° southern latitude.   Beyond this, only the hardiest lichens, and the very lowest order of plants, are seen.   Cockburn's Island, in latitude 64° 12′ S., and longitude 59° 49′ W., presents the last appearances of vegetation.   Unfriendly as are the soil and climate of this bleak spot, lichens are found here as high as fourteen hundred feet above the sea; but coldness and moisture seem to be far less prejudicial to their growth than the warmth of the sun, which causes them to become crisp and parched, so that they crumble in pieces at the slightest touch.

The animal kingdom is much better represented.   Here may be seen the extensive "rookeries," as they are termed by seamen, of countless numbers of seals; the feeding-grounds, abounding with animalcules and crustacea, of whales who have never yet been disturbed by their great enemy, man; and the teeming abodes of penguins and petrels, whose cries are ever heard rising shrill and clear, as if in proud defiance, above the wild howling of the wintry blast.   There are many of the large hunch-back and sperm whales, and it is almost impossible to count the numerous seals, that may be discovered on a pleasant sunny day, enjoying their favorite pastime of basking on the ice.   Sea-lions and sea-elephants are abundant.   The former is a large earless seal, having a heavy mane like the lion : the latter also belongs to the seal family, and is sometimes called the elephant seal; it is from twenty to thirty feet long, and from fifteen to eighteen feet in circumference; the full-grown male possesses the power of elongating his nose into a proboscis, or trunk, about twelve inches in length, and hence the appellation which it usually bears, has been bestowed upon it.   The Antarctic seas are filled with the molluscous and minute marine animals on which the whales feed.   One of the most remarkable varieties of the finny tribe found in their waters, is the "killer :" this is a fish about twenty feet long, of a brownish color on the back, and white on the belly, having a long dorsal fin, an possessing immense strength ; it often attacks one of the largest whales, catching him by the throat, and worrying him to death, but, as the whalers say, it contents itself with devouring the tongue of its victim—thus indicating, savage and ferocious as it may be, the possession of a most refined epicurean taste.

Among the wild fowl are albatrosses, Port Egmont hens, and petrels, in great abundance. Large flocks of cape pigeons are often seen. The edges of the cliffs are filled with the nests of the pintado birds and rapacious skua gulls ; and the loud coarse notes of the innumerable penguins make an eternal din. The largest of the penguins found here weigh upwards of sixty pounds each : their flesh is of a dark color, and has a rank fishy flavor.

(9.) On overhauling the Peacock at Sydney, it was found that extensive repairs would be necessary. She therefore remained here, with orders to follow the squadron to Tonga-taboo, while the Vincennes sailed for New Zealand on the 19th of March. In the morning of the 30th instant, the latter entered the Bay of Islands, and came to anchor in the Kawa-Kawa river, where she found the Porpoise and Flying Fish, and the scientific corps, looking for her with some anxiety. The Peacock, having completed her repairs, and replenished her stock of provisions, sailed from Sydney, on the same day, for the Tonga Islands.

13

CHAPTER XII.

(1.) It has been well said that England girdles the world with a chain of fortifications. At home, though small and diminutive in area, she bristles with bayonets, and forts, and armaments, and from her prolific hive sends forth army after army of soldiers; yet the vicissitudes of climate, and the chances of war, seem never to diminish the supply. Her vessels, too, are dispatched to every clime, and when new discoveries are made, they are promptly occupied by her people. Her indomitable will and untiring energy are rarely foiled; and whatever spot on the habitable globe, in the possession of a weaker race, excites her cupidity, or appears to be necessary or convenient for the accomplishment of her projects, it is doomed, sooner or later, by peaceable or forcible means, to fall under the dominion of her flag.

In the East Indies she is supreme, and in China her power has been felt, and is now tremblingly acknowledged. In the Eastern Archipelago she knows no rival; and from the Lion's Rump at Cape Town, she looks forth over the broad ocean, with the air of a conqueror, whose superiority none question or dispute. She has planted herself firmly on the coasts of Africa, and of North and South America; and the best of the West India islands are hers. Malta is no longer held by the knights hospitallers of St. John of Jerusalem, but the pride of the Mediterranean has passed into the hands of the Briton.

The rock of Gibraltar, occupied by the soldiery of England, like the Acropolis of Corinth, throws its shadow over two seas ;* and the banner of St. George, waving in sullen majesty over the rock of St. Helena, is seen far out in the Atlantic.

\ (2.) One of the most recent acquisitions of the British government, is New Zealand, which consists of a group of two large and several smaller islands in the Southern Pacific ocean, lying between the parallels of 35° and 47° of southern latitude, and 166° and 179°, east longitude. Tasman, in 1642, was the first discoverer of New Zealand, but he obtained very little information in regard to its extent and character. Captain Cook, however, made two voyages hither, in 1769 and 1774; his examinations of the islands and the neighboring waters were carefully and critically made, and the real merit of the discovery may, therefore, with much justice, be claimed for him. At any rate, its substantial advantages have, after some delay, accrued to the government by which he was commissioned.

It is mentioned as a singular fact, that the natives had no name originally for either of the islands, or for any part of the country. Cook and d'Urville were evidently ignorant of this, and gave them appellations which they had heard among the natives, and supposed to be applied to the islands. Until the English occupation, the two larger islands, however, were generally designated among sailors and whalemen, as the North, and the South Islands ; and the small island, still further south, was called Stewart's Island, after the master of an English vessel, who assisted the natives of the northern island in a bloody foray among the inhabitants of South Island. The present masters of the group have latterly provided names for their new acquisitions. North Island is now called New Ulster ; the middle, or South Island, New Munster ; and Stewart's Island, New Leinster. New Ulster is the widest of the two principal islands, being about three hundred miles in its greatest

" Quâ summas caput Acrocorinthos in auras
Tollit, et alternâ geminum marè protegit umbrâ."
P. Statius, *Thebaid.*, lib. vii.

breath, but New Munster is considerably the largest. The area of all the islands is estimated at about 86,000 square miles.

Along the centre of New Munster, throughout its whole extent, and along rather more than the southern half of New Ulster, runs a mountainous range, from south to north, which has every appearance of having been once continuous. Subordinate hilly ranges lie on either side, and, here and there, are detached outliers of vast dimensions. Along the line of the main cordillera are tall mountains, overtopping their companions, and lifting their heads into the region of perpetual snow. The loftiest peaks are the 'Lookers-on,' and Mount Egmont, lying near the southern extremity of New Ulster, which are supposed to be from eight to fourteen thousand feet high. The country at the bases of the mountains is made up of plain, pasture, marsh, and woodland. Some of the hills are barren, or covered with a thick growth of fern, but they are generally wooded to their very summits; and there are immense forests spread out along the flanks of the cordilleras, which climb the sides of the highest mountains, and encircle their snow-tipped peaks with rich fringing borders and belts of evergreen.

All the islands, so far as known, are well watered. Small brooklets thread their way down the sides of the great central mountain range that intersects New Ulster and New Munster, and singing ever so many a pretty refrain, as they wind out and in among the nooks and fissures, or spring from rock to rock, finally descend to the plain beneath. Here larger streams are formed, by the union of several of the smaller torrents, which proceed on their oceanward course,—now lazily crossing some sandy barren, now flashing through the interstices of the leafy forest, now half hidden beneath the long waving fern, and now leaping gayly forth into the sunlight, and bounding over the rocks and precipices, in picturesque falls and charming cascades, till at length they mingle their waters with those of " the dark, deep sea."

Five principal rivers, and numerous minor streams, debouch

into the Bay of Islands. The names of the former are Kawa-Kawa, Kiri-Kiri, Loytangi, Waicaddie, and Warooa. There are some fine cascades in the last mentioned stream, and in the Kiri-Kiri there is a magnificent waterfall to which the natives have given the poetic appellation of *Wani-Wani*, or "the waters of the rain-bow." One hundred and forty miles south of the Bay of Islands, is the Thames, or Waihou, and on the west side of the island is the Hokianga, both of which are considerable streams. The tide flows up many of the smaller rivers, and the larger ones are navigable for some distance by vessels of heavy burden. The Hokianga, however, has a bar at its mouth which obstructs the navigation, though it is ascended by boats as high as tide water, thirty miles up.

(3.) Perhaps there is no country in the world, having an equal extent of coast, that possesses more or finer harbors and roadsteads. This is especially true of New Ulster, whose shores are generally iron-bound, and quite dangerous to those not familiar with the channels and openings. Its harbors are principally formed by indentations in the coast. The chief importance is justly attached to the Bay of Islands, on the eastern shore. This is shaped like an open hand in the act of grasping the island, and derives its name from the great number of rocky islets with which it is studded. At its entrance, which is about eleven miles in width, it has Cape Brett on the south, and Point Pocock on the north. It is spacious and commodious, affording ample room for vessels to beat in, and is surrounded with bays and inlets, some larger and some smaller, extending in every direction, and presenting secure places of retreat when the winds mutter their hoarse wailings, and the loud roar of the beating surge is echoed from headland to headland.

Within the Bay of Islands, the anchorages most frequented are the roadstead of Tepuna, on the north side of the bay, and opposite to the mission of that name; and the Bay of Kororarika, and the Kawa-Kawa river, on the southern shore. Other numerous inlets and indentations afford deep and safe anchorage grounds. An occasional patch of marshy ground may be seen along the shores of the bay, but the scenery is for the most part bold and picturesque,—the surrounding hills averaging from three to five hundred feet in height, and at the head of the bay attaining an elevation of one thousand feet. Forests of magnificent timber, and pretty groves, amidst which the beautiful cottages of the foreign residents are tastefully disposed, give to all a most pleasing effect.

Wangarara Bay, thirty miles south of Cape Brett, is said to be still safer than the Bay of Islands. It is a deep indentation running parallel to the coast, and is separated from the ocean by a narrow belt of high and rocky land. The anchorage is good six miles from the entrance, which, though but one mile in width, is deep and free from danger.—Cloudy Bay, near the south end of New Ulster, is a great place of resort for whalers, many of whom live there; and Port Cooper, on the north side of Bank's Peninsula, is also an excellent harbor.

First in commercial importance, of the towns in New Zealand, is Kororarika, on the southern shore of the Bay of Islands. It has the deepest water, in its bay, and is the best sheltered from the wind. It contains over one hundred houses, and other buildings, among which is a Roman Catholic chapel, and is filled with a heterogeneous population, numbering about one thousand, and made up of civilized and uncivilized natives, foreign residents, escaped convicts from the British penal settlements, and runaway sailors. So famous was it, at one time, for the scenes of iniquity and degradation it constantly presented, that it was called " Black-guard Beach ;" but since the British government have taken possession, a police similar to that at Sydney has been introduced, and a much better state of things now prevails.

Pahia, on the opposite side of the bay, is very pleasantly situated : the principal missionary establishment of the Episcopal church is located at this place ; and here are the residences of those attached to the missions, and their printing presses. East of Pahia is a new town, called Victoria, which at first grew, under the impetus of speculation, with considerable rapidity. Its progress has since been checked to some extent, but it must eventually become quite a town. Eleven miles from the Bay of Islands, up the Waicaddie river, is Waicaddie Pa, probably the largest native town in the islands. It is a neat and cleanly place, and, as might be presumed from this fact, has a prosperous mission establishment.

Auckland, the capital of New Zealand, is situated on the Waitemata river, which affords it a spacious harbor, in latitude 36° 51′ 27″ S., and longitude 174° 45′ 20″ E.: it is a thriving town, and contains between two and three thousand inhabitants. The other principal stations are Port Nicholson, which has upwards of five thousand inhabitants, Port Nelson, and New Plymouth.

(4.) Volcanic phenomena may be witnessed almost everywhere in the interior. There is an active volcano on the Bay of Plenty, on the east coast of New Ulster, and at the northern extremity of the island there are a great number of conical hills, from three to five hundred feet high, with small cavities in their tops, which appear to be extinct craters. Cellular lava, and lava in boulders, are abundant. In those districts, too, where these indications of a volcanic origin are more conclusive, there are hot springs, resembling the geysers of Iceland, the waters of some of which rise to the boiling point, and are used by the natives in cooking.* The coasts are lined with dark basaltic rocks, which are worn into various shapes by the constant attrition of the waves. Quantities of pumice stone are found, and it is used by the natives for polishing their spears. Quartz, iron, and iron pyrites, have been discovered imbedded in the soil. Coal is plentiful in the middle island, which also furnishes the green talc, both in lamins and of a loose form, of which the natives make some

* About fifteen miles west of the Bay of Islands is the hot spring of Taiaimi, which is said to be an emission of heated gas bubbling up through the water, and thus giving the latter a boiling appearance. Sulphur is abundant in the vicinity, and a slight crust of alum is formed. The water is strongly impregnated with iron. The gas has no smell, neither is it inflammable.

of their weapons and ornaments.   Manganese, alum, sulphur, slate, copper, whinstone, granite, and marble, are quite common ; and clay, suitable for making bricks, is easily obtained in every part of the islands.

In the vicinity of the Bay of Islands, the rocky subsoil is compact and argillaceous, and it is covered with a layer of stiff clay.   In the neighborhood of the craters the land is much more productive than elsewhere.   On the ridges and elevated plains, the upper stratum is thin, on account of its being washed into the valleys and gulleys, that divide or intersect them, by the frequent rains.   Marshes alternate now and then with the rocky bluffs and precipices along the coast, and are often met with on the banks of the streams.   In general, the soil may be said to be a rich yellow loam or vegetable mould, very fertile, and well adapted to the production of all the vegetables, and most of the grains, raised in Europe and America.

Though the climate of New Zealand is changeable, it is temperate and healthy ; being analogous to that of France, southern England, and the middle states of our own country, and therefore well adapted to European constitutions.   At Auckland, the mean annual temperature is about 59° ; in the summer months it averages about 67°, and in the winter about 52°.   The oppressive heats of the mid-day at Sydney, and the long continued droughts that parch and wither up the vegetation of the Australian continent, are unknown.   Of moisture there is a great abundance.   North-easterly and south-westerly gales prevail at every change of the moon, and almost always bring heavy rains, particularly in the winter season. In the interior, the weather is much colder, but is also more equable.

Nevertheless, on the whole, the climate may be pronounced salubrious, and decidedly favorable to longevity.   In some situations scrofulous and glandular affections are common ; pectoral diseases, rapid consumptions, phthisis, pleurisy and rheumatism, are by no means rare ; yet, after all, most of the prevalent forms of disease have been either introduced by

Europeans, or occasioned by the habits and vices which they have imported.

(5.) It admits of great doubt, whether the native population of New Zealand comes up to 150,000, which is the number usually fixed upon, though some estimates reduce it nearly as low as 100,000. The white, or European population, occupying New Ulster, which has alone been regularly colonized, is not far from twenty thousand.

At the general peace in Europe, the claims of Great Britain to the different islands included in the term of New Zealand, under and by virtue of the discovery of Cook, were recognized. No effort was made, however, to enforce them by occupation and possession, till the year 1833, when a resident, subordinate to the authorities of New South Wales, but clothed with limited powers, was sent thither. The islands had already become infested with runaway convicts and sailors, and marauders of every dye and description. Outrages were daily committed on the persons and property of the natives; the latter were fast learning to imitate the vices and crimes of the outlaws, who both persecuted and demoralized them; and drunkenness, with its consequent evils, crimes, and wretchedness, was becoming everywhere prevalent. Here and there, where the missionary stations were established, and their influence felt, bright spots appeared amidst the moral darkness that overshadowed the land; but beyond their limits, there was nothing to relieve the general depravity, and sensuality, licentiousness, and excess, rejoiced in one continued holiday.

British, American, and French whalers, frequently visited the islands, but they were liable to be molested by the freebooters and their native retainers; resistance often provoked renewed aggressions; and they were sometimes attacked and plundered.

Combinations were likewise formed, principally in New South Wales, to purchase land of the natives. Associations of this character, by the grossest swindling and imposition, obtained the control of extensive tracts in the northern island.

13*

Influenced by their representations, settlers emigrated in considerable numbers from New South Wales, and the other Australian colonies; but colonization, so far from keeping pace with speculation, was completely distanced by it.   Matters were in this position, in 1839, and would probably have continued to remain so; but at that time it was reported, either with or without sufficient cause, that the French government contemplated taking possession of the southern island, and planting a colony there.   The British authorities promptly interfered; a colonial organization subordinate to that of New South Wales was formed in January, 1840; and Captain Hobson, of the Royal Navy, was appointed lieutenant governor of the new dependency.

On the arrival of the lieutenant governor at the Bay of Islands, he issued his proclamation, announcing that all future purchases of land from the aboriginal inhabitants would be absolutely void, unless made through the British local government.   A commission was then appointed to inquire into the validity of all claims to land, under instructions to recognize and confirm those only which were founded on just and equitable considerations, with the proviso, also, that no claim should be allowed for a greater extent than twenty-five hundred and sixty acres.   The lieutenant governor likewise obtained from the principal chiefs, a cession to the British monarch, of the paramount right of sovereignty in the islands, and extinguished the native titles to large bodies of land. These government lands were divided into suitable tracts, and disposed of at auction, to the settlers, and the immigrants who were daily arriving.

Since this formal occupation by the British, a more healthy state of things has existed in New Zealand.   In April, 1841, it was separated from New South Wales, and placed under a governor possessing similar powers with the chief executive officers in the colonies of Great Britain.   With the governor, the colonial secretary and treasurer, the attorney general, and three senior justices of the peace, constitute the legislative council, by whom all laws and regulations, of minor importance, are enacted. The annual expense of administering the government exceeds fifty thousand pounds sterling.

(6.) Ethnologically considered, the native New Zealanders may be classed as belonging to the Malay family, and they are undeniably the best specimens of the race. The men are tall, well-formed and athletic; many of the chiefs are upwards of six feet high; and all possess great strength and activity. The women are likewise well shaped, but they lack the fulness of muscle, and the soft rounded contour, witnessed among other Polynesians. Their color varies in individuals, from a dark chestnut to a light copper or brunette, and resembles very nearly that of the European gypsy, or the Eurasian in India. They have round faces, high foreheads sloping backwards, aquiline noses full at the point, large lips, and fine white teeth. Their eyes are black, strong, and piercing. Their hair is black and commonly straight, but sometimes thick, bushy, and curly; that of the women is frequently fine, soft, and silky. Some crop their hair, leaving only a small bunch on the top of the head, and others suffer it to grow long. Whiskers and beards are not considered at all in good taste among the New Zealand exquisites. Tattooing is practiced, by all who can afford the expense, and often gives a dark expression to the countenance, where it does not really exist. The men ornament their faces and arms, and their whole bodies and limbs, from the navel downwards; but the women rarely tattoo any other parts of their persons except the mouth and the pubes—the latter taking place on their arrival at the age of puberty—though a few ornamental devices about the wrists and ankles are occasionally seen. They pay little regard to personal cleanliness, rarely ever bathe, besmear themselves with grease and dirt, and seem to delight in being filthy.

Portions of the middle island, or New Munster, are said to be inhabited by individuals evidently of the Papuan race, who differ widely from the true New Zealanders, and bear a strong resemblance to the natives of Australia, and the islands of the Eastern Archipelago.

We have different accounts in regard to the character of
the New Zealander; some pronouncing him vindictive, crafty,
and treacherous; and others again insisting that he is frank,
generous, and confiding. Probably all these traits are by
turns displayed. The fierce and bloody conflicts, which are
known to have taken place between the different tribes, indicate a warlike disposition. They are exceedingly proud,
and when insulted, inclined to be revengeful; yet they are
hospitable to strangers, and seem to know how to appreciate
kind treatment. Though practicing infanticide, to a greater
or less extent, they are strongly attached to their children.
Honesty is not one of their failings; but they are somewhat
given to trickishness in their dealings, and their intercourse
with the whites has hardly contributed to divest them of it.
The men are capable of enduring fatigue, yet as their wants
are few and easily supplied, they are naturally indolent; the
labor and drudgery, as is generally the case in Polynesia, and
among all savage races, being performed by the weaker, more
suffering, yet less complaining, part of humanity.

A fondness for curiosities and ornaments is characteristic
of both sexes. Besides tattooing their persons, they bore
holes in their ears, in which are inserted small rings of jade
or talc, or shark's teeth; these are tipped with sealing wax,
or ornamented with white and red, or other bright colored
feathers. The principal chiefs and their wives wear green
talc stones, called *heitikis*, depending from their necks; these
are carved so as to resemble a human figure sitting crosslegged; they are held very sacred, and with the *meära*, a
short cleaver or club, are handed down as heirlooms, from
father to son. Acquisitiveness is a prominent trait among
them, and they are always ready for trading and bartering.
They will sell everything they have, even their sacred
heitikis. At one time a considerable trade was carried on
in New Zealand curiosities, which were purchased at the
islands, and exported to Australia, Europe, and America.
Prominent among the articles of traffic were the tattooed
heads of their chiefs, which commanded very high prices;

but the supply has recently been cut off, in consequence of the absolute prohibition of the sale of them by the British authorities.

Comparatively few of the vices usually witnessed among a savage people, are observed here. Cannibalism and infanticide were formerly very common, and they are now practiced in those districts remote from the white settlements, though they are gradually decreasing. The New Zealand chiefs, and many of the common people, are polygamists, yet always having one favorite wife. They are very jealous of their marital rights, and adultery is punished by the death of the offending parties, and often of their friends. The effects of dissipation are plainly visible among those natives who have adopted the habits and imitated the practices of the abandoned whites. Since 1815, missionaries have been laboring among them with considerable success. In 1843, there were a bishop and twelve clergymen of the established church, and about seventy ministers of the Roman Catholic, Church Missionary, Wesleyan and Scotch Churches. Wherever the influence of the missionaries has extended, though their labors have not been as practically directed as they might have been, a marked change is observable. As the natives have been so much accustomed to receiving presents, they sometimes expect to be paid for their good conduct, and their zeal in attending to their devotional duties. Gifts and proselytes are often made at the same time. But all those who have embraced christianity, or regularly attend church services, are much more virtuous and happy than the other natives; the men are more industrious, and more ready to share the burdens of their wives, while the latter are better-looking and lighter of heart, and no longer seek to check the jocund sprightliness of their daughters, by pointing them to a sad destiny—a dark future of misery and care.

In intellectual endowments they are by no means deficient. They possess a great deal of mechanical skill and ingenuity, though exhibiting it, hitherto, rather in the construction of their richly carved and ornamented canoes, and their fine and

delicate mats, than in the erection of their habitations. They
have shown a singular aptitude in accustoming themselves to
the usages of civilized life. Of poetry they have an abundance, chiefly of a lyrical kind ; rude it is, indeed, yet they
are not entire strangers to metre and quantity. They have
a passionate attachment for music, and, in fact, noise of any
kind. is scarcely ever unwelcome to them. Their voices are
monotonous, and when singing pitched in a high key. They
have their war dances and love dances, and sometimes sham
fights : these are much like exhibitions of a similar character
throughout Polynesia, very picturesque by candlelight, but
not bearing the full glare of day, and always tiresome on
repetition.

It is customary, however, among the New Zealanders, on
almost every occasion of ceremony, be it a funeral festivity,
or a dance, to intersperse the proceedings with discharges of
fire arms, the noise produced by which seems to afford them
real delight.

Surprising though it may be, they have a kind of astronomy
among them ; and like all Polynesians, they appear to have a
faint, though imperfect idea of the creation. In regard to
their own origin, they have no tradition, except that their ancestors came from the east in canoes, sewed together with
sennit.* While they have given no names to their islands,
strangely enough, there is not a single thing in the animal or
vegetable creation, for which they have not a distinct appella-
tive term by which it is generally known.

There was not originally, at the time of the discovery, any

---

* They have likewise a tradition, that their *kumara*, or sweet potato, was
brought from the east. Might not these islands, then, have been visited by
South American Indians, who found them peopled with Malays, or Papuans,
and from whom the present inhabitants have descended ?—or did the ancestors
of the latter come from some of the intermediate isles of the Pacific ? The ease
with which the New Zealander and the Tahitian converse, on first meeting each
other, has before been remarked,(*anté*, p. 178) ; and it is by no means improbable,
that the canoes, the memory of which is preserved in the traditions of the former,
may have originally come from the Society Islands. Nevertheless, how true it
is, that the more ethnology is studied, the more speculative it seems to become.

general head among the natives, even those who were evidently of the same race ; but they were divided into tribes, distinguished by separate names, which were governed by principal chiefs, or *arekees*, and between which fierce and exterminating wars often took place.   A very large proportion of the people were slaves, being subject to chiefs who were owners of the soil, and had the power to dispose of their lands, and alienate their servants, at will.   These chiefs were themselves dependent on the *arekees*, or head chiefs, but often proved refractory and disobedient subjects.

Fortified towns, called *pas*, are the permanent places of residence of the natives.   They consist of collections of huts or houses, built closely together, on high promontories or insulated hills ; such a position being usually selected as will afford the greatest natural resistance to an attacking enemy. These clusters of houses, or *pas*, are surrounded and protected by palisades, or upright stakes, perhaps ten feet high, driven firmly into the ground. Some of the inclosures contain as many as two or even three hundred huts.   The main entrance, or gateway, opening through the row of palisades, is commonly flanked with larger posts, on which are sometimes carved distorted representations of human figures.   Within the principal inclosure, there are frequently minor ones, containing five or six houses, separated from each other by intervening alleys or walks, from two to four feet wide.   Formerly, when the natives were ignorant of the use of fire arms, a *pa* may have been pretty secure against attack, but it would now form a feeble defence.

The huts of the New Zealander are most sorry affairs. They are of an oblong shape, low and small, blackened inside and out with soot and smoke, and defiled from top to bottom, with grease, filth, and dirt, of every kind.   Those of the largest class are only twenty feet long, by twelve feet broad.   In erecting them, they begin with the frame, which consists of four posts driven into the ground at the corners.   These project from two to five feet above the ground, and are connected by horizontal beams firmly secured in their places with twine or sennit. The rafters are laid upon the horizontal beams, and ascend upwards by a slight slope to the ridge pole, which is laid upon two or three posts set on a line running through the centre of the building. The roof descends on all sides, and is composed of rush thatching. Smaller poles fastened to the upright posts, with interstices of a foot in width, form the sides of the building. Twigs are sometimes wattled with the poles to fill up the chinks, or mats are hung up as screens. The doorways are under the eaves at the gable ends, over which mats are hung, though good and substantial doors of deal may now be occasionally seen. A few mats, a number of bark dishes and baskets, two or three fishing nets, an old sea chest in which the household goods are deposited for safe keeping, an iron pot that does all the cooking, and an old-fashioned rusty musket, or double-barreled gun, are about the usual assortment of furniture. Outside the house, there may be a few fruit trees growing, and sometimes a small garden spot can be discovered, though it is more common to see nothing but the former.

Mats, called *kakahus*, made of flax and braided by hand, are worn by both sexes. Those of the men are often very fine, and are sometimes interwoven of various colors, or beautifully embroidered. The women of the lower classes wear coarse corn leaf mats, particularly when at work. The *kakahu* is worn tied round the waist, or thrown over the shoulders. Short cloaks, or *patutus*, about three feet long, made of mat, coarse cloth, or dogskin dressed with the hair on, are worn by the chiefs. Loose slips of calico drawn about the neck, resembling the ancient *tiputa* of the Tahitian female, are frequently displayed by the women. Latterly European fashions have been introduced. Sailors' jackets and trowsers —and often the former without the latter—may sometimes be seen adorning the person of a swarthy New Zealander. Blankets, too, have been introduced, and they are now worn in the same manner as the *kakahu*.

Pork, fish, and potatoes, are the chief articles of food among the natives; and when other vegetables fail them, they

have recourse to the roots of the fern. They are quite partial
to rice, and as fond as bears, of sugar, molasses, and other sweet
things. The Polynesian mode of cooking was formerly in
vogue, but it has now given place to the iron pot, in which
everything is boiled. Where the influence of the missionaries has not proved sufficient to restrain their appetites, they
are much addicted to the use of spirituous drinks, and scenes
of revelry and debauchery, in which both sexes participate,
are often witnessed in the native *pas*. They also make for
themselves a very pleasant beverage, resembling spruce beer,
and having slight intoxicating properties, which they call
wai-maöri. They are quite fond of tobacco, and often use it
to excess.

The custom of *taboo* has yet the force of law. It is for
the most part enforced with great strictness, and carefully
observed ; and it is found exceedingly useful in protecting their
kumara-patches and vegetable gardens.

Funeral ceremonies are noisy enough ; a few rounds of
musketry being always regarded as a *sine quâ non*. When
a chief dies, unusual attention is paid to the rites of sepul-
ture. A small canoe is cut through the middle, and the two
sections being joined together, the body is placed in the cavity.
These receptacles of the departed chiefs are painted some
bright color, and ornamented with feathers. Instead of being
deposited in the ground, however, they are placed beneath
sheds, round about which are fence inclosures.

(7.) Owing to the prevalence of the dark green foliage of
the evergreens, New Zealand wears the appearance of perpetual vegetation. Yet the islands are not within the tropics,
neither do they possess the fruits or vegetables indigenous to
countries so situated. Barren wastes alternate with their
dense forests ; and nowhere is there exhibited the exuberance
of growth in the vegetable kingdom that may be witnessed
in warmer latitudes. Scandent and parasitic plants, which
always add so much to the beauty of tropical landscapes, are
rarely met with ; though now and then a tree may be seen
completely garlanded over with vines. The timber trees

nevertheless are really magnificent; they are mostly of the
pine species, and are regarded as among the most valuable in
the world for ship building.   The Kauri pine attains an enormous size: in 1841, one was cut and shipped which measured twenty-five feet in circumference at the base, and was
one hundred and fifty feet long; and quite lately there was
another standing on the eastern coast of New Ulster, seventy-
five feet in circumference, and estimated to be considerably
more than two hundred feet high.   The Kaikotia pine does
not grow as large as the Kauri, but it is highly valued for
spars.

The plains and low lands of New Zealand, in their natural
state, are overrun with masses of tall impenetrable fern
(*pteris esculenta,*) and with thick bushy shrubs, while the
swamps and marshes produce rushes and the native flax
(*phormium tenax*).   From the latter is procured what has
already become, and what will henceforth be, one of the most
important staples of New Zealand.   The flax is obtained from
the leaves, and not the stem, of the plant.   It is remarkable
for the length, strength, and flexibility of its fibres; and when
the necessary improvements shall have been introduced in its
preparation, it must yield a handsome profit to the grower.
The preparation is now left to the native women, who cut it,
and after dividing it into strips an inch wide, separate the external epidermis, while still in a green state, from the inner
fibres, by means of a muscle-shell or a piece of glass.   Great
care is required to keep the inner fibres straight, in order to
preserve their beauty; and when the separation is completed,
they are hackled and divided, washed, and then bleached in
the sun.

Among the other indigenous products of New Zealand, are
the kumara, or sweet potato; a species of arum esculentum,
known as coccos or eddoes; several varieties of gourds; and
the *tetragonia expansa*.   The last is the well-known New
Zealand spinach, which has been introduced into Europe and
America.   It is a succulent trailing plant, having no pretensions to beauty, but possessing this advantage over the com-

mon spinach—that, if well watered, it will produce leaves of
the greatest juiciness during the entire summer.   It is said
that a bed of twenty plants will afford a supply sufficient for
a large family.

The natives are not ignorant of the art of cultivating the
soil.   When Cook first visited the islands, he found that they
turned up the earth in their kumara patches with sharp-pointed
sticks and other rude implements.   Of late years spades and
plows have been introduced.   A great incentive to industry
is furnished by the almost indestructible native fern.   It springs
up everywhere where the forests have been cut down, or in
the open ground where its cultivation is neglected.   When it
has once established itself, it is with difficulty extirpated; and
it can never be got rid of except by plucking it up by the
roots, and burning it.   Even then, wherever there is careless-
ness in tillage, it again makes its appearance, as if it were a
judgment or a punishment for indolence and neglect.

Before he sailed from the islands, at the time of making
his discovery, Captain Cook planted, and left with intelligent
natives, the seeds of wheat, peas, cabbages, onions, potatoes
and turnips.   All these soon run out, with the exception of
the turnips and potatoes; the latter of which is the chief dependence of the New Zealander during the winter season.
In those soils where black loam, vegetable mould, or decomposed basalt, predominates, most of the cerealia flourish,
though Indian corn is the principal grain that is cultivated.
Sometimes wheat is sowed where the fern has been dug up
and burned, yet it rarely yields over fourteen bushels to the
acre, and after it is reaped the ground is seeded down to grass.
Of native grasses there are scarcely any, but the foreign
grasses thrive well.   The New Zealanders themselves do not,
in general, raise over two crops from the same ground, but
after tilling a piece for two seasons they prefer breaking
up new soil.   Apples, peaches, grapes, cape-gooseberries,
and many kinds of melons and other vegetables, have been
introduced and cultivated with success.   The apples and

peaches are very fine, but the grapes do not succeed very well except on volcanic soils.

There being such an excess of moisture in New Zealand, it is quite doubtful whether grain growing, unless it be for home consumption merely, will ever prove very profitable, but for pasturage the climate is decidedly favorable, and the rearing of stock will undoubtedly make handsome returns.

It is a singular fact, that when these islands were first discovered, they possessed no indigenous mammalia whatever ; the only quadrupeds, in fact, being a few species of lizards that were objects of terror and veneration to the natives. The hog, the dog, and the rat, were early introduced. The first was allowed to run wild, and multiplied so rapidly that the islands were soon well stocked. The hogs are very fond of the roots of the fern, which is so exceedingly abundant. When required for food, they are caught by the dogs. The flesh of the rat was esteemed a great delicacy by the natives, and it is now the principal species of game. Cattle, sheep, and goats, were imported by the missionaries, and large additions have been made to the stock of the first two, since the formation of settlements by the whites ; excellent browsing is afforded by the immense thickets of shrubs, where grass cannot be procured, and both appear to thrive unusually well.

Fish abound on the coast. Whales are taken in great plenty ; but it is said their numbers are diminishing, in consequence of the indiscriminate massacre which has been going on for so many years. Smaller fish are taken by the natives with hooks and nets ; they also catch great quantities of shell-fish for food, and there is a clam, called *pipi*, which they esteem highly delicious.

Of the bird kind, there are parrots and parroquets, and wild ducks and pigeons, of large size and fine flavor, in the forests ; and there is an abundance of sea fowl on the coasts. Poultry have been introduced, and are now reared in considerable numbers. The principal singing birds are the native nightingale and the *tui*. The latter is also called the "parson-bird," probably for the reason that its loud, screaming, and not very pleasant notes, resemble the declamatory articulations of the Wesleyan missionary.

(8.) The chief articles of export from the islands, are flax, spars, pine timber, potatoes, and kauri gum. The last is obtained from the pine tree of that name, and is shipped to New South Wales and Europe, where it is made into excellent varnish. In return for their commodities, the inhabitants of New Zealand import, or purchase from the trading vessels in exchange for their products, domestic goods, blankets, guns, powder, lead, agricultural implements, rice, sugar and molasses. At one time the whale fishery was the most profitable employment connected with commerce, and both French and American vessels participated largely in it; but since the establishment of custom houses, and a regular government, they do not visit the islands as much as formerly, and from the causes before mentioned, the fishery is said to be less valuable, though numbers of persons are still engaged in it.

Though exhibiting so little skill or taste in the construction of their mean, low, and dirty houses, the native New Zealanders in reality possess great mechanical ingenuity. This is displayed in their preparation of the flax, in their beautifully woven mats, in their canoes, which are carved and ornamented with great care, and particularly in the aptitude with which they imitate the whites in the use of weapons, tools, or implements. For common purposes, they now use whaleboats instead of canoes; and have substituted the square sail for the triangular one. They have no outriggers on their craft, and though liable to accidents, they show themselves to be expert seamen in their management of them. Their war canoes are from forty to seventy feet in length, with prows extending up to the height of ten or twelve feet, and adorned with waving tufts of bright-tinted feathers, and richly carved ornamental work.

Mills have been set up in New Ulster, and there is a great abundance of water power for propelling machinery on all the larger islands. In the opinion of Mr. Terry, when they

become cultivated and stocked with cattle, and, as an immediate consequence, when the necessaries of life, and labor,
grow cheaper, they must be the seat of extensive manufactures. "In addition," says he, "to moderate wages and cheap
food, there would be the further important auxiliaries of coal,
timber, and clay, with endless excellent localities, having
water communication. New Zealand would then bring into
profitable production her timber, for ship-building; flax, for
canvas, ropes, &c.; copper, for sheathing her ships, and all
other purposes; sulphur, for brimstone, &c.; alum and dye
woods, in manufacturing the wool of Australia or the cotton
of India; tan, for leather from the hides of her own cattle, or
from Australia and South America; tobacco, which could be
manufactured; breweries and distilleries, for barley and hops
of native growth, &c. But it is far more rational to conceive that, instead of attempting fruitlessly to compete
in the exports of raw produce, the colonists, in the first instance, will endeavor to render themselves independent of any
other colony for the supply of food; and when food and labor
are cheap, they will direct their capital and energies to bring
into play the other national products, in manufactures for
their own wants, as well as to supply Australia, India, China,
and Spanish America, all of which are not far distant." *

(9.) Having completed their repairs, all the vessels belonging to the American Exploring Squadron, with the exception of the Peacock, left the Bay of Islands on the 6th day
of April. Prosperous breezes wafted them rapidly on their
way; no incidents of special importance occurred on the passage; and on the 22d instant they made the islands of Eooa
and Tongataboo. On the 24th they came to anchor off
Nukualofa, the principal town on the latter island, and on
the 1st day of May they were joined by the Peacock.

* Terry's New Zealand, etc., pp. 260, 261.

CHAPTER XIII.

(1.) The Tonga Islands.—(2.) Physical Geography. Climate. Productions.—
(3.) Population. Character and Appearance. Dress. Customs. Superstitions.—(4.) Houses. Canoes.—(5.) Missionaries. Wars between the
Christians and the " Devil's Party."—(6.) Sailing of the Squadron, and
Arrival at the Feejee Group.

(1.) AMONG the many other important discoveries of the
eminent Dutch navigator, Abel Janssen Tasman, were the
Tonga Islands, or Hapaï Group. He touched at Tongataboo
in 1642, and afterwards visited the Feejee Group; but in
conformity with the general policy of his government, the
world was not enlightened in regard to his discoveries, till
other navigators had found their way to the islands. Captain
Cook first saw the Tonga Islands in 1773; he spent considerable time in the group, and in allusion to the kind and hospitable treatment he received from the native inhabitants,
named them the Friendly Isles, by which term they are now
most commonly designated.*

There are six principal islands :—Eooa, Tongataboo,
Hapaï, Vavaö, Keppel's Island, and Boscawen,—besides
which, there are a number of small and uninhabited isles,
visited by the natives only for fishing and obtaining *biche de
mer*. Eooa, and Tongataboo, or Tonga, are the southernmost
of the group, and the others lie further to the north; all being included between the parallels of 17° and 22° south latitude, and 172° and 176° west longitude. A strait eight
miles in width, separates Eooa from Tonga, and the other

---

* The term " Friendly Islands" is often applied, as a general appellation, to
the extensive group embracing the Navigators', Feejee, and Tonga Islands.

islands are divided in the same manner by deep sea channels, of greater or less width, in which vessels are often protected, in a degree, from the violence of the waves in the open ocean, by the immense coral reefs that encircle the group. These are low and sunken in many places, and unless provided with a correct chart, or the weather be particularly favorable, it is dangerous for a strange vessel to attempt to pass through the openings. Passages of this kind, however, are quite numerous, and once inside the reefs, still water may frequently be found, even when the storm rages the most fearfully without.

(2.) Quite a variety of scenery is presented in this group of islands. Eooa is rocky and barren, and rises to the height of six hundred feet above the level of the sea. Tofooa, one of the smaller islands, attains a still greater elevation, and is the highest of the group. Hapaï, Vavaö, and Tonga, are much lower, and far more fertile. Some of them are of volcanic origin, and exhibit all the distinctive features peculiar to that formation ; but the only active volcano is on the island of Tofooa. Others are the work of the coral. Tonga is low and almost level ; there being only here and there a small hillock from twenty to forty feet high, and near the northern extremity of the island a conical hill about sixty feet in height. It is not far from one hundred miles in circumference, and has a shallow lagoon, like those in the atolls of the Paumotu Group, extending some ten miles into the interior, though, of course, surrounded by a much greater mass of elevated ground.

Hurricanes and earthquakes are frequent, and the former are very destructive. Rain falls in great quantities, and heavy dews descend at night. The mean temperature in the summer months is about 80°, and the thermometer often rises to 98° in the shade. In consequence of the moist atmosphere, the oppressive heat, and the sudden transitions from the extremes of temperature, the climate is not at all healthy, though the natives, where their habits are regular, frequently live to an advanced age. Fevers, with the exception of intermittents, are not unusually prevalent, but colds, coughs, influenza, and consumption, are common. Glandular swellings and eruptive complaints, superinduced in many cases by intemperance and excess, are more or less prevalent.

Tonga is, perhaps, justly entitled to be called the garden of the group, since it is the most fruitful, and exhibits a greater exuberance of foliage. Yet all the coralline islands are covered with a deep and rich vegetable mould, containing very little sand, which is highly productive. They are beautifully feathered with bread-fruit and cocoas, and adorned with the graceful and majestic trees of the tropics, whose boughs are often interlaced with luxuriant vines and creepers, and with shrubs and plants, in all stages of growth, desirable either for their utility or for ornament. Like the happy valley of Cashmere, each is a paradise rejoicing in " perpetual spring," and when fanned by the soft breezes of summer, wafting the many odors of its perfumed flowers among its sister isles.

All the principal tropical productions flourish on these islands in great abundance. Yams, sweet potatoes, bananas, taro, bread-fruit, cocoa-nut, sugar-cane, shaddocks (*citrus decumana*), limes, papaw, or Carica papaya, and the ti, are the most important indigenous products. The sweet orange of Tahiti has been introduced by the missionaries, and appears to be well adapted to the soil and climate, but the fruit is almost always destroyed by an insect that deposits its larvæ on it, which cause it to fall before it becomes fully ripe. Pine-apples, water-melons, cabbages, turnips, mustard, peppers, maize, a species of chirimoya, and the North American papaw, or custard-apple, have likewise been introduced, and richly reward the time and labor expended in their cultivation. The heathen cultivate the tobacco-plant with great success. The ahia, (*eugenia malacconsis,*) producing a pulpy fruit something like the apple in shape, is occasionally found. There are several species of palms, and different varieties of cane and reeds. The casuarina affords the material for the native clubs, the shafts of their spears, their drums,

and some of their culinary utensils.   There is a species of
nutmeg-tree, yielding an abundance of fruit, which is upwards of forty feet in height.   Specimens of the ficus-tree
may be seen here, having trunks, as it were, composed of in-
tertwining roots, one hundred feet in circumference.   Ornamental shrubs and climbing-plants, euphorbias, tournefortias,
the apapa, and the faifai, are quite common.   The pandanus
is also plentiful, and great care is taken by the natives to
prune it, and otherwise encourage its growth, as all their mats
are made from its leaves.

Most of the fruits and other edible productions of the Tonga
Islands are cultivated by the natives, though they have latterly
become less industrious than they once were, probably for the
reason that they have contracted many of the bad habits of
the whites, and not a few of the vices of their neighbors of
the Feejee Group.   Still, their yam-grounds, and their sweet-
potato patches, receive a great degree of attention, and are
often objects of pride, especially since the substitution of more
modern agricultural implements for the rude ones formerly
in use.

(3.) Like most of the island-groups of Polynesia, the population of the Tonga Islands has been much overrated.   It has been
estimated as high as fifty thousand, but the missionaries located there, who have had ample means of observation, do not
think it can possibly exceed twenty thousand.   Almost one
half of this number are inhabitants of Tongataboo, or, Tonga ;
Hapaï and Vavaö each contain near four thousand inhabitants ; and the remainder are scattered about among the
different islands.

The Tongese have a strong resemblance to the people of
the Samoän Group, and the evidences of a generic affinity between the two are very striking.   The former are more fair,
perhaps ; but their countenances have the same general cast
and expression.   The men have large and powerful frames,
with an abundance of bone and muscle.   Many of the women
and children are almost white, and the Tonga maidens are
remarkable for the possession of great personal beauty.   Their

hair is straight and fine, and naturally of a dark color, but the frequent use of lime-water and lime turns it red ; yet they have black, expressive eyes ; their oval faces are just tinged with olive ; their busts and shoulders are well developed, their forms rounded and full, but not gross, and their limbs neatly turned. These are certainly attractive charms, and when united to an intelligent expression of countenance, gavety, but not frivolity of heart, frank and easy manners, and a true inbred modesty, almost always proof against temptation, surely entitle their possessors to an enviable distinction.

Cleanliness is characteristic of both sexes. The habit of frequent bathing is early acquired, and not often neglected. They are a cheerful and light-hearted people ; fond of music, dancing, and other amusements ; docile ; ingenious ; apt at imitation ; and great chafferers in making bargains. Generally speaking, they are virtuous and industrious ; but, though not yielding so much as might be expected to the enervating influences of the climate, they cannot resist the temptations placed before them by the whites or the neighboring islanders. They are usually quite happy in their domestic relations ; the attachment between husband and wife is strong, and the " olive branches" that twine themselves about their hearts, serve to knit them more firmly together, and render the tie that binds them to each other nearer, dearer, and more indissoluble.

A warlike disposition does not appear to have been originally characteristic of the Tongese, but they have imbibed it in their intercourse with the natives of the Feejee Group, and with it, have learned to be crafty, cunning, and treacherous. They are courageous, however, and are well acquainted with the use of fire arms. Muskets are quite plenty among them. Their other principal offensive weapons are clubs and spears, commonly made of the casuarina, or iron-wood.

Many of the natives possess European articles of dress, of which they are exceedingly proud, yet it is not usual for either sex to wear anything but the *siapo*, a sort of short petticoat made of *tapa*, and descending from the waist half-way down the thighs.   The *parçu* is also worn, and the missionaries have prevailed upon the christian women to arrange its folds so as to cover their bodies as high as the neck, but they do not like to conform to this new custom, and very often disregard it.   Neither sex wear a covering on their heads, upon ordinary occasions, and the children are rarely incumbered with any clothing whatsoever; but the latter have their hair cropped close, except a small lock over each ear, to keep out the vermin.

When the native warriors array themselves in their martial costumes and war-paint, and put on their richly ornamented mats, and their gay belts and turbans, they present a most striking and picturesque appearance.   A sight like this was witnessed during the visit of the American Exploring Squadron, which is thus described by Captain Wilkes in his narrative :—" I was now surrounded by large numbers of warriors, all grotesquely dressed and ready for the fight, with clubs, spears, and muskets.   In addition to the usual tapa around their waist, they had yellow and straw-colored ribands, made of the pandanus-leaves, tied around their arms above the elbows, on their legs above and below the knees, and on their bodies : some had them tied and gathered up in knots; others wore them as scarfs—some on the right shoulder, some on the left, and others on both shoulders.   Some of these sashes were beautifully white, about three inches wide, and quite pliable.   Many of them had fanciful head-dresses, some with natural and others with artificial flowers over their turbans (called sala) ; and nearly all had their faces painted in the most grotesque manner, with red, yellow, white, and black stripes, crossing the face in all directions.   Some were seen with a jet black face and vermilion nose ; others with half the face painted white.   When a body of some eight hundred of these dark-looking, well-formed warriors, all eager for the fight, and going to and fro to join their several companies, is seen, it is hardly possible to describe the effect."*

Beating *tapa*, and weaving mats of pandanus leaves, and

---

* Narrative of the Exploring Expedition, Vol. III. p. 8.

baskets of the same material, or of reeds or cane, with the performance of the necessary household duties, are the chief occupations of the women. All the out-door .work is performed by the men. They cultivate the yam and sweet potato patches, gather the bread-fruit and cocoa-nut, build houses and canoes, weave sails of pandanus leaves, and hunt and fish. They also display a great deal of ingenuity in making boxes of their beautiful woods, baskets of cane and reeds, and miniature canoes. Rat-catching was once a favorite amusement, and when the animals were captured they were often eaten uncooked. But the natives now subsist mainly on the produce raised by themselves, and the fruit of the cocoa and bread-fruit. Hogs and poultry are reared among them, and are gradually becoming quite plenty. Fish are abundant, especially the edible kinds, though sharks and whales are likewise numerous. Birds of different species, abound along the coasts, and in the groves and forests of the interior,—the most conspicuous among them being the tropic bird, woodpecker, turtle dove, and parroquet (*trichoclossus*), — but though often hunted, and killed or snared, they are not much eaten. The mode of preparing their food is similar to that practiced in the Samoän Group.

Among the heathen, smoking tobacco is a common practice. The leaf of the plant is cut, and rolled up inside of one of the finest and most delicate pandanus leaves, like a cigar. They are also fond of foreign liquors, and often drink to excess. These indulgences are forbidden to the christians ; they do not smoke, yet they occasionally give way to their love for ardent spirits. The fondness for *ava* is universal, it being drank alike by christian and heathen. It is prepared from the *piper mythisticum*, and the natives frequently meet together in small parties, to drown their sorrows, or heighten their joys, in the flowing ava-bowl.

Singing is a favorite diversion with all classes. The voices of the females are very musical, and all take great delight in displaying their powers. Both men and women have their tunes, appropriate to the employment or occupation in which they may be engaged. These are hummed or sung, when at labor, whether it be beating *tapa*, weaving mats, plucking the bread-fruit, or sculling the canoe. The heathen have their war and love dances, as among the Samoäns; but they are by no means so beastly or sensual in their habits and appetites, as the same class in the Navigator Group. Their principal musical instrument is the drum, or *toki*, which is made of the half section of a circular hollow log of hard sonorous wood.

No general head is recognized in the Tonga Group, though the king of Tongataboo and the southern islands is usually regarded as superior in rank to the other kings and chiefs. There are different tribes, often on the same island, and notwithstanding there may be a nominal king to whom all pay allegiance, their loyalty is not of the most devoted kind, being neither very loud in its profession, nor enthusiastic in its manifestation. All business affecting the general welfare, is transacted in the *fonos*, or councils.

Tonga was originally the sacred island of the group, and here were the principal *morais*, and temples, to which the natives of the other islands were obliged to bring their votive offerings. These temples are now maintained by the heathen in some of the districts, yet ancient superstitions and observances are fast losing their hold upon the minds of the people. The religion of the heathen is not exactly féticism,—though they have images of some of their gods,—for most of their divinities are purely imaginary, and many, perhaps, are the distinguished heroes and kings of Tonga in former days, apotheosized by their countrymen for their good deeds and qualities, whether real or fanciful. They worship a great number of deities, who are fabled to possess unlimited power over them, for good or for evil. These are called the gods of Bulotu, or Atua faka Bulotu, and are supposed to be immortal. Their oldest god was Maui, who drew the islands out of the sea with a hook and line; he and his two sons live under the earth, and when he turns over he produces earthquakes; the worship of this divinity is now entirely neglected. Tangaloä is their second god, who resides in the skies and is esteemed equal to Maui in dignity. Hikuleö is the god of spirits, and is the third in order ; he dwells in a cave on the island of Tonga. The gods who produce evil are called Atua Banuu.

Bulotu, however, is the principal deity. He inhabits a cave on a fabulous island bearing his name, which lies at a considerable distance north-west of Tonga. In consequence of his long tail he is unable to leave the cave, but holds his feasts there, and solaces himself with a great number of wives. He possesses absolute power over all, but is destitute of either love or goodness. The most valuable presents are deposited in his spirit-temple, and human sacrifices are offered to him, when an act of sacrilege has been committed, within the *morais*, or sacred inclosures. Other gods inferior to Bulotu reside on the same island. When the natives of the lower class die, they remain in the world, and feed on ants and lizards, but the spirits of the kings, nobles, and *matabooles*, or inferior chiefs, are wafted to Bulotu—" the island of the blessed." This island is supposed to be larger than the whole Tonga Group, and to be well stocked with useful and ornamental plants, in a high state of perfection. It produces the richest fruits, and the most beautiful flowers, always imbathed in fragrance. Brilliant-tinted birds fill the air with their melody. There is also an abundance of hogs and other animals. Neither fruit nor flower ever fades; but if either be plucked, another starts forth, its exact image, in the very place it occupied. So, too, the birds and animals are immortal. If one of the former be destroyed, ere its song be hushed, its rich melody is continued, without the loss of a single note, by another warbler that instant called into existence. If a hog be killed for the use of the gods, its place is supplied in a moment, and the occupants of porkerdom, like the birds, and fruits, and flowers, never diminish in numbers.

It is supposed by the natives, that the air of Bulotu cannot be inhaled by mortal bodies without producing speedy death, unless the gods so will ; that it is dangerous to go

thither in their canoes, that they cannot reach the island, or
if safely arriving there, return again, except through the same
special interposition of their deities. Yet it is said, that a
party of Tongese once visited this enchanted spot, and were
delighted with its beauties, but on attempting to pluck the
luscious bread-fruit, it eluded their grasp; and they walked
through the trunks of the trees, and the houses, which were
built after the Tongese fashion, without encountering any
resistance. Trees and dwellings, fruits and flowers, birds
and animals—all appeared but as shadows to those who were
strangers in this spirit-land.

(4.) When speaking of the dwellings in the Samoän Group,
it was remarked that they had borrowed their style of house-
building from the Tongese. The houses of the latter are of
an elliptical form, twenty feet long by fifteen wide, and about
fifteen feet high under the ridge-pole. The posts are either
of cocoa-nut or bread-fruit, and are set in the same manner as
has been previously described.* Indeed, the houses are constructed similarly to those of the Samoäns, in every respect,
except that the sides are made of wicker-work, composed of
the slender stalks of the sugar-cane firmly wattled together.
Glazed windows are nowhere seen except in the residences of
the missionaries. Mats are hung at the doors, and sometimes
they are made use of within, to divide a house into several
compartments. The floor is also covered with mats; coarse
ones being commonly used, and the finer ones kept in reserve
for extraordinary occasions. In the centre of the house, a
small space of ground is left uncovered, where the cooking is
performed. Clubs, spears, muskets, fishing gear, an occasional
shelf, the ava-bowl, a supply of mats, drinking-vessels made
of cocoa-nut shells, earthen jars dried in the sun, a few cooking utensils, and a chest or box to contain all the principle val-
uables, are the ordinary embellishments and articles of furniture found in a Tongese habitation. Besides their more
common mats, they have stiffer ones about two feet wide,
made to stand on the edges, supported by scrolls at either end;

* *Anté*, p. 209 et seq.

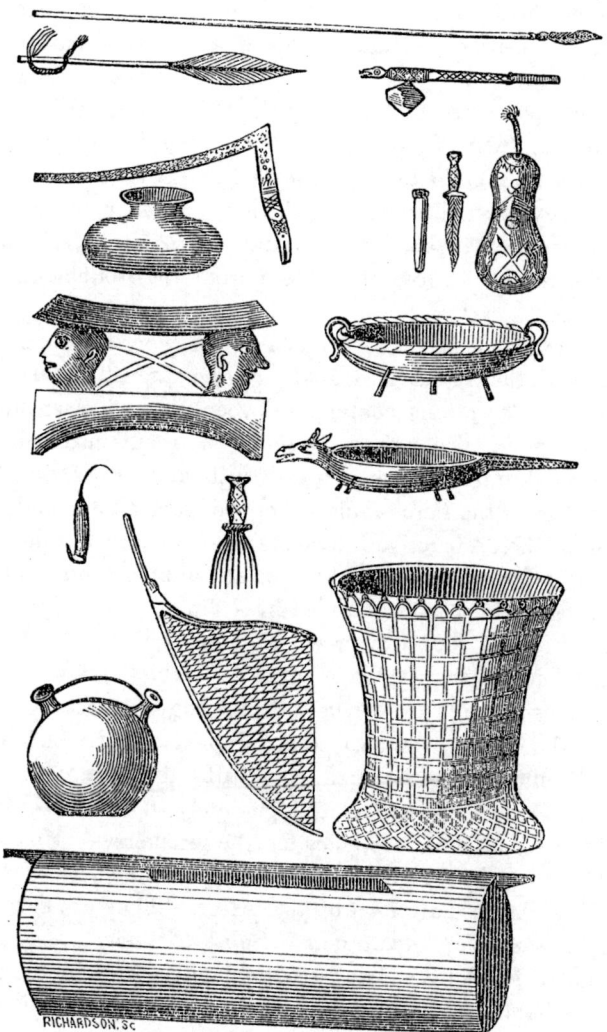

IMPLEMENTS AND UTENSILS OF POLYNESIANS.

these are curled about the young children when laid down upon the larger mats, or are used as screens by the females, to hide their persons when seated on the floor and engaged at their occupations. Fans are made of the same material with the mats, and both are often highly ornamented. In addition to their other uses, the mats of the Tongese are their couches at night; their pillow is made of a strip of bamboo, supported on legs from eight to ten inches high; if the weather be very cool they cover themselves with their lighter mats, and in the summer they are obliged to swathe fine *tapa* cloth about their limbs and bodies to protect them from the troublesome musquitoes.

Nukualofa, near the northern end of Tongataboo, and Lefooka on the island of Hapaï, are the largest towns in the group. The former contains between six and seven hundred houses, and is situated on the hill before mentioned, being half imbosked amid a grove of bread-fruits and cocoas, which protect it from the fierce radiance of the tropical sun, and shelter it from the destructive hurricanes. This is a fortified town, being defended by a high wall or embankment made of earth and logs, which is surrounded by a ditch. On the top of the parapet there is a wicker-work fence, from five to eight feet high, and in some places of several thicknesses. Narrow openings through the glacis, terminating in gateways admitting the passage of two persons abreast, and which can be easily filled up with earth, constitute the entrances to the fort. Hollow logs are placed obliquely in the embankment which are used as loop-holes for the musketry. Most of the other towns in the group are similarly fortified.

The Tongese are fond of the water. They are daring and expert sailors and swimmers. Some of their canoes are one hundred feet long. They are made like those in use among the inhabitants of the Feejee Group. The double canoes will often hold from forty to fifty persons; they consist of two single ones united together by a deck or platform projecting two or three feet beyond the canoes on each side. One of these canoes is smaller than the other; it serves the purpose of an outrigger, and is always kept toward the weather side.   There is a single mast, usually about thirty feet high, which is supported by guys, and has a long yard bearing a huge triangular sail or mat.   On the platform there is a house or cabin, for shelter in stormy weather, the roof of which is flanked by railings, and constitutes a sort of hurricane-deck. There are small hatchways at each end of the double and single canoes.   The Tongese have a mode of sculling that seems to be peculiar to them and the Feejees.   The oar is confined in a hole in the platform, behind which stands the sculler, who holds his implement perpendicularly, and bears his whole weight upon it.   Canoes are propelled in this manner with great rapidity, often making three miles in an hour. Both kinds of the Tongese craft leak badly, and though managed with great skill, they require constant bailing.

(5.) In 1821, the Wesleyan missionaries first began their labors in the Tonga Islands, but permanent establishments were not made till 1829.   In the last mentioned year stations were formed on Tonga and Hapaï, and in 1830, on the island of Vavaö.   The smaller islands are under the care of native teachers.   About one quarter of the inhabitants of the group are professed christians, one half of whom are church-members.   Not only have the islanders benefited by the religious instruction of their spiritual teachers ; numbers of them have been taught to read and write, and to understand the first principles of geography and arithmetic, while many of the females have learned to knit and sew.

As a people, the Tongese are much attached to their ancient customs, and fierce and bloody contests have taken place between the heathen and christian parties.   The missionaries have not always been the friends of peace.   When the American Squadron touched at the islands, the hostile factions were marshalling their forces for battle.   Captain Wilkes made an ineffectual attempt to procure a pacific arrangement of all difficulties, but his efforts were not very well seconded by the missionaries, who seemed perfectly willing that there should be a trial of strength between the rival bands. The " Devil's party" were completely successful in repelling an assault made upon their fortifications, and after various conflicts and reverses, peace was restored. Though the intercourse of the Tongese with the natives of the Feejee Group has had the tendency to impair or detract from the influence of the missionaries, they have much to encourage them ; and, if pursuing their labors with patience and perseverance, they may at no distant day accomplish the complete civilization and moral regeneration of the inhabitants of the Tonga Islands.

(6.) Early in the morning of the 4th of May, the Exploring Squadron got under way, and sailed out of the harbor of Nukualofa. The Porpoise was detached, under the command of Lieutenant Ringgold, with orders to proceed to the eastern group of the Feejee Islands, and to examine and survey the long line of islets and reefs extending to the north, between the 178th and 179th meridians. The other vessels pursued a north-westerly course, towards the main Feejee Group ; and on the 8th of May the Vincennes and Peacock came safely to anchor in the harbor of Levuka, on the east side of the island of Ovolau. The Flying Fish did not arrive till the 11th instant, having been delayed in her passage by running on a coral reef off the island of Nairai, and carrying away a portion of her false keel. Preparations were forthwith made, upon the arrival of the vessels, to proceed with the examination of the islands, and to make an accurate survey of all the reefs, coasts, and harbors.

MURDER OF Lieut. UNDERWOOD.

CHAPTER XIV.

(1.) But very few years have elapsed since any considerable amount of information has been obtained in regard to the Feejee Group. Tales of the covetousness, treachery, and barbarity of the inhabitants, were often heard. Occasionally it was said that an European or American vessel had been cast ashore, or had touched at the islands to obtain water or supplies, and that it had been attacked and plundered, and its crew murdered and their bodies devoured at the horrid cannibal repasts of the natives. In consequence of these stories, which were rife in the Pacific, whalers and traders were careful how they ventured thither; and those who were compelled to do so for the purpose of procuring the provisions with which the islands were bountifully stocked, wary and cautious as they might be, rarely escaped without the loss of one or more articles of property, or some member of the crew. Hidden coral reefs, too, were known to abound in the vicinity of the group, upon which vessels were frequently wrecked, and the dangers of the navigation, therefore, also deterred strangers from venturing too far where the sailing was so intricate.*

* Between the years 1828 and 1840, eight vessels, five of which were American, were lost in the Feejee Group, and twelve vessels ran ashore, within the same period, and were more or less damaged.

Tasman first discovered this group of islands, in 1643. When Cook was at Tongataboo, in 1773, he heard of their existence, but did not visit them.   Captain Bligh fell in with the eastern group, in 1791, when on his westward passage in the launch of the Bounty, after being set adrift and abandoned by his crew.   Captain Wilson touched at the islands, in the ship Duff, to land some missionaries, in 1797 ; but on account of the difficulty of the navigation, and the hostile and threatening appearance of the natives, he felt constrained to abandon his original intention.   D'Urville visited the group on his first expedition, and gave them the name of the Viti Islands: he was there again in 1839, and to him and Captain Wilkes is the merit due, of having made the first critical and scientific examinations and accurate surveys of the islands.

There are three divisions of the Feejee Islands, which are disposed in the form of a semi-circle, whose base is in about 19° 30′ southern latitude.   On the east, or weather side, is the Eastern Group ; on the north are Vanuä-levui, and Vuna; and on the west are Viti-levui, Ovolau, and Kantavu.   Other islands of less importance serve to complete what is almost a continuous chain.   That portion of the ocean included within the periphery is called the Sea of Goro.   The group is quite numerous; it is said to comprise over one hundred and fifty different islands, sixty-five of which are inhabited—all lying between 15° 30′ and 19° 30′ southern latitude, and longitude 177° E. and 178° W.   The uninhabited isles are often resorted to by the natives to obtain cocoa-nuts, and to take fish and *biche de mer*.   Most of the islands belonging to the eastern division, consist of chaplets or rings of coral inclosing high and broken volcanic peaks or bluffs.   The northern and western islands are bold and mountainous in the interior ; but the peaks and ridges are flanked by broad slopes, and separated by wide valleys, covered all over with the profuse vegetation of a tropical clime.

All the islands are surrounded in great part by coralline reefs, whose beautiful tints, and varied and delicate structure, always excite admiration : some of these are covered with a sufficient depth of soil to support vegetation ; and others are half concealed by the combing waves that spend their fury in impotent efforts to destroy the labors of the tiny zoöphyte. In addition to the reefs, there are sunken patches of branching coral, whose brilliant colors of pink and purple, brown, green, white, and yellow, seem like reflections in the clear water, or like the enchanted palaces of tritons and mermaids.

The most important islands of the eastern group are Fulanga, Kambara, Lakemba, and Vanuä-valavo. Fulanga is of a semi-circular form, and is rough and uneven ; its bluffs rising to the height of one hundred and fifty feet above the level of the sea. Kambara is three and a half miles long and two miles wide : it is three hundred and fifty feet above the ocean, and clothed to its topmost heights with the richest verdure. Lakemba is the largest island in the eastern group ; its highest peak has an altitude of over seven hundred feet ; it is five miles long and three in width, and is well wooded and highly productive. Quite a number of converted Tongese reside on Lakemba, and their example, with the efforts of the missionaries, has produced a most happy change in the conduct and appearance of the native population. Vanuä-valavo is in the shape of a half-moon ; it is quite narrow, but fourteen miles in length, and beautifully fringed with bread-fruits, cocoas, and palms.

Vuna is twenty-five miles in length, from north to south, and five miles wide. It is separated from Vanuä-levui, or the "large land," by the straits of Somu-Somu, which are five miles in width at the narrowest point. It has a central ridge, over two thousand feet high, almost always shrouded in dense masses of clouds, which slopes down gradually on every side to the beach ; but it is generally far more level than the other islands, and in consequence contains a much greater proportion of land adapted to cultivation.—The general direction of Vanuä-levui is from east to west : it is shaped like an elongated heart, with its opening, Natava Bay, facing the north-east ; and including all its indentations, it cannot be far from two hundred and fifty miles in circum-

ference. The coast country partakes of the same general
features characteristic of the other members of the group ;
mud flats alternating with swelling bluffs along the shore,
but soon giving place to a succession of richly carpeted hills
and plains stretching away to the lofty volcanic peaks of the
interior, that tower above the surrounding landscape to the
height of four or five thousand feet.

Viti-levui, about thirty-five miles south of the western end
of Vanuä-levui, is somewhat smaller and less hilly than the
" large land." It is nearly of a circular form ; on the west
the country is comparatively low, being broken only by a
few hills, scarcely ever rising above the height of five or
seven hundred feet ; but far in the interior there are lofty
ranges of blue mountains, running from north to south, that
attain an elevation of four or five thousand feet.—Ovolau
lies off the east end, and in sight of Viti-levui : it is eight
miles long, from north to south, and seven miles in width ;
it is intersected by a range of mountainous peaks, the tallest
of which is twenty-three hundred feet above the sea, and
from its base, gently undulating slopes, divided by lovely valleys, all adorned with magnificent groves of bread-fruits and
cocoas, stretch down to the sea-shore.—Malolo, lying off the
western point of Viti-levui, and inside the same great reef, is
a small circular island, remarkable only for the unfortunate
celebrity it has acquired as the scene of the murder of two
of the most promising officers of the American Exploring
Expedition.

The island of Mbenga, five miles south of Viti-levui, is
five miles long and three wide ; the land rises boldly on all
sides towards the interior, terminating in two prominent basaltic peaks thirteen hundred feet above the sea level. Twenty-
six miles further to the south is Kantavu, one of the most
important and densely populated islands in the whole group ;
it is likewise high and mountainous, and about twenty-five
miles in length.—Twenty miles a little to the south of east
from Ovolau, is Nairai, an oblong island seven miles in length
and from two to three miles wide, and particularly famous

for its manufacture of mats and baskets ; it has two elevated peaks, and its scenery partakes of the same general character of that of the other islands.—Goro, about fifteen miles north of Nairai, is one of the most fruitful of the Feejee islands ; it is nine and a half miles long and four miles wide ; the surface is high but not much broken, and from the tops of its loftiest hills to the foaming breakers, it presents a most abundant vegetation.—From fifteen to eighteen miles west of Viti-levui, is a long chain of rocky islands, all of volcanic formation, extending in a north-easterly direction from thirty to forty miles, which are classed together as the Assuä Group. There are fewer reefs to obstruct the navigation in the vicinity of these islands, and on the west there are no sea-reefs of importance.   Many of them are inhabited, but all are rugged and broken, their mountain peaks sometimes rising to the height of sixteen hundred feet.

Almost all the islands are well watered.   The numerous valleys that intersect the slopes and plains along the coasts, often form the channels of streams that carry off the surplus waters of the interior, of which there is usually an abundance, and dispense their grateful moisture, lavishly and without stint, as they wend their way to the ocean.   In the two larger islands there are several considerable rivers, which may be navigated for some distance in boats.   Mbua Bay, at the western end of Vanuä-levui, receives the waters of two or three large rivers, one of which is two hundred feet wide at its mouth.   Wai-levu river is the most considerable stream on the island of Viti-levui: it rises in the mountains, and, after tumbling over a precipice seven hundred feet high, divides into two branches, about forty-three miles from its mouth, the larger of which enters the sea at Rewa on the southern shore of the island, and the other at Indimbi, ten miles further to the west.   For eight miles above Rewa, the river is lined with rich alluvial flats, intersected with a great number of creeks, either tributaries to the main stream, or diverging from it.*

* The boats of the American Squadron ascended the Wai-levu for a distance

(2.) Most of the harbors in the Feejee Group are, like those of the Society Islands, mere indentations in the coast outline, protected by the encircling reefs of coral. Probably the best of them all is that of Levuka, on the east side of Ovolau, which is safe and easy of access for vessels of the largest class. The town contains about forty houses, and, after the prevailing fashion, is located in the midst of a grove of bread-fruits and cocoas, whose feathery canopies afford a most delightful shade ; its site is a beautiful valley, through which courses a fine stream of fresh water, opening to the ocean, flanked on either side by verdant hills, and rising by a gradual ascent to the lofty peaks of basalt that bound the view to the west. Most of the foreign residents make this their place of abode, and the society is altogether better than that of any other place in the group.

In the two principal islands there are a number of large bays. Vanuä-levui has Natava Bay on the east, Savu Bay on the south, and Mbua, or Sandal-wood Bay, at the west end. Natava Bay is much the largest of the three, and has a number of towns on its borders ; it is bounded on the south-east by Rambe Island, and by Point Unda on the north-west ; it is spacious, and sufficiently easy of access, but contains a great many hidden reefs and sunken patches of coral. Savu-Savu Bay is ten miles long, from east to west, and five miles in breadth ; it is a fine sheet of deep water, surrounded by high broken ridges which unite in the rear in a saddle-shaped peak. There are several towns in the vicinity, and the district contains over two thousand inhabitants. It was at one time more thickly settled than it now is, and the remains of some of the strongest fortifications in the Feejee Group may be seen here. Its principal attractions, however, are the hot springs, impregnated with salt and sulphur, which ooze from the ground like those of New Zealand, and cover an area of nearly half a mile square. They lie

of forty-eight miles from its mouth. The natives informed the party that it was the outlet of a large lake in the interior, but the formation of the country does not favor the idea in the least.

directly upon the bay, and close beside them is a stream of fresh water. The natives resort to these springs to boil their food: particularly when they make,great feasts; one of them is held sacred, and none but human victims, whose bleaching bones are piled around in heaps, are cooked in it; they also attribute healing qualities to the waters, which are doubtless real to some extent.—Mbua Bay was formerly much frequented by foreigners to procure the odorous sandal-wood that was once found in abundance on its borders, but the supply is now nearly exhausted, and it has consequently diminished in importance. The bay is of a circular shape, and affords ample anchorage at some distance from the shore; yet it is filled with reefs, and the country around is quite low, though soon rising into picturesque ridges and peaks as you advance into the interior. The principal town in the adjacent district is Vaturna, which lies about a mile up the large river before mentioned: it contains from fifty to sixty houses, and several *mbures*, or temples; the inhabitants are more kind and hospitable than in many of the other towns, which is probably to be attributed to their frequent intercourse with the whites. Muthuata, on the north side of Vanuä-levui is a pretty town, having a fine harbor, which is protected from the north winds by an island of the same name.

The most important harbors in Viti-levui, are the Bay of Ambau, and the roadstead of Rewa, at the mouth of the Wai-levu river. The former is at the south-eastern point of the island: the anchorage is much obstructed by the coral reefs and shoals, and vessels of large draught cannot approach near the shore. Within the bay are two small islands, Ambau and Viwa, connected with the main land, which is about a mile distant, by coral flats or reefs. Both are well covered with houses, but the town of Ambau is considerably the most populous, and in a political point of view possesses greater importance than any other town in the Feejee Islands. The harbor of Rewa is just round the point of the island from Ambau, but hardly ten miles distant from it over land. It is formed by two small islands and their reefs, fronting the

debouchure of the Wai-levu river. There are three passages
through the encircling reefs, inside of which the water is
deep and the anchorage secure. The town of Rewa is three
miles up the river, on an island, in the midst of an alluvial
tract formed of the *detritus* washed down from the highlands
in the interior. This low ground, though subject to frequent
inundations, is exceedingly productive. Dense thickets of
mangrove-bushes, in some places almost impervious, alternate
with copses of palms, and groves of bread-fruits and cocoas ;
the valleys and ravines that divide the hilly range along the
coast are concealed beneath the thrifty vegetation ; and above
them are spread out the wide patches of deep green verdure
extending to the red cliffs of the distant mountains. In the
vicinity of the town there are cultivated gardens and fields,
not, indeed, affording very strong evidence in favor of the
skill and industry of the husbandman, but, as if in sheer spite,
fairly teeming with their almost spontaneous products. The
open spaces are crowded with bananas ; the shade trees afford
both protection and nourishment, and

> " rich fruits o'erhang
> The sloping walks, and odorous shrubs entwine
> Their undulating branches."

Rewa contains a larger population than Ambau ; the number of its inhabitants is about five thousand, while that of
the latter is only three thousand. The natives there also
seem better disposed, and a residence among them is more
desirable, inasmuch as there are a number of abandoned
whites at Ambau who have corrupted the original inhabitants,
and made them, if possible, still worse than they formerly
were.

Mbenga is nearly divided in two by the harbor of Sawau,
which faces to the north, and is about two miles deep. The
entrance is narrow, being only a quarter of a mile from headland to headland, but it immediately opens out to a mile in
width, and contains from four to ten fathoms of water.
There are several small villages lying around the harbor, each

imbosomed in its pleasant grove of tropical fruit-trees. Kantavu has merely a harbor formed by the coral reefs. Near the centre of the island is Malatta Bay, whose shores are bordered with an abundant growth of pine timber, which is highly esteemed for masts and spars; and most of the large canoes in the group are built here. There are upwards of forty towns on the island, containing, altogether, from twelve to fifteen thousand inhabitants. There are many snug bays in the Assuä Group, upon which, on the steep and precipitous bluffs, are situated most of their little villages or towns.

The largest town and best harbor on Nairai is Toaloa, at the north end of the island. Vuna has a very good harbor at Somu-Somu, on its western shore. The town of the same name, which is a missionary station, is divided into two parts; one lying on the beach, and the other on the bluffs above, nearly screened from view by the thick foliage of the numerous bread-fruits, cocoas, palms, and bananas. There are no very important harbors in the Eastern Group. On the south side of Lakemba there is a slight indentation, in front of which is a coral reef, but there is not sufficient depth of water for a vessel of over one or two hundred tons burden. Situate on the harbor is a small town containing six hundred inhabitants, which can likewise boast of a church and a mission house. The former is eighty feet long by thirty-two feet wide, twenty-five feet high, and well carpeted with mats.

(3.) Evidences of the volcanic origin of this group are so abundant and so general, that it is hardly necessary to refer to them in detail. There are a number of tall, sharp-pointed, conical hills, of basaltic formation, which at no very remote age were the craters of active volcanoes, although no running streams of lava have been discovered, and the only indications of volcanic heat are at the hot springs of Savu-Savu. The islets of the eastern group are mostly composed of scoriaceous materials. There are extensive beds of ferruginous marl on the island of Ovolau, above which are masses of black lava and pudding stone, and lofty blocks of basalt. Volcanic conglomerate, scoria, agglutinated basalt or tufa, porphyritic pumice stone, and sandstone, are found throughout the group.

There can be no richer soil than that afforded by the decomposition of these formations, especially when mingled with the vegetable mould constantly accumulating in such vast quantities. This is shown in the rapid and thrifty growth of everything adapted to the climate. The dark green mangroves that cover the marshy and alluvial flats along the coasts, and at the mouths of the rivers; the graceful palms that adorn the acclivities of the hills, and the slopes and valleys; and the tall and gloomy pines that cast their deep shadows along the mountain sides—all denote the capacity of the islands for the production, with ordinary culture, of an almost exhaustless supply of tropical fruits and vegetables. The proportion of the unproductive land to that suited for tillage is very small. The general character of the soil is a brownish yellow, or red loam; in some few places a kind of indurated blue clay, containing nodules of grit, is found; and, only here and there, are occasional barren patches of gravel.

In respect to climate, too, these islands are highly favored. Of warmth and moisture there is no deficiency, except that on the leeward side of the islands, as is always the case in the larger and mountainous groups of Polynesia, showers are much less frequent, and sometimes long continued droughts occur, during which the vegetation often assumes a burnt appearance. Still, there is a great quantity of rain falls. There is a good deal of thunder and lightning; severe gales and hurricanes are frequently experienced; and earthquakes are not uncommon, though the shocks are usually quite slight.

Over the verdant hills and lovely valleys of the Feejee Group, there generally rests a soft and pure atmosphere, and even in the winter months, when it is the most rainy, the weather is remarkably fine. A cloudless sky is soon darkened, it is true, but when the sun shines forth again, and nature glistens through her tears, everything seems brighter and fairer than it is wont to do, and the laughing hours glide smoothly on, filling each heart with new-born gladness and joy.

The extremes of temperature during the year are from 58° to 100°, in the shade. The nights are cool, frequently even when no dew falls. In the summer months the heat continues very intense for many days in succession, but it is often moderated during some part of the day by the delicious sea breezes.

Colds, coughs, influenza, and acute diseases of the lungs, are quite prevalent. Ulcerous affections and rheumatism— the latter being principally confined to the women—are not uncommon. Cases of syphilis are exceedingly rare, and fevers are unknown. Elephantiasis does not prevail to any great extent. There is a singular disease, resembling syphilis, called by the natives *dthoke*, which is supposed to be peculiar to these islands. It attacks both children and adults, and commences with rheumatic pains and swellings, followed by the appearance of ulcerous pustules on the body. If the eruptions do not appear, or dry up too soon, the disease is pretty sure to terminate fatally.

All the ordinary productions of tropical climes may be found in the Feejee Group. Among the larger trees are the bread-fruit, cocoa, toa, or casuarina; several varieties of palms; a species of pine called *dackui*, resembling the kauri of New Zealand; the hibiscus tiliacus, pandanus, tamanu, rata, or native chestnut, plantain, banana, and Carica papaya. There are nine different kinds of bread-fruit, and three of cocoas, but all resemble one another in their general properties. The value of the annual product of these two trees alone must be enormous: they furnish the native with bread and clothing, and from them also he obtains a great proportion of the materials for his habitation. The cocoa does not flourish very well above the elevation of six hundred feet; but below that level its luxuriance of growth is unsurpassed. Besides the ordinary preparations of the bread-fruit, the natives scrape off the rind, and pack it in earthen jars, or bury it in pits lined with banana leaves and covered with thatch, where it ferments and forms an incrassated mass like cheese, which they call *mandrai ;* a similar preparation is also made of unripe bananas; both are cooked with cocoa-nut milk, and are exceedingly palatable and nutritious. It is said that *mandrai* will keep for a number of years, and a supply is always kept on hand for a season of scarcity.*

Bananas and plantains are very plentiful, but not highly prized, though they are more or less cultivated, and grow with great rapidity ; in a few years after the plants are set out, they form delightful umbrageous groves round the homes of the islanders. Besides the common plantain, the wild species, or *fei*, is also cultivated. Among the other trees that afford sustenance to the natives are the shaddock, tara-vou, or native plum, Malay apple, and indiva. The bitter orange is indigenous, and both the lemon and sweet orange have been brought here from Tahiti. On the uplands the wild nutmeg is found in considerable abundance, but the kernel does not possess much aromatic flavor. Plantations of the paper mulberry receive a great share of attention, as the bark of the young trees is manufactured into *tapa*, by scraping it with a conch shell, macerating, and beating it on a log with a grooved mallet. The *tapa* is afterwards bleached in the sun, and dyed to suit the taste of the person making it. Mats are made of pandanus leaves, bands and sashes of the bark of the hibiscus, and baskets of willow and rattan.

Building materials are principally obtained from the cocoa, bread-fruit, tree-fern, and palm. Bamboo and hibiscus are also used for the sides of the houses : of the former light rafts for taking fish, torches, and drinking vessels, are also made. When the joints of the bamboo are burned as torches, they are first saturated with cocoa-nut oil, and the twisted leaves of the cocoa are likewise used for candles. The mangrove completely covers the low grounds, if pains are not taken to

* The taro, and other fruits, are often preserved in the same manner. The term *mandrai* appears to be a general one; for instance, the preserved bread fruit, which is like the *mahi* of Tahiti, is called *mandrai-uta*, the banana *mandrai-vundi*, the native chestnut *mandrai-sivisivi*, and the taro *mandrai y taro*.

extirpate it, or keep it down, and where there is room for a single shoot to grow, it will spring up and flourish; the flexible twigs of this shrub are employed in wattling, and the tough and elastic roots are made into bows. The *toa*, or iron-wood, is manufactured into clubs, spears, bowls and other vessels, and articles of furniture; it is also used for arrows,—the strips of wood being charred and inserted in pieces of cane Spears are also made of the cocoa-nut wood: they are ordinarily ten or fifteen feet in length, sometimes wound with sennit, and either tipped with bone or charred at the point.

Pine timber is quite plenty, and is chiefly used in building their canoes; for masts and spars it is very valuable. The sandal-wood, or yase, is almost exhausted.

Edible roots of different kinds are in great abundance, and most of them are cultivated. The most important of these are the yam and the taro; the kawai, resembling the Malay batata; the ivia, arrow-root, and ti. Other wild roots, and wild berries growing on the mountains, are eaten when there is a failure in the supply of other products. Turmeric is cultivated for cosmetic purposes, and the sugar cane is found, both in a wild state, and in the gardens and plantations of the natives. Two varieties of the *gossypium* are indigenous; one producing a nankeen-colored, and the other a clear white cotton of fine and even texture. The cotton-tree, (*bombax*) is also found growing to the height of fifteen or twenty feet. Tobacco is grown in considerable quantities, and smoking is one of the chief enjoyments of the Feejeean. Melons, cucumbers, pine apples, guavas, capsicums, cape-gooseberries, and native tomatoes, are abundant; and nearly all of the most valuable foreign vegetables found in the tropics, or in the temperate zone, have been introduced here and cultivated with success.

Flowering plants and shrubs are quite common. The scarlet flowers of the callistemon, and the bright yellow blossoms of the cordia, everywhere peep out from amid the dense mangrove thickets. Acacias, gorgeously decked with

15

the rich and variegated dyes of innumerable creepers, are scattered over the landscape. Here and there may be seen the rich orange-colored fruit of the xylocarpus, or the white tufts bursting from the capsules of the cotton-tree. The numerous family of the orchideæ are lavish in the display of their charms. Beautiful mosses cling to the tall forest-trees, whose dark foliage contrasts so well with the gay parterre smiling in beauty and loveliness beneath them. Arborescent and trailing ferns adorn the acclivities of the mountains. Mingled with all these varied forms of vegetation, there are aromatic shrubs dispensing their fragrance on every hand; and while the beholder feasts his eyes on the beauties before him, he inhales an odor delightful as the ambrosia of Olympus.

Agriculture is one of the principal employments of the poorer class of natives; the chiefs and higher dignitaries being relieved from the necessity of labor, by the exactions imposed on those below them in rank and position. The earth in their plantations, and their yam and taro patches, is dug up for the most part with sharp-pointed sticks, though spades and shovels, usually made after a very rude fashion, have been introduced to some extent. Before working the soil, in new ground, they set fire to the underbrush, or the dry native grass, (*scirpus*,) which is coarse and thickly matted, and often spreads over large tracts of country. The young banana or mulberry trees, or the cane sprouts, are then set out, and the yam and taro planted. So far the labor is mainly performed by the men; but the women do most of the weeding, and when the yams and taros are dug, or other fruits gathered, they are obliged to carry them to the places where they are deposited for safe-keeping. In fact, nearly all burdens are borne by the women on their backs, in jars or baskets, which are secured from falling, by cords passing round and under the shoulders. Often may a Feejee woman be seen staggering under a heavy load, like the squaw of the North American savage, while her lord and master saunters leisurely along at her side.

(4.) All the quadrupeds, except the rat, which, as in New Zealand, is considered *game*, are of the domestic kinds. Cattle, hogs, and fowls, have been introduced by the whites, and thrive very well. The first should, perhaps, be excepted from this general remark ; for, though the islands abound in excellent pasturage, they do not appear to multiply very fast ; but this is probably owing to the want of due attention, or the improper selection of food. There are but few reptiles—lizards and snakes being the most common ; the latter are often worshipped as spirits.

Numerous whales frequent the neighboring waters for three or four months in the year ; their teeth are highly prized by the natives, yet, notwithstanding their skilful seamanship, they seem to be utterly ignorant of the mode of capturing them, and only secure those which are driven on shore. Hawk's-bill and green turtles are abundant ; and the tortoise shell obtained from the former is one of the most valuable articles of traffic to be procured in the islands : these animals are caught in nets of sennit made of the husks of the cocoa-nut, and are kept in pens. The average weight of the shell is about fourteen pounds, and it is often stripped off without killing the animal. Crustacea are in great abundance, and the most delicious crabs are found among the mangrove bushes. Shellfish of all kinds are obtained in plenty. The conch shell is the native trumpet or horn. Other beautiful varieties of shells, and especially the *cypræa ovula*, are collected in large quantities for decorating their canoes, the ridge poles of their houses, and other ornamental work. Fish are plentiful in the ocean, and in the rivers and streams ; they are speared, or taken with bone hooks or in nets of sennit ; and sometimes they are driven into pens formed of rocks and stones in the shallow water, where they are easily speared or caught by hand, or they are poisoned by throwing the stems and leaves of the glycine, a climbing plant, into the water where they abound.

A green salt water worm, called balolo, is eaten by the natives, and is considered quite a delicacy. But the *biche de mer*, or sea slug, is the most highly prized of the animals of this genus. It is from two to nine inches in length, resembles a caterpillar in its motions, and feeds by suction. There are several different sorts, and they are of various colors, being red, white, gray, yellow, brown or black. They live among the rocks and in the holes of the coral reefs, where the water is from one to two fathoms deep, and are caught by the natives, who either dive for them, or fish by moonlight or torchlight. Traders frequently visit the islands, and make arrangements with a prominent chief for the services of the natives in procuring the desired supply. After the animals are caught, they are placed in bins, where their entrails are ejected; the next process is to cut them open, and they are then boiled, and thoroughly dried in a building erected for the purpose by the person engaged in the fishery. When completely cured in this manner, they are fit for market, and find a ready sale in China, where they are esteemed as one of the richest ingredients of their soups. Some of the species of *biche de mer* are eaten raw by the natives of the Feejee Group.

There is an abundance of singing birds in the group. There are parrots and parroquets, of the most beautiful and richly variegated plumage. Wild ducks and pigeons, too, are quite common. All the different kinds of sea fowl usually seen in the Polynesian groups, may be found on the coasts.

(5.) A disciple of Lavater would form a pretty correct idea of the Feejee Islander from his physiognomy. The remarkable prominence of the cheek bones, and the projection of the jaws, indicative of the coarse and animal natures of the possessors, would not escape notice. The organs of taste and smell are unusually developed. In their countenances the distinctive features of the Malay and the Papuan seem to be blended. There are different shades of complexion, generally many degrees darker than that of the Tonga Islander, some being as fair as the lightest mulatto, and others dark as the sootiest negro. Their foreheads are high, but often narrow; their noses well-formed, though large; and their teeth white and evenly set. Their eyes are black as night, and when kindled with the demoniacal passions so easy to be inflamed, they glow like coals of fire. The forms of both sexes are cast in a fine mould, and corpulence is almost unknown. Their hair is naturally black, but it is so much discolored by the use of the ley obtained from the ashes of bread-fruit leaves, lime, white clay, and other substances, to destroy the vermin, that it often assumes a reddish appearance. The women, too, dye their hair with various pigments for the sake of improving their beauty, of which last commodity, however, they do not ordinarily possess a superabundance, although now and then a tolerably pretty and pleasing face may be seen. If they were confined more to their houses they might improve in this respect, but as they are now employed for a great part of the time out of doors, and almost in a nude state, whatever personal charms they naturally possess soon become impaired. They are the mere creatures and slaves of their husbands, yet from custom and habit seem to bow themselves willingly to the yoke.

It is usual among the Feejeeans to wear moustaches, and to allow the beard to grow long. The hair of the boys is kept cropped short, in order to keep out all strange intruders, with the exception of a single lock which is allowed to grow, till they arrive at man's estate, when it is spread out in a mop-like form, and often frizzled with great care and skill by the native barbers. Instead of the curling-irons of the *friseur*, a long and slender hair-pin, made of tortoise-shell or bone, is used for this purpose. Some of the chiefs keep several barbers among their retainers, and spend a great deal of time in dressing their heads, and their beards and moustaches. Cocoa-nut oil, scented with sandal-wood, is liberally applied to their hair. This singular mode of wearing that useful appendage gives the Feejeean dandies a most strange appearance ; but they pride themselves much on the exquisite finish of their toilet, and like other fops, will spend hour after hour in surveying themselves in a mirror. The loss of the hair is esteemed a great misfortune, and its place is always supplied by wigs, in the manufacture of which the native barbers display considerable skill, and often imitate nature so closely that it is impossible to distinguish the counterfeit except by careful observation.

The girls wear their hair long, and are fond of ornamenting it with pretty flowers. After they are married, however, their locks are cut off, and their hair frizzled like that of the men.

It is not difficult for the Feejeean to put on a friendly manner, even when the demon of malice and revenge is lurking in his heart. He is proud, irascible, treacherous, and vindictive; haughty to his inferiors, and abject and servile to those who are above him. When he speaks fair words, he is rarely to be trusted. He will lie and steal with the utmost effrontery; and if anything excites his covetous disposition, he will commit any crime to obtain it. He is changeable in mood; at one time appearing jocose in disposition and fond of merriment, and at another sullen, morose, and reserved, or giving way to the fierce passions that may be smothered for a time, but are always kept alive in his bosom. He can be kind and hospitable to a guest, and will not molest him at his own fireside, but once across his threshold, he will murder him with as little compunction as a tiger devours its prey.

The common people, or *kai-sis*, are more industrious than the Tahitian, and all possess greater activity and energy of mind and body; but they are nearly as licentious, and many of the chiefs are equally indolent. The domestic affections are not strongly manifested, though instances of devoted personal attachment are by no means rare. They will not tolerate drones among them, and deformed children, and old and infirm people, are put to death: this is often done by the nearest relatives, and not so much from a want of affection, as for the reason that they wish to relieve themselves from a burden, and to save their victims from living on in misery or distress. Their appetites are grossly sensual, and their tastes depraved. They wear very little clothing, but are careful not to expose their whole persons in public; yet the women are not over chaste, and the men will prostitute their wives and daughters for a compensation, or sometimes from motives of friendship. Their cannibal propensities are unusually strong, and they feed upon the bodies of their victims with a hearty relish. These are obtained in war, or are selected by the chiefs. If a canoe be upset, the occupants are prize to those who rescue them; and when a chief launches a new vessel, he slaughters a number of his retainers, or the prisoners he may have taken for the purpose, on its deck, after which their corpses are cooked and served up in a horrid repast. Great feasts are often made, for which human victims are provided: when the bodies are cooked, they are dissected with as much skill as could be displayed by a surgical operator, and distributed among the guests. Women are frequently captured when they have strayed away from home, and killed and eaten: their flesh is more highly prized than that of the other sex; and there are choice portions of the body, such as the fleshy part of the arm and the thigh, which are always preferred. Unnatural as it may seem, it cannot be doubted that they are really fond of this sort of food. The earthen pots in which it is cooked are used for no other purpose; it is esteemed as a luxury; and women, therefore, are forbidden to eat it, though it is said the wives of the chiefs often partake of it in private.*

Wars between the various tribes, or inhabitants occupying different districts, are very frequent, and serve to increase the natural ferocity of their dispositions. These often grow out of difficulties in regard to women, for, though prizing them at such little value, the men are prone to jealousy where their rights are invaded without their consent, and will promptly resent the taking away their wives and daughters by force. Their wars are sometimes protracted for a great length of time, and are commonly fierce and bloody. When one of the rival par-

---

* The Feejee chiefs are as proud of the heads of their enemies whom they have slain and eaten, as the North American savage of the scalps he has taken on the war-path, and it is customary to preserve them in earthen jars, as the trophies of their ferocious warfare.

ties acknowledges itself vanquished, if peace cannot be obtained on any milder terms, the chiefs and leading men crawl on their hands to the conquerors and humbly sue for mercy. This is not always accorded, but the victors generally content themselves with taking the daughters of the chiefs, who are brought by the suppliants and tendered to the vanquishers, and selecting some of the lower class of the people for victims at their cannibal feasts.

The Feejeean is not deficient in intelligence; he is shrewd, apt to learn, skilful, and cunning. But his soul is uninformed by that moral beauty which might relieve or conceal the dark and repulsive features of his character. In this respect, how great is the contrast between him and the matchless scenery by which he is surrounded, whose purity he has desecrated, and whose beauty sullied, by crimes the most odious, and customs the most abhorrent. In the midst of all that can please the taste, or charm the fancy, or gratify the imagination—where everything is fair, and bright, and beautiful—where the dreamy haze of a tropical clime rests lovingly on hill-top and valley—where the sun smiles in gladness upon landscapes picturesque and charming as the sweet spots, buried in foliage and flowers, that nestle in the bosom of the Italian Alps— where brook and fountain send forth unrestrained their unceasing melody—where the breezes are soft and balmy, and the perfumed breath of an unending summer fills the air with its intoxicating odor—man is alone debased. Nature displays her brightest charms, and revels in her gayest attire— but God's own image is loathsome and deformed!

Here is, indeed, a field for the missionary,—and laborers are not wanting. In fulfilment of the divine command— "Go ye into all the world and preach the gospel!"—the humble, self-denying, and persevering followers of Wesley, have found their way to this group. At Lakemba, Somu-Somu, Levuka, and Rewa, they have permanently established themselves. Hitherto their labors have been attended with little success, except among the natives of the Eastern Group, but it may be as true in the moral condition of man, as it is in nature, that "the darkest hour is that which just precedes the dawn." At least, if they accomplish nothing more, they may produce an impression on the rising generation, who are willingly placed under their instruction, that will be lasting and beneficial in its effects.

(6.) In the whole Feejee Group, there are about one hundred and fifty thousand inhabitants. Vanuä-levui and Viti-levui contain about forty thousand each, Ovolau eight thousand, Kantavu fifteen thousand, Vuna seven thousand, and Nairai seven thousand. The population is divided into five classes—the kings, chiefs, warriors, landholders (*mantanivanuä*), and common people, or slaves, called *kai-sis*. The *kai-sis* are by far the most numerous class, but they are much oppressed by their superiors, and sometimes rise in rebellion : this class, too, in appearance and character, resemble the Papuan, while the others are more like the Malay.

There are a number of kings in the group, and there are several on the two principal islands. They are nominally independent of each other, but many of them pay tribute to their brother sovereigns. Ambau is the great centre of power, and the king of that district is generally feared and respected throughout the group. The political power is wielded mainly by the kings and chiefs, who are complete despots so far as they can be, and the warriors and landholders are more or less under their control. As in many other countries more advanced in civilization, the influence of the native priests is exerted to sustain the government, and prevent the spread of disaffection among the lower classes.

(7.) The males, among the common people, rarely wear any other article of clothing except the *maro*. The chiefs have the ends of the *maro* lengthened before and behind, so as to nearly touch the ground, when it is called *seavo*. Sometimes the *seavo* is fifty yards long, and on state occasions is upheld by a train-bearer. *Pareus*, similar to those of the Samoäns, are also occasionally worn by the chiefs ; but their principal distinguishing mark, so far as regards dress, is the turban, or *sala*, which is made of the finest *tapa*, of gauze-

15*

like texture, and worn about the head in several folds. Thus furnished, the Feejee chief looks much like a half-naked Moor. Wreaths of flowers are frequently wound round the *salas*, or the feathers of the parroquet attached on the inside by the gum of the bread-fruit tree. Necklaces of shells, or the teeth of the whale, or those of human victims; and armlets made of the trochus-shell ground down into rings; likewise adorn the persons of the chiefs. Single shells of the valuable kinds are worn by the high chiefs, depending from their necks, and are handed down from father to son. They have a comb, or hair-pricker, made of bone, or stiff splints of reed, which is worn by the king as a coronet in front of his mop of hair; the chiefs wear their combs a little at one side, so as not to interfere with the prerogative of royalty; and the *kai-sis* stick it behind their ears.

One only garment, and that very diminutive in extent, is worn by the women. This is the *liku*, an elastic band, bordered on the lower side with fringe dyed either red or black, which is neatly braided of the bark of the hibiscus. It is worn about the loins, and for a maiden is only three inches wide, but married women, after they have borne children, lengthen it considerably. Tapa cloth is absolutely forbidden to be worn by the softer sex. They sometimes wear necklaces of shells, and adorn their persons with wreaths of flowers. Both sexes bore holes in the lobes of their ears,— which are often distended so as to admit the whole hand,— and insert in them gay feathers and beautiful flowers.

As has been before remarked, their toilets occupy a great share of the time and attention of the natives, considering the small quantity of clothing which they wear. Dressing the hair, combing, frizzling, greasing it with cocoa-nut oil, and daubing it over with ivory-black or some other dyeing material, are all matters of the first importance. Bathing is attended to punctually by all sexes and classes, after which their bodies are anointed with oil and turmeric, to prevent taking cold, and for the sake of beauty. Paint is lavishly used by both sexes on the face; no color is ever absolutely discarded, but vermilion, for ornamenting the tip of the nose, is considered almost priceless,—and the surest way to win the favor of the Feejeean is to present him with a small quantity of this pigment.

Tattooing is performed only on the females, by persons of the same sex. It is mainly confined to the lips and corners of the mouth, and the parts covered by the *liku*—the latter only being the most commonly tattooed. Ornaments about the wrists and ankles are rarely seen. This decoration of the body is regarded as highly important; it being thought essential to the safe passage of the women to the other world. It is performed about the age of puberty (usually fourteen years,)—and this period is celebrated by the young damsel and her associates. Circumcision is practiced on boys, as part of the ceremonies at the burial of chiefs, or on other great occasions, and it is said that a similar custom is observed with regard to the other sex in some districts.

In sitting down the males rest their bodies on their haunches, and dispose of their limbs by curling them up in front. The women assume a sort of oblique kneeling posture, so as not to expose their persons, sitting, as it were, on the calves of their legs.

Baked pig, bread-fruit, taro, and yams—the last three prepared in various ways,—are the articles of food most commonly eaten. They have also several agreeable preparations of the cocoa-nut which are made use of. Bananas and plantains are eaten, but are not so highly prized as the other edible productions of the group. The food of the common people is principally of a vegetable character. Fish and fowls often appear on the tables of the chiefs. Human flesh, as has been mentioned, is a rarity. Their cooking is principally performed by steam. For this purpose they use earthen pots made by themselves, in which their food is placed with a small quantity of water. These pots are manufactured by women who follow this employment only; they are made of clay, which is first fashioned into nearly the desired shape with the hand; a smooth round stone is then inserted, and the clay beaten or moulded about it with a mallet. If the vessel is to have but a small opening, it is first made in two or more pieces, which are afterwards joined together with great skill. Figures are traced upon them, if required, with the fibres of a cocoa-nut leaf. The pots are now baked before an open fire, and finished off by glazing, or varnishing them, with the resin of the Feejee pine, mixed with a decoction of the mangrove bark.

In serving up their food, the natives are certainly very neat, as everything is nicely wrapped up in fresh banana leaves. There is as much regularity in the courses, at the tables of the chiefs, as in the fashionable hotels of Europe and America; and when a new dish is to be brought on, the mats and other appendages previously used, are first removed. They usually eat with their fingers. Their principal meal is at the close of the day, or in the evening. The common people are, of course, obliged to work most of the time; but the aristocracy spend the greater part of the day at their toilets, and in visiting.

Ava-drinking is a national vice. The ava is prepared in the familiar mode common throughout Polynesia; their bowls are sometimes over three feet in diameter. Partaking of this beverage is quite a ceremony in the houses of the chiefs, and it is always brought to an end by a shout and a general clapping of the hands on the thighs.

Dancing is esteemed a great accomplishment, and there are regular dancing masters and mistresses employed to perfect the young men and maidens in this art. Terpsichore would be shamed, however, could she witness the manner in which her votaries display themselves in these islands. Their motions are mere writhings and contortions of the body, accompanied with monotonous chants, clapping of the hands, and beating of the hollow drum. Other amusements are resorted to among them to pass away the time agreeably; the young women have a kind of game, like forfeits; and the young men practice archery and throwing the spear. Hunting and fishing are favorite pastimes. The former is now often done with the musket, with the use of which they have become pretty well acquainted.

The language of the Feejeean has most of the characteristics usually noticed in the dialects of Polynesia. It is exceedingly full and copious. They have an appropriate term for every passion and emotion of the mind, and for every species of plants, trees, fruits, flowers, and animals, that is found in the group.

Polygamy is common. Every man has as many wives as he can afford to keep. The higher chiefs sometimes have from one to two hundred : but the middling classes content themselves with ten or a dozen ; and the poor *kai-si* is unable to indulge in the luxury of more than one. Wives are procured by making presents to the parents, or by capturing them from a hostile tribe. The marriage ceremony is performed by the priests, who enjoin upon the parties the duty of loving, honoring, and obeying, very much in the same manner as in civilized countries. Adultery is punished by the injured husband, if he possesses the power, with great severity, often in a mode too disgusting to be mentioned. When a chief dies some of his wives are usually strangled, either with or without their consent, and buried with him. Old people are frequently put to death, at their own desire, to escape decrepitude, and are sometimes forcibly strangled, or buried alive, by their children. Persons in an infirm condition, or sick of a lingering disease, are often served in the same manner.

The women are the mere slaves of their husbands, and are beaten by them at pleasure. From fear, rather than affection, they are generally faithful. Parturition is not severe among them, probably on account of their active habits of life ; and some women will resume their ordinary occupations within an hour after their delivery.

The Feejeean has a great number of divinities. The principal one is Ndengei, who is worshipped in the form of a large serpent. There are many subordinate deities, some good and others evil. They have a tradition that all men are descended of one pair of parents, and that they are darker colored than the Tongese, or the whites, because they have behaved so badly. They have likewise a tradition of a great deluge happening many years ago, which destroyed all the persons on the island except eight. *Mbures*, or spirit-houses, are the temples in which they deposit their offerings to their gods. These are held very sacred, and women are not allowed to enter them. Their priests, called *ambati*, constitute a separate and distinct class, and possess great influence over the lower orders of the population. Human sacrifices to their deities are quite common. They have also a great festival, or harvest moon, to celebrate the ingathering of their fruits.

After death, the natives of this group believe their spirits go immediately to Ndengei, by whom they are judged; some of them are allotted to the devils, who roast and eat them, and others are sent to an island, variously located by the different tribes, where they remain for a certain period, and are then annihilated. There are, of course, various shades of belief, and modifications of their superstitions, prevailing in the group; for instance, there are some who think the spirit is purified by Ndengei, after which it returns to hover about its former place of abode. The idea of a second death, however, in some form or other, is common throughout the islands.

(8.) The houses of the Feejeeans are of an oblong form, except in the Eastern Group, where they are oval. They are from twenty to twenty-five feet long, and usually about fifteen feet wide. The harems of the chiefs, however, are often huge barn-like structures, from one to two hundred feet long. They consist of a frame-work of cocoa-nut posts and sills, with rafters ascending to a ridge pole as in American houses. The roofs have a steep pitch, and are thatched with wild cane. The ridge pole projects several feet at either end, and is often fancifully adorned with the *cypræa ovula*, or other beautiful shells. The sides are filled in with reeds and cane woven neatly together. All the lashings are of sennit, and considerable pains are often taken in ornamenting the fronts of the houses with prettily braided lattice work of the same material, or of willow or cane. On the island of Vanuä-levui, it is customary to allow the eaves of the houses to project till they touch the ground. Sometimes, too, they are built in an elliptical form, like those of the Tongese, but the ridge pole always projects. They have yam-houses, which are elevated on four posts to keep out the rats and mice, and covered with thatch, to preserve the roots dry.

Mbures, or spirit-houses, are constructed after the same general fashion, except that their roofs are steeper. They are sometimes circular, and are placed either on stone platforms, or large timbers laid across each other in a rectangular form. Many of the towns, or *koros*, as they are called, are fortified with embankments of earth and cocoanut palisades with openings or *crénelés*, for musketry; and they are provided with gateways, as in the Tonga Islands. Fortifications are likewise erected, to which they retire for safety when attacked by their enemies, which consist of stone walls, composed of blocks of basalt, four or five feet high, and surrounded by moats ten feet wide, and from five to six feet deep. Bridges, also, are frequently built over their streams, on piles made of cocoa-nut wood.

Inside the houses there is a plentiful supply of *tapa* mats, and other similar articles. Earthen jars, drinking vessels, clubs, spears, muskets, and bows and arrows, are the ordinary embellishments. At one side of the centre, is a pit, or platform of stones, where the fire is built, and the cooking performed. The rest of the floor is for the most part covered with mats, and one end is elevated like a dais, by the same means, where the couches for repose are arranged. This portion of the apartment is often separated into divisions by *tapa* mats or screens, and liberally provided with musquito nettings. They sleep on mats, with pillows of bamboo resting on four legs. The latter often produce a scirrhous lump at the back of the head where it joins the neck, and it seems strange enough that the natives do not substitute in their stead the softer material of their *tapa* mats.

Their canoes are of superior construction, and are managed with more than ordinary skill. The bottom consists of a single plank of pine timber, or bread-fruit, dovetailed to the sides, which surround a frame-work of ribs lashed securely together with sennit. The joints and chinks are closed with the gum of the bread-fruit tree, with which also the sides are varnished. In other respects they resemble those of the Tongese, before described;* indeed, that people have imitated the Feejeeans, and frequently resort to this group to construct their craft. The canoes are likewise managed in a similar manner with those in the Tonga Islands. They are often fancifully ornamented with the shells of the *cypræa ovula*, and have beautifully white, or party-colored sails of *tapa* cloth, decorated with long pennants and streamers. When scudding before the wind, though trembling like an aspen leaf at every plunge, they present a most magnificent appearance.

Great ingenuity and skill are exhibited by the natives in building their houses and canoes; and their mechanical expertness is far superior to that of most other Polynesians. Prior to their intercourse with the whites, they had only a few rude tools, among which were an adze, and a hatchet, made of bone ; a knife of bamboo cut down to an edge when green, and afterwards dried and charred ; gimlets of bones, and the long spines of the *echina ;* and carving instruments of the teeth of rats and mice set in pieces of iron-wood. They now make their adzes of plane-irons lashed to crooked sticks with sennit, and use hatchets of American or European manufacture when they can be obtained.

(9.) Tortoise shell, *biche de mer*, and the whales frequenting the neighborhood of the Feejee Islands, are the only inducements for vessels to make voyages thither, except it be merely to obtain water and provisions. Tortoise shell sells readily in Europe and the United States for seven or eight dollars the pound, and a picul† of *biche de mer* brings from fifteen to twenty dollars in the Chinese market. Axes, hatchets, plane-irons, gimlets, scissors, knives, beads, vermilion, muskets, powder, trunks and chests, looking-glasses,

---

* *Anté*, pp. 321, 322.   † The picul is about 133⅓ pounds avoirdupois.

buttons, bottles, and brushes, are the articles best suited for traffic in these islands.

(10.) Shortly after the arrival of the American Squadron in the Feejee Group, a prominent native chief, by the name of Vendovi, who had been one of the chief instigators and actors in the murder of a part of the crew of an American vessel, several years previous, was captured by the address of Captain Hudson.* This had the effect to intimidate the natives, to some extent, and the friendly footing established by Captain Wilkes with the king of Ambau, served for a long time to protect the American vessels and their crews from molestation. But it was natural, perhaps, that the many new articles which the savages saw should excite their cupidity; and on the 12th of July, a cutter was lost on the reefs in Sualib Bay, twenty-five miles east of Mbua Bay, in the island of Vanuä-levui. Parties of natives had been hovering along the shore all day, and when they discovered that the cutter had grounded, they rushed forward and captured it with everything it contained, except the arms and chronometers, with which the crew succeeded in making their escape. Restitution, and prompt satisfaction for the outrage, were forthwith demanded by Captain Wilkes. After some parleying the boat was restored, but without the property. Becoming satisfied from the numerous prevarications of the natives, that they were trifling with him, the American commander ordered Captain Hudson to land with an armed party and destroy the town of Tye on Sualib Bay, where the natives concerned in the capture of the cutter were known to have collected. This was effected on the 13th of July : the natives were driven from their *koro*, which contained about sixty houses ; and the buildings were then fired and burnt to the ground, together with a number of yamhouses in the vicinity. Several chiefs were captured, but, it being ascertained that they were not concerned in the outrage, they were restored to liberty.

* Vendovi was brought as a prisoner to the United States, where he sickened and died.

This summary chastisement prevented any further acts of aggression in that quarter; but on the 24th of the same month, a still more lamentable incident occurred at the island of Malolo. Strict orders had been issued by the commander of the Squadron, in regard to their intercourse with the natives, while engaged in prosecuting the survey of the group; but on the morning of the 24th, Lieutenant Underwood went ashore from the first cutter of the Vincennes, to obtain provisions, unfortunately for himself neglecting to take with him a sufficient number of men or weapons. On discovering that the natives manifested symptoms of hostility, a hostage was seized and sent on board the cutter, which now drew in towards the shore, to be detained as a prisoner while the party were engaged in bartering with his fellows. Considerable time was spent in chaffering, and the natives gradually collected around the little party of Lieutenant Underwood. In the meanwhile the latter were joined by Midshipman Henry in a canoe. One or two attempts were made by the hostage to escape, and he at length succeeded in plunging into the water, when he struck out for the shore. Shots were fired at him, but without effect.

This was the signal for the attack, which had no doubt been premeditated. Lieutenant Underwood and his party were instantly beset by the natives. They were at first kept at bay, and the Americans attempted to retreat to the small boat, which they had left over six hundred yards from the beach, on account of the shallowness of the water on the reef. But the savages were not to be balked, and they now pressed eagerly on the feeble band, using their clubs and spears with great dexterity and effect. Both Lieutenant Underwood and Midshipman Henry defended themselves gallantly, and with praiseworthy intrepidity, but overpowered by superior numbers, they were unable to make their escape, and were at length knocked down and killed by the natives with their clubs. Others of the party were severely wounded, but none fatally except the two officers. Lieutenants Emmons and Alden had witnessed the beginning of the affray from the cutter, and instantly pulled in to the shore in their small boats. But it was too late to rescue their companions, and they had only the melancholy satisfaction of recovering their dead bodies.

On the reception of this sad intelligence, with a promptitude and decision worthy of commendation, Captain Wilkes determined to chastise the murderers in a manner that would long be remembered. The first duty, however, was owing to the dead. The bodies of the ill-starred officers were buried on one of the deserted islands of the group, and the cutters and boats of the Squadron then in that vicinity were stationed around Malolo, so as to prevent any persons making their escape. This being done, the Americans landed on the island in two divisions—one commanded by Captain Wilkes in person, and the other by Lieutenant Ringgold—early in the morning of the 26th of July. Two of the native towns, the only ones upon the island, were completely destroyed, and the plantations of the inhabitants laid waste. One of the *koros* was strongly fortified, and offered an obstinate resistance to the party under Lieutenant Ringgold, who had been ordered to attack it. A warm skirmish ensued, which was maintained for some time with spirit and bravery by the besieged as well as the assailing force. The American tars were not to be resisted, however; unharmed by the missiles showered upon them, they pressed forward to the ramparts, applied torches to the bamboo work, and drove the enemy from every part of their defences. About sixty of the savages were killed, and a great number wounded. Of the Americans but one was wounded, and he not dangerously. On the following day, the remainder of the natives, who had made their escape to the hills in the interior, appeared before Captain Wilkes effectually cowed down, and sued after their own abject fashion for mercy and forgiveness. This was accorded, but accompanied with a wholesome admonition for the future. It is almost unnecessary to add, that the Americans were not again molested while they remained in this vicinity.

All the islands and reefs of the Feejee Group were carefully examined and surveyed by the Squadron, with the exception of a part of the southern shore of Kantavu, which was known to have been included in the surveys of M. d'Urville ; regulations in regard to vessels frequenting the islands, for traffic or other purposes, were also adopted and signed by the principal kings ; and on the 11th of August, the Americans finally took their departure for the Sandwich Islands, with hearts saddened by the recollection of the severe loss which they had sustained.

SCENE OF CAPTAIN COOK'S MURDER.

CHAPTER XV.

(1.) WITH the acquisition of California by the government of the United States, and the introduction of steam navigation in the Pacific, commences a new era in the history of the Sandwich Islands. Heretofore this group has been the mere dépôt of stores and supplies for the whalemen of the Pacific, but, for the future, a new career opens before it. A glance at the map will show the favorable and important position which it occupies with reference to other countries. Midway it is placed, directly on the track of communication, between two worlds,—one passing, it may be, into decline, yet still teeming with the rich products of the Orient—the other, in the newness and freshness of youth, possessing mineral and agricultural resources without parallel in the world, inhabited by a persevering, energetic, and industrious people, and advancing on the road to greatness and prosperity with the vigor and stride of a giant. On the one hand are the silks, the teas, and the spices, of China and the East Indies; on the other, the treasures of the Siérra Neváda, and the cotton and corn of the valley of the Mississippi. These must be exchanged; and San Francisco and Canton must one day become to the Pacific, what New York and Liverpool now are to the Atlantic Ocean. This immense trade will, of necessity, pass directly through or by the Sandwich Islands. Whatever, then, may be their fate, in a political sense,—

whether, fully redeemed from the darkness of Paganism, they take their stand permanently among the nations of the earth, or fall under the dominion of some foreign power,—their destiny is fixed.

The Sandwich, or Hawaiian Islands, as they have been more appropriately termed by the missionaries, were discovered in the year 1778, by Captain Cook, who gave them the name by which they are generally known, in honor of the Earl of Sandwich, then first Lord of the Admiralty. Here, too, on the shore of the bay of Kealakekua, upon the west side of the island of Hawaii, that eminent navigator came to his tragic and untimely end, on the 14th day of February, 1779.

These islands are eleven in number, and are many hundred miles distant from any of the other Polynesian groups. They lie in the North Pacific, between latitude 18° 50' and 22° 20' N., and longitude 154° 55' and 160° 15' W. Their general direction is from southeast to north-west,— Hawaii, the southernmost of the group, being about two hundred and eighty miles distant from Kauai and Niihau, tho two islands lying furthest to the north. The total area of all the islands is about six thousand square miles. The principal members of the group are Hawaii, Maui, Kahoolawe, Lanai, Molokai, Oahu, Kauai and Niihau : the remaining three, Molokini, Lehuä, and Kaula, are mere rocky and barren islets.

Hawaii, formerly known as Owhyhee, has an area of four thousand square miles, being about two thirds that of the entire group. It is eighty-eight miles in length, by sixty-eight in breadth. The surface slopes up gradually from the beach towards the interior, which is a broken, elevated plain, three thousand feet above the level of the sea, with here and there a tall conical mountain-peak rearing its jagged front to the height of thirteen or fourteen thousand feet. Overlooking Waiakéa, or Hilo Bay, is Mauna Kea, flanked on either hand by similar peaks of less altitude, which attains an elevation of 13,953 feet; and just to the east of Kealakekua Bay, is the towering dome of Mauna Loa, 13,760 feet above the ocean, forever belching forth its volcanic fires, and casting its unearthly, waving shadow, far and wide over the broad ocean.

Maui is thirty miles north-west of Hawaii. It is forty-eight miles in length, and twenty-nine in breadth, and consists of two parts, each containing its separate ridge of mountains, which are united together by a belt or isthmus of low ground. Originally, there were, in all probability, two distinct islands, the space between which has been filled up by the scoria and lava thrown from their respective volcanoes when in a state of active operation. West Maui is considerably lower than the eastern part of the island, but both are high and volcanic, and, like Hawaii, rise gradually from the shore to the mountainous ridges in the interior. The loftiest peak on the island is Mauna Haleakala, or the " House of the Sun," whose cleft summit overlooks the eastern and southern shores of East Maui, and is 10,200 feet above the level of the ocean.—West of Maui, and separated from it by a strait averaging about twelve miles in width, are Lanai and Kahoolawe. The former is seventeen miles long, and nine miles wide ; it is shaped like a dome, and in the centre, or highest part of the island, attains an elevation of sixteen hundred feet. Kahoolawe lies opposite to the southern coast of Maui, and has Lanai on its north ; it is eleven miles long, and eight miles wide. It is a low, uninviting spot, covered with barren peaks and ridges, none of which attain a greater elevation than two hundred feet, and is tenanted only by a few miserable fishermen, and now and then an exile sent hither by order of the government.

Eighteen miles north of Maui and Lanai, and separated from them by the Pailolo channel, is Molokai. This island is forty miles long, from east to west, and nine miles wide : the western portion, embracing about one third of the whole extent, is a barren waste ; and the remaining two thirds is mountainous, in some places rising to the height of twenty-eight hundred feet, with the exception of a narrow strip of land on the south side, which has a most favorable exposure, and is highly productive.—Oahu lies about thirty miles north-west from Molokai, and, both politically and commercially, is the most important island in the group. It is forty-six miles in length, and twenty-three in breadth. Like Hawaii, it rises on all sides from the ocean, to an elevated plain in the interior, that is dotted with numerous mountain peaks, none of which, however, exceed four thousand feet in height. Indeed, the general character of the surface of this island is level in comparison with the other islands, and a very good carriage road might be constructed from one end to the other without much difficulty.

Kauai is between seventy and eighty miles still further to the north-west. It is nearly circular in shape; its greatest length being thirty-three miles, and its greatest breadth twenty-eight. Its scenery resembles that of the other islands, but is more delightfully varied. It is considerably broken, and has mountains towering to the height of five thousand feet. The climate is very fine; agriculture is here in a most flourishing state; and this, in connection with its natural attractions and advantages, has rendered it a favorite place of retreat during the hot summer months.—Niihau, sixteen miles south-west of Kauai, is eighteen miles long, from north to south, and seven miles wide. It is much lower than any of the other principal islands, having no elevation above eight hundred feet, but its surface is quite rocky and uneven. It is celebrated chiefly for the beautiful mats manufactured by its inhabitants, and is likewise said to be a fine place for making salt.

The same general features, in respect of scenery, characterize the whole group. Coral reefs encircle the coasts, with frequent openings,—and occasionally they wholly disappear. In some places the shores are low, and this is most commonly the case; but in others, the ocean waves are dashed against rocky piles of lava, and tall cliffs of basalt. Belts of tropical vegetation, of the most exuberant growth, begirt the islands, just inside the fringe of snowy breakers; beyond these are strips of fresh green verdure,—plants, and shrubs, and vines, and grasses, all mingled confusedly together,—which creep up the slopes of the hills and mountains to the height of two thousand feet; here the productions of a new climate display their manifold beauties, and the dark foliage of the cone-bearers, and other trees belonging to the lower part of the temperate zone, imborders the loftiest peaks, up to the elevation of six thousand feet; and above all, stretch upward to the region of eternal frost, the magnificent cones, with their fluted sides and perforated summits, like stupendous monuments reared by the art of man.

Numerous small rivers and streams have their sources in the mountainous ridges, and carry off the surplus waters which fall during the frequent rains, to irrigate the low levels, and add freshness and beauty to the diversified landscapes through which they wend their way, or to mingle again with the ocean. Some of these rivers, or brooks, are very considerable streams, and may be navigated for a short distance in boats. They often form picturesque falls and cascades, where they descend from the elevated plateaus to the coast level; and in a few instances their utility has been demonstrated by the employment of their waters in propelling machinery.

Evidences of the volcanic origin and character of this group meet the eye wherever it is turned. Wide fields and plains of lava, regularly piled strata of volcanic rock and cinders, and vast columnar masses of basalt, are scattered everywhere throughout the islands; although blocks of sandstone, and compact limestone with a stratification of pebbles, may occasionally be seen. But the most decisive indications of the geölogical formation, as well as the most prominent features of the islands, are the numerous conical craters, and the lofty hills of scoriaceous lava evidently poured forth from the bowels of the earth during some volcanic cataclysm. Most of these craters are now silent; their quaquaversal beds of lava no longer glow with fervent heat; their fires are slumbering, perhaps forever,—it may be, to gather new strength, and break out once more with redoubled fury.

The only active volcanoes are those of Mauna Loa and

Kilauéa, on the island of Hawaii. The first, which has been
before referred to, is much higher than the other ; but Kilauéa
is by far the most striking and peculiar. It is totally unlike
other volcanoes, and exhibits no permanent jets of fire, or flam-
ing cones, or eruptions of heated stones ; but it consists of a
vast depression, or basin,—on the flank of Mauna Loa, four
thousand feet above the ocean, and about twenty miles east of
the main volcano,—within which is a seething cauldron in a
constant state of terrific ebullition, where the boiling waves of
molten lava are continually surging to and fro, while they howl
and hiss like angry demons. This, in olden time, was the abode
of the great *Pele*, the principal goddess of the Hawaiian ;
and it is scarcely to be wondered, that the pagan should have
associated his chosen deity with a phenomenon that filled
him with so much awe, terror, and astonishment.

It is not far from one thousand feet, from the crest of the
overhanging bank down to the surface of this fiery lake.
The crater is of an oval figure, and is three and a half miles
long and two and a half miles wide. It is surrounded by
drifted heaps of scoria, and massive piles of lava, among
which are frequently found bundles of capillary glass, called
" *Pele's hair*" by the natives, springing from the crevices
and fissures, and waving in the wind like long threads of the
softest cotton. An occasional aperture from which the hot
steam escapes,—now quite often employed in cooking food by
strangers and natives, both alike indifferent to the good
pleasure of mistress *Pele*,—breaks the surface of the mountain.
Vegetation is but scanty. A few ferns, that derive their
principal sustenance from the vapors rising from the lake beneath, take root in the crannies amid the ledge of basaltic
rocks that surrounds the crater ; and in their rear are stunted
shrubs, and tall and sickly tufts of grass, which dot the sides
of the mountain, at wide intervals, down to the dark line of
vegetation that encircles its base.

Nearly seven hundred feet below the outer bank is a black
ledge of indurated lava, to which the mass boiling in the pool
below occasionally rises, and having lost a great part of its

volume by an eruption, subsides again to its customary limits. The pool is about fifteen hundred feet long, and one thousand feet across.   It is dangerous to descend from the black ledge to the border of the lake itself, although it has been done; for the reason that the thin crust of lava, formed above the glowing furnace, sometimes gives way.   The descent from the outer bank to the black ledge is comparatively easy, as the declivity is very gradual, and presents few obstructions.   The ground beneath is coated with a crust of vitreous or scoriaceous lava from half an inch to an inch thick.   Below the ledge there are many beautiful cones and jets of hardened lava scattered about in different positions.   Suspended over the blazing pool, in mid air, is a cloud of vapor, by day assuming a silvery appearance, and by night resembling a sea of fire.

The pool or lake undergoes frequent changes on its surface.   Besides rising and falling, as has been mentioned, sometimes a great number of cones start up from the midst of the liquid mass, and like miniature volcanoes eject red-hot stones, and streams of smoke and flame; then all at once they are silenced, and crumble down into the lake from which they had risen, while its fiery waves sweep away every trace of their existence.   But whatever be its condition, and in whatever aspect it is observed, the beholder is startled by the grandeur and sublimity of the scene; and the unearthly sounds that meet his ear, as if the whole brood of Cyclops were thundering at their subterranean forges, serve to heighten the emotions that steal upon him.   "The fiercely whizzing sound of gas and steam," says Mr. Bingham, "rushing with varying force, through obstructed apertures in blowing cones, or cooling crusts of lava,—the laboring, wheezing, struggling as of a living mountain, breathing fire and smoke and sulphurous gas from lurid nostrils, tossing up molten rocks or detached portions of fluid lava, and breaking up vast indurated masses with varied detonations,—all impressively bade us stand in awe."*

(2.) When the Sandwich Islands were first discovered, it

* Bingham's Sandwich Islands, pp. 387, 388.

was computed that they contained at least two hundred thousand inhabitants. Subsequent to that time a great part of the population fell victims to the bloody and devastating wars waged between the rival tribes and factions; and even after peace and harmony were restored by the benign influence of Christianity, who, with her twin sister Civilization, dispensed innumerable blessings throughout the group, and awakened new hopes and aspirations in the breasts of the illiterate and benighted pagans, other causes contributed to produce the same result—the rapid and alarming diminution of the native population. Foreign diseases and vices have been introduced, and have swept away their thousands. Infanticide, and the abandonment of children, have been almost done away; but in their stead, there has been a marked indifference to the welfare of their offspring manifested by the natives of the islands, and every year witnesses the death of a great number of infants, solely from the inattention and neglect of their parents.* Superadded to this cause of the reduction of the population, is the somewhat singular fact, that sterility, occasioned either by indulgence in pernicious habits and vices, or by the settled gloom and melancholy that have taken possession of the Sandwich Islander, is unusually common. Both these causes combined must, of necessity, lead to the result which has been witnessed here, among any people; if the species is not reproduced in sufficient numbers to supply the inroads made by time, in the ordinary course of nature, utter annihilation will be the inevitable consequence.

In 1832, the population of the group was about one hundred and thirty thousand; in 1836, it had dwindled down to about one hundred thousand; and in the winter of 1849, it was supposed not to exceed eighty thousand. Nearly one half of the whole number reside on Hawaii. Ever since the first settlement of the missionaries in the islands, the foreign population has been steadily increasing, and immi-

* Cases of abortion are not rare in some districts, though they can hardly be said to be of frequent occurrence in the group.

grants are now annually arriving in greater or less numbers. But the additions made in this manner, fail to make good the deficiencies in the native population, about one sixth of whom die every year. In some of the districts, the families of the ancient chiefs are almost extinct, and in nearly all they are much less numerous than they formerly were.

The foreign population of the group is composed of the most heterogeneous materials, and in Honolulu and some of the other towns the most striking contrasts are exhibited. There are phlegmatic Dutchmen, beer-drinking and pipe-loving Germans, mercurial Frenchmen, conceited and self-opinionated Englishmen fresh from the paradise of all true Cockneys, calculating down-east Yankees, western hoosiers, California Indians, greasy Mexicans, and last, but not least, in this hotchpot of humanity, veritable flat-nosed and sallow-faced Chinamen with the long tails and singular costume peculiar to the natives of the Celestial Empire.*

There is a close resemblance between the natives of the Society and Sandwich Islands. Those inhabiting the latter are several shades darker in complexion than the Tahitian, but their features are very similar. Their color is a brownish olive; they have dark hair, expressive and intelligent eyes, and more firm and muscular limbs than the natives of the Society Islands,—resembling more nearly, in this last respect, the people of the Samoän Group, to whom, also, they appear to be related. Both sexes of Hawaiians are inclined to become corpulent as they advance in life. The females do not possess much personal beauty, and their features are generally coarse

---

* " A *Bakery* has been established here [Honolulu] by ‘ Sam & Mow,’ bakers from Canton, where bread, cakes, and pies, are manufactured in every variety, and of excellent quality. Their advertisement contains a classical allusion in the last line, which will not be readily perceived, except by those who are aware of the arrogance of the *Celestial* Empire.

> ‘ Good people all, come near and buy
> Of Sam and Mow, good cake and pie,
> Bread, hard or soft, for land or sea,
> ‘ Celestial’ made ; come buy of we.’ ”

Olmsted’s Incidents of a Whaling Voyage, p. 213.

and disagreeable.   Between the two classes of the population
—the chiefs and the *kanakas*, or common people—there is
the same striking difference observed throughout Polynesia,
although each has some characteristics in common with the
other.   The former are more active in their movements than
the latter; they have lighter complexions and more harmonious features; and they are more graceful and stately in
their gait, and less embarrassed in their address.

Equally with the Society Islanders, the Hawaiians are
naturally indolent.   This predisposition has been in some
measure overcome by the missionaries, and the necessity of
cultivating the soil to supply their wants has rendered them
more energetic and industrious.   But they are far from being provident, nor do they show any particular desire to accumulate property.   A sufficiency of food and clothing, usually limited within the narrowest bounds, is all they care to
possess.   They are not as sensual as the Tahitian, but licentiousness is still quite prevalent, and excess in eating and
drinking is one of the chief causes that are accelerating the
steady decrease of the population.   They are tolerably
honest and hospitable; possess a respectable share of intelligence; and are quick to learn, and apt at imitation.
They are daring and courageous, and completely reckless of
life; yet they do not possess the frankness and generosity
which often accompany those traits.   On the contrary, they
are extremely selfish, and have very little natural affection;
there are striking exceptions, of course, to this general rule,
but infidelity, infanticide, and the abandonment of children,
are not looked upon with that abhorrence which they naturally excite in a well-educated and right-feeling community.
Parents, and mothers in particular, are exceedingly neglect-
ful of their offspring; the pleasurable cares and anxieties of
true affection, for them have no alleviation; and when they
are able to put their children out to nurse, which is frequently
done, they feel relieved of a most grievous burden.

Of national pride, the Sandwich Islander cannot boast.
Whether, since he has become partially enlightened and civil-

ized, the comparison he has been able to draw, between his own and other countries, has created an unnatural loathing towards his race, or that memory still clings with regret to the customs and associations of former days,—certain it is, that despair has cast its dark shadow over his countenance, and, like the vulture, is forever gnawing at his heart. Some few there are, who, not indifferent to the rapid dwindling away of their people, look forward to the future in trustful hope and confidence, and are zealous in urging forward those reforms and improvements that afford the promise of bettering their condition and checking the progress of decay ; but the great mass, when not under the influence of the temporary excitement produced by amusement or intoxication, are sorrowful, moody, and melancholy. It is painful to contemplate the sad expression of the common people, when at work, or when resting from their labors ; and when those possessing greater intelligence, and occupying a higher sphere, reflect on the alarming decrease of the native population, their thoughts are not pleasant ones. Civilization seems to them to have been a bane as well as a blessing ; they have been redeemed from the darkness of heathenism, but the full light of day has overpowered them, and like Semelé, they are perishing in the embraces which they courted.

European, or peculiar national costumes, prevail among the foreign residents. The greatest incongruity is exhibited in the apparel of the natives, especially in the seaport towns. The better classes often appear well clothed, in a manner similar to the whites ; the women in flaring chip bonnets, and silk or satin dresses, though sometimes accompanied with the coarsest brogans drawn over a stockingless foot ; and the men in broad-leafed straw hats, and nankeen jackets and trowsers. A great effort has been made by the missionaries to do away the primitive style of dress altogether, but they have not been entirely successful. The common people, or *kanakas*, still adhere to the *maro*, and both males and females can with difficulty be persuaded to put on anything else when they are at work. Sometimes, on Sundays or holidays, the former conceal their nether limbs in a pair of pantaloons, if fortunate enough to possess them; and provided the state of their wardrobes permits the indulgence, a coarse cotton shirt is added. On a week day, a native may often be seen clad simply in a shirt, or sailor's round jacket, with the indispensable *maro*. *Pareus* are likewise occasionally worn by both sexes. Since the missionaries have established themselves on the islands, they have persuaded the females, at least when they appear in public, to put on long gowns, like the loose morning dresses of our own American ladies. These are confined at the waist, if at all, by embroidered, or party-colored *tapa* scarfs or shawls.

Articles of apparel made of *tapa*, are, however, much less common now than they formerly were. Mantles, called *kapas* or *kiheis*, are still made of this material; and there are girdles, or *malos*, also, of the same fabric. The mantle is passed over the right shoulder of the wearer, and knotted under the opposite arm. Besides the *tapa* shawls, bright yellow or scarlet ones, of foreign manufacture, are frequently displayed.

The king, Kamameha III, usually wears the European dress,—consisting of a blue broadcloth coat, and white vest and pantaloons; but for great occasions he has robes of state, made of *tapa*, and adorned with rich yellow or scarlet feathers—the latter obtained from the beautiful *melithreptes Pacifica*. His royal spouse ordinarily appears in public with an embroidered shawl of scarlet crape thrown over her silk or satin dress; and when still greater state is desired, she, too, displays a gorgeous robe, showily, if not tastefully trimmed with feathers. Costly tiaras of yellow or scarlet feathers are, likewise, indicative of high rank. The chiefs wear helmets made of linen network, with brilliant feathers inserted, and the chiefesses, as they are called, pretty wreaths, either of feathers or flowers, or, sometimes, of both intermingled.

Ornaments are not very common. Amulets of bones or ivory shaped like a hook, or carved after some other pattern, or beautiful shells, are often seen. Necklaces of braided hair, or of the bright red fruit of the pandanus, sometimes tinged with orange color, and strung by the women on a cord, are worn about their necks.   Wreaths of flowers were formerly much worn by the females around their heads, but these have been interdicted by the missionaries, and are, therefore, pretty generally discarded.   Very little attention is paid by either sex to the hair : the males, among the higher classes, wear it cropped short, and the females gather it up in dark masses on the top of the head. Tattooing is almost abandoned, though now and then a native damsel will be seen, with her dusky legs and ankles prettily ornamented, " as a sort of substitute for open-work hosiery."   The *kanakas* commonly go barefooted, though when travelling over the rough paths in the interior, they put on sandals made of ti leaves.

Ancient manners and customs are nearly done away, and the natives are gradually accustoming themselves to the habits of the whites.   Some few of their amusements—the relics of former times—are still preserved.   They are an amphibious race, and being totally fearless of danger, will spend hours at a time, disporting themselves, in the most furious surf.   In bathing, each person is usually provided with a surf-board.   This is from six to nine feet long, and from twelve to eighteen inches wide.   It is from one to two inches thick in the centre, but quite thin at the edges.   Throwing himself flatwise upon this, the bather plunges forward from the shore on the top of the recoiling surf.   When he meets a roller he dives under it, and emerging on the other side, darts ahead once more with great rapidity, till he gains the outer line of breakers, from a quarter to half a mile distant from the shore.   Now watching the opportunity, he mounts one of the loftiest waves, balancing himself on his board on his hands and knees, or extended thereupon at full length.   With the speed of a maddened courser he darts towards the shore, his shout of triumph ringing loud and clear, and distinctly heard above the roar of the surge, if he is so fortunate as to distance his companions.   Accidents sometimes occur, but if the bather is dismounted from his board, or thrown from the wave on which he has placed himself, nothing daunted by the failure, he attempts to reach another, and though still unsuccessful, will persevere till he is obliged to return to the beach, at which he often arrives panting for breath and completely exhausted by his efforts. This is esteemed glorious sport by all ages and classes, and both sexes engage in it indiscriminately, with nothing on but the *maro.*

Lascivious dances, or *hulas,* are not uncommon, though the civil authorities and missionaries make every exertion to prevent such displays. Their music consists principally of drumming on hollow vessels or calabashes, or on the native drum, which is made of a hollow log, with a piece of shark skin drawn over the end. Foreign instruments have been introduced, as a matter of course, and the violin, the pipe, and the trumpet, may now frequently be heard in the fashionable assemblies held in the drinking houses of Honolulu.

Riding on horseback is as much of a passion with the Sandwich Islander, as with the sailor when ashore. All classes and conditions look upon this as their favorite pastime. They will mount without saddle or stirrups—the women sitting astride like the Peruvian señoríta; anything serves for a bridle; and once fairly seated, away they go with a loud hurrah, dashing over hill and plain at a furious rate.

All who are not restrained by their religious principles, or through fear of the missionaries, are much addicted to gambling, either with cards or dice, in the use of which many of the natives have become very expert. They have, also, a kind of *thimble-rigging* among them, which is called *buhenehene :* in this game a stone is hidden underneath various colored piles of *tapa* by one of the party, and the others guess where it is concealed, each player pointing to the pile where he supposes it to be hidden with a short stick. Throwing quoits, too, is much practiced; and there is another game, called *maiku,* which consists in hurling stones in a narrow trench dug in the ground, sometimes a mile in length,—he who can throw the furthest being considered the best player. This last amusement, however, is giving place to bowling, alleys for which have been erected at Honolulu, and some of the other seaports.

The young people amuse themselves at a sort of see-saw, not dissimilar to that seen among us. A long pole is extended across a forked stick, planted upright in the ground, on either end of which two or three of the company place themselves, and the great object is to see which party can throw the other the soonest.

One of the ancient sports was *hoolua*, or sliding down hill; and many of the natives are still as much attached to their mode of "coasting," as was the young Albanian in days of yore. The Sandwich Islander, of course, practiced his recreation without the accessory of snow or ice; but, in its stead, he placed a thin layer of grass along a broad smooth furrow made down some steep declivity, and prolonged for a short distance across the level ground at its foot. Light built, and long, and narrow sleds, were used in this sport. Grasping his vehicle in his hands, the player planted himself a few paces in rear of the starting point : then suddenly darting forward at his utmost speed, as he reached the brow of the slope he threw his sled forward, sprang headlong upon it, and darted down the hill. This was once a very common mode of gambling—the person who went the greatest distance the most frequently being considered the winner of the game.

When the missionaries first arrived in the islands, the ancient custom of *taboo*, or *tabu*, was the law of the land. It was the instrument of gross oppression and wrong; it had reduced the common people to a state of abject servitude ; it encouraged the gratification of every whim and caprice on the part of the kings or chiefs ; it entered the lowest hut, and restrained its occupant from the gratification of his simplest wishes, as well as from indulgence in connubial pleasures ; and, at the same time, it forbade the wife from eating with her husband, in order that he might enjoy his amours with other objects of his desire, unabashed by her presence. The marriage relation was scarcely acknowledged, and where the tie existed at all, it was regarded but as a rope of sand. Polygamy, or concubinage of the grossest character, was common among the higher chiefs throughout the group. Almost the first changes brought about by the missionaries affected the relations between the two sexes, and proceeding from one step to another, they finally caused it to be enacted, that marriages should not be solemnized between parties who were unable to read. It is somewhat doubtful whether this law is not too severe, and by its great stringency often lead to illicit connections. It is very natural that it should have that tendency; and it is certainly no reproach to the missionary, that his theory, however correct in itself, does not always prove beneficial in practice. The law has been hitherto enforced, however, pretty strictly; and adultery and fornication are punished with considerable severity. Persons found guilty of these offences are imprisoned in the forts or otherwise confined, and put at hard labor—the women being compelled to work with wreaths of flowers about their heads.

Most of the prisoners are employed on the roads, and in quarrying coral stone from the reefs for governmental purposes. There are particular days, also, called *pahau* days, on which the *kanakas* are obliged to work for the government. This class of the population have received altogether more credit than they really deserved for their industry. It is but their humiliating and debased condition, nevertheless, that produces the apathy, indifference, and indolence, which they show in every feature of their countenances, when collected together in groups, or arranged in long files, in the streets of Honolulu, and sitting squatted upon their hams— their favorite attitude—perfectly listless and immovable, until the voice of the overseer or director arouses them for the resumption of their task. Mere machines, endowed but with life, they have nothing to live or to hope for, except the gratification of the animal passions and appetites. No system of society can be sound, or permanently prosperous, that tolerates such debasement of its members, and here we have another important cause of the degeneracy and decay of the Hawaiian race.

Fish and taro are the chief articles of food among the natives. One of them will make a meal from a small fish, either dried or roasted, and a little *poë*. The latter is commonly eaten by thrusting the finger into the vessel containing it, and turning it round until a sufficient quantity is gathered, when it is carried to the mouth, and the paste sucked off very much as American youngsters eat treacle. Pigs and poultry, and most of the fruits and vegetables common in the tropics, or the lower part of the temperate zone, are more or less eaten by all classes of natives. Their mode of cooking is after the true Polynesian fashion ; the articles being placed in a hollow, or pit, dug in the earth and lined with heated stones. The *taro* is converted into *poë* in this way : the root is baked in the ground, in the manner above mentioned, till it becomes dry and mealy, when it is mixed with a little water, and beaten with a smooth stone, or pestle, until it has the consistence of bookbinder's paste ; it is now set aside for twenty-four hours, at the expiration of which it has a slightly acidulous, but agreeable taste, and is fit for use. It is also made in a harder state, for sea voyages or long journeys by land. At such times, jerked beef, prepared from the flesh of the wild cattle that roam at large through the pasture grounds in the interior of the larger islands, is used instead of fish.

All sexes and classes are much addicted to smoking, and even the poorest *kanaka* carries his short pipe, with a quantity of tobacco, wherever he goes. At night, too, the natives will frequently get up, light their pipes, take a few puffs, and then lie down again for another nap. When they smoke they often blow the vapor down through their nostrils.

Frequent bathing is practiced by the Sandwich Islanders, and they are tolerably cleanly in their habits. When a person is fatigued, they have a practice of rubbing and kneading him, called *lomi-lomi*, which is quite refreshing.

Whenever any one dies, a great outcry is made ; and the

relatives lament the loss they have sustained, by wailing for several days and nights in succession over the corpse of the deceased.   The most doleful cries are uttered at these wakes, and should one of the royal family be the object of their lamentations, the sad *auwe* is echoed from every town and hamlet throughout the group by a whole nation of mourners.   Joy at the meeting of friends after a long separation is expressed in a somewhat similar manner.   They take each other by the hand, rub their noses together, and at the same time utter the word *aloha*, in a low wailing tone.

(3.) When these islands were first discovered by Cook, they were governed by different chiefs or sovereigns, but after a series of long and bloody wars, they were reduced by the great Kamameha, the founder of the present dynasty, under one general head.   He was succeeded in 1819 by his son Kamameha II, under whose auspices *taboo* was abolished; the accustomed sacrifices were withheld from the gods, or *akuas;* and pleasure, licentiousness, and intemperance, engrossed the time, and occupied the thoughts, of the whole people.   Matters were in this condition when the first missionaries, sent out by the American Board of Foreign Missions, arrived at the islands, in March, 1820.   They were kindly, if not cordially received, and permitted at once to enter upon their labors.   Though, like others of the same class, they seem to have long entertained the hope of converting the Hawaiian Islands into a real, and not visionary Utopia, their efforts have, nevertheless, been far more practically directed, than those of missionaries generally in the Polynesian groups.   Well knowing that idleness was the fruitful parent of irreligion and vice, they commenced instructing the natives in the useful arts, and endeavored to create incentives to the prosecution of industrial pursuits.   In procuring the abolition, however, as far as was possible, of the ancient customs and amusements of the people, without substituting something of a similar character in their stead, they have, perhaps, committed an irreparable error; but if it be such, the motives that animated them have been pure and noble. He who passes, by a sudden transition, from the darkness of slavery to the full light of liberty, may remain a freeman, but he is liable to degenerate into a ruffian; instantaneous changes can never be made with safety, especially among an uneducated people; and if the recreations and indulgences to which they have been long accustomed, are denied, without a suitable and gradual preparation for so great an innovation, it is but natural that they should either revolt against the authority enforcing these restrictions, or sink into a melancholy lethargy from which it may be impossible to arouse them.

The last is the present condition of the inhabitants of the Sandwich Islands. A noble work was attempted by the missionaries, and they have, in reality, accomplished an untold amount of good. But they aimed too high—their error was one into which mere schoolmen were very liable to fall; they set up the standard of perfection, and acted upon the supposition that they could bar the doors, and keep vice and temptation away from the natives, and at the same time render them a happy, industrious, and contented people. Amusements and pastimes, sports and recreations, the song and the dance, were abolished; and the wreath of flowers, to which God himself had given beauty and freshness, was made the emblem of shame. For these were substituted the plain and simple mode of worship and of life so well adapted to the Puritan character, but here requiring some modification to render it less repulsive. Liberty and enjoyment were to be instantly exchanged for a rigid sobriety and sedateness. What could be the result of these errors, but that which we now witness—one half of the nation abandoned to intemperance and excess, and the other half struggling almost hopelessly against the melancholy and gloom that have overshadowed their hearts?*

* Of late years, a powerful attempt has been made to introduce the Roman Catholic religion into the islands. It is not denied that the natives have been much struck by the splendid shows and attractive worship of that church; and there is a moral in this fact, of vital importance to the missionary.

Doubtful as is the prospect for the future, there may still be a remedy, and the missionary may yet be spared the pain which he certainly must feel, when he reflects that he has aided in christianizing a people, only to fit them for their burial.   Upon the present generation, but little impression can be made ; yet, by providing social, and strictly moral amusements, for the young, by banishing sadness from their countenances, and substituting the light and life and joy springing from happy and contented hearts, much good may be effected.   The encouragement of intermarriages with foreigners, for the improvement of the race, may also be beneficial.   But, above all, it is necessary, that the practical, though not nominal, union of church and state, should be absolutely dissolved.   The missionaries may then confine themselves to their appropriate sphere, and leave politics and legislation, where none of the great principles of the christian religion are involved, to those who are responsible for the civil administration of the government.*

For some years after the arrival of the missionaries their progress was quite slow; but in 1822 they established a printing press, and commenced the publication of the bible and such tracts as were calculated to do good among the heathen. In 1823, the government publicly acknowledged the christian sabbath, and required all ordinary business and sports to be suspended on that day.   In 1824, Kamameha II. was succeeded by his brother, Kamameha III.   The latter being but a mere lad, at the time of his accession to the throne, the government was administered by Kaahumanu, one of the wives of his father, as regent, during the first eight years of his reign.   Many important and valuable reforms were introduced during her regency, and when the youthful monarch assumed the reins of government, in 1832, he continued the

* The Rev. Mr. Bingham, in his " Residence in the Sandwich Islands"—a work from which I have obtained much valuable information—insists (p. 278 et seq.) that the charge, or assertion, of a union of church and state in the Hawaiian Group, is utterly erroneous.   In theory, this is doubtless so ; but it is scarcely possible for an unprejudiced reader to examine his book, without coming to the conclusion that in practice it is directly the reverse.

good work which had been commenced. The repeated strifes between the foreign residents, and particularly between the agents of France and Great Britain, to obtain a controlling ascendency in the islands, operated very unfavorably, both to the missionary cause, and to the improvement of the social and political condition of the people.

At length, in October, 1840, a written constitution, modelled in many of its features after those of the United States and Great Britain, was adopted by the kings and chiefs, through the instrumentality of the missionaries, and publicly promulgated. This constitution contains the following declaration of rights, which, while acknowledging the divine authority, seems to afford an ample guaranty of protection to the rights and interests of the common people :

" God has made of one blood all the nations of men, that they might alike dwell upon the earth in peace and prosperity. And he has given certain equal rights to all people and all chiefs of all countries. These are the rights or gifts which he has granted to every man and chief of correct deportment, —life, the members of the body, freedom in dwelling and acting, and the rightful products of his hands and mind : but not those things which are inhibited by the laws.

" From God also are the office of rulers and the reign of chief magistrates for protection ; but in enacting the laws of the land, it is not right to make a law protecting the magistrate only and not subjects ; neither is it proper to establish laws for enriching chiefs only, without benefiting the people, and hereafter no law shall be established in opposition to the above declarations ; neither shall taxes, servitude, nor labor, be exacted, without law, of any man, in a manner at variance with those principles."

Under the Hawaiian constitution, the government is in the nature of a limited monarchy. The sovereignty is declared to exist, forever, in Kamameha III, and his heirs, to be designated by him and the chiefs during his life-time, or, in default thereof, by the nobles and representatives. A premier, or prime minister, appointed by the king, is associated with him in the executive administration. Lands cannot be alienated without the consent of the king, and where there are no persons to inherit real estate, it reverts to him. No law, at variance with the word of God, can be enacted; and no man can be punished without due trial and conviction. Representatives are elected by the people to a national legislature, or parliament; and there is also a public council, the members of which are the chiefs. No law can be enacted without the consent of a majority of the representatives and counsellors, respectively. The king appoints four governors under him,—one for Hawaii, one for Maui and the adjacent isles, one for Oahu, and one for Kauai and the adjacent isles. The supreme court consists of six judges, four of whom are appointed by the elected representatives, and the other two are the king, who is the chief judge, and his premier. Subordinate judges are appointed by the governors. Tax-officers receive their commissions and authority from the monarch and premier.

After the adoption of the constitution a new code of laws was established, under which strangers, as well as residents and natives, are amply protected in their persons and property. Indeed, none of the other groups in Polynesia, afford as great security in this respect. The authorities, in the main, are very impartial; and an excellent police has been organized. Whenever a vessel is landing her cargo at Honolulu, two or three constables, who carry canes as the badges of their authority, are posted along the wharfs, to keep off all intruders. The intrigues of foreign agents have occasionally disquieted the country, but as its independence has been guaranteed by France, Great Britain, and the United States, there can be no immediate danger of an overthrow of the existing government. Should the native population ultimately dwindle away altogether, and the foreign residents be left in the occupancy of the islands, although they may not seek any more intimate connection with the United States, the tone of the government, and the national character, will be decidedly American.

Taxes, in the Sandwich Islands, are paid, for the most part, in kind. There is also a land tax occasionally imposed, when the exigencies of the state require it. At one time the poll tax was very heavy on fathers of families; but latterly this has been changed, and encouragement has been given to raising children, by providing that where a man has a certain number, he shall be exempt from paying taxes.

Public and charity schools for the instruction of the children of the common people, are located all over the islands; and there are higher seminaries for the education of the sons and daughters of chiefs—for the males at Lahainaluna, and for the females at Wailuku, on the island of Maui. The observance of the Sabbath is strictly enforced by the authorities, and all offences and misdemeanors are punished with great promptitude. There are upwards of twenty churches in the group, and full one third of the native population are church members.

Two weekly newspapers have been established at Honolulu, and have a pretty extensive circulation. Most of the chiefs, and the principal members of the legislature, are men of very good education, and possess a respectable degree of judgment and intelligence. They take a deep interest in the welfare of their own country, and exhibit a pretty correct knowledge of the affairs of other governments.

(4.) The lofty mountain peaks of these islands, which are mainly destitute of vegetation, or, if really existing, not perceptible at a distance, give an aspect of barrenness to the country that is scarcely warranted by the fertility of the lovely valleys lying sweetly imbosomed amid the broken hills and ridges. Few more beautiful spots can be found in the world than these charming valleys; that of Nuuanu near Honolulu, and that of Manoä, in the rear of Waikiki, have excited the admiration of every traveller who has visited them. The scenery of the other islands is similar; and where the hoary mountains, rising amid the fields of indurated lava, attain the loftiest elevation, and display upon their summits the snow and frosts of cold and dreary winter, around their feet are garlanded the richest fruits and flowers, mingled with the greenest verdure, of a tropical clime. On the hill sides the soil is very often a hard red clay, which can never produce anything but grass for pasturage ; but in the valleys and low grounds it consists of decomposed lava and vegetation, intermixed with coral sand, and the *detritus* washed down by the mountain torrents. This last is highly productive, though, in dry weather, it is easily converted into dust, and is sometimes quite annoying.

None of the Polynesian islands can boast of a more delightful climate. The purity, elasticity, and equability of the atmosphere, are unsurpassed. The nights, in particular, are very fine. The ordinary range of the thermometer is from 65° to 86°. Showers are not very frequent directly along the coast, but clouds are continually forming in the mountains, and are driven by the winds over the delightful valleys upon which they discharge their refreshing tribute. In some seasons, the condensation of vapor constantly taking place in the mountains is remarkable ; drizzling mists are ever descending in the upper ravines, and in the intervals and plains beneath, rain rapidly alternates with the sunshine. It might be supposed, from this fact, that the climate must become so moist as to be prejudicial to health ; but as the islands are situated within the northern trades, blowing from the north-east to the south-west, the fierce winds, called by the natives *momukus*, prevent this result. On account of the prevalence of these winds, it is much more pleasant on the leeward side of the islands, than on the opposite side, and the vegetation has not that peculiar burnt appearance often noticed to windward, but looks fresher, greener, and more thrifty. Earthquakes occur somewhat frequently, but the shocks are usually quite slight, and it is very seldom that they produce any great damage.

Pulmonary affections, and scorbutic complaints, are quite common. The principal diseases are asthma, consumption, croup, influenza, catarrh, dropsy, fevers, apoplexy, diarrhea, dysentery, inflammation of the viscera from over-eating and excessive drinking, cutaneous eruptions, ophthalmia, fevers, inflammatory rheumatism, ulcers, scrofula, and syphilis. Biliary complaints and hepatic diseases are very rare. Previous to the arrival of the missionaries very little was known about medicine, though there were native physicians who practiced a great deal on the credulity of their countrymen. Almost the only remedies then prescribed in cases of sickness, were doses of salt water, or decoctions of the candle-nut, the bitter calabash, the seeds of the castor-oil nut, or the ipomœa, as cathartics. The want of proper medical attendance is now generally felt throughout the islands, although the missionaries render all the medical services in their power, without charge. The mortality among the native children is very great, and it is computed that full one sixth of the population die annually. The foreign residents, however, appear to enjoy excellent health ; and the climate seems to be exceedingly well adapted to persons born in the United States.

(5.) Almost all the choice fruit and timber trees of the tropics are found in the Sandwich Islands. The bread-fruit and cocoa flourish very well along the coasts ; they are as tall and as stately, but not so umbrageous, as in the Feejee Group or the Society Islands. The other important trees are the koa (acacia), ahia, pandanus, hibiscus, and tuitui ; of the wood of the koa, the finest panel work of the native churches, and the best and most beautiful furniture, are made. The shady tuitui is also a most valuable tree ; oil is obtained in great quantities from the nuts ; they are also roasted and eaten ; and they are strung on a straw, or a fibre of the pandanus leaf, and burned as torches. The *yase*, or sandal-wood, was once quite plenty, and this valuable timber was at first the main attraction that drew foreigners to the islands ; but it is now nearly extirpated, and there are only a few scraggy bushes to be found. The dark evergreen mangrove is spread all over the low country, and the sides of the mountains, above the customary strip of woodland, are covered with ferns of every variety, the roots of which are edible, with whortleberries, called *ohea* by the natives, and wild rasp and strawber-

ries. The ti (*dracæna*) has been found very useful for
hedges, as the bushes will grow closely matted together.
The tacca grows wild in considerable abundance, yet there is
comparatively but little arrow-root manufactured.

Bananas, melons, pine-apples, grapes, figs, plantains, rose
apples (*eugenia*), yams, and other rich fruits and vegetables,
are raised in great variety. The sweet potatoes produced
here are unusually fine ; they are like the delicious amor-
phous yams of the West Indies, and of every shade of color,
from dark purple to red, green, or yellow. Irish potatoes
have been acclimated and succeed well. Indian corn is extensively cultivated. The coffee bush, and the indigo and
cotton plant, are admirably adapted to the soil and climate,
and come forward vigorously, with very little trouble or attention. The same may be said of the sugar-cane, large
plantations of which can be seen on the alluvial flats in all
the principal islands. Thirteen varieties of the taro are cultivated, both on the uplands, and in low wet places. They
are more plentiful in the latter, and the wide green patches
are the most conspicuous objects to be seen along the shores
of the islands. This plant requires a great quantity of moisture, and the land where it is grown is frequently irrigated
during the dry weather,—the water being pumped from the
ponds and reservoirs by means of windmills.

The black mulberry is a native of the islands. Several
years since an extensive silk plantation was established by a
company of foreigners, on the island of Kauai, and quantities
of the *morus papyfera* and *morus alba* were imported, and
set out with the native mulberry. The trees grew with extraordinary vigor and luxuriance, and the *morus multicaulis*
was subsequently introduced. Some difficulty was experienced in acclimating the cocoons, but on crossing the American breed with the Chinese, everything promised well.
Machinery was now constructed, and steam power provided.
But the sanguine expectations of the projectors of this enterprise were doomed to a sudden disappointment. In 1840 a
severe drought came on ; the trees at once began to wither ;

aphides, in countless numbers, attached themselves to the limbs and trunks, and exhausted the juices ; and myriads of spiders threw their webs over the leafless branches, and completed the work of destruction. Utterly despairing of success, the company relinquished the undertaking in the following year, and turned their attention to the cultivation of the sugar-cane.

One of the most useful, if not the most valuable products of the Sandwich Islands, is a species of calabash-tree, the fruit of which is very large and more flat than the common varieties. The calabashes are often from eighteen to twenty inches in diameter, and some of them are said to be large enough to hold two bushels. They are much used by the common people, in conveying fruit, vegetables, and other light articles. For this purpose they are suspended in a network attached to the extremity of a pole, which the *kanaka* balances over his shoulder. At the other end of the pole there is usually a similar network, containing, also, one or more well-filled gourds, or a large stone, to preserve the equilibrium.

Rich succulent grasses carpet the plains and valleys, from the low grounds where the cocoa displays its long and elegantly shaped fronds, and the waving plumes of the breadfruit are lifted by the tropical breezes, to the elevated regions where the beautiful outlines of the graceful koa are distinctly traced against the light reddish background of the distant mountains. Excellent pasturage is therefore afforded, in the interior of Hawaii, for considerable herds of wild cattle, originally, it is said, imported from California.

Among the many plants and shrubs that add so much beauty and loveliness to the flora of the Hawaiian Group, are numerous arborescent and shrubby geraniums, vacciniums, and daphnes. There are the most beautiful amaranths ; and the crimson flowered dock, the white viola, the orange and scarlet clusters of the agati grandiflora, and the dark crimsom and lilac blossoms of the pelargonium, with the varied hues of many a more humble plant, lend their rich dyes to deck the Hawaiian valleys with mantles of the most gorgeous embroidery.

(6.) Singing birds, and others whose tones are not melodious, but displaying the most beautiful plumage, abound in the groves and forests. Of aquatic fowl there is also an abundance. Tropic birds, whose brilliant-colored tail feathers adorn the robes of royalty, are very common; and everywhere along the coral reefs, and upon the rocky islets,

> " Up and down! up and down!
> From the base of the wave to the billow's crown,
> And amidst the flashing and feathery foam,
> The Stormy Petrel finds a home."

Among the fish are whales and sharks, which frequent the coasts at certain seasons, and the black-fish, bonito, ray, rock-fish and albicore. Black-fish, and others of the smaller kinds, are taken in great quantities by driving them into pens made of stones in the shoal-water. They are also caught with nets and hooks, or with poisonous herbs. Shrimps are obtained in plenty, and the pearl oyster is quite abundant in Pearl river and its inlet, on the southern coast of Oahu. After the taro has been gathered, the patches are converted into fish-ponds, in which large supplies of fish are kept till they are required in the markets of the seaport towns.

Of wild animals there are none but rats and mice, except a few dogs who inhabit the caves in the mountains.* There are small herds of cattle, too, who are partially wild, in the mountainous regions of Hawaii, though they are said to be fast disappearing. Spaniards from California used frequently to come hither for the purpose of capturing them, after their own fashion, with the lasso. They are likewise often caught in deep pits, covered over lightly with brush and dirt, upon which the hoof-prints of a bullock are impressed. After they are taken, the cattle are marked by branding, and kept in

---

* Baked dog was once a favorite dish with the Hawaiian chief, and rats and mice were not unacceptable; but of late years, these dishes are no longer regarded as *luxuries.*

NATIVE CHURCH AT HONOLULU.

pastures, in readiness to supply the vessels touching at the island. Goats, hogs and poultry, are raised in considerable numbers on all the larger islands.

Musquitoes, fleas, scorpions, and centipedes, are very abundant, and excessively annoying. The natives insist that the musquitoes were first introduced there by stranger vessels ; and they stoutly affirm, also, that the flea is a foreign importation. The tradition in regard to the advent of the latter on their shores is as follows :—Many years ago a woman from Waiméa went out to a ship to see her lover, and as she was about to return, he gave her a bottle, saying that there was very valuable property (*waiwai*) contained in it, but that she must not open it, on any account, until she reached the shore. As soon as she gained the beach, she eagerly uncorked the bottle to examine her treasure, but nothing was to be discovered,—the fleas hopped out, and "they have gone on hopping and biting ever since."

(7.) Honolulu on the southern coast of Oahu is the seat of government, and the most important town in the group. It contains about ten thousand inhabitants, one fifth of whom are foreigners. It is prettily situated on a plain sloping gently down to the beach, and has a very good harbor, formed by a barrier reef of coral with a single opening, which is capable of accommodating from sixty to seventy vessels of five hundred tons burden. Groves of tall cocoas border the beach, and a few years ago they were the only shade trees to be seen, but now many of the streets are well ornamented with them. Its principal thoroughfare is called Main Street, and most of the houses on this street, or within two or three squares, are situated within neat inclosures, surrounded by *adobé* walls, and around them are well cultivated gardens, stocked with fruit trees, plants, shrubbery, and vegetables, that impart to them a cheerful rural aspect. On the outskirts of the town are the grass-thatched habitations of the natives. At the distance of half a mile in the rear of the town is the Puahi, or Punch-bowl Hill, an extinct crater rising by a steep ascent to the height of five or six hundred feet, which obtained its present name from the foreign residents, on account of the cavity at the top being shaped very much like a bowl. On the west are the mountains of Waianaë, and on the east is Diamond Hill, considerably larger and higher than Puahi, but of the same general character. On Punch-bowl Hill there is an apology for a fortification, consisting of a flagstaff, a rude stone wall, and a few natural embrasures in the lava rock, with a straw-built and mud-plastered powder magazine ; and on the flank of Diamond Hill is a battery, also in a state of dilapidation. These positions, however, command the harbor and its entrance, and if properly fortified would afford ample defence to the town.

There are three large churches in Honolulu, one of which is a thatched building, two hundred feet long ; another, whose walls are made of plastered *adobés*, is one hundred and twenty feet long and sixty feet wide ; and the third and more recent structure, which is built of coral stone hewn out in entire blocks, is two stories high, one hundred and forty-four in length and seventy-eight in breadth, and adorned with a tall tapering spire much like those of American churches.* Honolulu likewise contains a number of pretty school-houses with neat cupolas ; it has a charity school and an orphan school ; and, furthermore, it can boast of an Institute established for scientific investigation in Polynesia, which has a museum of curiosities and specimens of natural history, and a library of several hundred volumes. Besides these more important and useful structures and institutions, Honolulu contains a great number of grog-shops, billiard rooms, dancing halls, and sailors' boarding houses ; it has its hotels and livery stables, and if reports be true, its cock-pits and gambling saloons.

Waikiki, five miles east of Honolulu, is a very pleasant

---

* This edifice was erected mainly by the contributions of the natives, and it would seem that they are, as a general rule, very willing to bestow their labor and means on such objects. This is probably owing, in some degree, to the fact, that in former times, their *heiaus*, or heathen temples, were constructed in a similar manner ; each individual, from the highest to the lowest, being required to bring one or more stones for the erection of the contemplated building.

town; and Kailua, on the eastern coast, is delightfully situated amid a charming grove of waving cocoas. Near the
latter is a cavern extending for a distance of twelve hundred
feet under ground, and adorned with the most beautiful sta-
lactites.

Lahaina, on the western shore of Maui, opposite to the
island of Lanai, is the country residence of the king, Kamameha III. It is also a great resort for whalers frequenting
this quarter of the Pacific. It is built in a straggling manner, for three quarters of a mile along the beach, and has but
one principal street. Most of the private dwellings are built
of grass in the native fashion. The most imposing edifices
are the king's palace which is constructed of coral rock, his
storehouses for the reception of the royal revenue, and a rectangular fort, inclosing an area of about one acre, with walls
twenty feet high. About a mile and a half in the rear of the
town, at the foot of the mountains, is the seminary of Lahainaluna, the main building of which is two stories high and is
surmounted with a cupola. Wailuku, where the female
seminary is located, is on the opposite side of the island.

Hilo Bay, on the eastern side of Hawaii, is one of the best
harbors in the group. It receives the waters of the Wailuku
river, is easy of access, and quite spacious. Its shores are
thickly settled, and there are some fine native villages situated near or upon it. The town of Hilo, on the western side
of the bay, is, in the season, almost concealed amid the luxuriant growth of sugar-cane, which is extensively cultivated in
the vicinity. It contains the largest church on the island,
a thatched building capable of holding seven thousand persons. It has also a boarding-school for boys, and one for girls,
conducted on the manual labor plan. There are a number
of houses in this village which are built of coral or lava blocks,
and others neatly framed and put together, and there are a
few surmounted with zinc or shingle roofs. Waiakéa, on the
east side of Hilo Bay, is the best place for landing, and it is
quite prettily located and presents a neat appearance.

On the western side of Hawaii is Kealakekua Bay, the

scene of the murder of Captain Cook. It is narrow, and does not afford very good anchorage, but the scenery around it is highly picturesque. Napolo, on its southern shore, is a small but pleasant town, where there is a missionary station.

Waiméa, on the southwestern shore of Kauai, is said to have the best anchorage in the group, except when the trades are interrupted by the south-westerly winds, which is for near three months in the year. It contains about four hundred houses, and is situated on the right bank of the Waiméa river, at the mouth of which is the harbor, or roadstead, in the centre of a beautiful valley opening to the ocean and lavishly sprinkled with groves of bread-fruits, cocoas, bananas, and tuituis, or candle-nut trees. On the left of the entrance to the harbor, there is a rectangular fort, indented with embrasures and garnished with several pieces of cannon. The river is navigable for boats, only for a distance of three quarters of a mile. It has a course of about fifteen miles, and affords a number of excellent mill sites. At its head there is a fine cascade, the soft murmur of whose falling waters is borne sweetly along the valley, amid the groves that rejoice in their grateful moisture.

Most of the better class of dwelling houses in the group are built of coral or lava blocks, which are cemented together with a fine white plaster made of lime produced by burning coral. The foreign residents pattern after the styles of building peculiar to their respective countries. Glazed windows, porticos and chimneys, have become quite common. The roofs are made of zinc or shingles, or they are thatched with pandanus leaves. In Honolulu, and other seaports, many of the private dwellings have a cupola or look-out on the roof, to which the inmates betake themselves when a strange vessel is announced in the offing.

But the natives generally, and the *kanakas* in particular, prefer their old-fashioned grass-houses. The manner of their construction is thus described by Mr. Bingham :—" Round posts, a few inches in diameter, are set in the ground about a yard apart, rising from three to five feet from the surface.

WAIEMAIA.

RICHARDSON, SC

On a shoulder, near the top, is laid a horizontal pole, two or three inches in diameter, as, a plate ; on this, directly over the posts, rest the rafters. A point of the post, called a *finger*, rises on the outside of the plate, and passes between two points of the rafter projecting over the plate and below the main shoulder. The joint thus constructed is held together partly by the natural pressure of the roof, and partly by lashings of bark, vines, or grassy fibres, beaten, and by hand twisted and doubled into a coarse twine, and put on manifold, so as to act as four braces—two from the post, and two from the rafter, extending to the plate, all being attached six to twelve inches from the joint. Three poles or posts, about three times the length of the side posts, are set in the ground, one in the centre of the building, and the others at the ends, on which rests the nether ridge pole, supporting the head of the rafters. These crossing each other, the angle above receives the upper ridge pole, which is lashed to the nether and to the head of the rafters. Posts of unequal length are set at the ends of the building, sloping a little inward and reaching to the end rafters, to which their tops are tied. A door frame, from three to six feet high, is placed between two end or side posts. Thatch-poles are tied horizontally to the posts and rafters, from an inch to three inches apart, all around, and from the ground to the top ridge pole. At this stage the building assumes the appearance of a huge, rude bird-cage. It is then covered with the leaf of the ki, pandanus, sugar-cane, or more commonly (as in the case of the habitations for us) with grass, bound or in small bundles, side by side, one tier overlapping another, like shingles. A house thus thatched assumes the appearance of a long haystack without, and a cage in a haymow within. The area, or ground within, is raised a little with earth, to prevent the influx of water, and spread with grass and mats, answering usually instead of floors, tables, chairs, sofas, and beds. Air can pass through the thatching, and often there is one small opening through the thatch besides the door, for ventilation and light."*

* Bingham's Sandwich Islands, pp. 115, 116.

When these houses are first constructed, the smell of the sweet-scented grass is quite refreshing, but when they become old, the rats and other vermin harbor in them, and the thatching readily contracts dampness and mould. In the better class of native habitations, there are window frames, shutters, and partitions; but the *kanaka* is content with a single apartment, which is his kitchen, parlor and bed-chamber, and often his hen-coop and pig-sty. The natives sleep principally on mats of pandanus leaves, or *tapa*, neatly interwoven with colored straw, piled up several thicknesses deep. Since they have been able to procure iron tools and instruments, their mechanics manufacture a great many articles of furniture of the *koa* wood, such as tables, chairs, chests, and bureaux; and some or all of these are now frequently seen in their houses.

(8.) The supremacy of the law, at length permanently established, as it is believed, in the Sandwich Islands, must be of great benefit to them in a commercial point of view. To the whalers frequenting the Pacific this is of great importance, and it is to be hoped, for their sake, that the attempt of the French government to compel the authorities of this group to do away with the heavy duties on ardent spirits, now (1849) being made, may prove wholly unsuccessful. The position of the islands is favorable, not merely for whalers desiring to recruit or to obtain supplies, but for merchant vessels, proceeding by the shortest route, according to the principles of great circle sailing, from the American ports on the Pacific to China and the East Indies, to stop at for refreshments, or for steamers to obtain a new supply of coal from dépôts established here.* The capacity of the country

* About five hundred whaling vessels annually visit the Hawaiian Islands for refreshment. The average time of a passage from California to the islands is twenty days; from Astoria or Tahiti, twenty-five days; from China, sixty days; from Sydney, eighty-four days; from New York, by way of Cape Horn, one hundred and forty-six days; and from London, one hundred and fifty-nine days. Quite recently, a commercial treaty has been entered into, by commissioners representing the respective governments of the United States and the Hawaiian Group, under which a line of steamers to ply between San Francisco and China are to touch at the islands.

for the production of valuable articles of commerce is hardly yet ascertained, but these seem to be annually increasing in importance.

The chief products, besides the provisions and refreshments furnished to whalers and other vessels stopping at the islands, are sugar, cotton, tuitui oil, salt, hides, goat-skins, molasses and sirup, sandal-wood, leaf tobacco, sperm oil, and arrow-root. The exports, including with the above mentioned articles the supplies sold to vessels, amount annually to not far from two hundred thousand dollars. The imports often exceed six hundred thousand dollars in a single year; but about one half of this amount are purchases by traders designed for reshipment to the Russian and American settlements on the Pacific, and to the southern islands. It is estimated that there are twenty-five hundred tons of shipping owned in the islands; one half of this amount belonging to Americans, one third to Englishmen, and the remainder to the natives. Much the larger proportion of the foreign residents are Americans, and the trade of the islands is mainly in their hands. Nearly one half of the imports come from the United States, and the number of American ships arriving at the islands is more than double those from all other foreign countries. Now that California has attained so much commercial importance, this ascendency of the American interests in the Hawaiian Islands must be still greater.

But little attention has yet been paid to manufactures, although the numerous streams that descend from the mountain ridges in the interior of the islands, afford the finest water power. Great skill and taste are displayed by the native women in making their beautiful *tapas*, some of which are printed in close imitation of merino shawls and ribands. Cotton manufactories have been established, but none except the coarser fabrics have been made; though, with improved machinery and experience in its management, they will produce articles much superior to the *tapa* cloth, and the latter must consequently soon go out of use. Sugar mills are quite plenty. The salt works are very extensive on some of the islands. Between Honolulu and Waikiki, on the island of Oahu, there are a great number of ponds, where large quantities of salt are obtained by evaporation. Niihau is well adapted for this purpose, and affords every facility for embarking in the manufacture to any extent.

Building vessels and canoes, at this day, is far more of an art, and a great deal more neatly done, at the Sandwich Islands, than when they were first visited by the whites. Whaleboats are frequently used by the natives for short journeys along the coasts, though they still adhere, more or less, to the ancient canoe. The latter is much better built than formerly, and the lashings of sennit, and the gum of the breadfruit, have given place to good spikes and pitch. They are very narrow, and are usually provided with an outrigger,—which consists of two light sticks secured upon the gunwale of the craft, and projecting to windward from six to ten feet, where they are crossed and connected by another stick running parallel to the canoe. The outrigger serves to steady the boat, and prevent its upsetting; but if it breaks or gives way, when the huge sail is stretched by the fierce wind, woe be to the luckless mariner.

(9.) On the 24th day of September, the Vincennes came to anchor in the roads of Honolulu, and was joined by the Peacock on the 30th instant. The Porpoise and tender were employed for several days, subsequent to the departure of the two larger vessels from the Feejee Group, in examining Natava Bay and watching the conduct of the natives to the missionaries at Somu-Somu; but they also reached the Sandwich Islands in safety, early in the month of October. As the time for which the crews had originally engaged, was about expiring, they were here reshipped, with a few exceptions, for an additional period of eighteen months, and the complements were filled by the temporary employment of a suitable number of *kanakas*, who were to be discharged on the return of the Squadron from the north-west coast of America. The Porpoise, Lieutenant Ringgold, sailed on the 16th of November, to make a reëxamination of the Paumotu Group, which has been previously mentioned ; and on the 2d of December, the Peacock and Flying Fish, under the command of Captain Hudson, took their departure, to resurvey a part of the Samoän Group, and to look for doubtful islands to the north and west.   The Vincennes remained in the Hawaiian Group, mostly at Honolulu and Hilo Bay, during the winter.   On the 24th of March, 1841, the Porpoise rejoined the flag ship at Honolulu, and on the 5th of April they set sail, in company, for the American coast.   They were favored with a pleasant passage, and on the 2d day of May, came to anchor at Port Discovery in the Straits of Juan de Fuca.

17*

CHAPTER XVI.

(1.) RAPIDLY speeding on their way to the south, the Peacock and Flying Fish made the first land at Washington, or New York Island, in latitude 40° 41′ 35″ N., and longitude 160° 15′ 37″ W. This is a charming little islet, rising only about ten feet above the surface of the ocean, but fringed to the very breakers with the graceful cocoas, whose long trailing fronds are beautifully mirrored in the clear glassy waters of the ocean, and with numerous other tropical trees and plants, that fill the air with the perfume of their ripening fruit and odorous flowers. It is only three and a quarter miles in length, by one and a quarter in width, and is supposed to be uninhabited. The American vessels were unable to send a boat ashore in consequence of the heavy surf, but no evidences of its being occupied by human beings were discovered ; and the sea-birds are, in all probability, rarely, if ever, disturbed in the shady retreats where they have built their nests, and rear their young.

Continuing on his southerly course, Captain Hudson passed Jarvis Island, just south of the Equator, on the 20th of December, and on the 9th of January, 1841, made Enderbury's Island, belonging to the Phœnix Group. Passing through this cluster of coralline reefs and islands,—which lie just north of five degrees southern latitude, and west of the

170th meridian, western longitude, and are famous only for the quantity of turtles taken here by parties of Tahitians and Sàmoäns,—the Peacock and Flying Fish made the Duke of York's Island, or Oatafu, in latitude 8° 36′ S., and longitude 172° 23′ 52″ W., on the 25th day of January. On the 28th instant, they arrived off the Duke of Clarence Island, called by the natives Nukonono, a few miles further to the south-east.* Early in the morning of the 29th, having continued on their way in the same direction, they discovered a new island, to which the name of Bowditch Island was given, though the proper native appellation was ascertained to be Fakaäfo. These three islands form the Union Group.

(2.) The three islands last mentioned lie very nearly in a straight row or line, running from south-east to north-west— Oatafu being about one hundred and thirty-five miles distant from Fakaäfo, or Bowditch Island. These islands are of coral formation, and consist of rings or circlets of coral surrounding lagoons, like the atolls of the Paumotu Group. The reefs, which are in no place over ten feet above the water, are covered with a soil consisting of decomposed coral, vegetable mould, and guano ; and they are adorned with the most beautiful cocoa-nut trees, with the pandanus, the pisonia, the ficus, and the tournefortia. The most luxuriant parasitic ferns cover the loftiest trees, and the long delicate sprays of the jasmine depend here and there from the overhanging branches, and scatter their flowers and their perfume on every passing wind.

Oatafu is but three miles in length, from east to west, and two and a half miles wide, and contains about one hundred and fifty inhabitants. Nukunono is seven and a quarter miles long, from north to south, and five miles wide : it is also populated, and is supposed to contain two or three hundred inhabitants. Fakaäfo is the most important island of the three, and the great chief, to whom the natives of the group, or cluster, pay deference, resides here. It is called

* Lord Byron, the English navigator, discovered Oatafu and Nukonono, in 1765, and named them after the Royal Dukes.

by the inhabitants Fanuä Loä, or the " Great Land," to distinguish it from the other islands ; it is about eight miles long and four wide, and its population numbers not far from six hundred.

The people inhabiting these islands resemble, both in form and feature, the natives of the Samoän Group, and their dialect is also similar. Some of the young men and women are quite good-looking, and have very light complexions. They have had but little intercourse with the whites, and still entertain the notion that the latter came from the skies in their ships. They are a quiet, harmless, timid, and tractable people, but much addicted to thieving. The young persons of both sexes go entirely naked, but the adults wear the *maro*, which is made of pandanus leaves of the finest texture. The *maro* worn by the males is from six to eighteen inches wide, and is often bordered with fringe : that of the females resembles the *liku* of the Feejeean women, and consists of a great number of leaves tied to a cord, slit into fine threads, and made perfectly pliable by frequent oiling ; they form a thick mat about the body, and sometimes weigh as much as fifty pounds. Tattooing is practiced by both sexes ; their cheeks, breasts, legs and loins, being ornamented with the figures of turtles, fish, arrows, and divers other designs, some intended to imitate nature, and others originating with the fancy of the operator. On their heads they wear a piece of matting or tortoise-shell, shaped like the front of a cap, or an eye shade, to protect their faces from the scorching heat of the sun : some of them are adorned with the feathers of the tropic bird, to indicate the superiority of the wearer. For ornaments they have necklaces and ear-rings of shell and bone.

Their houses are built in clusters, or villages, surrounding an open space called *malæ*. They are of an oblong form, about fifteen feet high in the centre, and sloping down gradually with a slight convexity to within two or three feet of the ground. The rafters are secured to the supporting posts and to the ridge pole by lashings of sennit. At the gable-ends, the roof, which is a loose thatching of pandanus leaves, projects several feet, as a protection against the weather,—the sides and ends of the houses not being closed in. Like their persons, the houses of the natives are kept quite clean and neat. Their only articles of furniture are a few gourds and cocoa-nut shells, some boxes or buckets cut out of the solid wood and neatly fitted with lids or covers, and large mats woven of pandanus leaves, four feet square, on which they sleep at night, covering themselves, if necessary, with lighter mats made of the same material. They have, also, a reclining stool, or lounge, cut from a solid block of wood, and elevated at one end, by two legs, so as to form an angle of forty-five degrees.

On Bowditch Island is the house or temple of their god, Tui-Tokelau. It is of the same shape as the private houses, and is from thirty to fifty feet long, and twenty feet high. The roof is concave, and projects some distance at the eaves, where the pandanus leaves that compose the thatching are tied together at intervals, and present a notched or scolloped appearance. The sides and ends are open, with the exception of a low railing, only fifteen inches high. Within, there is an abundance of mats, and rudely fashioned benches carved out of the solid wood; also a number of gods, or idols, of wood or stone, from ten to fourteen feet high.

The natives of these islands seem to be ignorant of the uses of fire. They never cook their victuals, but subsist mainly on the fruit of the cocoa and pandanus, with the fish that they capture near the reefs, and in the lagoons, all which are eaten in a raw state. On the larger islands they dig wells in the ground, which are neatly walled up on the inside; but where the ground is very low, as is the case on Oatafu, they catch fresh water in excavations made in the body of the cocoa-nut trees, on the lee-side, and about two feet from the ground.

They have both double and single canoes, made of pieces of wood sewed together with sennit, like those of the Samoäns, and their paddles are of the same fashion. They have outriggers, likewise, but no sails; and they ornament their craft with the shells of the *cyprœa ovula*. These canoes are principally used in fishing, for which they have hooks of shell, bone, or shark's teeth, attached to long lines made of twisted bark. For the protection of their boats they have large quays built of coral blocks, containing slips ten feet wide, in which there are boat houses erected on poles and thatched with pandanus leaves.

Of mechanical ingenuity they possess a great share. Their houses, canoes, mats, stools, boxes, and fish hooks, all denote the possession of considerable skill by the makers. The instruments with which they work are saws and files, formed of shark's skins stretched on sticks, and a drill. The drill consists of a long stick passing through a flat circular piece of wood, designed to steady it when in operation : at the lower end a sharp-pointed stone is attached with bark twine, and the motion is communicated by means of a handle crossing the upright stick at right angles, near the centre, and secured in its place by a lashing of sennit.

They have a keen relish for the ridiculous, and are fond of dancing. Their dances are like those on the other islands of Polynesia. For music they have two different kinds of drums ; one made of a hollow log, like those of the Feejeeans and Tongese, and the other consisting of a cylindrical frame set upright in the ground, with a shark's skin drawn over it, as in the Hawaiian Islands. When they salute each other, or a stranger, they rub noses and chins together, and encircle the neck with their arms, uttering at the same time a low wail, like the *aloha* of the Sandwich Islander.

(3.) Captain Hudson remained but a short time at Fakaäfo, but continued without delay on his route to the Samoän Group, stopping on the way only long enough to survey Swain's Island, a circular coral islet, without a lagoon, but little over four miles in circumference, in latitude 11° 5′ S., and longitude 170° 55′ 15″ W. On the 5th of February the tall mountains of Savaii were discovered looming up above the southern horizon, and on the afternoon of the 6th instant, the Peacock anchored in the harbor of Apia, while the Flying Fish proceeded to survey the south side of the island of Upolu.

One of the chief objects of the second visit of Captain Hudson to the Samoän Group was to obtain satisfaction for the recent murder of an American seaman belonging to a whaling vessel. The murderer had been protected by Sangapolutale, the principal chief of the heathen towns of Saluafata, Fusi, and Salalese, on the island of Upolu, who refused to surrender him. On the 22d of February, Captain Hudson made an ineffectual attempt to capture the chief, with the intention of detaining him until the murderer should be surrendered. Failing in this, it was deemed important to inflict a severe punishment, in order that the crews of vessels visiting the islands might be secure from molestation. Accordingly, a party was landed at Saluafata on the morning of the 25th of February, the inhabitants having been first driven from the town by the guns of the Peacock, and that town, as well as those of Fusi and Salalese, were reduced to ashes, without encountering the natives or sustaining any loss.

From Apia Captain Hudson proceeded to Mataätu, on the northern side of the island of Savaii; and on the 6th of March he took his departure, with both vessels, for Ellice's Group.

(4.) At noon on the 14th instant, the island of Fanafute was made. This is one of Ellice's Group, or the Depeyster Islands, and is in latitude 8° 30′ 45″ S., and longitude 179° 13′ 30″ E. It is thirteen miles long and seven and a quarter miles wide, and consists of a series of small islets on a coral reef, with two openings on the west side, surrounding a lagoon that affords good anchorage. There are about two hundred and fifty inhabitants on the island.—Not far from forty miles to the north-west of Fanafute, or Ellice's Island, is Depeyster's Island, called by the natives Nukufetau. It contains one thousand inhabitants, and is eight miles in length, and about the same in width; and in its centre there is a lagoon, having from seventeen to twenty fathoms of water, and connected with the ocean by a deep ship channel.

Nearly thirty miles north-east of Nukufetau, is another atoll of about the same size, known as Tracy's Island among navigators, but called Oaitupu by the natives. The population of this island is said to be from three to four hundred. Near the sixth parallel of southern latitude, still further to the north-west, are three coral islets—St. Augustine, Spieden's Island, and Hudson's Island—the last two named, respectively, after the purser and commander of the Peacock. All three of these islands are inhabited, but the population cannot be very large.

The islands belonging to Ellice's Group are well-wooded with the cocoa-nut, pandanus, and pisonia. The inhabitants subsist on the fruit of the first two, together with a species of taro and another larger root, called pulaka, and the fish that they take in abundance from the neighboring waters; to which is now and then added a pig from the small stock on the islands. They are evidently descended from the natives of the Union Group, though they are far less reserved, and appear to have had more frequent intercourse with the whites. Their complexion is several shades darker than that of the Samoäns, but there is a striking similarity in their respective dialects. They are of middle size, slender, and well-proportioned, though not handsome; and their features are sharp and distinctly marked, like those of the Hawaiians. They salute strangers in the same manner as the natives of the Union Group, but they are more active and sociable, and, withal, more licentious. Their hair is fine, black, and glossy, and is worn long, sometimes hanging over the ears and shoulders, and at others gathered up in a number of puffs or rolls on the head. The men allow their beards and moustaches to grow, and seem to be as proud of these appendages as a Feejeean. Holes are bored in the lobes of their ears and distended, and tortoise-shell rings inserted in them.

Tattooing is quite tastefully performed among them. The men ornament their bodies, from the navel half-way down the thighs, principally with horizontal stripes; and the arms and legs of the women are similarly embellished. Both sexes wear the *maro*, which is made of the finest pandanus leaves, and prettily fringed; also a girdle, called *takai*, with a heavy fringe, two feet broad for the women, and from eight inches to a foot for the men; and some have mats as wrappers about their bodies. The women, too, often wear soft mats over their bosoms, and the men have similar articles sometimes thrown over their shoulders. The fringe of the *maro* and the girdle are usually dyed red, or some other bright color; and the fringes of the mats are tinged of various colors, in large squares or diamonds. A band of pandanus leaves is frequently tied about the head or waist, with the strips sticking out horizontally in every direction like so many horns or points.

Their canoes are rudely made. They are dug out of a single log, usually about twenty feet long, and have strips lashed on at the sides to raise them higher. Their sails are of a triangular shape, and their outriggers and paddles resemble those seen in other Polynesian groups. Their fish-hooks are carved out of wood or of shark's teeth. They have roughly hewn war-clubs and spears, consisting merely of poles of cocoa-nut wood sharpened at the point. Swords and knives are made of shark's teeth fitted into a stick, and fastened with gum and sennit.

(5.) Holding on his course to the north-west, Captain Hudson fell in with Taputeouea, or Drummond's Island, on the 3d day of April. This island, and fourteen or fifteen others, constitute the Tarawan or Kingsmill Group,* lying just west of the 175th meridian, east latitude, and stretching across the equator, from latitude 1° 20′ S. to about 4° N. They are of all sizes,—Drummond's Island, which is the largest and southernmost of the group, being thirty miles in length, and from a half to three quarters of a mile in width, and the smaller ones, or the atolls, having a diameter of from two to five miles. They are of coral formation, and none

---

* This group is also known as the Gilbert Islands.

of them rise more than twenty-five feet above the ocean.
The soil is but a few inches in depth, and is composed of
coral sand and vegetable mould : it is exceedingly productive, however, both in its natural state, and when cultivated.
Small pieces of pumice, that have probably drifted on the
islands, are found in considerable abundance, and are pounded
up and used as a manure.

Bread-fruit trees are seen on the islands north of the
equator, but not on those south of it. The cocoa and the
pandanus are very plenty, and the former is cultivated by
the natives, the trees being fenced in, and pounded pumice
mixed with the soil at the roots. On some of the islands
there is a great scarcity of shrubbery, the ground being
covered only with a scanty growth of dry grass (*sida*) ; but
on others, dense thickets of underbrush are scattered amid
the clumps of pandanus trees and cocoas. The pisonia,
tournefortia, cordia, boerhavia, urticæ, mangrove, scævola,
ficus, and hibiscus, are quite common, though they are
generally small in comparison with the specimens found on
other islands. There are two varieties of taro, and two of
yams. One species of taro (*arum cordifolium*), called by
the natives *pôipôi*, is extensively cultivated in deep trenches
excavated for the purpose. These are often placed near the
lagoons, and separated from them by a narrow embankment, in order that the water may percolate through the
coral sand. The api is also cultivated to some extent.
Purslane is abundant, and is much eaten in seasons of
scarcity. There is also a bush, bearing a fruit resembling
the gooseberry, which the natives call *teiparu*.

The climate of these islands is delightful. The heat is
of a high temperature, but not as oppressive as might be
expected. There are no sudden changes, and the range of
the thermometer is limited. Earthquakes, in which the
oscillations are rapid and powerful, occasionally occur, and
violent gales from the south-west are not uncommon. From
October to April there are frequent rains; but during the
remainder of the year the weather is fine, the air is pure

and elastic, the sky is rarely mottled with clouds, and showers and sunshine agreeably alternate with each other. In consequence of the equability of the climate, the inhabitants enjoy remarkable health, and suffer from but few diseases except those of a cutaneous character.

Rats in great numbers infest the islands. The other quadrupeds are a few dogs and cats. No land birds were seen by the American vessels, but white terns, golden plovers, noddies, curlews, turnstones, and tropic-birds, are very common. Whales, sharks, crustacea of different kinds, *biche de mer*, and numerous edible fish of the smaller varieties, abound in the vicinity of the group, and all are eaten by the inhabitants. Whales are often killed when they get aground on the shoals by the natives with their spears. Sharks are caught by dropping pieces of bait alongside a canoe, and when they rush forward to seize them, throwing a noose over their heads. Small fish are taken with scoop-nets, seines, hooks and lines, and traps made of withes and resembling eel-pots ; and they are also driven in shoals into large stone weirs or pens.

These islands are densely populated ; the whole number of inhabitants being estimated at sixty thousand, of which Drummond's Island alone contains about ten thousand. Their dialect differs essentially from that of the Samoän Group, but preserves many of the peculiarities of the great Polynesian root from which the various tongues are derived. Their features are small, but strongly marked, and indicate clearly their Malay origin.* They are of middle size, the men rarely

* The natives of these islands have a tradition that the first inhabitants came from Barness, or Baneba, an island said to lie to the south-west, in two canoes ; that they were subsequently joined by other persons, arriving from Amoi, an island lying to the south-east, also in two canoes ; and that after they had lived together in harmony for one or two generations, the male members of the two parties had a quarrel, in which those who had arrived first were successful and killed off all their opponents, after which they made wives of their women, who were better looking, and had fairer complexions, than the others. Amoi is supposed by Captain Wilkes, (Narrative, vol. v. p. 82.) and with good reason, to be the Samoän Group ; and he conjectures that Baneba may refer to Boneba, or Ascension Island, one of the Caroline Group, although its position does not correspond with the assigned locality. Bidera and Bouka, of the Solomon Archipelago, at the south-west, and Banda and Borneo (the latter not unlike Barness),

exceeding five feet eight inches in height; slender, but well proportioned; and lithe and active in their movements. Their cheek bones are prominent, and their noses slightly aquiline. They have large and bright black eyes. Their hair is also dark, and unusually fine and glossy. Their lips are full, and their teeth small and even, but often decayed. Their complexion, in general, is a shade or two darker than that of the Tahitian.

The young women are models of personal beauty, so far as mere softness of contour, and shapeliness of limb, are concerned. Their figures are slight, but as harmonious in their proportions as the finest statuary. Their full orbed eyes are alike beautiful, whether glowing with desire, or kindling with anger or jealousy. Long, glossy ringlets, glistening like' silver in the sunlight, and of ebon darkness in the shadow, float in ample profusion down their finely-rounded shoulders, and over the softly-swelling bust. Their forms taper gracefully towards the waist, and are supported on limbs turned with great neatness and delicacy. These charms, too, are not always

> "veiled and curtained from the sight
> Of the gross world."

They rarely wear any clothing whatsoever, and the simple *iriri* seems to be put on rather for ornament than concealment.

But the mothers of these Polynesian sylphs are as uncouth, not to say hideous, as their daughters are handsome. The wrinkles of age appear prematurely, and their features soon become distorted. This cannot be produced by out-door labor, for that is performed almost entirely by the men, but is probably owing in great part to the common practice of producing abortions. A woman seldom has more than two children, and never more than three; when she discovers herself to be *enceinte* for the third or fourth time, the fetus is destroyed by

in a westerly direction, are the only other islands lying in this part of the Pacific, whose names are in any respect similar.

a midwife, by external pressure upon the womb. This practice is not looked upon with the least abhorrence, and unmarried women always avoid having children in this way. Infanticide, however, is never known to occur. Indeed, parents are very fond of their children, and indulge them in every whim and caprice.

The inhabitants of Makin, or Pitt's Island, which lies furthest to the north, differ in some respects from the natives of the other islands, in their personal appearance. Instances of corpulence are not rare among the latter, but the former look much like over-fed porkers. Both men and women are exceedingly gross; but they are as good-natured and inoffensive as they are fat, and vessels stopping at the island are likely to meet with much better treatment than among the southern islands. Their faces are more oval, and they are somewhat lighter and fairer in complexion than the inhabitants of the other members of the group.

With the exception of the natives residing on Pitt's Island, the Kingsmill Islanders are all fierce and warlike in disposition. There are frequent bloody encounters between the inhabitants of rival towns, and the different islands. They are naturally intelligent, cheerful and sociable, and fond of mirth and merriment, though they sometimes give way to fits of sulkiness and despondency, and commit suicide by hanging themselves on trees. Among their own people they are both hospitable and generous, but treacherous and deceitful in their intercourse with the whites. They are also dishonest and thievish, inclined to be jealous, and very passionate. They are cruel and reckless of human life, but pay unusual respect to the dead,—washing their bodies and anointing them with cocoa-nut oil, and then burying them in the ground under their houses, with the head to the east, or wrapping them in mats, till the flesh decays, when the remains are exhumed, and the skulls preserved with great care. When they kill an enemy they dig out his teeth and string them in necklaces; the hair is also clipped off and twisted into wreaths, cords, and bands; and of the bones various instruments are made.

Chastity is not considered a virtue in either sex, and the want of it by an unmarried woman is esteemed no reproach. Fathers and brothers freely offer their daughters and sisters, to the crews of vessels stopping at the islands, for purposes of prostitution. Of their wives, however, they are more chary; and it is said that in the northern, or Pitt's Island, the men sew them up in mats so that they cannot give way to temptation.

The male population are divided into three classes: the *neas*, or *omatas*, who are the principal chiefs; the *katokas*, who are the landholders, not of noble birth; and the *kawas*, or slaves. On some of the islands there are kings, but the rank is mainly nominal, though tribute is paid to them by the several towns over which their sway extends. Each town is separate from the other in its municipal government. Public councils of all the different estates are held; but the political power and authority are mainly wielded by the *neas*, or *omatas*, who are all of noble birth as well as landholders. When a council is to be he'l, the oldest chief, who always presides at the meeting, sends out his messengers to summon the inhabitants by blowing conch shells. No regular vote is ever taken at these assemblages, but the opinion of the majority decides the subject matter under consideration. The distinction between those of high birth, and the ignobly born, prevails throughout the islands, but in some parts of the group the class of *katokas* is not recognized.

Slaves are regarded and treated as mere personal chattels. The chiefs have absolute power over their families and *kawas*. All minor crimes are punished by the person injured or aggrieved, or by his relatives; but more serious offences are brought before the council. Rank and property are hereditary. The son of a chief by the mother of the highest rank succeeds to his father's position. Where there is no inequality of birth, the eldest son either has twice as much land as the others, or succeeds to all the property, subject to the incumbrance of supporting and maintaining his brothers and sisters,

who are obliged to work for him, and the latter cannot marry
without his consent.

Most of the inhabitants go entirely naked, with the exception of a conical cap of braided pandanus leaves on their heads,
and the remainder have very little clothing. Among the men
this consists of a *maro*, covering merely a part of the back
and abdomen, and a small oblong mat with a slit in the centre,
which is put on over the head like a *póncho*. The appropriate dress of the women is called *iriri*, and consists of a fine
and beautiful fringe made of the softest cocoa-nut leaves split
into narrow strips; it is about a foot in width, and is dipped
in cocoa-nut oil to render it perfectly flexible; it is also dyed
and perfumed, and is often quite ornamental, though commonly worn so high up on the abdomen, like the *maro* of the
men, that it affords but little concealment to the person. Of
ornaments both sexes are very fond. They often wear a white
ovula shell attached to a wreath about the neck, made of the
pith of the scævola, and hanging down over the bosom. In
the lobes of their ears they insert shells and strings of leaves.
They have also necklaces of beads and shells, of shark's teeth
and small bones, and of human teeth or hair. Their beads
are made of the cocoa-nut and shell. Girdles of hair are likewise worn about their bodies. Tattooing, too, is general
among the higher classes, but not permitted to slaves: it is
considered essential, in order to enable the spirit after death
to be happy in Elysium, and is performed by professional
operators; the ornaments usually consist of short, oblique
lines, in parallel and perpendicular rows, at greater or less
distances apart, descending from the neck as low as the knees,
and sometimes to the ankles. The women are tattooed in the
same manner, but not so much, and they have frequently a
circle of spots surrounding the navel. The men do not shave
off their beards and moustaches, but they are not generally
of very luxuriant growth.

War is the favorite occupation of the inhabitants of the
southern islands. They have weapons both of offence and
defence. The former consist of spears, clubs, and swords.

The handles of the swords, the shafts of the spears, and the clubs, are made of cocoa-nut wood. Shark's teeth are inserted in the sword handles and fastened with gum, and barbs for the spears are also made of them. For defensive purposes, they have a sort of cuirass, like an ancient shirt of mail, covering the body as far down as the haunches, and rising above the back of the head from three to four inches: this piece of armor is drawn on over the head, there being holes for the arms; and it affords complete protection against the native weapons, as it is nearly half an inch thick, and is made of the fibres of the husk of the cocoa-nut closely matted together. They have, also, a similar defence for the arms, and cuishes and greaves for the thighs and legs, made of netted sennit; and the head is defended by a helmet consisting of the skin of the porcupine fish, with the tail sticking upwards like a crest.

When not at war, the men spend most of their time in taking care of their taro beds and yam plantations, and cultivating the cocoa and pandanus trees; or in building houses and canoes, taking fish, and fashioning their tools and weapons. Both sexes pay considerable attention to personal cleanliness, and wash their bodies daily, and anoint them with cocoa-nut oil. They rise at daylight, and after their morning toilet is performed, the men go out to work while the women pursue their in-door occupations, such as preparing food, and making mats, sails, baskets, *maros* and *iriris*. When the heat becomes too oppressive, which it usually does about nine o'clock, out-door labor is suspended, and the first meal during the day is then eaten. Sleeping, chatting, and light occupations inside of their houses, now occupy the time until four o'clock, when the rays of the sun begin to lose their power, and the men again sally out to continue the labors of the morning.

They have several divinities, the chief one of which is Wainangin, or Tabu-eriki, who is worshipped in the form of a coral stone, surrounded with the leaves of the cocoa, that are always changed when they begin to wither. Their principal female deity is Itivini: she is worshipped in a small circle, three feet in diameter, made of coral stones, and covered with white gravel ; in the centre of the ring is a cocoanut, which is bound round with leaves when prayers are offered up to the goddess. Almost every family of distinction has one of the stones typical of Wainangin, but some of the inhabitants do not recognize him, and worship birds, fish, animals, and the souls of their ancestors represented by their skulls, which are religiously preserved. Each family, too, in the higher ranks, has an *iboya*, or priest, to offer up prayers, and receive and eat the food presented to the tutelar deity. After death, according to the belief of the natives, their spirits ascend into the air—those of the children being carried by their female relatives—and are there tossed about for some time by the winds, until finally, if of high rank, they are wafted to Kainakaki, or Elysium ; but the shade of the poor *kawa*, or the person who is not tattooed (except in some parts of the group), is intercepted, and doomed by a large giantess, called Baine. The Kainakaki of the natives is supposed to be in the island of Tavaira, one of the group, where there are a number of curious oblong mounds, upwards of twenty feet high.

On a reef between the islets of Kuria and Oneöka, is a large flat coral stone, which the natives suppose to represent another female deity called Itituapéa ; and whenever they pass that way they invoke the protection of the goddess, and bestow upon her a portion of their food, if they chance to have any with them.

Children are named by the priest as soon as they are born ; but if they are soon taken sick, another name is substituted for the first, in the hope that it will prove more fortunate to the possessor. Females are betrothed immediately after their birth, or at a very early age. Polygamy is practiced by all the males of high rank, or who can afford to keep up a large harem. Some of the principal chiefs have from twenty to fifty wives, and they are pretty sure to monopolize all the comeliest damsels in their vicinity. The *kawas*, however, are denied the privilege of marrying, except with the consent

18

of their masters, though they sometimes form temporary connections with the unmarried females in the group.

Where a female is betrothed at her birth, no ceremony of marriage is requisite. In other cases the friends of the parties, who are left to choose for themselves, as women are not esteemed articles of traffic, assemble at the house of the bride's father, all clad in their gayest attire. The couple are seated on a mat in the midst of the company ; the priest then presses their foreheads together, pours a little cocoa-nut oil over their heads, and sprinkles their faces with the branch of a tree dipped in water, at the same time uttering a prayer for their happiness and prosperity. The friends now offer their congratulations and rub noses—the latter being their customary mode of salutation. The ceremony being completed, feasting and dancing succeed, which are commonly kept up till a late hour in the evening, and for several days in succession. On the third day, the bridegroom takes his wife to his own habitation, and for the first ten days the house where she lives is screened with mats, and she remains at home to receive the calls of her friends. Both parties are expected to contribute either land or household goods, or both, to the common stock ; but no questions are asked by the suitor, in regard to the dowry of an intended wife, of her parents, till after the consummation of the marriage, and sometimes not until shortly before the birth of the first child.

Playing at foot-ball, sailing miniature canoes, swimming in the surf with a board like that of the Hawaiians, and flying kites made of split pandanus leaves drawn over a frame, are the principal amusements of the men. The other sex join them in singing and dancing, of which they are extravagantly fond. Most of their dances resemble those of other Polynesians, consisting of violent motions of the bodies, rocking themselves to and fro, and clapping their hands together and slapping them upon their thighs. They have, however, a peculiar dance that consists of a combination of fencing and singing with dancing. They often collect in large parties for dances, intermingled with songs, in the evenings, and protract their sports to a late hour by the light of the moon or of a large fire. They have feasts, either public or private, quite often, but the only periodical one is at the full of the moon.

The dwelling houses of the natives are peculiarly constructed. They are of an oblong shape, and ordinarily about sixteen feet wide and twenty feet long. The frame work consists of cocoa-nut posts, and beams, supporting high sloping roofs, which descend from the ridge pole to within three feet of the ground, and are thatched with pandanus leaves. At the gable ends the roof is perpendicular for about one third of the descent, and then slopes off as at the sides. The ridge pole is from fifteen to twenty feet above the ground, and the rafters and cross-pieces are small poles only an inch or two in diameter. This main building—for there are two stories—rests on large beams of cocoa-nut wood, which are supported by four round posts of the same material, one at each corner, and made perfectly smooth so as to prevent the rats from climbing up. These posts are but three feet high, and within them is the basement of the house, which is used exclusively for sleeping. The upper apartment, where all the valuable goods and chattels are kept, is floored with pandanus boards resting on cross-beams. The sides of the houses are inclosed with mats or thatching, and they are entered by a square hole that serves the purpose of a door.

Besides the private dwellings of the inhabitants, each town has a *mariapa*, or council-house, which is built like the former, but of much larger dimensions, and frequently supported on blocks of coral. There are *atamas*, too, where the chiefs receive company and the natives meet to exchange their commodities : these are constructed after the same general fashion, but have no upper apartment. In some parts of the group the towns are surrounded by pickets and palisades of cocoa-nut wood ; and within the principal inclosure, there are smaller ones containing ten or twelve houses belonging to the same family, as in the *pas* of New Zealand.

Baskets, made of twigs or leaves woven firmly together,

fans, screens, mats, cocoa-nut shells, wooden bowls and troughs, spoons fashioned out of human ribs, and the skulls of their enemies, used as drinking vessels, are the principal articles of furniture in the habitations of the Kingsmill Islanders.　Some of their mats are very beautiful, the bright yellow of the young pandanus leaves contrasting finely with the dark brown of the older ones, and the clear white of those that have been bleached, with which they are interwoven.　They always have an abundance of conch shells in their houses, and they use the *tridachna gigas*, which are found here of an enormous size, for troughs to catch rain water.

For cooking, the natives have stone ovens built above the ground, and they roast the bread-fruit on hot stones.　Their food consists chiefly of fish of all kinds, from a whale to a sea-slug, of the cocoa and pandanus nuts, bread-fruit and taro. Yams and purslane are eaten when other articles of food are scarce.　Of the pandanus-nut they make a preparation which will keep for several years ; the edible portions of the nut are first pounded to the consistence of dough, and then baked in an oven, after which they are reduced to powder and fashioned into rolls, or *karapapa*.　The taro, too, is often baked hard, and grated to a powder, which is dried and formed into rolls, called *kabuibui*, which keep for a long time.　Another preparation, called *manam*, is made of baked taro and cocoa-nut, grated fine, and then mixed together and rolled up in large balls.　They have no intoxicating drinks, but they procure a toddy, called *karaca*, from the spathes of the cocoa-nut ; the formation of the fruit being prevented by tying a bandage of sennit tightly around the spathe, and then cutting off the end of the latter.　When this sap is first obtained it is like the milk of the young cocoa-nut, but it soon ferments and forms a pleasant acidulous beverage.　Of the *karaca*, a molasses is made called *kamoimoi*, by boiling the former down in cocoa-nut shells placed on hot stones, which in color and flavor resembles that obtained from the cane.　The *kamoimoi* is eaten with the preparations of pandanus, bread-fruit, taro, and cocoa-nut, and when mixed with water forms the common drink at their feasts, and is called *karave*.

Since the natives have had intercourse with the whites, they have become exceedingly fond of tobacco, which they call *tebake*, and chew and swallow it as if it were really delicious.

The canoes belonging to these natives differ from those seen in the neighboring groups, and are quite ingeniously built. They have frames, about which strips of board, usually of cocoa-nut wood, are arranged in nearly the same manner as the planking of large vessels. The boards are sewed together with sennit, and have strips of pandanus leaves inserted in the seams to prevent leakage. The canoes are from twelve to fifteen feet long, two or three feet deep, and from fifteen inches to two feet wide. They have small outriggers and narrow platforms. The masts rake considerably, and carry sails of moderate size and a triangular form. The natives manage their craft with great dexterity when under sail ; but their paddles are miserable things, consisting merely of a piece of cocoa-nut board or tortoise shell, perhaps six inches square, attached to a round stick, and they are not over expert in the use of them. Near most of the towns there are wharfs built of coral blocks, for the convenience of landing from the canoes.

Hatchets and adzes, roughly made of bone or stone, and knives and saws of shark's teeth, are the principal tools of the natives, but they are used with much skill and ingenuity, as is evinced by the buildings, canoes, and other articles manufactured with them.

(6.) While lying off the town of Utiroä, on Drummond's Island, a seaman belonging to one of the American vessels was inveigled away by some means from the party with whom he had landed, and was supposed to have been murdered. Repeated demands for the restoration of the missing man were made, but without success,—the natives assuming a blustering appearance, and displaying themselves clad in their armor and with their weapons. Captain Hudson thereupon sent a party ashore under Lieutenant Walker, who drove the savages from the beach, killing twelve of their number, and set fire to and destroyed the town.

The survey of the Kingsmill Group was not completed till the close of the month of April, and the American vessels then steered to the north. On arriving among the Radack, or Mulgrave Islands, Captain Hudson found that the time specified for his absence from the rest of the Squadron was fast drawing to a close. He therefore bore away for the Sandwich Islands, and on the 14th of June arrived off the port of Honolulu. On the 21st instant, he sailed for the Columbia river. Cape Disappointment was made by the Peacock on the afternoon of the 17th of July, and on the following day Captain Hudson attempted to enter the mouth of the river, being governed by the directions obtained from the commander of a merchant vessel by Captain Wilkes, which were supposed to be reliable but unfortunately proved deceptive. The Flying Fish entered in safety, but the Peacock, which preceded it, struck on the bar, amid the raging breakers, shortly after she commenced standing in, and in a few hours was made a complete wreck,—the officers and crew, with the ship's papers and other light articles, being with great difficulty saved in the small boats, and landed at Astoria. Having completed his examinations in northern Oregon, Captain Wilkes joined Captain Hudson early in August. The Vincennes was now dispatched to San Francisco to survey the Sacramento river, and the officers and crew of the Peacock were transferred to an American merchant brig, purchased for the occasion, to which the name of " Oregon" was given. After surveying and examining the Columbia river and valley as critically as time would permit, Captain Wilkes proceeded down the coast with the other vessels of the Squadron, and on the 19th of October anchored beside the Vincennes in the Bay of San Francisco.

CHAPTER XVII.

(1.) WHILE the diplomatists of Downing Street and Pennsylvania Avenue, and the legislators of St. Stephen's and the American Capitol, were unsuccessfully engaged, through a long series of years, but with greater or less intervals, in the attempt to terminate the qualified joint occupancy of the Oregon territory by Great Britain and the United States, and to establish a definite boundary line between their respective jurisdictions, the ultimate destiny of the country was being pretty surely fixed, by the immigration, subsequent to 1840, of great numbers of American settlers,—some of whom were sent out under the auspices of the Foreign Missionary Society and the board of missions of the Methodist Episcopal Church, and others were attracted by the glowing reports which had crossed the Rocky Mountains in regard to the rich tracts of farming land lying in the great basin of the Columbia river.

But all the numerous vexed questions in difference, growing out of the conflicting claims based upon the discoveries of Drake, Cook, Gray, and Vancouver, the Louisiana purchase, and the explorations of Lewis and Clarke—all which had been rendered but the more intricate by protracted negotiation—were finally settled in amity, by the treaty of 1846, under which the northern boundary line of the United States was extended from the Rocky Mountains west, along the 49th parallel of north latitude, to Queen Charlotte's Sound, and then through the Straits of Juan de Fuca to the Pacific ocean,—with the further stipulation, that the navigation of the Columbia river below 49° should be free to the Hudson's Bay Company during the continuance of their charter.

It is computed that there are from three hundred to three hundred and fifty thousand square miles contained in the area, or tract of country known as Oregon territory, lying between the boundary before mentioned and California, the Rocky Mountains and the Pacific. This extensive territory is divided into three belts or sections, rising like terraces one above the other, by different ranges of mountains running nearly parallel with the shore of the Pacific. The coast section is from one hundred to one hundred and fifty miles wide, and is bounded on the east by the Cascade Range, which is continuous, except where it is divided by the channels of streams, and frequently rises into tall conical peaks, from nine to ten thousand feet high, whose summits are bathed in perpetual snow.* The middle section lies between the Cascade Range and the Blue Mountains, and is of irregular width, varying from one to three hundred miles: the Blue Mountains are often interrupted, and deviate from their usual course, the spurs sometimes running off, nearly at right angles to the general direction, for a considerable distance, beyond which are occasional detached outliers. Beyond the Blue Mountains, and between them and the lofty barriers of the Great Cordillera, which tower upward to the height of sixteen thousand feet, is the third or eastern section, whose average width is not far from five hundred miles. Notwithstanding the Rocky Mountains are here a continuous chain, in general, the long reach, trending away on the one side to the frozen regions of the north, and on the other to the sunny plateaus of Anahuac, is occasionally interrupted by passes through which roads are practicable. The North

---

* The line of perpetual snow in this latitude, is about 6500 feet above the level of the sea.

Pass, discovered by Lewis and Clarke, is in latitude 46° 30′ N.; the Middle Pass is in about 44° 30′ N.; and the South Pass, which was made known by Colonel Frémont and is decidedly the best of the three, is in latitude 42° 30′ N., where the headwaters of the north fork of the Platte are separated by a narrow watershed from those of the Snake river. On the southern border of the territory is the Klamet range, running from east to west, near. the parallel of 42° N. latitude, which separates it from California.

At the foot of the Cascade Range on the west, the soil is well adapted to raising the cereal grains, peas, apples, pears, and other hardy fruits; but much the greater portion of the western division south of the Columbia is occupied by low prairies and interval lands liable to inundations, yet possessing a fine soil and producing heavy burdens of the richest grass. The valley of the Willamette, or Multnomah river, in this section, contains some of the finest land in Oregon, and for beauty and fertility is not often surpassed in the older states and territories of the American Union. North of the Columbia, and beyond the immediate valley of the river, which is also well calculated for grazing though very liable to inundations, the country is rough and much broken, but thickly covered with gigantic forest trees.

The soil of the middle section is a sandy loam, very light on the hills and only fitted for grazing, but in the valleys there is a large mixture of alluvial deposit. The eastern section, between the Blue and Rocky Mountains, is high, broken, and barren; there are but few level tracts, which are sparsely timbered, and, where not rocky, the soil is light and sandy. But the desert character of this interior basin should not be allowed to cast any doubt upon, or detract from, the capacity of the western portions; for though they contain, here and there, a few barren patches, the productiveness of their extensive tracts of prairie and interval land, and the value of their noble forests, must be sources of continued wealth and prosperity to the hardy pioneers who have located themselves in these remote regions.

In fossils, but little variety is presented. Basalt is the principal rock. Granite, limestone, and sandstone, are found in small quantities, and specimens of white marble have been obtained in the upper country, while at the extreme north freestone is abundant. Appearances would indicate the possession of vast stores of mineral wealth, but these are deceptive. Coal, however, exists in great abundance in the Cascade Range, and iron and platina have been discovered, though they cannot be said to abound.

(2.) In 1845, the Indian population of Oregon was estimated to be about twenty-seven thousand, and that of the whites at from three to five thousand. The numbers of the former, since that time, as in previous years, have been rapidly diminishing, mainly from disease, though the aggregate has probably been nearly kept up by the white immigration. The principal Indian tribes, commencing at the north, are the Spokans, Flatheads, Nisqually Indians, Cayuses, Nez Perces, Callapooah Indians, and Shoshones. Most of these tribes have generally been on good terms with the white settlers, and some of them have been partially civilized, have abandoned their roving habits, and commenced the cultivation of the soil; but the lawless bands of Cayuses roaming through the upper valley of the Columbia, were for a long time a source of great annoyance to the parties of immigrants arriving in the country, and the latter were repeatedly attacked by them. In November, 1847, the Presbyterian Mission at Walla-Walla was attacked by these savages, fourteen persons were killed and sixty-one wounded, and all the houses at the station burnt down or destroyed. Immediately upon the occurrence of this event, troops were raised in the lower towns, and in the following January, the Indians were defeated in a series of bloody engagements, and their villages burnt to the ground. Since that time peace and harmony have for the most part prevailed.

The white population is of a mixed character. There are immigrants from almost every state in the Union, *employés* of the Hudson's Bay Company, hunters, trappers, and half-breeds of every hue and stamp. For several years after the tide of immigration was turned in this direction, the inhabitants had no regularly constituted government, but for a portion of the time the affairs of the territory were managed by a legislative committee, consisting of nine members, and an executive council composed of three members. In August, 1848, however, a territorial organization was provided for them by a law of Congress, under which the government is now administered.

Astoria, on the southern bank of the Columbia, eight miles from its mouth, was first established as a trading port, by John Jacob Astor, the great New York *millionaire*, recently deceased, and is now the principal commercial town. Oregon City is the seat of government, and is situated on the Willamette, about one hundred miles from its mouth. The water power at this place is unusually great. The river is a fine, ample stream, and pours down at this place through three natural channels worn in the solid rock, with a descent of from thirty to forty feet. Just in rear of these channels there are a number of islands, upon which buildings for machinery, to almost any extent, can be erected. Portland, at the head of ship navigation on the same stream, also possesses a fine water power, and is a thriving town. Fort Vancouver, on the north part of the Columbia, opposite the embouchure of the Willamette, has been the chief station of the Hudson's Bay Company, and is surrounded by a wide extent of richly cultivated country, exceedingly well adapted for grazing. Fort Walla-Walla, at the junction of the Walla-Walla with the Columbia, and Fort Nisqually on Puget's Sound, are the only other important posts in the territory: the former is surrounded by some excellent farming land, and the latter is well situated for trading with the Indians, and for shipping the valuable timber of northern Oregon.

(3.) The noble Columbia is the great river of the territory, and is over one thousand miles in length. It has two principal affluents—the northern branch, and Saptin or Lewis river. The first rises among the Rocky Mountains, not far from the

52d parallel of north latitude, at an elevation of near four thousand feet above the level of the sea. Pursuing a southerly course, amid the lofty mountains, in the basins formed between which it sometimes expands into lakes, and constantly increasing its volume by the admission of numerous tributaries, it descends to Fort Colville, in about 48° 30′ N. latitude, where its bed is still over two thousand feet above the ocean. From hence it pursues a circuitous westerly and southerly course till it unites with Lewis river just above the 46th parallel; the latter having already traversed a distance of five hundred and twenty miles from its distant source near the South Pass. Just below the junction of the two main branches, the Columbia turns to the westward and descends over twelve hundred feet in its passage to the ocean. In passing through the Cascade Range it forms a series of picturesque falls and cascades—from which the neighboring mountains derive their name—that are entirely impassable even in the highest stages of water. Below the cascades the channel is unobstructed for forty miles, where there are other rapids that interrupt the navigation; but from thence to the ocean, there is a long reach of one hundred and twenty miles, in the course of which the waters of the Willamette come in from the south, navigable for vessels drawing twelve feet of water.

Small vessels can ascend the Willamette, which runs nearly parallel with the coast, from south to north, to within three miles of the falls, though that stream, as well as the Columbia, are obstructed by the sand bars constantly forming, which are difficult to pass except at high-tide. Near the southern boundary of Oregon is the Klamet, or Too-too-tut-na river, which rises in the Klamet range, and pursues a westerly course to the ocean. A short distance north of the 43d parallel is the Umpqua river, running in the same direction with the Klamet, which has its rise at the foot of the Cascade Range near the headwaters of the Willamette. There are numerous other minor streams south of the Columbia, all which, like the Willamette, are bordered by the finest tracts of timbered land, and the most fertile prairies and intervales.

The coast outline of Oregon is bold and rocky, and there are but few indentations forming harbors sufficiently large for vessels of any considerable burden, and as most of them are openings at the mouths of rivers, they are usually obstructed by sand bars. The straits of Juan de Fuca, however, form the noble entrance to a chain of magnificent harbors on its southern coast, prominent among which is Puget's Sound, consisting of an inlet that stretches into the interior for about one hundred miles parallel to the ocean. The entrance to the straits is easy, the shores are bold, and the anchorage deep in the main channel. For the greater part of the year the winds are favorable, and the navigation is not often obstructed by the ice descending from the upper rivers. There are no shoals in the straits, and the harbors are accessible to vessels of any burden, spacious, and perfectly secure.

Gray's Harbor is the only one of importance south of Cape Flattery, at the entrance of the Straits of Juan de Fuca, and above the mouth of the Columbia. This has a narrow opening, however, with dangerous breakers on either side, and though it immediately opens out, it is filled with mudflats, which confine the anchorage within narrow limits. Various opinions are entertained in regard to the entrance to the Columbia river, which affords deep and secure anchorage in abundance inside its bar. For twenty miles above the ocean this river widens out like a bay, and at its mouth is seven miles across, from Cape Disappointment on the north to Point Adams on the south. Here, where its mighty tide meets the rolling surge of the ocean, sand bars have been formed stretching out for a great distance on both sides, and leaving but a narrow channel through which a vessel can enter. And even this cannot always be reached, as the cross tides changing every half hour often render it impossible for a ship to maintain her position. At some seasons, and, as it is said, for the greater part of the year, it is highly dangerous to attempt entering or leaving the river. From one shore to the other a foaming line of breakers is formed, which, in a few moments, will rend the stoutest craft in pieces, when it has once grounded upon the bar.*

From fifty to sixty miles south of the Columbia is Kilamuke Bay, which is spacious in extent, but presents the same difficulties as Gray's Harbor, and can be entered with safety only by vessels of light draft. South of the Kilamuke are Celeste and Yacquina bays, both of which are small, but the latter has no dangerous bar at its entrance, which is three quarters of a mile wide, and is perfectly sheltered from the ocean winds. At the mouth of the Umpqua river, also, there is a wide bay, but it is difficult for vessels of very heavy burden to cross the bar.

(4.) Oregon boasts of a fine climate, not more favorable to the health of the inhabitants than to the growth of agricultural products. In the elevated sections of the interior, east of the Blue Mountains, snow lies nearly through the year; there is very little rain, and no dew. Here the thermometer has a wide range during the day; the temperature at noon often being forty degrees higher than at sunrise. But this portion of Oregon is regarded by the inhabitants as an 'outsider'; and when they refer, as they can do with justice, to the evenness and salubrity of their climate, they have in view the western and middle sections of the country, where the brown-colored hills, the dark evergreen forests, the rolling prairies, and the richly-carpeted valleys, are bathed in the clear blue haze, mingled with bright tints of purple, of an almost perpetual spring.

The range of the thermometer in the valley of the Willamette, is from 30° to 96°, up to the 45th parallel, and above this it is not often much colder. The winter is short, commencing the last of December, and continuing only until February. During this time snow falls but rarely, never to the depth of more than three or four inches, and soon disappears. The nights are cold, and frosts occur early, sometimes

* In the opinion of Captain Wilkes (Narrative, vol. iv. p. 491,) the safest time to cross the bar is "when both the tide and wind are adverse."

towards the last of August ; but the latter are owing to the proximity of the mountains, which cause a fall in the temperature, yet they are never severe.   Rains are quite frequent, especially from November till March, though not often heavy.   It is well known that isothermal lines, or lines of equal temperature, traverse the earth with varied eccentricity ; and it is much warmer on the Pacific coast, than in the same latitude on the Atlantic ; hence, fruit trees blossom early in April at Nisqually, and green peas and strawberries are abundant in May, while south of the Columbia grass grows all the winter long, and the cattle are not housed, and only confined in pens at night to protect them from the wolves and other wild animals.

Fever and ague, occasioned by the decomposition of the vegetable matter turned up by the plow on the prairies, and some pulmonary complaints, are the principal diseases to which the inhabitants are subject.   The first is quite fatal to the Indians, solely on account of bad treatment, however ; and small-pox has made dreadful ravages among them.

Most conspicuous among the productions of Oregon are the timber trees.   These are truly giants.   Near Astoria, in the primeval forest, there are fir trees over forty feet in circumference, three hundred feet long, and rising to the height of one hundred and fifty feet without giving off a single branch. A pine in the same vicinity, measured by the officers of the Exploring Squadron, was thirty-nine feet six inches in circumference eight feet above the ground, two hundred and fifty feet high, perfectly straight and sound, and had a bark eleven inches thick.   On the banks of the Umpqua, a fir tree is said to have been measured that proved to be fifty-seven feet in circumference, and two hundred and sixteen feet in length below its first branches.   Among the evergreens are the pine, fir, spruce, arbutus, arbor vitæ, cedar and yew. The principal deciduous trees are red and white oaks, hard and soft maples, the alder, poplar, elm, and cherry.   The ash, here and there, scatters its winged seeds upon the wind ; and in the forests of southern Oregon, the long strings of balls of the sycamore, and the feathery scones of the cotton-wood, wave above a dense undergrowth of willows, hazels, and wild roses, amid which occasionally glisten the silvery trunks of the birches, "the ladies of the wood."

South of the Columbia river, however, there is, comparatively speaking, but little forest-land. But in northern Oregon there is an abundance of timber for home consumption, as well as for exportation; and since the discovery of the gold mines of California and the rapid population of that territory, the value of the timber has enhanced in a wonderful degree. California is almost entirely destitute of timber for building, and for years to come, the chief supply must be obtained from the exhaustless forests of Oregon, where the immense water power renders every desirable facility for getting it out in any quantity.*

All kinds of grass—timothy, clover, and blue grass—grow with the greatest luxuriance in the valleys of the Columbia, Willamette, Umpqua, and other streams in the eastern section. Indeed, the country seems to be peculiarly well adapted to their growth, and it can scarcely be excelled in the Union for good pasturage. There are two crops of rich, juicy grass, produced on the river prairies; one in the spring, and the other after the overflow subsides, in July or August. Yet there is very little hay made; the scythe and the rake, and the toil and sweat of the mower, are rendered almost unnecessary by the kindness of nature. The growth of the grass is so rapid in the early summer, that the subsequent heats convert it readily into hay where it stands, without the loss of any of its juices. Upon the second crop the stock feed during the winter.

The soil of the prairies and interval lands contains an abundance of silex, and where it is sufficiently dry produces

* In September, 1849, timber was worth from forty to fifty dollars per thousand feet, in Oregon, for exportation to California, and will probably never rule below twenty dollars, even when prices fall back to their proper level. Beef, pork, grain, butter and cheese, indeed all kinds of agricultural products raised in Oregon, will doubtless find a ready market in California for many years to come.

fine crops of wheat,—the yield varying from twenty to fifty bushels per acre, often of more than sixty pounds weight. There is no such thing as a complete failure of the wheat crop ; but as the waters of the rivers are quite cold, and possess little or no fertilizing properties, it is liable to be injured by the inundations, in all low exposures. Indian corn and oats do not succeed very well ; the former suffering much during the cold nights, and the latter producing small heads in comparison with the stalk. For peas, beans, potatoes, and most garden vegetables, the soil is superior.

As the labors of the farmer are lightened in the summer season by the absence of a necessity for securing a supply of hay for his stock, so he is relieved during the winter from providing them with a shelter, except a few pens or inclosures into which they may be driven at night, and from bestowing upon them any extraordinary care. The horses and cattle thrive well, and look unusually fat and sleek. Merino sheep are not suited to the climate, but the California breed, crossed with the Leicester, Bakewell, and other stout and hardy breeds, prosper finely, yeaning time occurring twice a year, and at the shearing exhibit fleeces weighing from eight to twelve pounds. Hogs require but little care : they are generally fattened on wheat, which is said to make the finest pork.

Oregon is not deficient in fruits. Apples, pears, and currants, have a thrifty growth, and yield plentifully; and the indigenous fruits, including gooseberries, strawberries, blackberries, serviceberries, cranberries, crab apples, wild cherries, wild peas, and thorn apples, are very prolific.

In former times, the abundance of game found in this region made it a favorite resort for the hunter and trapper ; but the animals valuable for their furs are fast disappearing, and the buffalo is now rarely seen. The principal animals found are the black-tailed and common red deer, the grizzly and black bear, three different species of the wolf, the wild cat, panther, antelope, mountain sheep, beaver, and otter. Squirrels, foxes, rabbits, racoons, hedgehogs, and weasels, are abundant. The streams of Oregon produce excellent fish, and great quantities of salmon arc annually taken in the rivers discharging their waters into Puget's Sound. All the birds commonly found on the Atlantic coasts in about the same latitude are seen here, and on the ocean shores there are an abundance of gulls, frigate-birds, villula, and other aquatic fowl.

(5.) California, formerly designated as Upper California, was first discovered by Cobrillo, a Spanish navigator, who visited the lower portion of the country in 1542. Sir Francis Drake discovered the upper part in 1578, and called it New Albion. It was colonized, however, by the Spaniards, in 1767, and formed a part of the territory of New Spain—subsequently the Mexican Republic—till the year 1848. By the treaty of Guadalupe Hidalgo, concluded on the 2d day of February of that year, it was ceded by Mexico to the United States. But little importance was then attached to it, except for the fine harbors it contained; but within a few months after the cession, the whole American Union, and a great part of the world, were electrified by the unexpected discovery of vast stores of mineral wealth in this new acquisition. As the circumstances attending this discovery have been described by me in detail, in another work;* and as I do not know that I should desire to change anything there written; in any particular, I transcribe it here:

Vague rumors in regard to the mineral treasures locked up in the volcanic mountain ranges of California—at certain times attracting greater attention than at others, but never receiving much credit—have been circulating throughout the world for centuries. Among the first trophies brought to Cortés, after the conquest of Mexico, in 1521, were samples of Californian pearls; and it was then reported, that gold and gems were to be found in the regions at the north, which had not yet been visited by the Europeans. Two expeditions were fitted out by Cortés, in 1532 and 1533, and sent on voyages of discovery to the north-west. The latter crossed the Gulf of California, called by the Spaniards, in honor of the illus-

* History of the War with Mexico (sup. nota.), p. 507, et seq.

trious discoverer, *Mer de Cortés*—the Sea of Cortés—and effected a landing at the modern port of La Paz. Shortly after this, the Conqueror himself embarked with a squadron, and planted a colony at the same place. His attempts to settle the country, however, were unsuccessful, and the colonists eventually returned to Mexico. In 1539, he dispatched another expedition, under an officer by the name of Ulloa, who sailed to the head of the Gulf, doubled the peninsula, and ascended along the western coast, to the twenty-eighth or twenty-ninth degree of north latitude, but was never afterwards heard of.

Nothing daunted by his ill success, Cortés projected still another expedition ; but his enterprise was now checked by the viceroy Mendoza, whose mind had been inflamed by the golden reports of an itinerant monk sent to convert the Indians of Sonora, and who had penetrated far into the interior of California. The viceroy claimed the right of discovery, and Cortés appealed to the Emperor. The premature death of Cortés, pending the appeal, put an end to all his ambitious hopes, and, in a considerable degree, to the discoveries which he and others had anticipated.*

Various expeditions were subsequently undertaken, but with little or no success. The energetic spirit of the great adventurer and discoverer had died with him ; the glittering realms, where gold and precious stones were said to abound in exhaustless profusion, were never reached ; and the descendants of the *Conquistadores* were obliged to content themselves with the far less valuable silver mines of Mexico.

The pearl fisheries in the Gulf of California, however, were soon made available, and formal possession of the peninsula was taken by the Spanish authorities, in 1569. Not quite fifty years later, the Jesuits established themselves in the country, and gradually extended their missions to the north. They were, no doubt, aware of the existence of gold and silver in California ; yet they dissuaded the Indians from digging

---

* Prescott's Conquest of Mexico, Vol. III, p. 333, et seq.—Greenhow's History of Oregon and California, p. 22, et seq.

after the minerals—probably for the reason that they did not suppose there could be sufficient quantities found to render the search profitable—and encouraged them to devote their time to herding cattle and other agricultural pursuits. In 1767, the Jesuits were expelled from the possessions of Spain, and were succeeded, in California, by Franciscan and Dominican friars. Deprived of the fostering care, the energy and industry, of the followers of Ignatius Loyola, the mission establishments began rapidly to decline, and the discoveries which might ultimately have been made, under their auspices, were reserved for a more enterprising people than the white inhabitants who now made their way to the Californias.

Adventurers from Mexico, from Spain, and the United States, American and European seamen, emigrated thither, and founded settlements on the inner shore of the Gulf, and along the iron-bound coast of the Pacific, from Cape San Lúcas to the Bay of San Francisco.* Some few among them appear to have been active and industrious, but the great majority speedily relapsed into habits of indolence and slothfulness. No extraordinary efforts were made to develop the resources of the country; considerable silver was discovered, but as there was no mercury to purify it, that obtained was of an inferior quality, and afforded a trifling profit. A rich mine, called San Antonio, near La Paz, was wrought for several years, and is said to have yielded handsome returns. But the political dissensions that agitated the southern departments of Mexico were felt in the Californias, perhaps more than all, in the baneful influence which they exerted in repressing the energies of the inhabitants, and curbing the little spirit of enterprise that had previously animated them.

For many years, there was scarcely the least improvement in Upper or Lower California; and if any progress was made, it was at a snail's pace. Hides and tallow formed the principal articles of exportation from the upper province; but the trade was small, and liable to frequent interruptions, by reason

* The mongrel white population of Upper California was computed, in 1842, to be about 5,000, and the Indians 33,000.

of the struggles between the different factions for the ascendency.　Matters remained pretty much in this condition, till
after the termination of the war with the United States, and
the cession to them of Upper California.

This territory, now belonging to the American Union, embraces an area of 448,961 square miles.　It extends along the
Pacific coast, from about the thirty-second parallel of north
latitude, a distance of near seven hundred miles, to the
forty-second parallel, the southern boundary of Oregon.　On
the east, it is bounded by New Mexico.　During the long
period which transpired between its discovery and its cession
to the United States, this vast tract of country was frequently visited by men of science, from all parts of the world.　Repeated examinations were made by learned and enterprising
officers and civilians; but none of them discovered the important fact, that the mountain torrents of the Siérra Neváda
were constantly pouring down their golden sands into the
valleys of the Sacramento and San Joaquin.　The glittering
particles twinkled beneath their feet, in the ravines which they
explored, or glistened in the water-courses which they forded,
yet they passed them by unheeded.　Not a legend or tradition
was heard among the white settlers, or the aborigines, that
attracted their curiosity.　A nation's ransom lay within their
grasp, but, strange to say, it escaped their notice—it flashed
and sparkled all in vain.*

The Russian American Company had a large establishment
at Ross and Bodega, ninety miles north of San Francisco,
founded in the year 1812 ; and factories were also established
in the territory by the Hudson Bay Company.　Their agents
and *employés* ransacked the whole country west of the Siérra
Neváda, or Snowy Mountain, in search of game.　In 1838,
Captain Sutter, formerly an officer in the Swiss Guards of
Charles X, King of France, emigrated from the state of
Missouri to Upper California, and obtained from the Mexican
government a conditional grant of thirty leagues square of

---

* A gold *placéra* was discovered some years ago, near the mission of San Fernando, but it was very little worked, on account of the want of water.

land, bounded on the west by the Sacramento river.   Having purchased the stock, arms, and ammunition of the Russian establishment, he erected a dwelling and fortification on the left bank of the Sacramento, about fifty miles from its mouth, and near what was termed, in allusion to the new settlers, the American Fork.   This formed the nucleus of a thriving settlement, to which Captain Sutter gave the name of New Helvetia.   It is situated at the head of navigation for vessels on the Sacramento, in latitude 38° 33′ 45″ North, and longitude 121° 20′ 05″ West.   During a residence of ten years in the immediate vicinity of the recently discovered *placéras*, or gold regions, Captain Sutter was neither the wiser nor the richer for the brilliant treasures that lay scattered around him.*

In the year 1841, careful examinations of the Bay of San Francisco, and of the Sacramento river and its tributaries, were made by Lieutenant Wilkes, the commander of the Exploring Expedition; and a party under Lieutenant Emmons, of the navy, proceeded up the valley of the Willamette, crossed the intervening highlands, and descended the Sacramento.   In 1843–4, similar examinations were made by Captain, afterwards Lieutenant-Colonel, Frémont, of the Topographical Engineers, and in 1846, by Major Emory, of the same corps.   None of these officers made any discoveries of minerals, although they were led to conjecture, as private individuals who had visited the country had done, from its volcanic formation and peculiar geölogical features, that they might be found to exist in considerable quantities.†

---

* Farnham's Adventures in California.—Wilkes' Narrative of the Exploring Expedition.—Frémont's Narrative.

† See Farnham's Adventures, Wilkes' and Frémont's Narratives, and Emory's Report.— In 1846, Eugenio Macnamara, a Catholic priest and missionary, obtained a grant of a large tract of land between the San Joaquin and the Siérra Neváda, the Cosumnés and the Tulares in the vicinity of San Gabriel, from Pio Pico, governor of the Californias, for the purpose of establishing upon it a large colony of Irish Catholics; but the grant was not ratified by the Central Government, and the project was not carried into effect.   There is no evidence that Father Macnamara was aware of the existence of gold in the valley of the San Joaquin.

SUTER'S FORT.

As is often the case, chance at length accomplished what science had failed to do. In the winter of 1847–8, a Mr. Marshall commenced the construction of a saw-mill for Captain Sutter, on the north branch of the American Fork, and about fifty miles above New Helvetia, in a region abounding with pine timber. The dam and race were completed, but on attempting to put the mill in motion, it was ascertained that the tail-race was too narrow to permit the water to escape with perfect freedom. A strong current was then passed in, to wash it wider and deeper, by which a large bed of mud and gravel was thrown up at the foot of the race. Some days after this occurrence, Mr. Marshall observed a number of brilliant particles on this deposit of mud, which attracted his attention. On examining them, he became satisfied that they were gold, and communicated the fact to Captain Sutter. It was agreed between them, that the circumstance should not be made public for the present; but, like the secret of Midas, it could not be concealed. The Mormon emigrants, of whom Mr. Marshall was one, were soon made acquainted with the discovery, and in a few weeks all California was agitated with the startling information.

Business of every kind was neglected, and the ripened grain was left in the fields unharvested. Nearly the whole population of Upper California became infected with the mania, and flocked to the mines. Whalers and merchant vessels entering the ports were abandoned by their crews, and the American soldiers and sailors deserted in scores. Upon the disbandment of Colonel Stevenson's regiment, most of the men made their way to the mineral regions. Within three months after the discovery, it was computed that there were near four thousand persons, including Indians, who were mostly employed by the whites, engaged in washing for gold. Various modes were adopted to separate the metal from the sand and gravel—some making use of tin pans, others of close-woven Indian baskets, and others still, of a rude machine called the cradle, six or eight feet long, and mounted on rockers, with a coarse grate, or sieve, at one end, but open at the other. The washings were mainly confined to the low wet grounds, and the margins of the streams—the earth being rarely disturbed more than eighteen inches below the surface. The value of the gold-dust obtained by each man, per day, is said to have ranged from ten to fifty dollars, and sometimes even to have far exceeded that. The natural consequence of this state of things was, that the price of labor, and, indeed, of everything, rose immediately from ten to twenty fold.*

As may readily be conjectured, every stream and ravine in the valley of the Sacramento was soon explored. Gold was found on every one of its tributaries; but the richest earth was discovered near the *Rio de los Plúmas*, or Feather river,† and its branches, the Yubah and Bear rivers, and on Weber's creek, a tributary of the American Fork. Explorations were also made in the valley of the San Joaquin, which resulted in the discovery of gold on the Cosumnés and other streams, and in the ravines of the Coast Range, west of the valley, as far down as Ciúdad de los Ángelos.

Sometimes the gold has been found encasing a bright, sparkling crystal of quartz, but no accounts have been received up to this date (January, 1849) indicating that it has been encountered in its matrix, or the place of its original production. In the "dry diggings," or ravines, it is obtained in grains, averaging from one to two pennyweights; but in the swamps, and on the margins of streams, it is procured in small flat spangles, six or seven of which are required to make one grain. Specimens of the metal have been assayed at the mint in Philadelphia, under the direction of Professor Patterson, and the average fineness ascertained to be 894 thousandths, being a little below the standard, which is 900, but fully equal

---

* Official Dispatch of Colonel Mason, Commander of the 10th Military Department, August 17, 1848.—Letters of Thomas C. Larkin, U. S. Consul at Monterey, to the Secretary of State, June 1, and June 28, 1848.

† Feather river is the first considerable branch of the Sacramento below the *Prairie Buttes*. It has a course of about forty miles, and empties into the main river about fifteen miles above New Helvetia. Though the Sacramento is navigable for vessels only to that place, boats can pass up one hundred miles further.

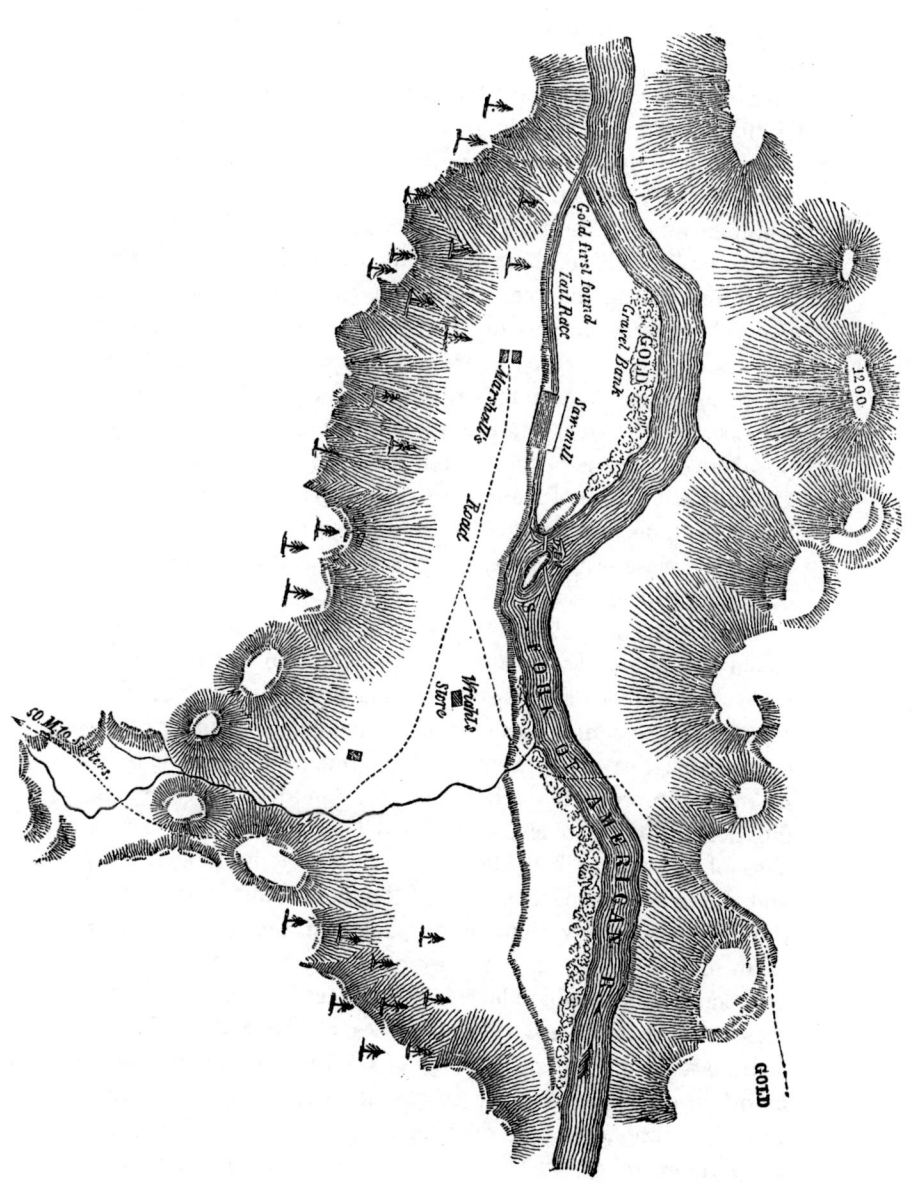

MAP OF THE GOLD PLACÉRA FIRST DISCOVERED.

19

to that obtained in the southern states, and nearly as good as the best gold procured in Africa.

In regard to the productiveness of the gold *placéras* of California, it is difficult to make any estimates, or form any conjectures.   In a Memorial of the citizens of San Francisco, dated in September, 1848, praying Congress to establish a branch mint in the territory, it was estimated that the sum of five and a half millions of dollars would be removed from the mines during the year ending on the 1st of July, 1849. But this calculation was evidently predicated on the number of persons then engaged at the washings.   Since that time, there has been a vast influx of *gold-hunters* from Oregon, Mexico, South America, and the Sandwich Islands.   Large numbers of citizens of the United States have also set out for California, by way of Cape Horn, the Panamá route, or overland from Independence.   It is, therefore, not improbable, that before the close of the year, the population may be trebled, or even quadrupled.

It has been predicted by some, that the washings in California would soon be exhausted, as were those of Brazil, from which ten millions sterling were once annually sent to Europe.   The volcanic character of the country, and its geölogical peculiarities hardly confirm this opinion, although it is by no means improbable.   Gold has been found, or there are indications of its existence, at different points along the western base of the Siérra Neváda, for nearly seven hundred miles, and it has been discovered east of the mountains, on the Great Salt Lake, and at various other places in the great interior basin of California.   If we may place any reliance upon the inferences fairly deducible from these facts, it may be safely presumed, that the rugged buttresses of the Siérra Neváda contain a vaster deposit of mineral wealth than has yet been found in any other locality in the known world—in extent and productiveness far excelling the Andes of Peru, the Carpathian range of Hungary, or the Ural mountains of Russia.*

* The peaks of the Siérra Neváda are from ten to fifteen thousand feet above

In addition to the gold mines, other important discoveries have been made in Upper California. A rich vein of quick-silver has been opened at New Almadin, near Santa Clara, which, with imperfect machinery,—the heat by which the metal is made to exude from the rock being applied by a very rude process,—yields over thirty per cent. This mine—one of the principal advantages to be derived from which will be, that the working of the silver mines scattered through the territory must now become profitable—is superior to those of Almadin, in Old Spain, and second only to those of Idria, near Trieste, the richest in the world.* It is more than probable, also, that other veins will be opened, as the soil, for miles around, is highly impregnated with mercury.

Lead mines have likewise been discovered in the neighbor-hood of Sonoma, and vast beds of iron ore near the American fork, yielding from eighty-five to ninety per cent. Copper, platina, tin, sulphur, zinc, and cobalt, everywhere abound; coal exists in large quantities in the Cascade Range of Oregon, of which the Siérra Neváda is a continuation; and in the vicinity of all this mineral wealth, there are immense quarries of marble and granite, for building purposes.

Colonel Mason expresses the opinion, in his official dispatch, that "there is more gold in the country drained by the Sacramento and San Joaquin rivers, than will pay the cost of the [late] war with Mexico a hundred times over."† Should this even prove to be an exaggeration, there can be little reason to doubt, when we take into consideration all the mineral resources of the country, that the territory of Cali-fornia is by far the richest acquisition made by this govern-ment since its organization. All that is needed, to render these resources of incalculable benefit to our people, is to dis-

---

the level of the ocean; the Carpathian mountains, seven thousand five hundred feet; and the Ural mountains, between four and five thousand feet.

* The mines of Almadin yield only ten per cent; and those at Idria range as high as eighty per cent., although ores containing only one per cent are worked. Specimens of cinnabar from California have been examined at the Philadelphia mint: the red ore yielded over thirty-three per cent, and the yellow ore over fifteen.

† Letter to the Secretary of War, dated August 17, 1848.

countenance from the outset the system of monopoly which proved so ruinous to the interests of Spain in Mexico and Peru; to foster individual enterprise; and to open a more direct communication with California, by a railroad across the isthmus of Panamá, as is now contemplated, or some similar work.

Since the foregoing account was written, the valleys of the Sacramento and San Joaquin have been inundated with gold-seekers; some of whom were doomed to disappointment at the outset, while others have been exceedingly fortunate, though but a very few, perhaps none, have quite equalled their expectations. Those who first arrived in the country, with those on the spot at the time of the discovery, have been the most successful. One *placéra* after another, literally teeming with wealth, have been discovered; rich deposits of the precious metal have been disclosed in every *gulche* and *cañon;* and the glowing statements of Sir Francis Drake, hitherto so commonly discredited, seem to have been actually verified.* Quite recently gold has been found in its matrix, on the banks of the Mariposa, one of the tributaries of the San Joaquin: here there has been a fine vein opened, which has been traced for two leagues, and appears to have an average breadth of one hundred and fifty feet, and to dip only about 20°; the metal occurs in strata of reddish quartz, and eight ounces of pure gold are obtained from one hundred pounds of rock.

The extent of the mineral resources, and more particularly of the gold deposits of California, is still a matter of conjecture; but there is every reason to suppose that the time for accumulating fortunes in a day has nearly gone by; and unless still greater discoveries should be made, at the close of another mining season, with the vast addition which will un-

---

* "The country, too, if we can depend upon what Sir Francis Drake or his chaplain say, is worth the seeking and the keeping—since they assert that the land is so rich in gold and silver, that upon the slightest turning it up with a spade or pick-axe, those rich metals plainly appear mixed with the mould."— Pinkerton's Voyages, vol. ii. p. 172.

doubtedly be made to the number of persons operating in the mining districts during the past year, the *placéras* will be so much exhausted, that they cannot be profitably worked without cheap labor and expensive machinery. Should other deposits of the metal be found, however, equalling or nearly approaching in richness, those which have been already disclosed, it would be idle to predict when these discoveries will end. It is far better, nevertheless, that too sanguine expectations should not be formed, for disappointment, come when or how it may, needs nothing to heighten its poignancy.

It is computed that the value of the gold taken from the mines during the first twelve months subsequent to the discovery, was not far from thirty millions of dollars. Of this amount only about six millions of dollars have reached the Atlantic sea board; some ten or twelve millions have been carried to foreign countries; and the balance still remains in the territory. At first, many of the miners obtained an ounce of gold per day, but the general average has not been five dollars per day to each person while actually at work. Taking into consideration the enormous prices to be paid for every article of necessity or luxury, this return is by no means flattering; for there is a great portion of the year during which the mining operations are for the most part suspended, by the recurrence of the rainy season. While such prices are maintained, the yield of gold should amount upon an average to at least five dollars per day to every individual in the territory, including as well those engaged in trade and furnishing supplies, as those at work in the mines. According to the latest accounts from this auriferous region, the rich washings on Feather river and some other streams have been measurably exhausted, though with good machinery and Indian labor still yielding a fair remuneration.* In some instances, the courses of the streams have been turned, or their

---

* Individual miners have so far succeeded much better with a common tin pan, or basin, for washing their gold, and it is full as popular at the *placéras* of California as is the *gamella* at the washings of Brazil. Small parties still prefer to adhere to the rocker or cradle.

waters dammed up, in order to examine their beds, and valuable deposits of gold have been found ; but similar attempts have, in other cases, often proved unsuccessful.

But even amid the golden sands of California, man cannot escape from his destiny. Toil is his allotment there as everywhere. Working in the *placéras* is no boyish pastime. None but those inured from early life to the severest labor and hardship can pass through the ordeal unscathed. Whether moiling in the earth in the dry diggings, beneath the blistering rocks, and amid the scorching sands, or standing up to the knees in the ice-cold waters of the mountain torrents, with the blazing orb of day pouring down hour after hour his burning rays against which there is no shelter or protection, the powers of endurance are taxed to the utmost. The climate is not unhealthy, it is true, but the heat is oppressive, and when this relaxes the system, exposure to the cold night-air pretty surely brings on disease. Added to this, the miner rarely enjoys any of the comforts, and is frequently deprived of the necessaries of life. Still, those who find their physical powers equal to the task, and continue their labor in spite of every hardship and trial, do not go unrewarded.

Fortune, however, smiles less kindly on those who undergo the greatest fatigue, and perform the severest labor, than upon those who profit by their necessities. The toil and sweat of the former often go to enrich the cunning trader and the shrewd speculator. The prices of food and clothing, of luxuries and necessaries, of everything that can please the fancy, or gratify the appetite, are from one to ten hundred per cent higher than in the Atlantic states ; and those engaged in providing supplies for the miner are in a majority of cases accumulating large fortunes. Yet it is to be regretted that the rage for speculation has already extended so widely in the territory, for, though of little importance at the outset, it soon becomes as incapable of control as the raging whirlwind, and, like that, always leaves desolation and ruin in its track. Within a twelvemonth after the first discovery of gold, the credit operations of the citizens of the territory amounted to one hundred millions of dollars, resting for support upon a metallic or specie basis of only ten millions. City and town lots, houses and farming lands, food and raiment, everything that man needs or desires, are the objects of speculation. What will be the result of all this, the future only can determine. Those who keep aloof from the whirlpool, or pause in time, may reap a rich harvest; but if California herself, or the older states in the Union that become too intimately connected with her, are ultimately benefited, it will be an anomaly in the history of the world.

Yet the mineral resources of California are unquestionably great; and even the smallest rivulets that course down the corrugated sides of the Siérra Neváda are richly impregnated with gold, silver, and platina. But although these deposits of wealth may be nearly, or quite inexhaustible, when the treasures which have been accumulating for so many years near the surface have been gathered, as they soon must be, labor, be it ever so industrious and enterprising, will reap no more abundant harvests at the *placéras* of California, than, if properly applied, it can obtain from the rich farming lands in the Atlantic states and the valley of the Mississippi.

(7.) Previous to the cession of Upper California to the United States, there were, as has been remarked, something less than forty thousand persons in the territory. The population is now estimated at over one hundred thousand. Up to the first day of November, 1849, about five hundred vessels, containing more or less passengers, besides their crews, had arrived at San Francisco within the preceding year; and there were at that time upwards of two hundred vessels, each having its cargo of living freight, on their way from the Atlantic states. Numerous caravans of immigrants have crossed over land, and adventurers by scores have gone by way of Panamá. Around Cape Horn, across the isthmus, and over the desert prairies and bleak mountains of the far west, the tide has swept like the waters of the sea. Danger in every form has been defied. Animated by the all-pervading, if not unhallowed thirst for gold—*auri sacra fames—*

peril and hardship have been cheerfully encountered. The ocean tempest has lost its terrors; the *vómito* of New Grenada is supposed no longer to possess the power to harm; and the horrors of Indian warfare or starvation, both equally dreaded in former times, no more affright the timid, or discourage the weak-hearted, as they wend their way, faint in body but stout of soul, across the trackless wastes of New Mexico and Deseret. And if, perchance, nature at length becomes exhausted and gives way ere the glittering prize has been clutched, the last thoughts of the wayfarer may dwell upon the home he has left, smiling with everything that could cheer or comfort him, and the sad faces and sadder hearts that witnessed his departure, yet with them are mingled feelings of regret that he was unable to reach the land of promise before him.

It might naturally be expected, that the population of California would exhibit a mongrel character. Almost every clime and creed under the sun has its representatives there. Yet it is a remarkable fact, and one highly creditable to the immigrants, that the state of society in the main has been, and now is, a great deal better than could be looked for among such an incongruous mass. Outrages and excesses have been committed, but they are daily becoming less frequent. For several months the citizens governed themselves, in a degree, by laws arbitrarily adopted, yet which were both appropriate and needful, and usually administered with impartiality and justice. On the 1st day of September, 1849, a convention of delegates elected in the different districts, in pursuance of a proclamation of General Riley, then acting as civil and military governor of the territory, assembled at Monterey, and on the 12th day of October following, adopted a state constitution, modelled, in all its general features, after the new constitution of the state of New York; and immediately after the adjournment of that body, all the necessary steps were taken to bring the question of their admission into the confederacy before the national Congress, at its ensuing session.

(8.) The eastern boundary of California established by

the convention, is the 120th meridian, east longitude ; but the other boundaries were left unchanged. The surface of the country near the ocean is much diversified, in some places rising in lofty ranges of hills, covered with patches of wild flowers, and grass, and low shrubs, and at others spreading out into broad plains, intersected with valleys, which are usually rich and fertile, though requiring in the dry season considerable irrigation to render them highly productive. North of the bay of San Francisco, the coast country is still more broken than at the south, but it is well adapted for the culture of grain and the rearing of cattle. From forty to fifty miles inland is the Coast Range, which is the first ridge of mountains, and the continuation of the central chain of Lower California. This ridge divides into several ranges as it trends to the north, and is finally lost in the Klamet range on the southern borders of Oregon.

Between the Coast Range and the Siérra Neváda, which runs nearly along the 120th meridian, the country consists of extensive plains and swelling hills, either well-wooded, or thickly carpeted with wild oats, whose yellow waves sweep far up the sides of the Snowy Mountains. In the midst of this section, near the lower end of California, are the Tulé lakes, which connect with the San Joaquin in the rainy season. That river has a northerly course of from one hundred and fifty to two hundred miles, and unites with the Sacramento in Suisun Bay. The Sacramento comes from the north, and has a course of not far from two hundred miles in extent. Both these streams have a number of affluents which bring down the melted snows of the Siérra Neváda, and the heavy rains that fall during the winter months. The banks of the two larger rivers are low, and for miles above and below the head of Suisun Bay, there are extensive marshes or *tulares*, covered with a species of bulrush, called *tulé*, which are overflowed in high water, and are finely situated for raising rice.

Besides the Sacramento and the San Joaquin, and the Rio Colorado of the west, which forms a part of its eastern

19*

boundary, California has no other considerable streams except it be the Rio de San Buénaventura. This last stream has a north-westerly course of upwards of one hundred miles, and discharges its waters into the bay of Monterey.

The bay of San Francisco is not only the best harbor in California, but it is one of the finest in the world. It lies parallel to the ocean, at a distance of from five to six miles, and is connected with it by a narrow strait from two to four miles in width. The bay is about forty-five miles long, and varies in width from four to ten miles. It affords abundant anchorage for vessels of the largest class, and is capable of sheltering the navies of the world from the waves and tempests of the neighboring ocean. At its northern extremity it is connected by a small strait with the bay of San Pablo, which is circular, and about ten miles in diameter. The latter is, in turn, connected with Suisun Bay, into which the San Joaquin and the Sacramento debouch, by the Straits of Karquinez. Vessels of light draught can ascend the Sacramento as high as Sacramento city. The San Joaquin is also navigable, in like manner, for some distance, varying with the different stages of the water.

Monterey has a bay, or roadstead, which is sufficiently capacious, and affords pretty secure anchorage in the southeast corner of the bight, inside of a line drawn from Point Año Nuévo through Point Pinos, but elsewhere it is not protected against the north-westerly winds. The harbor of San Diego is a semi-circular indentation of the coast; it is protected on the north and east by high bluffs, and is considered perfectly safe.

Since the discovery of gold in California, towns and cities have sprung up like mushrooms, and it would be useless and unwise to attempt to describe them, as the changes constantly taking place are so great, and of such a character. that a description, however faithful at the moment, could scarcely be written ere it would prove to be erroneous. At the time of the cession to the United States, the only places of any importance in the territory, were Yerba Buéna, or

San Francisco, which stands on the west bank of the bay of the same name, just below the opening of the strait leading to the ocean, and Monterey and San Diego on the coast. Ciúdad de los Ángelos, in the interior, and about midway between Monterey and San Diego, was also a town of some consideration; it being the capital of the two Californias while under the Mexican sway. All these places have come forward during the past year with astonishing rapidity. But little more than twelve months ago, either of them counted its population by hundreds, but now they are numbered in thousands. San Francisco has outstripped them all. She has over twenty-five thousand inhabitants; a dense forest of masts and spars may be witnessed in front of her wharfs; and from sunrise till sunset, the busy hum of a commercial town resounds upon a spot whose wild solitudes at a very recent period were scarcely disturbed by the footsteps of civilized man. The most important towns which have sprung up since the commencement of the gold excitement, are Sacramento city, at the junction of the American Fork and the Sacramento; Stockton, on the San Joaquin; New York-of-the-Pacific, on Suisun Bay, in the peninsula formed between the two rivers at their junction, and at the head of ship navigation; and Benicia, which lies on the northern bank of the straits of Karquinez, near the entrance into Suisun Bay, a distance of forty-five miles from San Francisco.

The climate of California is variable, but not unhealthy, and most of the diseases that prevail are not produced by its influence. It is much warmer, of course, than in the same latitude on the Pacific; and at the south, the heat is sometimes intense. Near the Colorado, the thermometer often rises to 140°; and in the valley of the Sacramento, to 110°, in the shade. Along the coast, it is not so warm. During the dry season, from the 1st of March to the 1st of November, the mornings are clear, and the heat generally intolerable; but at noon, the sky becomes overcast; the strong and unpleasant, but bracing north-westerly gales set in, and condense the vapors which have risen during the morning, and the thermometer falls very rapidly. The nights are almost always cool. During the rainy months, the plains and low grounds are usually enveloped in fogs and mists, and every little *arroyo* is swollen far beyond its ordinary limits, while the large streams roll down a vast flood of waters to the ocean.

(9.) Among the principal wild animals in California, are the fierce grizzly bear, the antlered elk, the black-tailed deer, the savage panther and puma, the Californian lion, the shy antelope, and the noisy coyote, or prairie wolf. The buffalo is an entire stranger in this quarter. Hares, squirrels, rabbits, and marmots, are abundant. The streams abound in fine-flavored fish; and the delicate and luscious salmon are quite plenty. Among the feathered tribes are the eagle, hawk, vulture, crow, pheasant, partridge, goose, duck, pelican, curlew, crane, turkey, pigeon, and plover.

M. de Mofras, one of the most learned and scientific travellers who have visited this country, insists, that all that part of California lying between the coast and the Siérra Neváda is "of admirable fertility, and perfectly proper for colonization."* Captain Wilkes also informs us, that the fertility of the soil is so great, that eighty bushels of wheat is the average yield, and that sometimes one hundred and twenty bushels—though this is not very common—are obtained.† But these statements must be taken with some degree of reservation. The hills and uplands afford the finest pasturage; but they are not calculated to produce anything else except gramineous plants. The elevated plains are covered with immense fields of wild oats and wild mustard, of a most thrifty growth, which often climb up the sides of the mountains to a considerable height. The soil of the low grounds is a rich, dark loam, that becomes dry like powder in the summer season; but the winter and spring rains soon convert them into blooming gardens. Irrigation will be needed all over the territory, in order to

* Exploration du Territoire de l'Orégon, des Californies, et de la Mer Vermeille, Tom. II, p. 40.
† Narrative of the Exploring Expedition, Vol. V, pp. 158, 159.

render agricultural enterprises eminently successful; but where this is practicable, abundant crops will be obtained. The *tulé* marshes could readily be converted into rice fields, and the interval lands will produce most of the cereal grains with but a tolerable culture. Blue flax and hemp are well suited to the country. In southern California, the vine (*vitis vinifera*) thrives wonderfully, and great quantities of brandy and wine are made : the volcanic soil is well adapted for vine-yards; and the attention of the inhabitants will probably be still more directed to the cultivation of the grape, whenever the excitement in regard to the gold deposits has subsided.

California cannot be termed well-wooded, although the high-lying sections, between the Pacific and the Siérra Neváda, are dotted quite frequently with forests of excellent timber, and the flanks of the mountains, and the deep *cañons* open-ing into the valleys beneath, are fringed here and there with strips of woodland. The courses of the streams, also, are usually lined with belts of stately trees, or thickets of shrubby undergrowth. The most valuable timber trees are the live-oak, ash, pine, cedar, cypress, sycamore, willow, and cotton-wood. Of the fruit-trees, pears, apples, plums, peaches, oranges, limes, figs, and olives, thrive with great luxuriance, where they receive proper care and attention. The pitahaya (*cactus pitajaya*) is very abundant, and bears a most delicious fruit. All the vegetables found in the same latitudes in other parts of the world, flourish here equally well.

The country is rich in flowering plants and creepers. Beautiful mosses exhibit their long trails from the tops of the highest trees, and the mistletoe shelters itself beneath the shade of the noble oak, climbs up its rugged trunk, and nestles amid its tufted canopy. Among the grasses on the damp flats, and the wild oats of the hilly slopes and moun-tain-sides, are mingled the most valuable bulbous roots, and the brightest and sweetest flowers. There are tulips and hyacinths; the lily and the narcissus; golden poppies and delicately tinted daisies; crimson and scarlet pinks; the fra-grant graphalium; and the medicinal canchalagua. And their beauty, too, is enhanced in a great degree, by the fine contrast presented by the snow-crowned peaks of the Siérra Neváda, that glisten like burnished silver on the very border of the dark line of vegetation, and, more than all, by the beautiful ultra-marine tints, which, in a clear day, dye the whole landscape from the ocean surf to the loftiest mountain height.

(10.) All the vessels of the Exploring Squadron having assembled at San Francisco, and the surveys having been completed, orders were given to make ready for sea on the 28th of October. On the first day of November, they sailed out of the bay, and proceeded to the Sandwich Islands, where it was necessary to stop in order to complete the supplies required for the return voyage to the United States. The whole Squadron were safely anchored in the inner harbor of Honolulu, early in the morning of the 18th of November, and on the 27th instant, the Vincennes and tender took their final departure for Manilla, where they arrived on the 13th day of January, 1842. The Porpoise and Oregon were directed to examine the shoals and reefs west of the Sandwich Islands, and then to proceed, through the China seas, to Singapore.

CHAPTER XVIII.

(1.) MANILLA, or Mañila, is situated on the island of Luzon,
upon the east side of the bay of Manilla, and about half a
mile from the mouth of the Pasig, a small river that winds
down through a narrow plain, terminating on the east in swelling hills, which gradually rise into lofty mountains, clothed
to the summit with the rich vegetation of the Orient. It
is built in a circular form, on the south side of the river, and
is connected with its suburbs on the right bank, by a handsome stone bridge, one hundred and forty-nine *varas* in length,
by eight in breadth. It is surrounded by strong walls, with
six gates, and a broad ditch; and at the mouth of the river
there is a small battery, and near the north-western extremity
of the town, the more imposing citadel of San Jago.

Most of the houses in the city proper, which is only about
two miles in circumference, are firmly built of the volcanic
tufa, the prevalent formation in the vicinity. They are constructed after the Spanish fashion, with *azotéas*, or flat roofs,
and balustrades, and are garnished with jutting balconies and
shady verandas. Few of them exceed two stories in height,
on account of the frequent occurrence of earthquakes. The
windows are protected by blinds or shutters, in which are inserted, instead of glass, thin pieces of semi-transparent shell,
a species of *placuna*, which, though not admitting the light so
freely, are valuable in repelling the fierce tropical heat, and,
unless the dark-eyed señorítas of this second Lima are not

belied, in permitting them to watch the passers-by without being themselves visible. In some of the suburbs, the houses are light, airy structures, built wholly of bamboo, in the Eastern mode, and resting on thick poles eight or ten feet above the ground.

Churches and monastic establishments are by far the most numerous structures of a public character in the city.* The cathedral and archbishop's palace are conspicuous buildings. There is also a missionary college, and several hospitals and orphan asylums. On one side of the *pláza mayór*, is the government-house, or palace, in which are the residences of the captain general, and the public officers. The square is about one hundred yards in breadth and length, and in its centre there is a bronze statue of Charles IV, mounted on a marble pedestal. The custom-house, or *aduana*, is a large building, constructed at great expense, but entirely out of proportion to the business transacted in it, and is tenanted for the greater part of the time, only by the numerous officials, whose high-sounding names and formal politeness always attract the notice of the stranger, and are quite sure to cause many an involuntary smile. On the great square is one of the royal cigar manufactories, in which three hundred and fifty males and two thousand females are employed ; and in the suburb of Bidondo, on the opposite side of the river, there is a similar establishment, in which there are said to be eight thousand females constantly kept at work. Each female makes about two hundred cigars in a day. The manufacture is a government monopoly, and the annual revenue derived from the two establishments is over half a million of dollars.

The streets are well laid out, and have carriage-ways, hardened by a mixture of quartz with the loamy soil. There are paths, also, for persons travelling on foot—an unusual mode of conveyance, by the way, with the aristocracy of " the celebrated and forever royal city of Manilla," by which sonorous distinction the capital of the Philippines is honored in

* This is not to be wondered at, when we consider that Manilla contains upwards of seven thousand clergymen, either natives or Europeans.

the charter of 1571. From the river, there are a number of side cuts diverging in every direction, that extend up into the town and suburbs, like the canals of Venice, which serve instead of streets, and are constantly filled with bancas, or small boats, plying to and fro, from one quarter of the city to the other.

Outside the walls, and beyond the suburbs, are fine carriage drives, bordered with rice-grounds and cotton plantations, with wide-spreading fields covered with the fragrant coffee-bush, with clumps of graceful cocoas, whose long branches bend with the weight of the ripening fruit, with gardens blooming with flowers and redolent of perfume, and with beautiful groves, where the areca,* the mango, and the orange, mingle their branches lovingly together, and

> "The tamarind from the dew
> Sheathes its young fruit, yet green."

Within the limits of the city-proper, there are only twelve or fourteen thousand inhabitants; but the total population, inclusive of all the suburbs, is estimated at about one hundred and fifty thousand, much the larger proportion of whom are *Tagalas*, or natives, who belong to the Malay race. With these are intermingled perhaps five thousand Spaniards and other Europeans, great numbers of Chinese, Malays, Papuan negroes, and the motley descendants of all the different races. The Spanish residents have given the tone and character to the society, and the higher classes spend their time nearly in the same manner as those occupying a similar position in the towns of old Spain. The men transact a little business, it may be, in the morning, while their wives are engaged at their toilets, or sleeping or lolling at home. After dinner, both sexes resort to the *prado*, for a drive or a promenade, amid the groups of smokers and gamblers who may always be seen lounging there; and the evening is spent at the gay *tertulia*, with its guitars, its dances and dulces, its wines and lemonade.

* The fruit of the areca is the betel nut, which is quite generally chewed by the natives in the East Indies, with the leaf of the pepper-betel, and lime.

The Europeans and their descendants dress principally after the Spanish fashion, but the ladies are so fond of displaying their finely-moulded arms and ankles, that sleeves and stockings are usually at a discount. The costume of the other classes is a sort of mixture of Chinese and Malay, blended together in different shades and forms.

Manilla possesses considerable commerce ; it is the capital of the Spanish settlements in the East, and the only port in the Philippines with which foreign vessels are allowed to trade.* Its exports amount anually to over two millions of dollars, and the imports are about one million seven hundred thousand dollars. The former consist mainly of sugar, hempen stuffs, rice, indigo, sapan and other woods, tobacco, cigars, hides, ebony, coffee, cotton, and tortoise-shell. The principal articles imported are iron, and all kinds of manufactured goods. The harbor of Manilla, which is formed by the river Pasig, is accessible to merchant vessels of six hundred tons burden, and those of three hundred tons can ascend as high up as the bridge. Beyond the bridge the stream is navigable for small boats to the lake in which it rises, a distance of about nine miles. Large vessels anchor in the roads, at from one to two miles off the shore, and discharge their cargoes into lighters, except during the prevalence of the south-western monsoons, in the months of July, August, and September, when they are obliged to anchor at Cavité, six or seven miles from the mouth of the river, where they are sheltered by a long neck of land from the fury of the winds.

(2.) The Philippine Islands were discovered by Magellan, in 1521, and were first claimed by the Spanish in 1565. They are the most valuable colonial possession belonging to Spain, with the exception of the island of Cuba. They lie between the parallels of 5° and 20° north latitude, and the 117th and 124th meridians of eastern longitude ; being separated on the north, from the Batanes and Basher islands, by the Balintang

---

* Previous to the Spanish invasion, Manilla was a native town of some importance. It was taken in 1571, when the Spaniards made it the capital of their Eastern possessions.

channel, and on the south, from the Sooloo archipelago, by the strait of Basillan. The total area of all the islands is one hundred and thirty-five thousand square miles, and the number of inhabitants is supposed to exceed three millions—composed, in great part, of Tagalas, Chinese, Malays, and Papuan Negroes, with comparatively few Europeans. Luzon, the largest of the group, is of irregular shape, and is about four hundred and fifty miles in length, and varies in width, from ten, to one hundred and forty miles. The other principal islands are Mindoro, Samar, Panay, Magindanao, and Palawan, all lying to the south of Luzon.

These islands are all of volcanic formation, and on Luzon there are several active volcanoes. The coasts are bold and rocky, but indented with numerous bays and gulfs. In the interior there are lofty mountainous ridges, the peaks of which sometimes attain an elevation of six thousand feet. But the proportion of arable land is large, and is usually of great fertility. The hilly districts are well wooded; and the savannas in the vicinity of the numerous lakes, of which most of the islands have several, and the plains and valleys along the rivers and small streams, are covered with a deluge of vegetation—with succulent grasses and perfumed flowers, with aromatic shrubs and luscious fruits, and with all the rich products of a tropical clime. Most conspicuous among the last are the sugar-cane, rice, indigo, tobacco, coffee, hemp, millet, maize, and the shrub-cotton. The sugar of the Philippines is excellent, and is the most important article of exportation. Of rice there are several varieties, both for the uplands and the low grounds; this is the chief reliance of the inhabitants for food, and large quantities of it are shipped to China. Tobacco is well adapted to the soil and climate, but its production is entirely controlled by the government, as it is allowed to be manufactured only into cigars. Of the hemp, which is obtained from a species of plantain called *abaca*, excellent cordage and a kind of strong, coarse cloth, are made by the Malays.

Bananas, cocoas, shaddocks, pine-apples, the bread-fruit, the areca, the clove-tree, and the mango, are in great plenty, and

are either indigenous or have been introduced and cultivated
with success. Sago, of a very fine quality, is produced in
abundance on Luzon, but is not exported to any great extent.
Sapan-wood and bamboo are the principal timber trees. The
former is a species of Cæsalpinia; it is highly valued as
a dye-wood, and in its color and properties resembles Brazil-
wood. The bamboo grows to an extraordinary size, the bolls
of the trees often being as thick as a man's thigh.

There are no beasts of prey on the islands, but caymans
are plentiful in the rivers and lakes. Wild fowl, and the domestic kinds, are quite numerous. There are also great
quantities of swallows, whose nests are esteemed edible by the
Chinese and Malays, and form an important article of traffic.
The buffalo is a native of the islands, and was once used as a
beast of burden, and in the cultivation of the soil; but latterly
oxen have been introduced, as the former was found to be too
sluggish in his movements, by the industrious Malays, who are
the principal tillers of the ground. Horses, of a small but hardy
breed, goats, sheep, and pigs, are raised in considerable numbers. All kinds of edible fish, the pearl oyster, and the *biche
de mer*, abound in the vicinity of the islands, and the land
tortoise is also very abundant.

On account of the great extent of these islands, the climate
is quite variable, notwithstanding they lie so near the Equator.
At Manilla, the mean temperature of the hot season, from
August to October, is about 82°, though the heat is sometimes exceedingly oppressive to those unaccustomed to a tropical climate; and for the remaining part of the year, the thermometer ranges but little above or below 70°. The south-
western monsoon always brings an abundance of rain, and the
savannas and valleys along the rivers are then inundated with
water; to which circumstance the great prevalence of agues
and dysentery, especially in the marshy districts, is attributed.
While the north-eastern monsoon continues, it is usually quite
dry. From May till December, Luzon is subject to be visited by the destructive typhoons of the Chinese Seas. Manilla has several times suffered from earthquakes, though

they have rarely damaged any other buildings except the churches.

Nearly all the trade of the Philippines is carried on through Manilla, the extent of whose commerce has been already mentioned. Besides the manufacture of cigars, under the auspices of the government, which gives employment to so many of the native females, great numbers of them occupy themselves, principally at home, in weaving cotton and hempen cloths and silks, and in plaiting rice straw, and splints of wood, into hats, cigar-cases, and matting, of various patterns. From a species of pine-apple, produced in abundance on the island of Panay, a thin, gossamer fabric, called *pina*, of a yellowish color, is manufactured also by the women. The web of the *pina* is so fine, that it is necessary to weave it in a room from which all currents of air are excluded, by means of gauze screens placed in the windows. It is richly embroidered, and made into dresses, scarfs, caps, collars, cuffs, and pocket-handkerchiefs, which are very beautiful, and highly expensive, and much sought after by foreigners and residents who possess the means to purchase them.

The Philippines are nominally under the dominion of Spain, and her authority is exerted throughout the greater part of the group. Two of the largest islands, however, Palawan and Magindanao, are chiefly inhabited by Malays and Papuans, who have never been subjected by the Spanish, and claim to be entirely independent of them, acknowledging no allegiance except to their own chiefs. The group is divided into thirty provinces, sixteen of which are on the island of Luzon. At the head of the government, as the representative of the Spanish sovereign, is the captain-general, or governor, who resides at Manilla, and deputes his authority to lieutenant-governors on the other important islands. Every province has its alcalde, and is sub-divided into pueblos, each of which has its separate intendant.

(3.) But little time was spent by the American vessels at Manilla. They left the bay on the evening of the 21st of January, and proceeded to the southward. Passing through the straits of Mindoro, the tender directed her course towards Singapore, and the Vincennes bore away for the Sooloo archipelago, the survey of which, as far as was practicable, was one of the objects of the expedition; and on the 3d day of February she came to anchor in Soung Harbor, at the island of Sooloo, in latitude 6° 01′ N. and longitude 120° 55′ 51″ E.

The Sooloo Islands extend in a north-easterly direction, between the 4th and 7th parallels of north latitude, and 120° and 123° eastern longitude. There are about sixty different islands, in the centre of which is Sooloo, the largest and most important, like a hen in the midst of her brood. The population of the group is about one hundred and thirty thousand. The inhabitants are of the Malay race. Their complexion is of a light tawny color, and their hair black, soft, and thick. They are tall, and well-formed, and have tolerably fine features. In character they are not courageous, yet they are confirmed thieves and pirates. They are passionate and treacherous, and much addicted to sensual pleasures, and to smoking opium and chewing the betel nut. Most of them are Mohammedans, and their sovereign is called a sultan; his authority is limited, however, by the power and influence possessed by the subordinate chiefs, who are called *datus*.

In their manners and customs the Sooloos differ but little from the other nations in the East Indies. They build their houses of bamboo, elevated on poles if near the water side, or imbosomed amid thickets of cocoas. Their dress resembles that of the Chinese, consisting in the main of loose calico gowns, silk sashes, wide breeches and slippers; the attire of a man not being considered complete unless he has a huge *kreese*, or knife, stuck in his belt, in a wooden scabbard. Polygamy is not generally practiced, though the sultan has a number of wives of whom he is quite proud. The women are not generally celebrated for their chastity, yet it is said that they possess great influence over their husbands.

Sago is one of the principal products of the islands, and

is the chief article of food upon which the inhabitants subsist.   All the tropical fruits and plants flourish here in great
luxuriance and beauty.   Rice, sweet potatoes, and yams, of
the finest quality, are very abundant.   The commerce of the
islands is principally carried on with the neighboring islands
of Celebes, Mindanao, and Borneo, and occasionally with the
Chinese traders who visit the archipelago.   The most important products which they have for trade are pearls,
mother-of-pearl, and cowries.   The cowry is the shell of a
small muscle, (*cypreæ moneta*), of an oval shape, and
usually about one and a half inches long.   It is extensively
used throughout the East Indies, instead of small coin,
though the value affixed to the shells is but small, being only
about three cents per pound.*

Captain Wilkes found himself so limited in time, that he
was unable to remain but for two or three days at Soung.
As this was the residence of the sultan, he had an interview with him, and succeeded in concluding a treaty providing for the protection of American merchant vessels trading
in this quarter against the attacks of the Sooloo pirates, and
from molestation and ill-treatment when they touched at the
islands.   Little faith can be placed on the ability or disposition of the sultan to control the crews of the piratical proas,
but if the first infraction of the treaty be visited with severe
and speedy punishment, a most salutary effect will, without
doubt, be produced.   The Vincennes left Soung Harbor on the
6th of February, and crossing the beautiful Sooloo sea, whose
waters are rarely disturbed by the swell of the ocean, passed
through the straits of Balabac, and in the afternoon of the
19th instant joined the other vessels of the Squadron then
lying at anchor in Singapore Roads.

(4.) Singapore is one of the most important commercial
emporiums, or entrepôts in the East.   It belongs to Great
Britain, and was purchased of the Sultan of Johore by the
East India company, in 1819.   It is situated on the south side
of a small island at the southern extremity of the Malay pen-

---

* Cowries are found in great plenty everywhere in the Indian seas.

insula, from which it is separated by a narrow strait, one quarter of a mile in width, in latitude 1° 17′ N., and longitude 103° 51′ E. In the centre of the town are the dwellings of the merchants and the military cantonments; the Malay quarter is on the east, and the Chinese quarter, which is the business part of the city, on the west. The streets are well laid out, and all the better class of houses are built of brick. The only public buildings of any importance are the government house, jail, custom-house, the Armenian church, the Missionary chapel, and the Singapore Institution, founded for the purpose of affording instruction in the Eastern languages.

The island on which the town is situated is composed principally of laterite, sandstone, and granite. Iron ore is abundant, and tin is also said to exist. The island is twenty-seven miles long from east to west, and eleven miles wide. The surface is for the most part low and undulating, here and there rising into dome-shaped hills, whose summits are sterile, but whose slopes are thickly covered with jungle patches, while the intermediate plains and valleys are carpeted with a most profuse vegetation, whose freshness and beauty are preserved throughout the year by the frequent showers. The climate is hot, but the range of the thermometer is unusually limited, being only from 71° to 89°. Nutmegs, coffee, pepper, and gambier catechu, thrive very well on the island, but the clove does not seem adapted to the soil or climate. Most of the principal tropical fruits and vegetables are raised in considerable quantities. There are no quadrupeds on the island, except a few small deer, the otter, the porcupine, one or two others of no great importance, and the domestic animals that have been introduced. Birds and reptiles are quite plentiful, but the swarms of insects that usually constitute so great an annoyance in Eastern countries are unknown. White ants, however, are abundant, and exceedingly destructive to the crops in the interior.

There are about thirty thousand inhabitants on the island, three fourths of whom are Chinese and Malays, and the remainder are natives of the East Indies with a few Europeans. Every variety of costume is witnessed in the streets, and the manners and customs of the inhabitants differ as widely as their dress. Chinese and Malay artisans pursue their occupations in the streets of Singapore, and the salt river or inlet on which the town is situated, is crowded with junks and sampans, all freighted with their living cargoes. The principal language spoken among business men is the Malay, though a majority of the shopkeepers, and the most valuable part of the laboring population, are Chinese.

It is chiefly, perhaps only, as the entrepôt for the commerce of the adjacent countries, that Singapore possesses so much importance. It is diminutive in area; produces but few articles of any moment; manufactures nothing except pearl sago, agricultural implements and arms, in small quantities, and consumes but little,—yet it is situated directly on the track of communication between the commercial towns of eastern and western Asia, and its annual imports and exports each amount to not far from seven millions of dollars.

(5.) While at Singapore, an examination was made into the condition of the Flying Fish, when it was found that she was totally unfit to make the voyage home, whereupon orders were reluctantly given by the commander of the Squadron to advertise her for sale at public auction. This was accordingly done, though much to the regret of those who had accompanied her through so many scenes, and shared with her so many perils.

The crew of the tender having been transferred to the other vessels, and the necessary stores obtained for the passage home, the little fleet, now consisting of only the Vincennes and Porpoise originally belonging to the Squadron, and the brig Oregon, sailed from Singapore on the 26th day of February. Passing through the Straits of Rhio, Banca, and Sunda, they entered the Indian Ocean on the 6th day of March. Gladly the heads of the vessels were now turned to the west, and all on board, from the highest to the lowest, hailed with joy the freshening breezes that bore them rapidly

20*

onward to the homes and hearts beyond the Atlantic which they well knew would almost leap to welcome them. Finding that the Vincennes made more rapid progress than her consorts, Captain Wilkes parted from them on the 7th instant, having given orders to their commanders to touch at Rio Janeiro on their homeward route, while he proceeded direct to the Cape of Good Hope.

On the 14th of April, the Vincennes came to anchor in Table Bay, amidst the fleet of boats always moving busily hither and thither in this harbor, and within view of the dark, reddish battlements, and noble outlines of Table Mountain, upon which the Titans might easily have taken their repast, of the pretty straw colored cottages at its base surrounded by a rich garniture of foliage and flowers, the short and dwarfish houses or "lockers" strung along the beach, the frowning castle with its mud walls and white tower, the long ox-teams hitched to the rude wagons with their gipsy tents, and the groups of Malay boys and corlies with their red kerchiefs and funnel-shaped straw hats, that form the *matériel* and *personnel* of Cape Town. But few days were spent here; and on the 17th instant, the Vincennes again got under way. On the 1st of May, she arrived off St. Helena, at which the Porpoise and Oregon had previously touched. Delaying but for a short time at this island, she soon shaped her course for the United States, and on the afternoon of the 10th day of June, 1842, was cozily moored at the Brooklyn navy yard, where the Porpoise and Oregon also arrived within a few days of each other,—thus terminating in safety, though it had been checkered with divers vicissitudes, their adventurous cruise of four years' duration.

CAPETOWN AND TABLE MOUNTAIN.

PART II.

EXPEDITION TO THE DEAD SEA

AND THE RIVER JORDAN.

EXPEDITION TO THE DEAD SEA.

CHAPTER I.

(1.) Destruction of the Cities of the Plain. Traditions. Peculiar Position and Character of the Dead Sea. Unsuccessful Attempts to Explore it.—(2.) Projected Expedition of Lieutenant Lynch. Departure from New York. Smyrna.—(3.) Firman of the Sultan. Beïrût. St. Jean d'Acre.—(4.) Preparations for the Overland March. The Escort. Bedawin.—(5.) Incidents by the Way. Arabian Villages. (6.) Arrival at the Sea of Galilee.

(1.) CENTURIES have been multiplied upon centuries, cycle after cycle has been numbered on the dial-plate of time, since the setting sun smiled for the last time on the fertile valley of Siddim, and threw its bright effulgence of mingled purple and gold far and wide over the groves, and gardens, and vineyards, blooming with freshness and beauty, that surrounded the lovely cities of the plain. Ere the morning's dawn, a little group, but four in number—the father, well stricken in years, and the wife of his bosom, with two young daughters, the pledges of their love—might have been seen hastening for their lives towards the gates of Zoar. None dared to look behind them, for the anger of the Most High was kindled—none save the mother, who, moved either by the curiosity perhaps unjustly attributed to her sex, or the yearning of her heart for the daughters and sons-in-law she had left behind her, turned to cast one more look on the fair scene which had been marred by the vices of man, and was now doomed of God. In an instant, the fountains of life were sealed up, and her frame hardened into a statue ; she no longer followed in the footsteps of her fleeing companions, but, transfixed to the spot—a pillar of salt—she stood there, where her feet had been planted, a lasting monument of the indignation of her Maker, and a continual warning against disobedience.

And now the fire and brimstone descended out of heaven, and " the garden of the Lord," the cities and their inhabitants, and the plain and everything it contained, sank beneath the burning and hissing waves, that surged up to the valley of El-Ghor; Sodom and Gomorrah, Admah and Zeboim—the people in the midst of their crimes—the substance which they had hoarded—their flocks and their herds—the fields and gardens teeming with the products of the earth, the fruits and the flowers, the noble groves of palms and sycamores, and the vine and the olive with their load of blushing honors,—all disappeared forever—"and, lo ! the smoke of the country went up as the smoke of a furnace !"

For thousands of years, sacred and profane history have preserved the traditions connected with this event. The chosen people of God were driven from the homes of their fathers by the legions of Rome ; the latter was deprived of her conquests by the Saracen ; and he, in his turn, was succeeded by the Turk. But ever since Titus planted his eagles in triumph on the crumbling ramparts of Jerusalem, and from the hour in which the edict of Adrian made the Jew an outcast and a wanderer,* whithersoever he has gone, wherever he has sought an abiding-place—whether amid the snows and frosts of northern Europe, or the soft and voluptuous climes along the classic shores of the Mediterranean—whether in the crowded capitals of the Old World, or the expanding cities of the New—he has clung, in every trial and vicissitude, through every peril and persecution, to the memories that time has hallowed, and which his religion has sanctified.

During all this period, too, Palestine herself has not been without witnesses. Though the Infidel is in possession of

* Jerusalem was taken by Titus in the 70th year of the Christian Era ; but the Jews were not banished from Judea until A. D. 136.

the desert plains, and the still fertile valleys, fanned but rarely
by the soft winds that blow

> "Sabean odors from the spicy shore
> Of Araby the Blest,"——

though new customs and new institutions have taken the
place of the old, the foot of the Gentile has not trampled out
the evidences that testify to this occurrence; and the scenes
and associations endeared to the Christian, though here and
there partially veiled in mystery, yet bask beneath the same
sunshine that lighted the nephew of Abraham in his flight
from that valley of wickedness and sin.   The follower of Is-
lam continues, to this day, to hand down to his children the
legends of the stranger race that once inhabited the soil which
he now treads as its master; and the fierce Bedawi, as he
looks down from the o'ershadowing heights upon the dank pool
lying inclosed between the barren hills of Judea and the stony
mountains of Arabia Petrea, utters the name of *Băhr-Lŭt.**

From the earliest period, the peculiar position and character of the Salt, or Dead Sea, have attracted the notice of
men of learning and intelligence.   In ancient times, Stephen
of Byzantium, Strabo, Diodorus Siculus, Pliny and Josephus,
regarded it as an anomaly in the physical composition of the
world, while Justin and Tertullian pointed to it as affording
the most conclusive evidence in favor of the great truths of
Christianity.   In later days, the scholars and *savans* of
Europe and America have made repeated efforts to obtain
the most careful and accurate information in regard to this
singular body of water, by personal examination and observation; and, in connection therewith, to ascertain by what mysterious agency, or in what mysterious manner, the judgment of
God was carried into effect in the destruction of the cities of the
plain.   Some of them have been partially successful, and others
have become disheartened almost at the commencement of their
task.   Pococke, Maundrell, Shaw, and Burckhardt,—Abbé

---

* Sea of Lot.

Martine, Châteaubriand, Lamartine, and the Count de Bertou, among Europeans,—and Stephens and Robinson of our own countrymen, have thrown a flood of light upon the subject. But all these travellers were, in one respect or another, deficient in the facilities that might have enabled them to perfect their investigations, and a great deal was still left undetermined as the fruitful subject of conjecture. An accurate survey of the lake, and a critical examination into the configuration of its shores, were essential. This was attempted by private individuals, but the results were neither complete, nor reliable. Two successive efforts were also made by British officers, but they too failed ; and it was reserved for Lieutenant William F. Lynch, of the navy of the United States, with the means placed at his disposal by his government, to achieve a far greater measure of success, in many particulars, than those who had preceded him.

(2.) In the spring of 1847, the idea of conducting an Expedition to the Holy Land, to circumnavigate the Lake Asphaltites, or Dead Sea, and explore the river ordan, suggested itself to Lieutenant Lynch. The project which he had conceived was immediately laid before the Secretary of the Navy and the President of the United States, and received a favorable consideration. Instructions were accordingly issued to him on the last day of July to commence his preparations ; and on the 2d of October following, the store-ship Supply was placed under his orders, to convey the men whom he had selected to accompany him, with the necessary stores, to the Syrian coast.

Besides furnishing himself and the members of his party, with a liberal supply of weapons, including a large blunderbuss, as a protection against the attacks of the savage Bedawin of the desert, the commander of the projected Expedition received permission to have two metallic boats constructed, one of copper and the other of galvanized iron, together with a couple of trucks and sets of harness, it being the intention to transport them overland from the Mediterranean to the sea of Galilee.* To these were added suitable tents for camping, cooking utensils, gum-elastic water bags, books and instruments.

Every requisite preparation having been made, on the 20th of November, the Supply dropped down from the Brooklyn Navy Yard, where she had been fitted for the Expedition, to the anchorage off the Battery. The unfavorable weather detained her here for several days, but on the 26th instant it changed for the better, and she stood down the Narrows and thence out to sea, with her sails distended by the prosperous breezes that wafted her rapidly along toward the storied land whither she was bound. Making brief stoppings at Gibraltar, Port Mahon, and Malta, on the 16th of February, 1848, she anchored in the harbor of Smyrna, the Ismir of the Infidel, lying in the midst of an amphitheatre of lofty hills, towering above which is the ancient *Mons Pagus*, on whose slopes are spread out the blooming environs, and the perfumed groves of citrons, oranges, and lemons, that surround it; on the north, the Mysian Olympus rearing its hoary summit to the clouds, on the south the peaks of Tmolus clothed with their dark canopies of sombre oaks and funereal pines and melancholy cypresses, and between them a varied scene of floral loveliness,—green hills fringed with the richest vegetation, intermingled with delightful valleys, where the nectarine and almond, the fig and plantain, the acacia, the palm, the olive, the mulberry and the mimosa, flourish and blossom in an atmosphere which the keen frosts of winter can never penetrate,—and by the water's side the long lines of flat roofed houses, some well built of brick, and others shabbily constructed of planks, and offering a strange contrast to the many colored domes and lofty minarets that surmount the temples of the Moslem, while far as the eye can reach in the interior the landscape is dotted with pillared kiosks and handsome villas sweetly embowered amid the most luxuriant foliage, and the most beautiful flowers.

* The boats were so made, also, that they could be taken to pieces, if necessary, and carried on the backs of camels.

But however beautiful and impressive may be the view of Smyrna from the bay, on entering the city and examining it closely, the pleasing illusion is soon dissipated. "The Frank quarter is dirty, ill-paved, and narrow; in addition to which, it is almost rendered impassable by long strings of camels and porters carrying huge bales of cotton. The houses (excepting those of the consuls and principal merchants, which are large and commodious,) are miserably built; the sides consist often of planks, and when of bricks, the walls are too thin to keep out cold and damp. Neither windows nor doors are made to shut close; and if locks appear on the latter, it is too much to expect that they should be serviceable. There is a great lack of accommodation for travellers. The only inn in the town contains but a single decent room; and the noise of revelry is incessant. Beside this, there are three boarding houses, but furnished lodgings are not to be procured, nor can furniture be hired for a few weeks or months. The apparatus commonly used for supplying warmth to the body in cold weather is a brazier placed under the table, which is covered by a large cloth held by each member of the family circle up to the chin, to prevent the heat from escaping. Grates and stoves have of late years been introduced, but they are still rare, and to be seen only in Frank dwellings. The shops are little dark rooms, but tolerably supplied with European articles. The bazars, with their long covered rows of stalls, built with sundry precautions against fire, whose ravages are awfully common, are secured by iron gates closed at night."*

Smyrna was one of the cities that contested for the honor of being the birthplace of Homer, and, also, the seat of one of the seven apocalyptic churches. It contains not far from one hundred and fifty thousand inhabitants, most of whom are Turks, and the remainder Greeks, Jews, Armenians, Syrians, and Franks. The society is said to be quite agreeable, and strangers are welcomed with a cordiality and hospitality not usual in Turkish towns. The Greeks have assimilated

* Elliott's Travels, Vol. II, p. 39, et seq.

to the manners of the Franks in many respects, and adopted in great part the costumes of western Europe; but among the other classes, with the exception of the Franks and Jews, the Turkish dress prevails. A clear white or party-colored turban, or the crimson *tarbûsh*, with its long silken tassel of blue or black hanging down nearly to the shoulder of the wearer, is worn by the males, while the females conceal their dark locks and sallow faces—all but the bright flashing eyes—beneath the folds of the thin muslin *yashmak*. When the condition of the weather requires it, the former envelop themselves in the *grego*, a long coat, made of a thick brown or maroon-colored woolen stuff, with a hood, and trimmed with scarlet cord and facings—while the latter hide their *embonpoint* figures, and their loose, flowing sacks, and embroidered *shakshen*, beneath their worsted *ferajes* of yellow or purple, with their wide capes drooping down to the ground. The Frank adheres to the costume of his fathers, and the Jew still hides his sharp, cunning features, and the well-filled gipsire in his girdle, beneath the folds of his dark serge or cotton gabardine.

For the greater part of the year the climate of Smyrna is very pleasant, and tolerably healthy, but in the midsummer months, from June till September, the hot rays of the sun are concentrated by the surrounding hills, and pour down their burning flood upon the city without mitigation. The intense heat is ordinarily modified or tempered by the *inbat*, or sea-breeze, but when this fails, the atmosphere is almost suffocating. At such times business is entirely suspended, and the Franks always confine themselves to the pleasant shades of their country houses.

(3.) Leaving his vessel at Smyrna, Lieutenant Lynch proceeded to Constantinople—the Stambûl of the Turk—in accordance with his instructions, to obtain the permission of the Sultan to pass through his dominions in Syria, to the Dead Sea. This was cheerfully granted, and the requisite firman, addressed to the governors of Saida and Jerusalem, was placed in the hands of Lieutenant Lynch, who immediately returned to his party.

On the 10th of March, the Supply again got under way, in order to proceed to St. Jean d'Acre, where it was designed finally to disembark. Shortly after leaving the Gulf of Smyrna, the vessel was driven by a fierce levanter to take shelter in the bay of Scio. From thence she attempted to pass through the Icarean Sea, but another gale obliged her to bear away for Scala Nova, the ancient Neapolis, near which are the ruins of Ephesus, and of the famed temple of Diana, fired by the ambitious Erostratus. Sail was once more made on the 18th instant, and after a pleasant run of near seven hundred miles, the morning sun of the 25th was discovered flinging his rosy beams over the noble range of Jebel-Liban, once adorned with those gigantic cedars that added beauty and strength to the temple of Solomon; but now "the glory of Lebanon has departed," and the clustering firs alone conceal beneath their umbrella-like canopies the deep ravines and beetling precipices beneath, and the caves and sepulchres in which the Jews and Christians sheltered themselves in former days from the fury of the persecutor, while far above them, in the clear sunlight, glistens the eternal snow.

Early in the morning of the 25th, the Supply anchored off the town of Beïrût, in order to enable Lieutenant Lynch to have an interview with the Pasha, and obtain the requisite instructions to the subordinates of the latter to afford him assistance and protection on his route through the country, if necessary, and to dispatch a messenger to the Pasha of Damascus for a similar purpose.—Beïrût is a small town, with a population of only twelve or fifteen thousand, consisting principally of Turks, Druses, Armenians, and Franks In the days of antiquity it was known as Berytus ($Bηρυτος$), and was celebrated for its law school, established by Alexander Severus. In the legends of the Crusaders it is famous as the scene of St. George's victory over the dragon. It was for a long time under the dominion of the Roman Emperors, but subsequently fell into the hands of the Saracens.

During the crusades it was frequently captured by the champions of the Cross, and as often retaken by the Infidel. In the 17th century it became the capital of the renowned Druse Emir, Fakir-el-Din, and was afterwards attached by the Pasha of Acre to his jurisdiction, though it now constitutes, with the adjacent country, a separate pashalic.

Beïrût contains no public buildings of importance, and its houses and bazars are much like those of Smyrna—Turkish towns always presenting a singular uniformity in this respect. It is the seaport for the exportation of the cotton and silks of the Druses, which are manufactured here in considerable quantities. The silk goods of Beïrût, and especially the sashes, are highly esteemed. The surrounding country is fertile, and is well watered by the river of Beïrût (Nahr-Beïrût). There are extensive plantations of mulberry trees in the vicinity,* upon the leaves of which the silk-worms are fed, and interspersed among them are gardens and groves, richly garnished with flowers, and well stocked with the orange and the olive, the almond and the tamarind. The heat of the atmosphere is often intense, yet it is considerably modified by the numerous wells in the town and suburbs; and as the streets are kept much cleaner than is common in Eastern towns, it is usually a great deal more healthy.

The costume of the inhabitants of Beïrût differs but little from that noticed in Smyrna. The *learned* Druse (*akout*) does not lay aside his white turban, nor does his wife ever part with her ungainly *tantûr*, but the Turkish dress, in some or all of its features, prevails among every class except the Franks. The *tantûr* is a singular, not to say hideous appendage, peculiar to the Druses women, though occasionally seen among their neighbors, the Maronites; it is worn only

---

* The mulberry plants are here set in rows six or eight feet apart, and they are always cut off at a corresponding height, none but the fresh twigs being allowed to remain. The owners of the plantations allow the peasants one fourth of the silk for reeling it, gathering the leaves, and taking care of the worms. The cocoons are kept in reed inclosures, called sheds, though they have no roofs.

by those who are married, or by the unmarried of the highest rank, and when once assumed is never laid aside. It is a tube, made of tin, or plated silver, or gilt, according to the means of the wearer, about eighteen inches long, and resembling a horn. At the base it is from three to four inches in diameter, and tapers gradually to the point where it is about an inch across. It is fastened to the head by means of a spring, balanced by three heavy tassels hanging down on the opposite side, and projects either from the centre of tl ˟o-head or from one side, at an angle of forty-five degrees, ʌ ˃ the horn of a unicorn. From the tip, depends a ʰite transparent veil, that floats down to the breast, and serves to conceal the features when desired.

In the afternoon of the 28th of March, the Supply once more got under sail, and, continuing her southerly course, past the memorable cities of Sidon and Tyre, anchored before the walled village of Haifa, under Mount Carmel. This steep promontory forms the south-western extremity bay of Acre, and is from fifteen to eighteen hundre above the level of the sea. Far to the east stretche plain of Jezrael, the ancient Megiddo, so often dyed wiᵗ blood of the warring hosts who have here contenᵈ the victory, while to the south lies the lovely valley of Sharon, inclosed between the hills of Samaria and Galilee, and adorned with the beautiful flowers of the cistus which have so often elicited the admiration of the traveller and the encomiums of the poet. On the opposite side of the bay, at a distance of sixteen miles, is St. Jean d'Acre, the Ptolemais of the Greek, and the Akka of the Saracen;* before whose walls the Lion-Hearted Richard and his gallant knights performed so many deeds of high emprise, and in later years the

---

* Upon the site of St. Jean d'Acre stood the ancient Hebrew, or Phœnician city, called Accho. From this the name of Akka was derived by the Saracens, and not from the church of St. Jean d'Acre, as Lieutenant Lynch erroneously supposes (Narrative, p. 122.) St. Jean d'Acre, the modern name of the town, was, of course, derived from the magnificent cathedral erected by the knights hospitallers of St. John.

" Child of Destiny," the future Emperor of France, was so completely foiled. It is famous, too, as the scene of the last desperate but useless struggle of the Knights of St. John.

St. Jean d'Acre once boasted of its handsome structures, uniting the grandeur and massiveness of ancient Gothic architecture, with the light arabesque work of the Saracen. All its fine public and private buildings were battered down and nearly destroyed, during the siege by Ibrahim Pasha, in 1 with the single exception of the white marble mosque of Djezzar Pasha, which is of a quadrangular form, and surmounted with a beautiful cupola supported on pillars brought from the ruins of Cæsarea. The cube-shaped houses are mostly built of stone, with flat mud roofs which form agreeable promenades.

(4.) The members of the exploring party, consisting of Lieutenant Lynch, Lieutenant Dale, Passed Midshipman Aulick, and eleven others, petty officers and seamen, landed at Haifa with their baggage and equipment—not forgetting the two boats—on the morning of the 31st of March, and encamped by the sea-shore.* The Supply then sailed for Jaffa, the ancient Joppa, and the seaport to Jerusalem, from whence the "military chest" of the Expedition was forwarded to the British Consul at the ancient capital of Judea.

Horses having been procured from Acre, the party commenced moving from their encampment on the morning of the 1st of April. But the Arabian steeds seemed to be conscious that the day was a privileged one, and so determined to fool their new friends " to the top of their bent." The boats were secured upon the trucks, and the horses duly harnessed; but when the word was given to start, the latter showed off all their fine points with perfect delight, except that of go-ahead-ativeness. They kicked and pranced, and foamed and reared, but not an inch forward would they

* In addition to the above, Henry Bedlow, Esq., and Dr. Henry J. Anderson, joined the party as volunteers, and rendered efficient service in conducting the scientific examinations made by the Expedition.

budge. Coaxing and beating were alike found of no avail, and the boats were then taken off and sent across the bay by water. The difficulty was not yet removed, however, and the brutes still protested against the unaccustomed load. Backed by a Bedawi on the desert they could outstrip the wind, but they were wholly unused to draught, and had no mind to change positions with the patient ox, and the stubborn, yet generally good natured mule. Still, after a long and tiresome struggle, by dint of supplication and entreaty, intermingled with kicks and cuffs without number, they were finally forced along within a couple of miles of St. Jean d'Acre.

While the necessary preparations for the overland march were being completed, the party encamped on the river Namàanè, or Belus. After a protacted and fruitless parley with Sa'id Bey, the governor of Acre, a private treaty was concluded with the Sherîf Hazzâ of Mecca, a lineal descendant of the Prophet, and 'Akîl Aga el Hasseé, a powerful border sheikh, who agreed to accompany the expedition, and to bring with them ten spears, for a reasonable compensation. The Sherîf was a fine old Arab nobleman, small in stature, but lithe and active in his movements, possessing intelligent features and a dark Egyptian complexion. 'Akîl was a sort of Murat of the desert, a model of personal beauty, and a noble specimen of the Arabian Bedawin. His complexion was a soft olive, whose feminine appearance was relieved by the dark flashing eye and swelling nostril indicative of the warrior's soul that beat within his bosom. In form he was another Antinoüs, presenting a muscular development in which elegance and strength were beautifully and harmoniously combined. Attired in a scarlet cloth pelisse, with its rich embroidery of gold—the dark masses of his glossy black hair half concealed beneath his crimson *tarbûsh*—and the long *ataghan* in his girdle ready to be clutched at a moment's warning—he seemed equally well fitted to enter the lists of Venus or of Mars.

In describing the Bedawin whom he saw during his tour through the Holy Land, the Rev. Mr. Fisk remarks,

that " they are for the most part, straight, upright, and gracefully formed. I have never met," says he, " with a lame or
deformed Bedawi. They are generally of a spare habit, muscular and sinewy. Their skins are of a fine, rich brown, very
like the color of the carefully roasted coffee-berry. Frequently
their skin has almost a transparent appearance, and is capable
of exhibiting emotion, in the rushing of the blood to the cheeks.
Their eyes are well set in their heads, and are sparkling, burning, quick, and intelligent. They have mostly thin spare
beards which they wear untrimmed. They possess immense
energy and activity, and are capable of enduring fatigue; all
of which their most abstemious habits tend to cherish. · Their
step, when in the desert, is firm, agile, and graceful. They
walk as nature intended. They have never been drilled into
awkwardness by dancing and posture masters. Every muscle,
tendon and sinew, performs its proper office. If asked to
mention, the best specimen of untutored, manly gracefulness
of bearing, I have ever met with, I would try and depict a
young, healthy Bedawi Arab. And their simple attire is as
graceful as their persons, though consisting of but slender
and uncostly materials. Next to the skin they wear a tunic
or shirt of unbleached, coarse linen, open at the throat and
chest, and extending a little below the knees, the legs being
left bare. The sleeves are wide and flowing, and admit of
being thrown up to the shoulder, so as to leave the arm unin-
cumbered, when needed for the use of the sabre. This garment is gathered round the loins by a broad, stiff leather
girdle, in which is fixed the long, crooked knife, with a blade
of about eighteen inches long—a fearful weapon in a dextrous
hand. From the girdle is suspended, also, the flint and steel
for firing their matchlock guns; and also a pouch for tobaccco,
commonly made of lizard skin. Slung from the neck, they
wear a belt containing several rounds of ammunition; while
by the side is usually suspended a strong iron-hilted sabre,
and behind the shoulders a long matchlock gun, sometimes
ornamented with bits of mother-of-pearl. On the head they
wear the *tarbûsh,* or skull cap, made of crimson felt, with a

blue tassel at the crown, round which is bound a shawl or turban. Some, instead of the latter, wear the *keffieh*, which is a handkerchief, often of rich colors, placed diagonally open over the head. The foremost corner is thrown back, and the whole is left to fall in graceful folds over the shoulder, and bound round the temples by a fillet of camel's hair twisted into a rope. This latter head-dress is far more common among the Arabs on both sides of the river Jordan, than among those of the more southern parts of the Desert. The attire of all Bedawin, except the very poorest, is completed by an outside flowing mantle, of a very graceful shape—sometimes blue, now and then crimson—but more commonly of a fawn color, marked with broad stripes of dark brown. The former are generally of woolen cloth; the latter of camel's hair. They commonly go barefoot; but those who can afford such a luxury, have sandals of fish skin, which are made at Tor, in the peninsula of Sinai. They, however, use them only occasionally, when the sands are intensely hot, or the mountain passes sharp and rugged. With such a costume—so picturesque and graceful, it is no wonder that they should produce, at first, a startling effect upon a European mind, when seen in connection with their *wild-bird-o'-th'-wilderness* bearing. Their garments appear as if they had never been new—they are so frayed and worn; and often are little better than rags—yet not the less graceful for that; and their weapons, doubtless, have passed from father to son, for several generations."[*]

The remarks of Mr. Fisk are more particularly applicable to those tribes inhabiting the peninsula of Sinai; the male members of which usually compose the escorts of caravans, or of parties of travellers, proceeding to Jerusalem, by way of Mount Sinai, Akabah, Wâdy Mousa, and Hebron. But all these different families of the descendants of Ishmael resemble one another in their more important and most striking characteristics; and each individual is a type of his class. Bold, fierce, and courageous; proud and intractable; possess-

* Fisk's Memorial of the Holy Land.

ing powers of physical endurance rarely equalled; prompt in danger; terrible in battle,—yet kind and affectionate in his intercourse with his family; ever ready to face any peril in defence of his creed, to accomplish revenge, or gratify his propensity for plunder; never-tiring and relentless in the pursuit of an enemy, but adhering to a friend with the devotion of a brother: murdering and robbing with impunity those not under his protection, but, where his word and faith have been plighted, faithful and reliable to the last—such, in brief, is the character of the Bedawi warrior, who roams at will through the desert wilderness of Judea, and along the sandy terraces overlooking the valley of El-Ghor.

(5.) It having been satisfactorily proved that the horses of Araby, however useful in their appropriate sphere, were wholly unfitted for hauling the boats over the mountain ridges between Acre and the Lake of Tiberias, though the distance barely exceeded thirty miles, Lieutenant Lynch had recourse to the never-failing "ship of the desert"*—the *jemel* of the Arab. A pair of camels were harnessed to each truck, and one attached in front as a leader; a number of the same animals were also provided to relieve the former, and to carry the baggage of the party, while each one of the officers and men was mounted on a fine Arabian *destrier*.

On the morning of the 4th of April, they commenced the overland march. Crossing the beautiful plain of Acre, empurpled with the glorious dyes of the anemone, and sprinkled all over with the beautiful blossoms of the daisy, the white and crimson and golden flowers of the aster, the pale asphodel, the scarlet pink, the variegated convolvulus, and the bright-tinted cyclamen,—they soon commenced the ascent of the hills

---

* According to Sir William Jones, the ancient Arabian poets were fond of comparing their favorite animal to a ship; and among the extracts which he gives, illustrative of this fact, are the following:—

"Long is her neck [the camel's]; and when she raises it with celerity, it resembles the stern of a ship, floating aloft on the billowy Tigris."

"Ah! the vehicles which bore away my fair one, on the morning when the tribe of Malee departed, and their camels were travelling the banks of Deda, resembled large ships."

beyond, which were richly carpeted along their slopes with the purest green verdure, and dotted with clumps of figs and apricots, and groves of olives and pomegranates, amid whose branches many a feathered songster discoursed "most eloquent music," and whose emerald foliage seemed so refreshing to the eye, in contrast with the glassy appearance of the ocean, and the hot sandy beach.

A short distance beyond Acre, in a south-easterly direction, was the village of Abelin,* the mountain fortress of the Sheikh 'Akīl, perched on its eyry-cliff high above the southern slope of the plain. Here the cavalcade was joined by the Arabian Escort. Including the Sherîf and 'Akīl, with their servants, there were, in all, fifteen Bedawin; this addition making the total number of the whole party, counting the interpreter and cook hired for the occasion by Lieutenant Lynch, to be thirty-one. 'Akīl was dressed in a long flowing *āba*, or cloak, of a green color, a red *tarbûsh*, and white trowsers of ample dimensions; while the Sherîf wore a rich cloak embroidered with silver, and underneath a spencer and trowsers of the finest olive-colored cloth. Their followers and attendants were enveloped in dark purple *ābas*, and their swart faces half hidden beneath their yellow *kōofeeyahs*, or *keffiehs*, which were bound round with cords of camel's hair, dyed black. All were armed with spears eighteen feet long, some of which were tufted with beautiful ostrich feathers.

When in motion, the united party presented an imposing and picturesque appearance. The Americans on their fine-spirited horses—the long line of camels—the carriages and boats, each of which bore its tiny flag of mingled stripes and stars—the Arabs on their caracoling steeds, leading the head of the column, or darting over the distant hills, in front, in

---

* Lieutenant Lynch hazards the conjecture, (Narrative, p. 140, note.) that Abelin may be the Abilene, or Abila, mentioned by St. Luke, (chap. iii. 1st verse.) As the former had previously exhibited (p. 43) his limited knowledge of history, in making Old Noll the successor of the Merry Monarch, Charles II, it is not strange that he should be equally mistaken in regard to Biblical topography. The true Abila, to which the apostle refers, was located to the north-west of Damascus.

flank, or in rear, as videttes—and the glistening carbines and flashing spears—all combined to produce a most attractive sight, which excited the curiosity, and called forth the wondering gaze, of the few *fellahîn* that were seen along the line of the route. Occasionally, an Arab village would be passed, and many a dark eye would then scan the equipments of the cavalcade, and watch its movements as it wound its way through the valleys and plains, through the rocky defiles, and over the hilly slopes.

Usually, the villages of the Arabian peasantry (*fellahîn*), as well as of the more aristocratic class to which 'Akîl and his followers belonged, who think it beneath their dignity to cultivate the soil, and spend most of their time upon horseback, and live mainly by plunder and extortion, are picturesquely situated, near the summit of some lofty hill, in a position not easily accessible to an enemy. Most of the houses are but one story in height. They are of a cubical shape, and built of uncemented stones, with flat mud roofs, sometimes surrounded with balustrades, two or three feet high, made of twigs wattled closely together. Inside they are most commonly quite mean and filthy. The floors are of mud, and the rafters begrimed with smoke and dirt. A pot of coffee is almost always simmering amidst the embers in the centre of the floor, but its delicious aroma is entirely lost in the fumes of tobacco proceeding from the *chibouque* or *narghilé*, or the odor of the burning camel's dung, which constitutes the only fuel used by the Arab, that impregnates everything, and taints the atmosphere for miles around. Each house has a dome-roofed oven near it, made of mud, in which the family bake their bread. Hovels for sheltering the favorite horse or horses of the Arab are seen once in a while, but they are extremely rare, and the same roof not unfrequently covers both the steed and his master.

(6.) After leaving Abelin, the Expedition crossed a ridge bounding the plain sloping down to the Syrian coast, and soon after entered the Wâdy en Nafakh, usually called the

Blowing Valley,* which is flanked by high hills covered with
an abundance of wild flowers and grass, and with white oak
trees of a stunted growth. In the midst of this valley, and
in the land of Zebulon, the party halted for the night. Early
in the morning of the 5th instant, the tents were struck and
the march resumed. Passing between Nazareth and Cana
of Galilee—the residence in early life, and the scene of the
first miracle of our Saviour—they encamped, about the middle of the afternoon, near Tŭrân, a fortified Arab village,
imbosomed amid thrifty groves and orchards of olives. During the day, a number of sharp and abrupt ridges had been
passed by the cavalcade. The road was a mere mule-track,
and it was often necessary to deviate from it. Where the
hills were so steep that the descent was difficult, the camels
were detached from the trucks, and the latter let down with
ropes.

On the 6th of April they passed through a rich undulating
country, dotted with uninclosed fields of horse-beans, wheat,
barley, and millet, and with patches of melons, pumpkins,
and cucumbers, alternating, now and then, with grassy
slopes, with dense clumps of the purple merar, and with
bright parterres sprinkled with the blue convolvulus and the
scarlet anemone, and with beautiful groves, where the white
blossoms of the olive, and the crimson flowers of the pomegranate, peeped out from amid the light green foliage of the
fig and the apricot, that shaded and relieved, but could not
conceal, their gorgeous dyes. About the middle of the afternoon, the summit of the dividing ridge was reached, and
glimpses were obtained of the Sea of Galilee, and the mountains of Bashan piled up to the clouds on its further shore.
The prevailing formation, hitherto, had been limestone, but
nodules of quartz were now frequently seen, and an abundance of trap entirely destitute of minerals. Far to the right
trended a long range of crateriform slopes, all indicating the
volcanic character of the country that lay beyond.

* The literal meaning of *Wâdy en Nafakh*, is " *The Valley, or Ravine, of the*
Winds."

Shortly after commencing the descent, and after threading with great difficulty a number of precipitous valleys, the vanguard of the party emerged upon the high road leading from Jerusalem to Damascus, near the ancient town of Magdalen. The silvery surface of the lake was now distinctly visible, and a few hours' ride brought them to the ancient city of Tiberias—the Tibaria of the Jew, and the Tŭbarīyeh of his Moslem oppressor and taskmaster.*

* Tiberias was originally built by Herod, and named in honor of Tiberius Cæsar.

CHAPTER II.

(1.) How great changes have taken place, what various incidents have transpired, on the shores of the Lake of Genesareth,*
since the galleys of the Jew and the Roman contended upon
its placid waters for the mastery! The flourishing cities
that once adorned its borders lie crumbling in ruins, or have
disappeared forever. Tiberias still remains—the wreck of its
former greatness; but the doom pronounced against Capernaum the proud, against Chorazin and Bethsaida, has been
fulfilled.† The original possessor of the soil has been driven
forth by the Gentile, or lingers amid the scenes around
which cluster so many bright and dear recollections of by-
gone days, to be the victim of oppression, or the object of the
scoffing gibes and contemptuous sneers of the stranger who
has deprived him of his inheritance. The snowy peaks of
"breezy Hermon" yet bound the vision on the north; on the
east, the barren hills and precipitous ravines of Anti-Libanus
wear the same dreary and desert aspect as in days of yore;
and on the west, the cultivated slopes are still adorned with
waving corn, with fragrant groves, and "radiant fields of
asphodel." But all beside is changed. The towns and cities
are no longer the same, and a new people have established
themselves in the land. The victorious banners of Tancred

---

* The Sea of Galilee is also called the Sea of Tiberias and the Lake of Genesareth (Gennezareth. Genesar, Chinnereth, or Cinneroth.)

† Matthew xi, 20–24.

and Saladin have been alike mirrored in the clear waters,— the Christian and the Infidel have rejoiced in alternate triumph,—the Frank and the Turk have each, in turn, succumbed to the other,—but after ages of war and bloodshed, the Mussulman is left in undisturbed possession of the sacred places of Israel.

The Sea of Galilee, or Lake of Genesareth, is, strictly speaking, an expansion of the river Jordan, occupying a basin formed amid the surrounding hills. It is about sixteen miles in length, from north to south, and between five and six miles in breadth. On the east it is bordered by precipitous mountains, for the most part rising abruptly from the water's edge; but on the west, the banks slope gradually upwards to the plain of Zebulon. As the shore outline is almost unbroken, and the margin nearly destitute of trees, while a boat, or sailing craft of any kind, is scarcely ever seen, the aspect of the lake is cheerless and monotonous, except when disturbed by the occasional squalls issuing from the ravines, similar to that which was hushed in an instant by the simple command of the Saviour, "Peace, be still!"—yet its broad and unruffled surface, "added to the impression under which every Christian pilgrim approaches it, gives to it a character of unparalleled dignity."*

During the rainy season, the depth of the water in the lake is considerably greater than at other times, but after a rise, the rapid evaporation which takes place in this warm climate soon causes it to fall. The greatest depth so far ascertained is one hundred and sixty-five feet. To the taste the water is cool and sweet, and it is said to possess medicinal properties. About a mile to the south of Tiberias are the hot baths or springs of Emmaus, the waters of which are salt and bitter, and strongly impregnated with sulphuretted hydrogen. Near them are several other springs, whose waters contain more or less mineral substances. Several varieties of the most delicious fish are found in the lake, which furnish the weary traveller with many an excellent repast.

* Dr. Clarke's Travels, Vol. IV, p. 216.

In regard to the geölogy of the surrounding country, the
general formation of the Libanus ranges is said to be car-
boniferous and mountain-limestone, and the higher parts seem
to consist of graüwacke, slate, and other transition rocks.
At the southern extremity of the lake, and on its eastern
shore, basalt, and igneous rocks of different kinds, are abundant.   The limestone is very porous, and easily affected by
air or water.   It abounds in fossil remains, and is rapidly worn
into hollows and caves, which have been formed into sepulchres, and in ancient days were the hiding places of the Jews
and Christians.   The soil of the slopes and terraces, and the
valleys and ravines, consists mainly of the decomposed *débris*
and *detritus* washed down from the mountains.   It is usually
quite productive; and were proper encouragement given to
the husbandman, or the requisite attention bestowed on the
cultivation of the ground, abundant crops would be obtained.
But agriculture is now in a languishing state, and the implements of husbandry are of the rudest description.   Acts of
oppression, of lawlessness and violence, are of frequent occurrence; and the poor *fellah* who plants his field of corn or
dhoura (*millet*,) or a patch of wild peas, (*kersenna*,) for his
camels, esteems himself quite fortunate if his crops are not
reaped by the rapacious Turk, or the wandering Bedawi.

In itself, the Sea of Galilee is by no means a striking feature in the scenery of Palestine; but there is scarce a mountain or a rock, a town or a ruin, a tree or a shrub along its
shores, but is vocal with its scripture legend.   Upon its western borders, in the city of Capernaum, dwelt Jesus himself.
On its verdant banks, fringed with the scarlet anemone, the
yellow marigold, and the pink oleander, he called his disciples,
and made them "fishers of men."   Here is the Mount of
Beatitudes, upon whose summit he delivered that noble sermon
which contains the whole duty of man.   Here he performed
the miracle of the loaves and fishes; here he healed the sick
and cleansed those who were diseased; and here he preached
the gospel of mercy and love.   In yonder field, now covered
with the growing corn, the famishing disciples fed themselves

upon the Sabbath day; and on that tufted hillock, where the *hedda** makes its nest, stood their Master, after his glorious triumph over death and the grave, when he bade them cast their net on the right side of the ship, and they should find.†

With the exception of Tiberias, there are no towns of particular importance on the banks of the lake, except as connected with the localities of Scripture. A short distance north of the former is the miserable village of Mejdel, the ancient Magdala, and the birth-place of Mary Magdalene; but all the other places of interest are in ruins, and in some cases it is difficult even to ascertain their sites with any degree of precision. Tiberias is a walled town, and contains from fifteen hundred to two thousand inhabitants; one thousand of whom are Jews, and the remainder are Mussulmans. It contains two synagogues, and a dilapidated fortification usually tenanted by a few Turkish soldiers. The private houses are built in the same manner as those of the villages in the interior, though they often have several rooms, and occasionally stone floors. The streets are crooked and narrow; and, as the owners of the fields lying in the immediate vicinity all reside within the walls, they are often obstructed with loaded camels, mules, and donkeys. Great numbers of swallows have their nests amid the ruins, and sometimes they are allowed to build their habitations inside of the occupied houses. Cleanliness is not one of the cardinal virtues of the inhabitants; vermin are pretty abundant; and Tiberias might be appropriately called, "the Paradise of Fleas."

(2.) Throughout Palestine, the condition of the Jews, as a general rule, is miserable in the extreme. In Tiberias, however, it is somewhat mollified; and though they are often made to feel the heaviness of the Turkish yoke, they are less exposed to indignities than in many of the other cities and towns in Palestine. This is one of the holy cities of the Jews, and is held in peculiar veneration by them. According to their traditions, Jacob resided here, and the advent of the expected Messiah is to take place on the shores of the

---

* The heron, or king-fisher.　　　　　　　　　　† John xxi, 6.

neighboring lake. Tibérias was an ancient seat of Jewish literature, and it now contains a sanhedrim consisting of seventy rabbis, who are constantly occupied in the study of the Talmud. They are supported principally by the contributions of European Jews, and to them are referred controversial matters of discipline by their brethren in all parts of the world.

It has often been remarked, that the snake-eyed and sharp-featured Israelite of the present day is very different, in personal appearance, from the tall and manly warriors who composed the armies of David, or the comely youth that graced the court of Solomon; and the male Jews, clad in their dark and unshapely gabardines, who may be seen in the synagogues of Tiberias, with their broad and narrow phylacteries, either plain or embroidered, chanting in a monotonous, but earnest tone, the lamentations of Jeremiah, do not constitute an exception to this remark. But the Jewish women, here as everywhere, are

> " Like a ladye from a far countree,
> Beautiful exceedingly."

Whether it be that the hardships and sufferings, the trials and perils, encountered by their race, have wrought less harshly upon their feelings, and that their fortitude and buoyancy of soul have proved sufficient to sustain them in every difficulty and adversity,—or that, as many among them still believe, they have escaped the curse pronounced upon those who reviled and scourged and crucified the Redeemer,*—it is undeniable, that in personal attractions, in gracefulness of form, in ease of movement, in beauty and symmetry of feature, and, withal, in kindliness and gentleness of spirit, they

---

* It is said that there was not a single Jewess seen among the crowd that scoffed at and maltreated the Son of God. A woman of Bethany poured upon his head the precious ointment, and wiped his golden locks with her hair. The daughters of Jerusalem wept over what they deemed his misfortunes. Holy women accompanied him to Calvary, and brought thither balm and spices: they sought him, too, at the sepulchre, and to Mary Magdalene was vouchsafed the privilege of first gazing upon those well-remembered features after he had risen from the dead.

far exceed their male companions. In the neighborhood of
the Eastern towns, at the wells and springs, groups of Jewish
damsels, or peasant women, may be seen, each one of whom,
in the style of her dress, in her complexion, manner, and appearance, will remind the Christian traveller of the Rebecca
whom Isaac loved. And it has been remarked by an intelligent female writer, who speaks from her own personal observation, that the common practice of carrying water on their
heads contributes a great deal to the uprightness and elegance of figure for which the women of Syria and Egypt are
remarkable. " So far from giving a curve to the spine, de-
pressing the neck, or in anywise shortening the growth of
the body, the resistance of the muscles seems to increase in
proportion to the pressure, and much elasticity of action is
the result. In some places, the springs are often a quarter of
a mile from the villages, and much below them, so as to render the ascent very toilsome : yet every day in the week may
be seen girls and women carrying these jars, containing not
less than fifteen quarts of water, on their heads, with a
natural grace not exceeded by the studied walk of a stage
dancer. A favorite manner with them, when seen by men
and when wishing to be coquettish, is to place both thumbs
through the jar handles, which has a very statue-like appearance. When unobserved, they generally tuck up their gowns
all round, showing their pantaloons. If in their best clothes,
they are seen with silver bracelets instead of glass ones,
and with similar rings round their ankles; with a silver relic
case hanging at their bosom; with long sleeves to their
gowns; and over it, if in winter, a cloth vest, if in summer,
one of bombazine; with ear-rings; and with a species of
ornament not known in England or France, silver rims of
mail or of coins which take in the oval of the face from the
temples to the chin, and have a very pretty effect. The girdles are fastened by two silver bosses as large as the bottom
of a tumbler, and they wear on their feet a pair of yellow
slippers." *

* Travels of Lady Hester Stanhope.

Very little change has been made for centuries in the dress of the Jewish women. The fabrics of which they are composed, are in some cases different, but the form and fashion are nearly the same. They wear short, narrow-skirted gowns, boddices, and wide pantalets gathered at the ankles. The boddice is left open in front, and underneath there is a thin gauze *chemisette* or stomacher, with pockets for the breasts—the shape of which is thus distinctly shown, and oftentimes the exhibition is so gross that it detracts very much from the appearance in other respects. The unmarried females wear their hair in tasteful plaits intermingled with ornaments, or suffer it to fall in long clustering ringlets over the neck and shoulders. But the married women are forbidden to expose their hair, though they make ample amends for regarding the prohibition, by ornamenting their heads with silver rims, and coins and gems, and with a great abundance of false curls.

(3.) 'The sacred Jordan' rises a few miles north of Bânias, the ancient Cæsarea Philippi, near the modern town of Hâsbeiya, in latitude 33° 26' N., and longitude 32° 35' E. It starts abruptly from beneath an escarped rock, forty feet high, on the western slope of Jebel-es-Sheikh, or Mount Hermon.* At its source, a small pool or fountain is formed, which is half hidden beneath the willow and plane-trees that twine their branches together above it, and beautifully fringed with wild roses and clematis, with white and pink oleanders, with the retem and the dianthus, with altheas and snap-dragons.

From its source at the foot of Anti-Libanus, the Jordan pursues a circuitous and impetuous course of more than forty miles, through the beautiful valley of Bakaäh, and the Ardh-el-Hŭleh (Land of Hŭleh),—receiving, meanwhile, the waters of the River of Bânias and its tributaries, and crossing the ferny lake of Hŭleh, the Merom of antiquity,—and, at length, opens out into the Sea of Tiberias, or Galilee, close

---

* The name 'Jordan' has been given to one of the tributaries of the main river, which is the outlet of a small pool, called Phiala; and the principal stream, which rises as stated in the text, is called the Hâsbeiya.

beside the ancient Bethsaida, whose reputed site on its eastern bank is still pointed out to the pilgrim. Throughout this whole distance, the valley of the river is enamelled with the brightest and most luxuriant vegetation. Mulberry orchards and olive groves cover the bottom lands, and the shelving slopes are adorned with fields of barley, wheat, and millet: with patches of vines and melons; and with beds of wild flowers, filling the air with their fragrance, and shaming with their richly varied hues the brilliant dyes of an Eastern sunset.

On its leaving the Sea of Galilee, the Jordan debouches shortly to the right, and then turning to the south, enters the narrow valley of El-Ghor. Henceforward it is even more sinuous than before; and, though it traverses only sixty miles of latitude in its progress to the Dead Sea, it actually makes full two hundred miles, according to the calculation of Lieutenant Lynch.[*] The Ghor is about three quarters of a mile in average width. On the east it is bordered by the barren mountains of Hauran, and on the west by a series of laminated hills worn by the rains into tent-like shapes, or truncated cones. The river has two banks,—one just above the channel which it has cut through the loose soil, and the other, something like five hundred feet above, running like a terrace along the rolling sand hills that form the surface of the upper plain.

The size of the stream, and the rapidity of the current, vary with the season. In February and March the floods occur, and its lower banks are then often overflowed by the melted snows of the Libanus ranges. In high water, it is from ten to seventeen feet deep, and the breadth varies from twenty-five to seventy yards. At one time it meanders slowly through a rich alluvial plain, and at another dashes

---

[*] Narrative, p. 265.—A proneness to exaggeration is characteristic of the statements of Lieutenant Lynch; and as he does not appear to have been very critical in the measurement of altitudes or distances, this estimate may be erroneous. Heretofore, the entire length of the Jordan has always been set down at one hundred and fifty miles.

swiftly between bold and precipitous banks from fifteen to thirty feet high.   Here it is a placid streamlet, softly laving the white fringy clusters of the asphodel, and the long plumy tresses of the willow and the oleander; and there, a mountain torrent, bounding and foaming and tossing over its rocky bed.

Numerous rapids and cascades obstruct the navigation of the river, and at its embouchure into the Dead Sea, where it is about one hundred and eighty yards across, it is thirteen hundred feet lower than its fountain head, at the foot of Mount Hermon.   In the course of its descent from the Sea of Tiberias to the Lake Asphaltites, it receives several tributaries. Those coming in on the west are mere torrents : the principal affluents on the east, are the Sheriat-el-Mandhur, (the ancient Jarmok, or Yermâk,) and the Jabok, which flows down through the Wâdy Zŭrka.   Below the mouth of this tributary, which is not far from twenty miles above the Dead Sea, the evidences of a volcanic formation multiply rapidly, and there seems to have been a depression of the whole bed of the river, south of this point, produced, as appearances would indicate, by some sudden convulsion of nature.   The water of the river is for the most part sweet; but now and then it is somewhat brackish, occasioned, doubtless, by the salt streams that mingle their contents with it.   Owing to the abundance of hot springs along the borders of the stream, and the heat of the climate, its temperature is quite warm.   It is usually of a white sulphurous color, and, except as has been mentioned, is free from any taste or smell.   According to the analysis of Dr. Marcet, it contains but about one three-hundredth part of the proportion of solid matter found in the water of the Dead Sea.*

To the biblical scholar, the Jordan is replete with interesting associations.   When Lot separated himself from Abram, he " chose him all the plain of Jordan."†   Its waters were divided when the Ark of the Covenant was carried into the stream, and the children of Israel, under Joshua their leader,

---

* Philosophical Transactions, 1807.   † Genesis xiii, 11.

"passed over right against Jericho."* Elijah performed a similar miracle just before he ascended to heaven in the chariot of fire, and, in company with Elisha, "went over on dry ground;" so, too, the latter, after the departure of his friend, with the mantle that fell from him, smote the waters, and "they parted hither and thither."† In later times, it has been celebrated as the sacred stream in which Jesus Christ received the rite of baptism from John the Baptist; and in commemoration of this event, at the Easter season, thousands of devotees, usually pilgrims to the Holy City, from every nation and clime in Christendom, repair to El Meshra'a, where it is said to have taken place, to bathe in the river on the anniversary, and "cleanse them from all unrighteousness."‡

(4.) After encountering and overcoming almost insuperable difficulties, the metallic boats transported by the American Exploring party overland from Acre, were finally launched upon the waters of the Sea of Galilee on the 8th of April. A third boat—said to be the only one on the lake—was purchased at Tiberias—in order to carry some of the lighter baggage, and the tents, after the arrival of the party at the Dead Sea. As the waters of the river were now subsiding, on the receipt of the firman, or *buyurŭldi*, of the Pasha of Jerusalem, addressed to "the Sheikhs and elders of the Arabs and keepers of the highways," requiring them to give assistance and protection, if necessary, to Lieutenant Lynch and his command, immediate preparations were made for the descent of the river. On the 10th instant, they left Tiberias,—Lieutenant Dale, with the Arabian Escort, and the scientific gentlemen who accompanied the Expedition as amateurs, following the right bank of the stream, and taking with him the loaded camels,—and Lieutenant Lynch accompanying the boats.

---

* Joshua, iii, 16. † II. Kings, ii, 8, 14.

‡ It has been quite fashionable to baptize the scions of royalty in water brought from the Jordan. That used on the occasion of the baptism of young Napoleon, was obtained by Châteaubriand. Some, or all, of Queen Victoria's children, have been similarly honored.

So tortuous was the course of the river, that at the close of the second day after leaving Tiberias, they were only twelve miles distant in a straight line from the Sea of Galilee. The boat purchased there was soon dashed to pieces amid the rocks and precipices over which tumbled the foaming waters; but the metallic ones suffered but little from the severe thumps which they received. No obstacle impeded the descent of the stream except the numerous rapids and cascades, many of which were from eleven to fifteen feet fall. In passing these, it was sometimes found necessary to attach ropes to the boats to lower them slowly down; at others, they made the leap boldly, trusting to fortune and the skilful hand that guided the helm; and at others still, while one or two remained in each boat, the rest sprang overboard, and clinging to its sides to steady it in the descent, floated along with it over the dangerous rapid or the plunging cascade.

A member of the party, in giving an account of the passage of one of these rapids, says :—" Presently we came near to the ruins of a bridge, in the immediate vicinity of which was a streaming rapid and a steep and dangerous fall; over this we had to pass somehow or other: there was no circumnavigating it: the fall was there, and we must dash over it at all hazard. We thought it right, however, first of all, to unload the boats on the banks, and then, ' neck or nothing,' firmly brave the danger: the word ' Ready !' was given— every precaution was taken—and with a thrilling interest the undaunted ' Yankee boys' guided the copper boat, for she took the lead, into the stream: and away they went, dashing ahead, all hands ready to jump overboard if she should strike the rocks and come ' broadside on' to the edge of the fall, and so slew round and capsize. But despite all their forethought and skill, ' she struck,' and slewed round with all hands in her, and dash she went into the midst of the fall. At this dangerous moment the little gig [the boat purchased at Tiberias] came over the rapid, jumping like a parched pea, and dashing at us, struck our boat ' amidships,' threatening to break us in two. We fortunately received no injury, but the poor little gig was broken to pieces. Then the iron boat dashed into the, midst of the stream, and leaped the dangerous fall without sustaining any damage."*

(5.) For several miles below the Sea of Galilee, the elevated plains lying along the valley of the Jordan are well cultivated, and fields of grain are quite abundant; but as you progress to the southward, this appearance of fertility gives place to a barren, and a wilder and more savage aspect. The terraces are now strongly marked, and continuous ranges of perpendicular cliffs, of a chalky color at the top, and a light brown at the base, border El-Ghor on either hand. Limestone is the prevalent formation, but huge blocks of trap and conglomerate, boulders of sandstone and quartz, fossil rocks, and perpendicular layers and columnar masses of basalt, are likewise found. The soil of the lower valley is a dark rich loam, or alluvion, occasionally interrupted by indurated clay and sand, which supports, for the most part, an exceedingly rank vegetation.

But although the upper plains along the southern part of the valley of the river are so deficient in vegetable life, a bright line of the richest verdure marks the course of the river throughout the whole distance. So luxuriant is this, that the stream itself is oftentimes completely hidden, and screened, by the dense thickets of trees and bushes, "the pride of Jordan," from the fierce sun that beats down in all its fury, as if in fulfilment of a curse, upon the barren hills and desert slopes of Palestine. Upon the borders of the stream, amid the mingled tufts of cane and reeds and grass, innumerable *wild flowers bloom and blossom. The scarlet anemone, the yellow marigold and daisy, the pink-flowered valerian, the* crimson *bâghuk,* the bright waterlily, the orange-colored *bisbâs* and *murur,* the white fringy asphodel, the purple clover, the medicinal briony, the pheasant's eye, and the scabiosa stellata, blend their choice dyes together. Tangled masses of shrubbery, of vines and osiers, shade or conceal the wild oats and mustard, the fennel and mallows, that grow beneath

* Montague's Narrative of the Expedition, pp. 156, 157.

them. White and pink oleanders display their clustering
flowers in every bight, and scent the air with their grateful
perfume. The beautiful acacia, and the stately plane-tree,
are occasionally seen. The tamarisk (*türfa*), and the willow
(*sifsaf*) abound through the whole length of the valley. The
swamp-like shores—often real jungles in appearance—here
and there present a lovely myrtle bower, and far inland may
be descried miniature forests of dwarf oaks and cedars.
Kelakh and *ghürrah* bushes are scattered along the terraces,
with the laurestinus, the arbutus, and the agnus castus.
The carob tree, the mala insana, and the pistachio, or tere-
binth (the *bütm* of the Arab) are seen, though but rarely;
and every turn of the river discloses the purple blossoms of
the osher tree, and the thorny branches of the *nübk*, or lotus.[*]

Few of the animals driven out from the thickets, in the
olden time, by the swelling of the river,[†] are now found in
the country. The principal ones at present known to exist,
are the gazelle, the fallow deer, the jackal, the panther, and
the *kelb-el-maya*, or water-dog. Wild fowl are tolerably
plentiful. The beautiful bulbul—its crimson wings and
scarlet head contrasting finely with the rich nutty brown of
its breast—trills its soft notes in the fragrant groves at even-
tide; and the sweet banks and woods echo till early dawn the
melodious songs of a thousand nightingales.[‡]

Wandering tribes of Bedawin occupy both shores of the
Jordan and the Dead Sea. At Kerak, near the eastern bank
of the latter, there are a number of Christian Arabs who
have a chapel of their own; but, generally speaking, all the
Arabs are Mussulmans. Some of them are bold, fierce and
warlike, and others timid, meagre, forlorn, and wretched
looking objects. All are treacherous and thievish. Ten

---

[*] This tree is also called by the Arabs the *sidr*. It is the *spina christi*, from
whose branches, as it is supposed, the crown of thorns worn by the Redeemer,
was plaited.

[†] Jeremiah, xlix, 19.

[‡]   "And Jordan, those sweet banks of thine,
          And woods, so full of nightingales."

                                        Lalla Rookh.

miles east of a line drawn from Jerusalem to Nabulus, they rob and plunder without fear or favor, except when intimidated by a display of superior strength, or when their good offices and their countenance and protection are secured beforehand by hiring them as an escort. The *fellahîn,* or peasantry, are miserable creatures. When it is stated that the poor *fellah* is the slave of the Bedawi or Turk, and that the *fellaha,* his wife, is also his drudge, nothing more need be added in regard to their condition. They live in filthy mud hovels, and subsist mainly on *pilau,* or boiled rice, which they eat by scooping it up and conveying it to their mouths in the hollow of their hands.

It is much the safest for travellers to pass down or ascend the Jordan, along its eastern bank, as the Arabs on the opposite shore are famed for their treacherous and cruel dispositions, and a score of other bad qualities; but on either route, a liberal distribution of presents or money can alone insure safety. The good will of the Sheikhs of the different tribes it is also important to secure, unless the escort is sufficiently strong to set at defiance the perils of the road.

(6.) In their descent of the river, the American boats passed safely over twenty-seven important rapids and cascades, besides a number of smaller ones. The voyage was not wanting, of course, in excitement; and whenever there was a lack of incident, the ruins of some old Roman bridge, or some locality celebrated in Scripture history, or an Arab village of mud houses, or goat's hair tents, filled with unkempt and unwashed children and slatternly Bedawîyeh, would be discovered, and suggest a hundred topics for discussion or reflection. Late in the evening of the 17th of April, they arrived at El-Meshra'a, the Pilgrim's Ford, but a few miles distant from the Dead Sea.

The morrow was the anniversary of the baptism of the Saviour. At three o'clock in the morning, says Lieutenant Lynch, " we were aroused by the intelligence that the pilgrims were coming. Rising in haste, we beheld thousands of torchlights, with a dark mass beneath, moving rapidly

over the hills.   Striking our tents with precipitation, we
hurriedly removed them and all our effects a short distance
to the left.   We had scarce finished, when they were upon
us:—men, women, and children, mounted on camels, horses,
mules, and donkeys, rushed impetuously by towards the
bank.   They presented the appearance of fugitives from a
routed army.   Our Arab friends here stood us in good stead;
—sticking their tufted spears before our tents, they mounted
their steeds and formed a military cordon round us.   But for
them we should have been run down, and most of our effects
trampled upon, scattered and lost.   Strange that we should
have been shielded from a Christian throng by wild children
of the desert,—Muslims in name, but pagans in reality.
Nothing but the spears and swarthy faces of the Arabs saved
us.   I had, in the meantime, sent the boats to the opposite
shore, a little below the bathing place, as well to be out of
the way as to be in readiness to render assistance, should
any of the crowd be swept down by the current, and in
danger of drowning.   While the boats were taking their
position, one of the earlier bathers cried out that it was a
sacred place; but when the purpose was explained to him,
he warmly thanked us.   Moored to the opposite shore, with
their crews in them, they presented an unusual spectacle.

"The party which had disturbed us was the advanced
guard of the great body of the pilgrims.   At 5, just at the
dawn of day, the last made its appearance, coming over the
crest of a high ridge, in one tumultuous and eager throng.
In all the wild haste of a disorderly rout, Copts and Russians,
Poles, Armenians, Greeks, and Syrians, from all parts of
Asia, from Europe, from Africa, and from far distant America, on they came; men, women and children, of every age
and hue, and in every variety of costume; talking, screaming, shouting, in almost every known language under the
sun.   Mounted as variously as those who had preceded them,
many of the women and children were suspended in baskets
or confined in cages; and with their eyes strained towards
the river, heedless of all intervening obstacles, they hurried

eagerly forward, and dismounting in haste, and disrobing with precipitation, rushed down the bank and threw themselves into the stream.

"They seemed to be absorbed by one impulsive feeling, and perfectly regardless of the observations of others. Each one plunged himself, or was dipped by another, three times, below the surface, in honor of the Trinity; and then filled a bottle, or some other utensil, from the river. The bathing-dress of many of the pilgrims was a white gown with a black cross upon it. Most of them, as soon as they were dressed, cut branches of the agnus castus, or willow; and, dipping them in the consecrated stream, bore them away as memorials of their visit. In an hour they began to disappear; and in less than three hours the trodden surface of the lately crowded bank reflected no human shadow. The pageant disappeared as rapidly as it had approached, and left to us once more the silence and the solitude of the wilderness. It was like a dream. An immense crowd of human beings, said to be 8000, but I thought not so many, had passed and repassed before our tents, and left not a vestige behind them."*

(7.) In their progress down the river, the Americans had occasionally been threatened with an attack from the roving Arabs, but thus far they had not been molested; and they continued on their way, after the departure of the pilgrims, without meeting any interruption. The gloomy mountains bordering upon the Salt Lake, had been visible in the after-noon of the previous day; and towards the close of the 18th of April, they reached the embouchure of the river, whose banks were here bordered with sedge and drift-wood, and presented a fit introduction to the dreary waste of waters that lay spread out in the dark chasm beyond. Proceeding directly to the western shore, the boats joined the land party at Ain-el-Feshka (the fountain of the Stride), and shortly after nightfall encamped in the vicinity of the fountain, and within hearing of the convent bell of Mar Saba.

* Narrative of Lieut. Lynch, p. 260, et seq.

CHAPTER III.

(1.) Lake Asphaltites, or the Dead Sea. Surveys and Explorations.—(2.) Dimensions. Depth. Analysis of the Water.—(3.) Physical Geography.—(4.) Animal and Vegetable Life.—(5.) Probable Position of the Cities of the Plain. Manner of their Destruction.—(6.) Return of the Exploring Party.

(1.) VARIOUS names have been given to the Dead Sea. Among the Jews, in earlier times, it was called the *Salt Sea*,* in allusion to the saline properties of its waters; and the *Sea of the Plain*,† probably with reference to the unfortunate catastrophe that occurred on the plain which it now occupies. At a later day, the prophets designated it as the *East Sea*,‡ in order to distinguish it from the Mediterranean, or West Sea. Josephus, and the Greek and Roman writers generally, call it *Lacus Asphaltites*, or the Asphaltic Lake, from the quantities of asphaltum, in a soft or liquid state, that float on its surface, and the inflammable bituminous stones found upon its shores. Its modern appellation of the "Dead Sea" (*Mare Mortuum*), is derived from the once popular superstition, that the atmosphere above and around it, like the fabled exhalations of the Upas tree, was tainted with poison, and that to drink of its water was certain death.§ In Syria it is known as *Al-Motanah*, or *Bähr Lüt*,

---

* Genesis, xiv, 3; Deuteronomy, iii, 17; Joshua, xv, 5.

† Deuteronomy, iii, 17; iv, 19.   ‡ Ezekiel, xlvii, 18; Joel, ii, 20.

§ "Reland, in his account of the *Lacus Asphaltites* (*Palæst. vol.* 1, *p.* 238), after inserting copious extracts from Galen, concerning the properties and quality of the water, and its natural history, proceeds to account for the strange fables that have prevailed with regard to its deadly influence, by showing that certain of the ancients confounded this lake with another, bearing the same appellation of Asphaltites, near Babylon; and that they attributed to it qualities which properly belonged to the Babylonian waters. An account of the proper-

—the latter being the term used by the descendants of Ishmael to perpetuate the remembrance of the escape of Lot from the fearful judgment of the Almighty.

Immediately upon the arrival of the American Exploring party on the shore of the Dead Sea, a dépôt was established at Aìn Jidy* (Engaddi), on the western bank, which was guarded by a few soldiers obtained from the Pasha of Jerusalem. The Sherîf and his servant remained at the dépôt, but 'Akîl and his Bedawin followers proceeded round the lake to Kerak, to establish a look-out for the party on the Arabian shore, and to make preparations for furnishing them with supplies, and ensuring their good treatment by the inhabitants, if they should decide to visit the land of Moab.

After a day of rest, on the 20th of April, the work of surveying and exploring the lake commenced. Diagonal soundings were made from shore to shore—a cast being taken every half-mile. The strait formed by the peninsula projecting from the eastern shore, was carefully and critically examined, in order to prove or disprove the existence of the ford mentioned by previous travellers in the Holy Land. Nothing of the kind was found. On the contrary, the bottom of the lake was ascertained to slope gradually upwards to its southern extremity. The boats proceeded as far in this direction as was possible,—the water having shoaled so much that they could go no further. Within three hundred yards of the southern shore, near the cave of Usdum (Sodom), the boats grounded in six inches; but several members of the party waded through the water to the land. The intense heat

ties of the Babylonian lake occurs in the writings of Vitruvius (8. 3), of Pliny (*H. N.* 35. 15) of Athenæus (2. 5), and of Xiphilinus, (p. 252.) From their various testimony, it is evident, that all the phenomena supposed to belong to the lake Asphaltites near Babylon, were, from the similarity of their names, ultimately considered as the natural characteristics of the Judæan lake—the two Asphaltites being confounded."—Dr. Clarke's Travels, vol. iv, p. 400.

* Lieutenant Lynch twice refers (Narrative, pp. 291, 323) to the "Diamond of the Desert," mentioned by Sir Walter Scott in his "Talisman" as being at or near Aìn Jidy (the fountain of the kid). He is certainly in error in this respect. The fountain in which Kenneth and Saladin reposed, was that of Aìn-es-Sultan, or the fountain of Elisha, near Jericho.

pouring down into this narrow chasm, and reflected from the smooth surface of the sea, and the barren mountain sides, soon forced them to retire, however; and on the 28th of April, the surveys being ended, they all returned to camp.

While occupied in the examination of the southern part of the sea, a singular curiosity was discovered on the western shore, at the foot of the salt mountain of Usdum, or Sodom, and about two miles from the south end of the lake. This is described by Lieutenant Lynch, as "a lofty, round pillar, standing apparently detached from the general mass, at the head of a deep, narrow, and abrupt chasm. We immediately pulled in for the shore," says he, "and Dr. Anderson and I went up and examined it. The beach was a soft, slimy mud, encrusted with salt, and a short distance from the water, covered with saline fragments and flakes of bitumen. We found the pillar to be of solid salt, capped with carbonate of lime, cylindrical in front, and pyramidal behind. The upper or rounded part is about forty feet high, resting on a kind of oval pedestal, from forty to sixty feet above the level of the sea. It slightly decreases in size upwards, crumbles at the top, and is one entire mass of crystallization. A prop, or buttress, connects it with the mountain behind, and the whole is covered with *débris* of a light stone color. Its peculiar shape is doubtless attributable to the action of the winter rains. The Arabs had told us in vague terms that there was to be found a pillar somewhere upon the shores of the sea; but their statements in all other respects had proved so unsatisfactory that we could place no reliance upon them."*

It is very probable that this is the same pillar which Josephus saw, and which he avers to be identical with that into which Lot's wife was transformed;†—but its position, on the opposite side of the lake from Zoar, shows plainly enough that his theory is incorrect. The supposed identity rests merely on traditionary authority, though many, doubtless, have believed in it, who were ignorant of the topography

* Narrative, p. 307.   † Antiquities of the Jews, book 1, chap. 12.

of the adjacent country, and whose credulity overbalanced their judgment.*

The task of surveying the lake, and making the necessary soundings, was found to be attended with a great deal of difficulty and inconvenience. The heat of the sun, whose burning rays were concentrated within the opening between the mountain walls bordering the lake on either hand, was almost overpowering; the arms and clothes of the party were completely coated over with the greasy salt; and their hands and faces, eyes, lips, and nostrils, smarted with the incrustations formed by the spray that dashed over them. On the 30th of April, Lieutenant Lynch crossed over the sea to Moab; several days were spent in visiting the interesting localities, and cruising along the Arabian shore; and on the 5th of May—the work of exploration being now nearly ended—he returned with his party to Ain Tŭrâbeh, whither the camp had been removed in charge of the Sherîf. While the Americans were on the eastern side of the sea, they were several times in danger of being attacked by the unfriendly Arabs, but the watchfulness of the party prevented a surprise, and the fidelity of 'Akīl and his little band, united to their own firmness and intrepidity, secured them from molestation.

(2.) Widely differing statements have been made, from time to time, in regard to the dimensions of this body of water,—some authorities making it fifty, others seventy, and others still one hundred miles in length, and from twelve to twenty-five in breadth. Dr. Robinson supposed it to be about fifty miles long and twelve miles broad. His observations are usually very accurate; but the actual measurements of Lieutenant Lynch and his party reduce the size of the lake

---

* Clemens of Rome mentions the same pillar referred to by Josephus. Justin the Martyr, Irenæus, and Tertullian, also speak of it; they allege that it gave periodical evidence of its feminine nature, and Irenæus seriously questions how its members remained so long entire. Reland, the learned orientalist, relates a tradition,—that whenever a part of the pillar was washed away by the rains it was supernaturally renewed,—which might have relieved the good and pious, but superstitious father, from his difficulty.

from even his estimate. According to those, it appears to be
a trifle over forty miles in length, and its average breadth is
between eight and nine miles. Undoubtedly, the dimensions
vary with the season; but they can never exceed those determined by the American Expedition, to any great extent,
as they were ascertained but a short time after the season of
floods, and before the volume of water swollen by 'the rising
of the Jordan' could have been seriously diminished by evaporation.

In regard to the depth of water in the sea, there has likewise been a great diversity of opinion. Some travellers have
fancied, from the whirlpools produced by the current flowing
in from the Jordan, and the returning eddy, that it was
bottomless; and others, with greater haste than wisdom, have
adopted the plausible supposition that, inasmuch as it had
no visible outlet, there must be some subterraneous communication with the Mediterranean sea, though the latter is thirteen hundred feet above it. The soundings of the American
Exploring party show that the greatest depth of the water—
at a point three miles distant from the Arabian shore and
twelve miles from the mouth of the Jordan—is two hundred
and eighteen fathoms, or upwards of thirteen hundred feet;
and that from this point, the bottom slopes upward on every
side, but more gradually towards the western shore and the
southern extremity of the lake.

The water of this sea is more salt than that of the ocean,
or of any other similar body of water in the known world.
It contains about one-fourth part of its weight of saline contents in a state of perfect desiccation, and forty-one parts in
a hundred in a state of simple crystallization. An analysis
of the water was made by Dr. Marcet, in 1807, who says
that it "is perfectly transparent, and does not deposit any
crystals on standing in close vessels. Its taste is peculiarly
bitter, saline, and pungent. Solutions of silver produce from
it a very copious precipitate, showing the presence of marine
acid. Oxalic acid instantly discovers lime in the water.
The lime being separated, both caustic and carbonated alka-

lies readily throw down a magnesian precipitate. Solutions of barytes produce a cloud, showing the existence of sulphuric acid. No alumine can be discovered in the water by the delicate test of succinic acid combined with ammonia. A small quantity of pulverized sea salt being added to a few drops of the water, cold and undiluted, the salt was readily dissolved with the assistance of gentle trituration, showing that the Dead Sea is not saturated with common salt."* As the result of his analysis, Dr. Marcet ascertained that the proportions of the following substances contained in one hundred grains of the water, were:—

		Grains.
Muriate of Lime - - - - - - -		3.920
Muriate of Magnesia - - - - - - -		10.246
Muriate of Soda - - - - - - -		10.360
Sulphate of Lime - - - - - - - .. -		0.054
		24.580

Similar results have subsequently been obtained by other scientific men who have examined and analyzed the water.

Its density, too, is greater than the water of the Atlantic. It was ascertained by Lieutenant Lynch, distilled water being regarded as 1, that that of the Atlantic was 1.02, and that of the Dead Sea 1.13. The boats of the Expedition drew one inch less water on the sea than upon the Jordan, and when they encountered the waves they seemed to strike against them with a dull heavy plash like molten lead. Such is the buoyancy of the water that it is difficult for a bather to dive, or to keep his feet down; and if he lies upon his back, and draws his knees up and places his hands on them, he can roll over with scarce any exertion. It was once said that nothing could sink in the bottom of this sea, but this, of course, is wholly fabulous.

To the touch the water seems greasy, and causes the hands and face to smart with a sort of prickly sensation. It is inodorous, except in the vicinity of the sulphurous thermal springs that abound along the shores; but it is always exces-

* Philosophical Transactions, 1807.

sively bitter and offensive to the taste. It likewise possesses petrifying qualities, and the stunted trees and bushes that grow upon its banks and die, and the drift wood brought down by the Jordan, are preserved for a long time from decay by the salts with which they become saturated.

"My friend and fellow-traveller, Mr. Erskine," says Mr. Fisk, "bathed in the Dead Sea, and found the water extremely buoyant. I could not quite make up my mind to the experiment; but I tasted the water. It is impossible to express the intensity of its nauseousness, when taken in sufficient quantity, and retained long enough to act upon the palate. It has two distinct flavors when first tasted, which soon unite and make a most loathsome compound. The first is of extremely pungent saltness, and capable of excoriating the palate. The other is sheer bitterness—and so bitter, that it seems to penetrate the skin of the mouth. Though I took no more than about half a wine glass full in my mouth, and did not swallow any, yet my palate was saturated with it, and the sensation remained during the day."*

As there is no outlet through which the waters accumulating in this reservoir can be discharged, the evaporation that takes place must be very rapid; for, in addition to the Jordan, it receives the contents of several other tributary streams, and there are a number of springs along its shores, some of which pour their waters into the sea, though others are absorbed by the sand. According to the estimate of Dr. Shaw, the Jordan alone discharges daily, upon an average, 6,090,000 tons of water. Lieutenant Lynch also made an estimate; but his figures appear to have startled him, and he has therefore withheld them from the public. "The streams," says he, "from the fountains of Tŭrâbeh, Aïn Jidy, and the salt spring near Muhăriwat, were almost wholly absorbed in the plains, as well as those running down the ravines of Sudeir, Sêyâl, Mubŭghghik, and Humeir, and the torrent between the Arnon and the Callirohoe. Taking the mean

* Memorial of the Holy Land.

depth, width, and velocity of its more constant tributaries, I had estimated the quantity of water which the Dead Sea was hourly receiving from them at the time of our visit, but the calculation is one so liable to error, that I withhold it. It is scarcely necessary to say, that the quantity varies with the season, being greater during the winter rains, and much less in the heat of summer."*

After the notion in regard to a subterraneous outlet began to be questioned, and the process of evaporation constantly going on came to be better understood, it was said that the rapidity of the latter was occasioned by the volcanic fires at the bottom of the sea. Scientific, as well as uneducated men, seemed determined to make what was peculiar still more strange and singular, and to explain everything, if the expression may be used, in as difficult a manner as possible. A simple fact, easy to be ascertained, puts an end at once to the theory of subterraneous fires. At the surface of the sea the water is from twenty to thirty degrees warmer than below, and at the bottom it varies but little from 50 deg. No doubt, the evaporation is very rapid; but we must remember that the sea is confined between two lofty walls of mountains, in a narrow chasm, and that during the greater part of the year, the burning rays of a tropical sun are poured directly upon it. No gentle breezes fan its waters and cool the air; but the hot simoom of the Arabian Desert that whistles through the dark gorges of Wâdy-el-Arabah, and disturbs its usually silent waters, produces the same effect with the intense heat.

Some idea may be formed with regard to the rapidity of the evaporation, from the fact that the atmosphere, within a wide circuit around the lake, is impregnated with the substances contained in its waters. The fetid smell noticed by every traveller was once supposed to be a property peculiar to the sea itself; but this is now admitted to be produced by the hot sulphurous springs on its margin. Everything metal-

* Narrative, p. 377.

lic exposed to the effects of the atmosphere is bronzed by it. The shores of the sea, the stones on the beach and in the torrent beds opening towards it, and the sides of the adjacent mountains, are coated with saline incrustations.* This is especially the case in the lower or southern part of the lake, where the mountains are more abrupt, and the water much shallower,—in general not averaging over thirteen feet in depth. A hazy cloud, as if of heated vapor, hangs suspended over the southern sea, and to the north there is a thin transparent cloud, of a purple tinge, almost always to be seen, except when driven away by the fierce sirocco.

Popular credulity at one time went so far as to maintain that the atmosphere in the vicinity of the Dead Sea, at certain seasons, was fatal to animal life. The mineral substances contained in its waters are certainly not poisonous, and there is no vegetable decomposition to render the air impure. The sulphur springs load the atmosphere with offensive odors, but it is far from being pestilential. Strangers visiting the sea complain of the drowsy feeling produced, and the oppressive sensation about the head which they often experience. But these effects are to be attributed as much to the heat of the sun as to the character of the atmosphere; and it is not at all strange that those unused to the climate should be attacked with fevers, occasioned by exposure in a place where its evils are enhanced in a tenfold degree.

Without a more careful and accurate analysis of the waters of the Dead Sea, and its tributaries, than has yet been made, it would be difficult to account satisfactorily for the existence of the saline substances found in the former; but there is every reason to believe, that the Jordan, and the other streams that flow into it, bring down a great proportion of them, and that the large deposit now there is the gradual accumulation of ages. This idea seems to derive strength from the fact, that this deposit is much the greatest at the

* Stones lying exposed on the shores of the Jordan, twenty miles above the Dead Sea, are often coated with salt; but this is probably a deposition of the atmosphere carried thither by the simooms which blow in this direction.

southern end of the lake, where the earthy matters and foreign substances would naturally be carried by the strong current flowing in from the Jordan.

(3.) From the dimensions of the sea, as previously given, it will be inferred that it is nearly oblong in shape; and it is rarely less than five, or more than eight or nine miles, in breadth, except directly at the ends. Its eastern and western shores run almost duly north and south. In the continuity of its plan, or the general regularity of its shape and form, there is a fault, occasioned by a peninsula, shaped like a foot and ankle with the toe pointing to the north, that projects out from the eastern shore about eight miles from the south end of the lake, and is separated from the western bank by a strait or channel averaging two miles in width, and between six and seven miles long. South of the peninsula the water is, upon an average, only thirteen feet deep; but in the northern sea the average is over one thousand feet. The bottom of the channel shelves gradually downwards from the shallow bed of the southern sea to the greater depth of the upper. Opposite the north point of the peninsula, the water is upwards of one hundred fathoms deep in the centre of the channel, and opposite the heel, or southern point, it is only three fathoms.

On either hand, the sea is flanked by lofty and arid mountains. On the west are the sterile cliffs of Judea, from one thousand to fifteen hundred feet high, in some places looking as if they had been scathed with fire, in others wearing a rose-colored or purple hue, and elsewhere presenting a chalky appearance. At the foot of these barren icinerated hills, are banks of sand and dust, impalpable as ashes, and innumerable boulders bleached by long exposure to the sun. Masses of conglomerate, too, may be seen, here and there, wasting away beneath the winter rain, or glowing in the hot sun that beats upon this desert waste during the long-continued summer. On the east, the sea is skirted by the rugged precipices and battlemented heights of Moab, that form the continuation of the Hauran range. They, also, are comparatively bare of

all vegetation, and cast their dark shadows, from an altitude
of between two and three thousand feet, far down upon the
dark and dreary pool imbosomed amid those calcined mountains—from year to year, from age to age, bearing testimony
to the truth, that although the judgments of the Almighty
may be delayed for long, they are nevertheless sure and certain.

The eastern shore is evidently of volcanic formation.
Trap, tufa, granite, gneiss, dolomite, and pieces of scoriated
lava, are found in considerable abundance. The prevalent
formation is brown limestone lying in horizontal strata above
yellow sand-stone. On the western shore, no sand-stone has
been discovered, but the mountains there are mainly composed of limestone. The rocks are, of course, much discolored
by the substances deposited by the atmosphere. In the
neighborhood of the sulphur springs, they are unusually dark
and gloomy, and elsewhere, particularly along the borders of
the southern sea, they are whitened with the incrustations of
salt. The peninsula before mentioned is a bold and rocky
promontory, from forty to sixty feet in average height, and
at its northern extremity or point attaining an elevation of
near one hundred feet: it is composed of limestone, with
loose calcareous marl, and soft chalky flints scattered along
the shore. Mud flats, sandy plains or deltas, at the openings
of the ravines and gorges, which support a scanty vegetation,
alternating with rocky precipices, and strips of low and marshy
or broken ground, covered with sand and gravel or minute
angular fragments of flint, or pebbles of bituminous limestone, form the immediate shore, or beach, of the lake.

On the east the shore is very bold and abrupt, the depth
of water in the northern sea averaging about ninety fathoms
within a quarter of a mile of the beetling cliffs ; and if the
Jordan once continued its course through the vale of Siddim,
its channel was probably on this side of the lake. The
bottom of the northern sea is composed of brown or blue mud,
sometimes but not usually hard, of sand and crystals of salt.
Mud and crystals of salt are found all along the bottom of the
lake, through the channel, and in the southern sea. In the

last, however, there appears to be a greater abundance of salt than is found in other parts of the lake; and at the extreme south end, there appears to be a layer of slimy mud, a foot deep, resting upon a thick crust of salt, beneath which is another foot of mud, and still below this is the firm bottom. At this extremity of the lake, there is an extensive mud flat, reaching to the foot of high hills bounding the basin occupied by the sea to the southward, in which there is an opening corresponding to El-Ghor at the north, which has led to the supposition that the Jordan once had a continuous course through this opening or ravine, to the Gulf of Akabah, one of the arms of the Red Sea. This ravine is known as Wâdy-el-Arabah, and the supposition connected with it will be hereafter noticed.

Salt is found so abundantly along the southern sea, that it is quite an important article of traffic. Most of the bitumen, also, that is met with in commerce, is obtained from this sea, and is hence called Jewish bitumen. Sulphur is plentiful, and it is sometimes procured on the shores of the lake in large lumps. There are indications, likewise, of nitre, gypsum, and alum. Bromine is contained in the water, and to the presence of this substance its caustic taste must in great part be attributed.

Besides the Jordan, the most important tributaries of the Dead Sea are the river Arnon, which enters it from the east, through a narrow opening in the mountains flanked by walls of naked rocks piled in ledges on either hand; and the Brook Kidron, which has its source in the vicinity of Jerusalem, and discharges its waters, usually very diminutive in volume, through the Wâdy-en-Nâr, or Ravine of Fire. There are, also, a great number of springs on the margin of the lake, the waters of most of which are absorbed by the sandy soil. The largest of these are the hot springs of Callirohoe on the Arabian shore, which discharges considerable water through their outlet, the Zŭrka Maìn. Almost all the springs, too, in the southern valley, north of Wâdy Tâlh, which appears at this day to be the dividing ridge between the waters of the Dead Sea and those of the Red Sea, flow into the former.

(4.) Few travellers have written more eloquently upon the Dead Sea than Châteaubriand, and few have made more grievous mistakes. "Its solitary abysses," he remarks, "can sustain the life of no living thing; no vessel ever ploughed its bosom; its shores are without trees, without birds, without verdure; its water, frightfully salt, is so heavy that the highest wind can hardly raise it." Fish are scarce, it is true,—being only found at or near the mouths of the tributary streams,—and occasionally a few shell fish have been seen along the shore. Panthers now and then disturb the solitude with their wailing cry, and once in a while a hare may be discovered darting in and out among the cane-brakes or the sedgy thickets in the ravines. Swallows and partridges have their homes in the cliffs above, and ducks and snipes dwell amid the tufts of cane and clumps of flags growing in the vicinity of the springs, and often sail out upon the lake or disport along its shores. Hawks and herons are not uncommon. Doves and catbirds, also, are quite plentiful. Several kinds of insects are found here, and butterflies are very abundant. The fabulous accounts of the olden time are therefore disproved, and though this scene be so drear and desolate, it is still the home of many a living thing.

At the bottom of the ravines and gorges, which, during the rainy season, or throughout the year, form the beds of tributary streams, there are plains or deltas, more or less extensive, frequently projecting for some distance out into the lake. The mountain sides and summits are, indeed, almost destitute of vegetation; but the ravines are fringed, here and there, with tamarisks and oleanders, with osher* and ghŭrrah

---

* The fruit of the osher is the genuine apple of Sodom, about which so much has been said, and which, according to Tacitus, (Hist. lib. v, cap. 7) is fair without, but within all dust and ashes. It is a tall, perennial plant, and has thick, dark-green, and glossy leaves. The flowers are interminal, umbelliferous, and of a purple color. They are succeeded by globose pods about the size of a large apple, which contain numerous flat brown seeds, each of which is furnished with a silky plume or pappus. If the bark be cut, or a leaf torn from the plant, a viscous, milky juice exudes from the wound, which is exceedingly acrid, and is used in Egypt as a depillatory.

trees, with the nŭbk, the palm, the olive, and the pistachia. Beds of yellow henbane, of nightshade and mignionette, not only destitute of fragrance but entirely scentless, are mingled with patches of prickly cucumbers; and in the moist places of the plains and deltas there are thickets of cane, and clumps of reeds and sedges, and tufts of fern and water lilies. But the foliage is usually of a tawny color, occasioned by the sulphurous vapors floating in the air; and the leaves and fruit of most of the shrubs and trees have a salt and bitter taste, and often seem to be completely saturated with the saline substances with which the atmosphere is loaded.

Tolerably successful attempts have been made, in some instances, to cultivate the plains and deltas along the borders of the lake, and very good crops of barley and dhoura have not unfrequently been obtained. Where irrigation has been practicable, still greater success has attended the labors of the husbandman. In the land of Moab, beyond the barren strip lying upon the shore of the sea, the country is tolerably fertile, in the low grounds and intervales; but it is liable to visitations from the locusts, which oftentimes commit dreadful ravages.

(5.) For centuries speculation has been rife with regard to the probable position of the cities of the plain, and the manner of their destruction. It has repeatedly been said, that their ruins have been observed near the western side of the Dead Sea, but this fact is not well authenticated. Josephus, indeed, avers, that the shadows of the five cities could be seen in his time, yet it is not at all clear that he intended to be literally understood.* Strabo professes to give the actual circumference of the ruins of Sodom as being sixty stadia,† but the correctness of his statement is more than doubtful.‡

* History of the Jewish War, book iv, chap. 8.

† Geographiâ, lib. xvi, cap. 2.

‡ The Geography of Strabo is of great value to the present age, but some of its statements are grossly erroneous. For instance, he asserts that there were thirteen cities in the plain now occupied by the Dead Sea (lib. xvi, cap. 2). Stephen of Byzantium is more moderate, and makes them only ten in number (art. Σόδομα.)—According to the Scriptural account, there were but five,— Sodom and Gomorrah, Admah and Zeboim, and Bela, or Zoar, (Genesis xiv, 2.)

The supposed site of the ruins has frequently been pointed out to travellers by the old inhabitants, though the former could never discover them.   Costigan fancied he had found the ruins of Gomorrah on the plain at the foot of Wâ·ly Mubŭghghik, five or six miles north of the salt mountain of Usdum, and on the western shore of the lake; but Lieutenant Lynch shows that they were merely the remains of an old aqueduct constructed for purposes of irrigation.*   It is far from impossible that the ruins of the doomed cities may actually have been seen at a remote day, and that they have been gradually covered up by the accumulated deposits collected at the southern end of the lake ; but the probability is, that the alleged remains were the fragments of some of the fortifications or other structures, erected by the Jews, or, at a later day, by the Romans, on the banks of the lake.

History and tradition, both sacred and profane, dating back for thousands of years, concur in the one great fact, that the Dead Sea, or the Sea of the Plain, covers the spot once occupied by the guilty cities.   Until quite recently, too, it has been pretty generally conceded, that the Jordan originally continued its course along the fertile vale of Siddim, after leaving the valley of El-Ghor, and then passed through the Wâdy-el-Arabah, whose general features have a striking resemblance to those of the former, to the Gulf of Akabah. But the examinations made by Dr. Robinson and the Count de Bertou—the latter of whom travelled through the Wâdy-el-Arabah—go to show that the level of the Dead Sea and the bed of the Jordan is below that of the Red Sea, and that the Wâdy-el-Arabah rises gradually as far south as Wâdy Talh, the dividing ridge.   This would indicate that a lake, or sea, without any outlet, has always existed where the Dead Sea now is; and that opinion has latterly been gaining ground.

An able and intelligent writer† has recently examined this subject with a great deal of care, and collated all the facts and circumstances favoring the opinion which he has adopted, as the result of his investigations,—that a lake, though of

* Narrative, p. 304.   † Rev. J. A. Wylie.

much smaller dimensions than the present, previously existed in the valley of Siddim. This supposition, he insists, is unavoidable. "The bed of the Jordan," he says, "is so far below the level of El-Arabah and the Red Sea, that it is impossible, in the nature of things, it ever could have flowed through that valley. And this, we conceive, implies the existence of a lake. But though we are obliged to suppose that a lake existed, we are not obliged to suppose that it was as large as it is at present. It is natural to think that so terrible a catastrophe happening on its shores would make some alteration in its dimensions, and most probably enlarge them. And if we examine the lake, we find that it is, in fact, composed of two lakes, an upper and a lower—the former being forty miles long, and the latter ten, assuming the whole at fifty. The division between the two lakes is strongly marked. On the shores the mountains approach, so as almost to separate them from above; and in the bottom a high ridge of ground runs across from shore to shore, so as almost to divide them below the surface. The water which covers this ridge is seldom more than two feet in depth, and the ford which the bottom offers, may be crossed by the Arabs at all seasons.* This ford is about three hours (nine miles) from the extremity of the lake, on the authority of Burckhardt. Now, if we suppose that the lake, in former times, terminated at this point, as the form of the mountains and the nature of the bottom seem to indicate, then, between the extremity of the lake, and the low range of hills which bound the valley of the Jordan towards the south, and from the head of El-Arabah, we have a level and fertile plain of seventeen miles in length, on which we suppose the cities

---

* The soundings made under the direction of Lieutenant Lynch have settled the fact that there is actually no such ford in existence. "We ascertained," says the Narrative (p. 303), "that there is no ford as laid down in the map of Messrs. Robinson and Smith. One of the Arabs said that there was once a ford here, but all the others denied it." At the narrowest part of the lake, where the mountains approach nearest to each other, the water is from two to three fathoms deep most of the way across; and yet, according to Burckhardt, this is the locality of the supposed ford.

stood. The south-eastern portion of this plain is still very fertile; the whole is abundantly irrigated. Its great depth draws all the streams of El-Arabah into it. Numerous rivulets descend on both sides from the hills; and to these causes, no doubt, it owed the fertile aspect in which it appeared to Lot, when he chose it for the range of his flocks.

"Moreover, it is more reasonable to suppose that the five cities stood on this plain, than that they were scattered over so large a space as that which is now occupied by the lake. Each of the cities, we are told, had a king; but the kings of those days resembled the village sheikhs of modern times; and even granting that the cities were opulent, and had dependent villages around them, still the plain was amply sufficient to maintain them. In the East, the towns were thickly planted, seldom at greater distances, as we learn from the ruins, than three or four miles—a space so large as that which the waters of the lake now cover, considering its great fertility, instead of containing five, would have contained fifty cities. From the expression frequently used in Scripture—'Sodom and her daughters,' and from the circumstance of the destruction of the cities being often mentioned simply as the 'overthrow of Sodom,' we infer that Sodom was the capital, or at least the principal city of the Pentapolis; and it is probable that the other towns which perished with her were ranged around her at no great distances. The exact part of the plain in which Sodom was situated, we do not know; but the following consideration will satisfy us, that its site could not have been far from what are now the southern limits of the lake.

"When Sodom fell, the little town of Zoar afforded refuge to Lot. The time which Lot occupied in going thither, will give us the distance of Sodom, the probable capital, of Zoar. We read that 'there came two angels to Sodom at even; and Lot sat in the gate of Sodom. And he said, 'Behold now, my lords, turn in, I pray you, into your servant's house and tarry all night.' During night, the angels disclosed the approaching destruction of the city, and enjoined Lot to leave it, which he did at day-break, but not earlier. 'When the morning arose, then the angels hastened Lot, &c.' Having set out, he reached the gates of Zoar at sunrise— 'The sun was risen upon the earth, when Lot entered into Zoar.' It thus appears that Lot occupied only two hours in travelling between the two cities—the time from day-break till sunrise. Sodom, consequently, could not have been more than six miles distant from Zoar; and thus, its site would fall within the limits of the lower lake; for the head of that lake is three hours from Zoar,—the site of Zoar, which is known at this day, adjoining the southern extremity of the lake. Now, if we suppose that Sodom was the capital of the cities, and had her tributary towns arranged around her, it will appear probable that the site of all these cities was comprised in what is now the basin of the lower lake. The ground on which they stood being depressed by their over-throw, the lake adjoining them on the north poured its waters over the low barrier, and covered from the eye of man, this scene of enormous wickedness. Every consideration tends to this conclusion. The geographical arrangement of the region, and the construction of the lake, indicate that at some former period it has been enlarged, and the traces of the pristine beauties of the plain, which are still to be seen in some places on its remaining portion, tell us that once it was 'well watered everywhere'—'even as the garden of the Lord.'"*

The survey of Lieutenant Lynch disproves one of the assumed facts upon which Mr. Wylie bases his theory, and on which he lays great stress—viz. that of the existence of a dividing ridge between the upper and lower lakes. As there is a strong current putting into the lake, which is deflected by Mount Usdum and the southern shore, it is likewise exceedingly probable, that the slime and mud accumulated here have been deposited in this manner.† Indeed, this is much more likely than that the bed of the southern lake was the

* Modern Judea, etc., compared with Ancient Prophecy.
† Lynch's Narrative, p. 295.

plain upon which the cities stood, and which was covered by the overflow of water from the upper sea. The fertility, too, mentioned by Mr. Wylie, as being characteristic of the south-eastern plain, is hardly consistent with the facts obtained by the American Expedition.

Lieutenant Lynch remarks that the mountains on all sides appear much older than the sea, and that the torrents, particularly those pouring into the upper lake, plunge down abruptly. His inference from the facts and appearances before him was, that the entire chasm was a sunken plain, and that the depression was greatest at the northern end. In summing up the conclusions at which he arrived, he says:— " The inference from the Bible, that this entire chasm was a plain sunk and 'overwhelmed' by the wrath of God, seems to be sustained by the extraordinary character of our soundings. The bottom of this sea consists of two submerged plains, an elevated and a depressed one; the last averaging *thirteen*, and the former about *thirteen hundred* feet below the surface. Through the northern, and largest and deepest one, in a line corresponding with the bed of the Jordan, is a ravine, which again seems to correspond with the Wâdy-el-Jeib, or ravine within a ravine, at the south end of the sea.

"Between the Jabok and this sea, we unexpectedly found a sudden break-down in the bed of the Jordan. If there be a similar break in the water courses to the south of the sea, accompanied with like volcanic characters, there can scarce be a doubt that the whole Ghor has sunk from some extraordinary convulsion ; preceded, most probably, by an eruption of fire, and a general conflagration of the bitumen which abounded in the plain. I shall ever regret that we were not authorized to explore the southern Ghor to the Red Sea.

" All our observations have impressed me forcibly with the conviction, that the mountains are older than the sea. Had their relative levels been the same at first, the torrents would have worn their beds in a gradual and correlative slope ;— whereas, in the northern section, the part supposed to have been so deeply engulfed, although a soft, bituminous limestone prevails, the torrents plunge down several hundred feet, while on both sides of the southern portion, the ravines come down without abruptness, although the head of Wâdy Kerak is more than a thousand feet higher than the head of Wâdy Ghuweir. Most of the ravines, too, * * * have a south-ward inclination near their outlets, that of Zŭrka Main especially, which, next to the Jordan, must pour down the greatest volume of water in the rainy season. But even if they had not that deflection, the argument which has been based on this supposition would be untenable ; for tributaries, like all other streams, seek the greatest declivities without regard to angular inclination."*

It is, indeed, to be regretted, so far as the elucidation of this subject is concerned, that Lieutenant Lynch felt restrained by his instructions from prosecuting his reconnais-sance through the Wâdy-el-Arabah, or lower Ghor, to the Red Sea ; for, unless such an examination, carefully made, shall disclose insuperable difficulties, it must still appear highly probable that there has been a depression, or subsidence, of the whole Ghor from the Jabok to Wâdy Tâlh ; and that the Jordan once flowed into the Gulf of Akabah, and carried with it the saline and other substances which, since the sudden convulsion that interrupted its course, have been accumulating at the southern extremity of the Sea of the Plain.

Taking the account given in Scripture as the guide, this inference appears to be the only plausible one. The same form of expression ("Bela, which *is* Zoar") used in Genesis xiv, 2, in describing the cities of the plain, is employed by the inspired historian in the following verse, when he speaks of the vale of Siddim, which, he says, "*is* the Salt Sea." Now Zoar was not known by that name till after Lot had taken refuge there ; and is it not fair—nay, even necessary—to infer, that the Salt Sea had no existence until the vale of Siddim was overwhelmed ? Furthermore, it seems strange, that Moses did not mention the Salt Sea, if it previously

---

* Narrative, p. 378, et seq.

existed, when he describes the country inhabited by the
Canaanites, which extended to Lasha, on the Persian Gulf;*
and is it not inconsistent with the fertile character of the
plain, to which he repeatedly refers, that it should be watered
by a stream terminating in a salt pool? After the quarrel
between the herdsmen of Abram and Lot, also, the latter
chose all the plain of Jordan, and journeyed to the east; but
no mention is made of his crossing any sea, as he would have
done, provided there had been one in existence.†

But it may be said, that the vale of Siddim occupied the
southern part of the basin, where the shallow lake now is.
This is hardly probable, however, although it is quite likely
that the five cities stood upon or near the south end of the
plain; for we are told that their kings went out to meet
Chedorlaomer "and the kings that were with him," who
were approaching from the north, and "joined battle with
them in the vale of Siddim."‡

With regard to the manner in which the cities were
destroyed, there has been a great deal of conjecture, for the
most part idly, or at least unprofitably hazarded. We know
that the Almighty usually operates with secondary causes;
and it may be that volcanic agency, as has been presumed,
was the physical instrument employed by him in this case;
that the Salt Sea was formed by the subsidence of the plain,
or from the damming up of the Jordan by a current of lava,
or both combined; and that the showers of fire and brimstone
were occasioned by the fall of volcanic ejections.§ But the
most reasonable supposition is, that, simultaneously with the
fire and brimstone rained out of heaven upon the doomed
cities, volcanic eruptions took place; that the slime pits, or
pits of bitumen according to the version of the Septuagint,
with which the plain was filled,‖ were inflamed; and that
the combustion of the soil or the underlying strata was
followed by the subsidence of the plain.¶

Be this as it may,—there lies that solitary and desolate

---

* Genesis, x, 19.   † Ibid., xiii, 11.   ‡ Ibid., xiv, 8.

§ See Daubeny on Volcanoes.   ‖ Genesis, xiv, 10.   ¶ Ibid., xix, 24, 25.

lake, the seal and the witness to the fearful judgment pronounced by Jehovah himself upon those who had erred past all forgiveness. Within its dark waters thousands of animate beings were suddenly engulfed—cut off, in an instant, while cherishing, as we can well imagine, many of the bright hopes and joys and aspirations that animate our hearts, yet so tainted with the leprosy of vice and crime, that Nature shuddered as she received them in her bosom. Both the infidel and the christian historian concur in the main facts connected with this catastrophe. The former may continue to scoff and doubt, yet his reflections will often give rise to emotions of fear; but the latter, though trembling with awe, consoles himself with the thought that God is merciful as well as just!

(6.) Warned by the rapidly increasing heat, and the debilitated state of his party, that the summer solstice was fast approaching, Lieutenant Lynch broke up his encampment on the shores of the Dead Sea, on the morning of the 10th of May. The boats were taken to pieces, and placed on the backs of the camels; and the whole party commenced their return journey to the Mediterranean coast, proceeding overland by way of Jerusalem, across

> "Those holy fields,
> Over whose acres walked those blessed feet,
> Which, fourteen hundred years ago, were nail'd
> For our advantage, on the bitter cross."

THE END.

Lightning Source UK Ltd.
Milton Keynes UK
UKOW04f1448230914

239027UK00007B/399/P